THE
Short Stories
OF
JAMES T. FARRELL

THE SHORT STORIES OF

James T. Farrell

THE SUN DIAL PRESS
GARDEN CITY, NEW YORK

NO PORTION OF THIS BOOK MAY BE REPRINTED
WITHOUT THE WRITTEN PERMISSION OF THE
PUBLISHER.

SUN DIAL PRESS Reprint Edition, 1945, by special
arrangement with THE VANGUARD PRESS.

COPYRIGHT: *The American Mercury*, 1932, 1933, 1935; *Pagany*, 1932; *This Quarter*, 1930, 1932; *The New Masses*, 1934, 1935; *Midland*, 1931; *Dynamo*, 1934; *Story*, 1932, 1933; *Best Short Stories of 1933*, 1933; *The Monthly Review*, 1934; *A Year Magazine*, 1933; *Tambour*, 1931; Harcourt, Brace and Company, 1936; *The Daily Worker*, 1934; *The Nation*, 1936; *The New Quarterly*, 1934; *College Humor*, 1937; *Fight*, 1934; *The Readies*, 1931; *Contact*, 1932; *The Dubuque Dial*, 1935; *Midweek Features* of *The Chicago Daily News*, 1931; *The American Spectator*, 1935; *The Partisan Review*, 1934; *American Abroad*, 1932; The Vanguard Press, 1934, 1935, 1937.

CL

PRINTED IN THE UNITED STATES OF AMERICA

TO
EARL *and* LORETTA FARRELL

All the characters in these stories are fictitious
and if the names of any actual persons occur,
it is by sheer coincidence.

Acknowledgment

THE kind permission of the publishers has enabled me to quote in the Preface from the following works:

A Handbook of Short Story Writing by John T. Frederick. Published by F. S. Crofts and Company, New York, N. Y.

A Book of the Short Story by E. A. Cross. Published by the American Book Company, New York, N. Y.

The Coming Struggle For Power by John Strachey. Published by Covici Friede, Inc., New York, N. Y.

A Handbook on Story Writing by Blanche Colton Williams. Published by Dodd, Mead and Company, New York, N. Y.

European Theories of the Drama by Barrett H. Clark. Published by D. Appleton-Century Company, Inc., New York, N. Y.

A Manual of the Art of Fiction by Clayton Hamilton. Published by Doubleday, Doran and Company, Inc., Garden City, N. Y.

Writing the Short Story by Edith Mirrielees. Published by Doubleday, Doran and Company, Inc., Garden City, N. Y.

Short Story-Writing by N. Bryllion Fagin. Published by Thomas Seltzer, Inc., New York, N. Y.

The Philosophy of the Short Story by Brander Matthews. Published by Longmans, Green and Company, New York, N. Y.

Short Stories, How To Write Them by Cecil Hunt. Published by George S. Harrap and Company, Ltd., London, England.

Short-Story Technique by Stewart Beach. Published by Houghton Mifflin Company, Boston, Mass.

J. T. F.

"But now that everything is torn down, and swords and capes rendered useless, it is time to base our works on truth. . . . There should no longer be any school, no more formulas . . . there is only life itself, an immense field where each may study and create as he likes. . . . I am expressing my profound conviction . . . that the experimental and scientific spirit of the century will enter the domain of the drama, and that in it lies its only possible salvation. Let the critics look about them and tell me from what direction help is to be expected, or a breath of life, to rehabilitate the drama? Of course, the past is dead. We must look to the future, and the future will have to do with the human problem studied in the framework of reality. We must cast aside fables of every sort, and delve into the living drama of the two-fold life of character and its environment, bereft of every nursery tale, historical trapping, and the usual conventional stupidities. The decayed scaffoldings of the drama of yesterday will fall of their own accord. We must clear the ground. The well-known recipes for the tying and untying of an intrigue have served their time; now we must seek a simple and broad picture of men and things. . . . Outside of a few scenic conventions, all that is known as the 'science of the theater' is merely a heap of clever tricks, a narrow tradition that serves to cramp the drama, a ready-made code of language and hackneyed situations, all known and planned out beforehand, which every original worker will scorn to use."

Emile Zola
Préface (to) Thérèse Raquin
(*1873*)

Preface

I

In our time, perhaps, more nonsense has been written about the short story than about any other literary form. Commentators long ago popularized the conceit that the short story is the typical American literary form. There was a time when short stories of a certain plot pattern were in great demand and, for that matter, we are not yet out of that period. The short story has been conceived by persons with "literary" aspirations as a means of making a good living, and it has been used by magazine proprietors as bait for procuring advertisements. To use plain language, it has often been employed as a kind of literary pimp. At the present time, scenario writing is viewed as the open sesame for the Get-Rich-Quick-Wallingfords of writing, and the plot short story is losing some of its commercial utility.

The short story, then—that so-called typical American literary form —became a business. And just as there are schools to teach accounting, stenography, salesmanship, hotel-keeping, and the like, so are there institutions teaching short-story writing. There are college courses dedicated to this purpose. A whole series of guides to short-story writing, handbooks on the short story, treatises on narrative technique with special emphasis on the short story, household hints in the production and marketing of the short story, tips, suggestions, charts, outlines, diagrams, maps, and prospectuses have flooded the market. The libraries are now glutted with such books.

In many instances, these books were written in order to keep flourishing the notion that the art and/or the technique of short-story writing could be learned, and that once it was mastered, it could be the means of a profitable and relatively easy livelihood. N. Bryllion Fagin's book, *Short Story-Writing, An Art or a Trade?* (a sincere and clever protest against such tactics), points out clearly that the ease of mastering the short-story technique (so-called) was stressed because of such reasons. By doing this, teachers were helping to give their own business the status of a going concern. Mr. Fagin quotes one of the instructors of this business as follows: "Given a reasonable intelligence and a sufficient patience, any man with the smallest gifts may learn to write at least marketable stuff, and may earn an honest livelihood, if he studies the taste of the least exacting portion of the public, and accommodates himself to the whim of the time." Blanche Colton Williams, head of the Department of English at Hunter College, City of New York, is one of the practitioners of this form of literary advice-mongering. She remarks in the preface to her *A Handbook on Story Writing:* "The story is so much a matter of form it can be learned. Conceivably it can be learned by persons who are endowed with no supreme literary gift." Nor has this business and its practices been confined to this country alone, the alleged home of the short story. Thus, an Englishman, Cecil Hunt, tells us in *Short Stories, How to Write Them* that: "Short-story writing is not easy money; it is not a fool's game; but, given the . . . qualities" of a desire to write, average capacity, enthusiasm, etc., "it can be learned as easily as most other occupations. It gives a higher return in money and in pleasure than many. What is more, it can be a delightful and remunerative hobby."

Upon examination, most of the short-story handbooks reveal that they are largely expansions and extensions of what the late Brander Matthews wrote some years ago in his *The Philosophy of the Short-story*. And it must be added that he wrote next to nothing of real literary worth, insight, or suggestiveness. He placed his emphasis on form, and thus he said: "The Short-story is nothing if there is no story to tell." And again: "A Short-story in which nothing happens at all is an absolute impossibility." He distinguished between the short story and the sketch, stating that "while a Sketch may be a still-life, in a Short-story something always happens. A Sketch may be an outline of character, or even a picture of a mood of mind, but in a Short-story there must be something done, there must be action." When he branched off to speak of content, he was downright silly. For instance, take this priceless observation: "While the Novel cannot get on easily without love, the Short-story can."

To repeat, most of the latter-day books on short-story writing are largely derivative from Matthews. They follow his definitions and demarcations of the story in terms of form. But that is only a prelude,

PREFACE

a breaking of ground for the real stuff—the charts, the formulae, the outlines, the plot diagrams, the analyses of methods of obtaining effects, the breaking up of narrative technique into its assumedly component parts, the presentation of an entire cabalistic ritual of writing. For example, there is one Stewart Beach, former Lecturer on Short-Story Writing at New York University. In his book, *Short-Story Technique,* he outlines a method that is particularly important for the neophyte. It is "the X-ray method." It "demands unity of focus" and "it is an ingeniously simple scheme which depends for its success upon the author's borrowing one leaf from the book of the theater and another from the clinical notes of the doctor. Instead of *telling* [italics in original] a story about a group of characters or about something which happened to some one, the author places one character under the X-ray and allows his readers to see his thoughts as well as his actions." He talks about "snares" to catch the reader's interest, tells us that the short story has a beginning, a body, and an ending, asks and learnedly discusses such questions as: "How is the author to know the actual point at which the beginning ends, and the action shifts over into the body of the story?", comments on the "piecemeal method of introducing exposition," and informs us that there are four essentials in plot building: "chief actor"; "basic characteristic" of the chief actor; "original situation"; "problem." He discusses the "mechanics of suspense" and points out that suspense grows from two roots, conflict and contrast. He lists the simple types of conflict under five headings: man with himself; man with his background; man with his situation; man with man; man with fate. Blanche Colton Williams goes him one better and catalogues six types of struggle (or conflict) : beast with beast; man with beast; man with natural forces; man with man (under which heading there are sub-categories from *a* to *g*); man with fate; man with supernatural forces. Beach's remarks in this connection are sufficiently momentous to warrant quotation: "Contrast is the stuff of *conflict,* but *conflict* is the stuff of *suspense."* (Italics in original—J.T.F.)

Then there is Professor E. A. Cross, whose *A Book of the Short Story* is full of a cabalistic lore all its own. Professor Cross goes to the heart of the matter by asking the question, what kinds of people should the short-story writer use? "In the first place, the characters must be real people." And he states that there are two methods of delineating character: *"direct"* and *"indirect."* His most notable contribution to this esoteric science, however, is to be found in his diagrams of plots. He is

xvi PREFACE

the man who has *demonstrated* the plot diagrams of stories. Thus, *The Piece of String* has a "stair-step" plot, and many of O. Henry's plots, when diagrammed, are of the "rocket" design. It is to be noticed in all these views that something called *form* is stressed. In other words, it can be said that the positive value here is that of *structure*. The philosophy of the short story, as outlined, is one in which structure is given positive value. (This situation is, incidentally, analogous to that in the contemporary drama.) We discover here the weakness in all approaches to literature that are purely formal. Form becomes a philosophy, a value. In the traditional American short story, this is precisely what has happened. A writer whose sole gift is technical facility will rise to the top. Thus the reputation of a writer such as Wilbur Daniel Steele is explained. His sole capacity is that of technical facility, and for the rest, he is sterile. He is, in my opinion, the example par excellence of the writer whose only positive value is form, structure. When form and structure become predominant values in literature, the material from life on which literature draws is falsified. Inevitably, there is a loss of concern with content. Content is altered—but not to gain that more concentrated effect and meaning which literature strives to achieve. It is changed, pieced together, in order to make it fit into an arbitrary structure. Life is falsified. A literature of hollow and straw men is produced.

It was Edward James O'Brien, I believe, who suggested that there was a peculiar faith in predestination to be found in the conventional and traditional conceptions of the American short story. He analyzed this phenomenon, however, as a product of the machine age, and of the standardization that develops in such an epoch. Here he tended to focus the questions within the confines of an arbitrary perspective. We find semblances of such an attitude in his books, *The Advance of the American Short Story* and *The Dance of the Machines* (which discusses the short story at some length). He polarizes man and the machine. According to his view, the standardization of the machine age has produced the standardized machine story. He neglected to realize that in previous epochs, before there was what properly can be called a machine age, writing was often equally as conventionalized as it has been in the representative American plot story. Previous to the romantic movement in English letters, there was standardization —the result, largely, of neo-classicism. In French painting there was a similar type of conventionalization. It was broken by Delacroix and other predecessors of the Impressionists, and then, more decisively, by the Impressionists themselves.

So the analogy with the machine is an unsatisfactory explanation of this phenomenon. The growth of science, on which the machine is based, has done more to liberate than it has to mechanize literature. However, Mr. O'Brien's suggestion that the traditional American short story exemplifies an inclination toward a faith in predestination is, to repeat, suggestive. To cite the best example that comes in mind, I shall have to go outside of the technical limits of the short story and examine a novelette, *The Go-Getter*, by Peter B. Kyne. Herein we find a typical illustration of the American faith in go-getting as it is incorporated into a story pattern. The outlook implicitly inculcated into the very pattern and movement of the story is that go-getting is automatically bound to bring success. Success is conceived in financial terms. The story contains a definite moral or theme. If you try, if you won't allow yourself to be licked, if you bend every effort toward doing your job in business—you will rise. You will be a financial success. You will move up the ladder. Also, of course, there is the additional suggestion that with this kind of effort, and the success that results from it, you will also obtain a wife. Professor Beach states that the "necessity of a definite conclusion" in the short story "naturally presupposes a story for which such a conclusion is possible." The conventional short story has been reduced largely to a proposition in *a priori* problem-solving. In this sense, it affirms an essentially Calvinistic faith in predestination.

Calvinism furnished the rising capitalism of another century with a religious justification. It served to bring the form of religion, a modification of, a mutation upon, medieval Christianity, into harmony with a rising capitalism. The ideological background of the conventional American short story has here one of its main sources. This form has now reached the stage of development where its positive affirmation, its implied view, is merely that of structure. This structure delimits the literary form and demands that certain things be done with characters and events that are utilized in this form. The content poured into this structure has been mainly of a kind that implicitly or explicitly affirms and enforces an acceptance of the aims and the ideals which are part of the ideological structure of capitalism. One of the products of the rise of capitalism and the ascension of the bourgeoisie to power as a class has been the development of a sense of the *self* and of the *individual* that is totally different from the view of the individual that prevailed in earlier epochs, such as those of the medieval and classic civilizations. With the Renaissance, the rise of the middle class, the development of modern science, a new view of the self came into the consciousness of men on a wholesale scale. Self-consciousness as we know it today developed. Man began to trust more and more to his own nature, his own impulses, his own resources and knowledge. Man began to view himself as self-dependent. Freedom of action in various fields of endeavor flows from this view of the self, and a constituent part of that freedom of action is freedom to buy and to sell.

Individualism in this more limited sense is the individualism that has been very often inculcated into the traditional American short story. The content of many such stories is formed from a simplified view of individualism. The individual is conceived as the best judge of his own wants. He must rely on himself. His future depends on what he does. If he is a go-getter, if he adheres to the prevailing views of life and the "worthy" goods of life, if he plays the game of capitalistic struggle, he will advance. He will be a success. Success will bring happiness.

Such is the typical content of many traditional American short stories. In others, there is a treatment of a related nature. Or there is a local-color content that tends to patronize those who are of a lower economic origin, or of a "socially inferior" race. One may cite as stories of the latter type the Octavus Roy Cohen series featuring Florian Slappey. Added to this simplified type of individualism there is a hygienic and largely Protestant morality, and a carry-over of the virgin complex that traces back to the medieval cult of the virgin. The ideal of life is success, and the fruits of success are marriage to an American virgin, a home in the suburbs that contains all the advantages, conveniences, gadgets, automobiles, radios, etc., that are to be found advertised in the magazines which have long specialized in printing precisely this type of story.

II

The history of the revolt against the traditional short story is familiar to most literate persons. It is part of the general revolt in American literature that has resulted in the realism to be found in the works of our leading fiction writers of this era. In part, this revolt took the form of turning upside down the familiar views, notions, ideals, and themes

PREFACE   xix

that had been dominant in our fiction during the early years of this century. For instance, one conventional view was that sin begot its own punishment ("the wages of sin is death") and that virtue was rewarded, not necessarily in Heaven, but also on earth. Dreiser's *Sister Carrie* reversed this maxim. Sister Carrie sinned, sacrificed her virtue, and reached a peak of worldly success. Dreiser's *The Titan* and *The Financier* and Sherwood Anderson's *Windy MacPherson's Son* are novels in which business success does not bring happiness and contentment. In some of the short stories of Ring Lardner, such as *The Champion*, as well as in his *You Know Me Al*, the heroism of the sport pages is reversed with biting irony. Besides overturning popular myths, the revolt in American writing threw overboard the plot conception of the short story and the happy ending, the traditional patterns of the English Victorian novel. It introduced new phases and new emphases of experience into our fiction. In early years, there was the literature of the American immigrant, of first-generation groups, written in an unreal and patronizing vein. The melting pot was a typical literary theme. The treatment in such works was without vitality, conventional, intended to be humorous. The stories contained little truth and were written from the outside. Writers played on variations of such themes as that of the stage Irishman who was manufactured by some nineteenth-century Irish novelists for English consumption. In a vulgar and insulting manner, such fiction sentimentalized Jewish characters. It was a literature of the Cohens and the Kellys, of Abie's Irish Roses, Uncle Remus, a literature of the upper classes and of good old Star-Spangled-Banner patronage. With this so-called revolt in American literature, several generations of writers arose and began articulating the experience of groups in America, of phases in American life that had hitherto received false and patronizing treatment, or no attention at all. Immigrant groups, the working class, the poorer elements in general began to receive some degree of realistic representation in American fiction. This tendency has now reached the point where, viewed sociologically, American writing treats of an infinite variety of types, racial and economic groups, and localities that go toward making up the totality of American life.

Most of the writing in this so-called revolt is usually described as realism, or as realism and naturalism. Naturalism in literature can be described as an attempt to embody scientific method in so-called creative writing. One of the foremost exponents of naturalism was Zola, who based his naturalism on an earlier view of materialism, a view that juxtaposed matter and spirit, environment and character. Theodore Dreiser has exemplified a similar naturalism in this country. This revolt, particularly in its earlier stages, involved the attempt to treat character as the product of environment. There were attacks on social conditions—witness *The Jungle,* by Upton Sinclair. Blows were struck at accepted social and moral attitudes—witness the work of Dreiser and Anderson, Masters' *Spoon River Anthology,* and innumerable other works in both poetry and prose, novels and short stories alike.

The revolt in American literature, and the revolt of the short-story writer, which was part of the more general revolt, have been, to a certain degree, victorious. We have beheld the introduction of profound changes in the form, so-called, and in the content, so-called, in the American short story. There is now the basis for a tradition in our short story which runs counter to that of the O. Henry and Bret Harte story, and, more generally, to that of the plot story. A number of works can be cited here as examples, stories such as Sherwood Anderson's *I'm a Fool,* and *I Want to Know Why,* Dreiser's *The Lost Phoebe,* Ring Lardner's *The Golden Honeymoon* and *Some Like Them Cold,* Ernest Hemingway's *Hills Like White Elephants.* But I need not further elaborate concerning this revolt. Although I do not always admire Edward James O'Brien's taste in the selection of short stories, the record of this change can be found in his yearly anthologies; these books are invaluable as source books revealing the history, the changes, the course and career of the American short story.

III

While the plot short story has been driven backward into a sucession of retreats, not all the effects of its earlier acceptance have been dissipated. For instance, in the drama today, the view of structure that enshrines it as a positive value persists. Play structure in some instances is elevated almost into a philosophy forming the basis for interpreting characters and events. Similar influences are being brought back into the stream of American literature through the medium of Hollywood. The same influences are still at play in the minds of masses of Americans. In consequence, the appreciation, not only of the short story, but also of all forms of literature, is deadened. The view of the short story in formal terms is still retained in whole or in part by many who consider themselves sophisticated book reviewers, critics, editors.

One discovers vestiges of these views if one reads reviews, criticisms, comments on short stories. As a rule, a short work of fiction is more of a test of a critic's capacities in appreciation than is a longer one. In a novel, the author has room for expansion. He can fully reveal and reiterate his way of seeing characters and events. His views of life are made more explicit. Repetitions and elaborations give a more definite sense of his intentions, his values, his conceptions than is possible in the necessarily more concentrated and simplified shorter work of fiction. Thus it is easier for the critic—and for the reader in general—to obtain some sense of the author's purposes in the longer work. It is also easier to talk about the "sociological" importance, background, meanings, and references of a novel than of a short story. The critic is often puzzled by a short story, because it is less adaptable as a springboard for a critical dive into Karl Marx, the Catholic Church, the depression, war and fascism, the Soviet Union, the Five-Year Plan, form and content, Henry James, and the like. So it very often becomes a kind of test of the critic's capacities in the *appreciation* of a work of literature.

Thus, we frequently find reviewers and critics dodging the task of *appreciation* of short stories by posing irrelevant questions. Is this specific work a short story? Are these particular pieces of fiction short stories, or are they not? Such a question is easily asked. It is an excellent question for the critic or reviewer who seeks to pad his review, to avoid *appreciating* a work, *judging* it, *evaluating* it. Several paragraphs, or even pages, can be spun around it, and then the critic can remark that the particular work or works are or are not short stories. Thanks largely to the popularity of writers such as Joyce and Proust, it is difficult for critics to employ the same subterfuge in discussing a novel. In consequence, there is a greater tendency to measure the short story in a formal manner than there is to measure the novel in this way. This tendency, of course, is largely a hangover from the days when the plot short story was leading the field.

IV

We come now to the question: "What is a short story?" There are definitions piled on top of other definitions, and I shall cite some. Professor Beach, the apostle of "the X-ray method" of writing short stories, has this definition: "The short story, in so far as its scope is concerned, is the simplest form of fiction. Unlike the novel, it lacks space to unfold a complex situation." John T. Frederick, editor of the defunct *Midland,* has written one of the more intelligent books in this field, *A Handbook of Short Story Writing,* although he also gives some of the usual synthetic advice on narrative technique and the like. He says: "The aim of short story writing must be no longer defined in terms of approximation of artificial canons of form and method, but primarily in terms of the sincerity of the writer and the significance of his material." Professor Cross, he who invented the "stair-step" and the "rocket" plot diagrams, says: "Like the novel, the short story is a piece of fiction producing a unified effect. Unlike the novel, the single effect is usually an *impression* [italics in original—J.T.F.], instead of a deliberate marshaling together of a large number of diverse elements into a unity. . . . The short story is a cross section of life . . . but of a single life or at most of the thread of life where it crosses and becomes entangled with one or two other subordinated threads—a section through the knot." Professor Cross also quotes Clayton Hamilton, another adept at this recondite wisdom, who says, in his *A Manual of the Art of Fiction: "The aim of a short-story* [italics in original—J.T.F.] *is to produce a single narrative effect with the greatest economy of means that is consistent with the utmost emphasis."* Edith Mirrielees, in *Significant Contemporary Stories,* quoted by Blanche Colton Williams, states: "In the first fraction of the twentieth century, a short story is a fiction in prose of a somewhat limited magnitude—that and no more." In her *Writing the Short Story* she has this definition: *"A short story is a brief prose narrative, primarily imaginative, which, by means of the adhesion of every part to one central purpose, renders a coherent and interpretative account of some phase of action, character, or mood."* [Italics in original—J.T.F.] Blanche Colton Williams (whose own book bears out the ironical remark of Edward James O'Brien that most of the handbooks are like treatises on bridge building because of their charts and diagrams) of course has her definition: "The short-story is a prose narrative artistically presenting character in a struggle or complication which has a definite outcome. If the action occurs in a brief time and a closely circumscribed space, the story approaches the extreme or ultimate form." Which of these definitions is best suited to the stories of Chekhov?—in my opinion the greatest short-story writer who ever lived. Or which one is most applicable to the stories in Joyce's *Dubliners?* To *Winesburg Ohio?* Amen. And again—*amen!*

V

To anyone concerned with the evaluation and appreciation of literature, it is not crucial whether a particular work be a novel, a condensed novel, a novelette, a story, a tale, a sketch, an anecdote, an incident, a dramatic dialogue or whatever other term be applied. What does matter is whether a specific piece of writing provides the reader with an *experience,* whether it increases his or her understanding, intensifies his or her consciousness, provides the reader with pleasure and refreshment. All of the definitions with which I am familiar are arbitrary. And when we refer them to our actual experience in reading, we readily perceive how arbitrary they are. For instance, some of the experts tell us that the short story creates a *single* or a *unified* impression. What is the meaning here of single? Of unified? When we look at a work of art, we learn that there are not just *single* impressions to be gathered from it. If we take a story such as Chekhov's *A Woman's Kingdom,* what is the single and unified impression which we gain from reading it? This is a story of class relationships in Tsarist Russia, and it is, literally, a cross section of many phases of the life of that place and period. One gets from it impressions of class relationships, of characters, of moods? What, then, of the singleness of impression? In fact, Chekhov's stories are an excellent refutation of all these definitions. His stories are, in my opinion, like doors of understanding and awareness opening outward into an entire world. How, then, can we speak of the *single* impression which they create? Perhaps this will explain why a pundit once boasted that Chekhov wrote sketches, but that we, Americans, write short stories.

In *The Coming Struggle for Power,* John Strachey writes with genuine insight into literature: " 'Literature' . . . is a great sea into which for centuries have been poured all those thoughts, dreams, fantasies, concepts, ascertained facts, and emotions, which did not fit into any of the other categories of human thought. Into literature have gone philosophical ideas too tenuous for the philosophers, dreams too literal for plastic expression, ascertained facts too uncorrelated for science, and emotions too intertwined with the particular instance to find expression in the glorious and precise abstractions of music." This statement is like a clear light exposing some of the purposes motivating the writing of shorter works of fiction. Fiction itself is a great sea of human experience, and part of that sea is the novel, part of it other forms. Into it is poured a complexity of human experience. The manner of presenting this experience is determined by many factors. There are, for instance, many impressions that do not, in terms of the writer's purposes, talents, values, way of seeing and feeling life, etc., merit being translated into more than a short piece of fiction, a story, anecdote, tale, incident, sketch, or whatever else it may be called. Form and content are functions of each other mutually interdependent, mutually related. They cannot be separated. If we approach shorter works of fiction with definitions and peer through these definitions as lenses, we shall turn literature into a parlor game of recognition. New writers will come along and smash our definitions—and we shall have to add new ones. Such a method suggests the old fashioned school of instinct psychologists. Their approach to psychology was *a priori*. They presented a psychological doctrine that was based on the assumption that there were a certain number of instincts in man. Soon these instincts were insufficient to explain human conduct. New ones had to be added. Psychology, thus studied, became an *a priori* task of multiplying instincts. Soon it was a chaos of instincts and an utter confusion. The actual material of psychology, man himself, was lost sight of, and his inner world was divided into an *a priori* collection of instincts.

VI

Reviewers who think themselves sociologically minded most frequently break their critical necks on short stories. This is perhaps particularly so of the pseudo-Marxians who infested the literary atmosphere until they were called off by the Kremlin and told, as a means of fighting fascism, to reverse their entire method of approaching literature. Their demand was that literature be didactic, and they called for a didactic type of story, which they labeled *proletarian*. Didacticism is particularly difficult, dangerous, and unproductive in a shorter work of fiction. There is not the space for it. The little left-wing magazines of a few years ago were flooded with didactic stories made to the pattern of the critics who were demanding just such writing, calling it *proletarian.* When they were given what they had asked for, they were disappointed. Instead of approaching the short story with definitions of form, they approached it with arbitrary conceptions of content, sacred cows, and the demand that a purely conceptualized, hypothetical, and non-existent worker be the hero. The stories produced in this movement were bad, lifeless, wooden. In place of the happy ending of *The Saturday Evening Post* variety, they had an "uplifting" conclusion based on a sudden conversion to the sole correct faith in progress and the future of humanity.

This is now all in the past. But these stories, and the now defunct magazines that printed them—most notably *The Anvil*—constitute a laboratory of interest to everyone who is concerned in noting how not to approach literature, how not to write. If one would learn how not to write, how not to understand, how not to appreciate literature, one can, on one hand, find excellent object lessons in the proletarian stories and in the school of criticism and politics that produced them, and, on the other, in the handbooks and guide books of the Blanche Colton Williams variety. The former hypostatizes, narrows, and freezes content; the latter achieves a similar effect with form. These two sources combined exemplify just about every conceivable *don't*.

VII

Literary criticism is the result of a somewhat different process than that which produces fiction. This preface has been written in my capacity as a critic, and not in that of one who writes fiction. It is not intended as a direct explanation or defense of the stories included in this volume. It relates to them only in the sense that it embodies views which I hold concerning the writing and appreciation of fiction. In that sense, it seeks to explain views, ideals, and aims that I seek to embody in my own writing. Only in that sense can this preface legitimately be taken as relating to my stories.

JAMES T. FARRELL

August 10, 1937
New York City

Contents

Preface *by the author* — xiii
Introduction *by Robert Morss Lovett* — xxix

CALICO SHOES

Helen, I Love You — 3
The Scarecrow — 10
Looking 'Em Over — 23
The Buddies — 35
A Front-page Story — 40
Just Boys — 48
Honey, We'll Be Brave — 58
A Casual Incident — 83
Clyde — 87
Jim O'Neill — 101
Twenty-five Bucks — 108
Mary O'Reilley — 116
Calico Shoes — 125
Sunday — 135
Well, That's That — 144
Meet the Girls! — 153

GUILLOTINE PARTY

Soap — 179
The Open Road — 184
Guillotine Party — 196
Big Jeff — 203
In Accents of Death! — 207

The Little Blond Fellow	214
The Merry Clouters	224
Reverend Father Gilhooley	239
Jo-Jo	254
All Things Are Nothing to Me	263
A Practical Joke	276
Wedding Bells Will Ring So Merrily	289
The Benefits of American Life	302
Nostalgia	311
For White Men Only	315
Footnote	322
Comedy Cop	325
Two Sisters	340
Studs	347

CAN ALL THIS GRANDEUR PERISH?

Can All This Grandeur Perish?	357
Mendel and His Wife	370
Precinct Captain	385
The Professor	394
Children of the Times	406
Wanted: A Chauffeur	418
The Scoop	430
In City Hall Square	434
Spring Evening	435
Mr. Lunkhead, the Banker	442
The Oratory Contest	445
Angela	455
A Noble Guy	462
A Hell of a Good Time	470
Curbstone Philosophy	477
Thanksgiving Spirit	483
Seventeen	488

Introduction

By Robert Morss Lovett

FIVE years ago the name of James Farrell was unknown. Today it is read on the title pages of five novels, three volumes of short stories, and a challenging book of criticism. It is signed to articles in numerous magazines, including those to which contribution is a matter of generosity and good will; and appears in lists of eminent sponsors to causes which used to be vaguely grouped under the general name of the uplift. Farrell himself is seen and heard at dinners and mass meetings in aid of the same causes. He was lately the recipient of a large amount of unsolicited advertising through the attentions of Mr. John S. Sumner of the Society for the Suppression of Vice and was the star in a *cause célèbre* in the legal history of censorship. He is among the foremost in the group of younger writers who are taking the stage in succession to those whom we already think of as the old guard: Theodore Dreiser, Upton Sinclair, Sinclair Lewis, Sherwood Anderson, and Ernest Hemingway. In his external career he recalls Dickens in the rapidity of his production and his sudden rise to notability as a writer and as a public figure—a defender of human rights.

My first acquaintance with Farrell at the University of Chicago was in connection with a letter which he wrote to the college newspaper protesting against the exclusion by the dramatic club of colored students from plays which introduced characters belonging to their race. At our second meeting he brought me the manuscript of a story about Studs Lonigan, a boy who grew up in the changing neighborhood a mile or so west of the University. If my recollection is correct—that I told him his material was fitted for longer treatment than the short story—I take it as an "appropriation to my own good parts." At all events, I soon

This article by Professor Lovett appeared originally in *The English Journal*, May, 1937.

which is determined with Calvinistic inevitability out of the factors given of heredity, environment, and circumstance. *A World I Never Made,* which opens a tetralogy based upon similar data of Irish-American family life, shows gain in firmness of texture and precision of drawing. The appearance of Margaret in her lovely nakedness is unforgettable. Here again convention has stored up dynamic power for the bold defier of it. Painters of the nude have discovered the difference between academic purity and realistic truth. Farrell merely follows them. The quarrel between Margaret and her mother in which each combatant fires volleys of verbal filth in the face of the other is a scene with the fine abundance of Fielding, though it will be long before this displaces the famous quarrels of Brutus and Cassius and of Marmion and Douglas as an appropriate exercise for graduation from high school.

Besides Dreiser the writers whom Farrell mentions with most approval are Proust and Joyce. These three were the literary gods in the years when he was beginning to find himself, and it is natural to see something of each in his work. The stern logic of the career of Studs Lonigan is comparable to that of *An American Tragedy,* but it may be inferred that in the more extensive and deeply implied human pattern which emerges in *Judgment Day,* with its ampler sense of "the individual human being in interaction with other human beings in society," we have the influence of Proust. Certainly the first volume of *A World I Never Made* suggests a definitely Proustian approach to a segment of society which the author knows from the inside. The external realism by which we follow the characters through the section of Chicago which lies between Washington Park and Wabash Avenue is reminiscent of Joyce's Dublin; and the stream of consciousness which carries us down the years of Patrick J. Lonigan's life, once in triumph in the first pages of *Studs Lonigan,* again in defeat in the last pages of *Judgment Day,* is suggestive of Mrs. Bloom. It may be added that Farrell's short stories are of the family of Joyce's *Dubliners.*

Farrell's short stories are chips off the blocks of his novels. They are sketches of characters and episodes, casual and often trivial, thrown off with the prodigality of a Chekhov. Two qualities which are implicit in all Farrell's work stand out more distinctly than elsewhere in these fragments of life: irony and pathos. Sometimes the mere factual statement carries the bitter meaning: the dull vulgarity of city life in Don Bryan's Sunday stroll in *Looking 'Em Over;* and the atrocious sacrifice, mediated by priestly teachers, of the young lives intrusted to their

INTRODUCTION

charge in the resolutions set for Alvin Norton to read in *Accents of Death*. The pathos of wasted youth in *A Front Page Story, Soap,* and *Honey, We'll Be Brave* is released the more effectively by the author's determined understatement. The reader knows, however, that behind the literal manner of the case reporter there is pity for the broken shards of humanity—a pity that has its most sustained expression in the drunken odyssey of the elder Lonigan, back through the years and the city of his success to the starting-point which now denotes failure —on the evening of his son's dying.

Mr. Farrell's later volume of short stories, *Can All This Grandeur Perish?*, shows a wider range of material, with no change of method. In particular, he gives several characterizations of adolescent girlhood as poignantly real as Studs Lonigan. In "Angela," an ill-favored high-school girl becomes a successful parasite at college by virtue of literary ambitions and radical pretensions. "Seventeen" is a story of precocious curiosity and passion, told against a background of cynical talk between two girls who call each other "Russell" and "McGowan." For another matter, Mr. Farrell shows a more sustained and mordant use of satire, directed, according to tradition, toward unmasking the pretensions and shams of an uncouth culture. It is to be feared that Mr. Farrell does not hold in high respect the literary education provided by the American college. "The Professor" is a cruelly revealing study through behavior and analysis. Here, for once, Mr. Farrell can be charged with animus which is usually absent from his work. The suffering which he displays with a lavishness almost medieval is not of his nature but of life's.

His admiration of Dreiser, Farrell limits by recognizing the inadequacy of his general ideas. In this respect the younger writer has already surpassed the older master, and, judging by his growth in intellectual power evinced by *A Note in Literary Criticism*, he bids fair to go farther yet. When the first volume of the *Studs Lonigan* series appeared it was recognized as a valuable contribution to the social problem of adolescence in metropolitan life. Professor Thrasher wrote in his Introduction:

> Life on the street is the most potent educative influence for the majority of boys in such areas and one which contradicts traditional definitions and values as represented by the home, the church, the social agency, and the school. The street gives no diplomas and grants no degrees, but it educates with fatal precision. In *Young Lonigan* there is clearly portrayed a process of

assimilation of boys to the attitudes and behavior patterns of the street and its characteristic playgroups, gangs, poolrooms, et cet., which represent the juvenile community in this type of area. The process of demoralization as it takes place in a natural and inevitable way among boys in such an environment is vividly illustrated in the life of Studs Lonigan and his *confrères*. The influence of the streetcorner tramp, the role played by social status in the gang, the neighborhood processes of rivalry and conflict, and the immense importance attributed to sex are revealed as important elements in the boy's social life. This is the process of informal education, the significance of which as yet has hardly penetrated the ken of psychologists and educationists, to say nothing of parents and teachers.

An aspect of urban life which appears with sinister clearness is the decline of institutions in their ability to hold or influence youth. The impotence of the church is always a theme of Farrell's social criticism. It is traced to one source in two short scenes from clerical life: *Reverend Father Gilhooley* and *The Little Blond Fellow*. A mild endorsement of its influence appears in the belief of Studs Lonigan's companions that Catholic girls do not fall as easily as others, but its services have become a bore and the confessional has no terrors. The school is an unexplainable trespass on personal liberty. The family is a field of wrangling in which parental authority is constantly flouted. A theme of great significance in late nineteenth-century literature is that of the revolt of youth seeking freedom from institutions of the past—the war between the generations—which received its classic treatment in Turgeniev's *Fathers and Sons*. The tragedy of Studs Lonigan is that he is not a rebel; not even a criminal. He does not war against his family and against society, though he preys upon both. His life is tragic because it is empty of any purpose whatever. His experience is terrible and pitiful to his audience because it is meaningless to himself. It is Farrell's ferocious indictment of American life.

As I remarked at the outset, Farrell's addiction to general ideas and social criticism is by way of making him a public figure concerned in various movements for the reform and renovation of society. He has, however, succeeded in keeping his fiction free from the entanglements of partisanship. It is perhaps as a prophylactic treatment against the infection of his art by the virus of propaganda that he wrote his *Note on Literary Criticism*. At all events, a reader sees in this unpretentious little book the evidence of the writer's assimilation of ideas from Marx, Engels, Lenin, Dewey, and others, according to their usefulness to him—

INTRODUCTION

self in making clear the purpose and necessary processes of his art.

Farrell begins by distinguishing between the aspects of literature as a fine and a useful art, according to whether it depends upon the aesthetic or the functional elements in human experience. Exclusive emphasis upon the aesthetic as represented by Pater or upon the functional as represented by St. Thomas Aquinas and Professor Babbitt he rejects. His chief battle is with the critics of the Marxist school: Granville Hicks, Michael Gold, Edwin Seaver, and others, who conceive literature largely in terms of economic environment and evaluate it according to its consciousness of the class struggle and the aid which it brings to one side or the other, bourgeois or proletarian. Against these interpreters of Marx, Farrell cites the authority of Marx himself:

Marx, then, conceived societies in motion, and he perceived that the factor of change is ever present in social relationships. Because of this factor, the effects of one set of relationships become casual factors for the next set, and thus there is ever evolving a whole network of influences; so that cultural manifestations, such as formal art, thought, and literature, which *may be* directly related to the basic material and economic relationships upon which a society is founded in one era, evolve away from that set of relationships as the process unfolds with the passage of time, and they in turn become part of the network of casual factors and conditioning influences in the general stream of social tendencies and forces.

This description, as Farrell points out, provides an explanation of the process "in which thought, art, and literature possess a carry-over value" from the past and bring aesthetic enrichment to the present as part of the inheritance of tradition.

The fact that Farrell is himself a Marxist in politics makes him the more anxious to defend his position that individual and collective, bourgeois and proletarian, as categories have no place as standards of judgment. He does not deny that a collective novel can be written but he rejects the notion that "the extent of the geographical territory covered in a novel and a prolixity of characters treated with relatively little detail will convey a stronger sense of the pressure of social circumstances and a stronger feeling of group or class or continent." His citation of John Dos Passos' *The 42nd Parallel* as an example of a so-called collective novel which "has to rely for unity on mechanical interlardings—his news-reel, his camera's eye, his use of free verse biographies of contemporary and historical figures," seems to me ill chosen. For

Dos Passos, unity depends on atmosphere diffused through a technique which Professor Joseph Warren Beach has happily called "breadthwise cutting," and further made palpable by the explicit interludes which remind us of what the country at large was reading, seeing, and thinking. Again one must agree with Farrell's protest that men have other interests besides the class struggle, and that to use "proletarian" and "bourgeois" as terms of eulogy or reprobation is to substitute labels for analysis. It is true, nevertheless, that experiments in fiction and drama which emphasize the concept of group or mass, and criticism which takes account of literary values to be found in the exploited class, whose immediate interest is bound up with a world-process leading to a classless society, are in accord with the great and characteristic theme of modern literature: the theme of human solidarity—of "social union in a rationally ordered state." That Farrell in his stories of the degradation of human beings under the decay of human institutions is contributing to the emergence of this theme is my own conviction. Within the categories of growth and decay in literature, to which he devotes his last chapter, I place his own work in that of growth.

Calico Shoes
AND OTHER
STORIES

"The world is so full of a number of things, I'm sure we should all be as happy as kings."

ROBERT LOUIS STEVENSON

"No sovereign, no court, no personal loyalty, no aristocracy, no church, no clergy, no army, no diplomatic service, no country gentlemen, no palaces, no castles, nor manors, nor old country houses, nor parsonages, nor thatched cottages, nor ivied ruins; no cathedrals, nor abbeys, nor little Norman churches; no great Universities nor public schools—no Oxford, nor Eton, nor Harrow."

HENRY JAMES

"For, in reality, the knowledge of an effect is nothing else than the acquisition of more perfect knowledge of its cause."

SPINOZA

Helen, I Love You

I

"You got a goofy look," Dick Buckford said.

"Yeh," Dan said.

The two boys stood in front of one of the small graystone houses in the 5700 block on Indiana Avenue, glaring at each other.

Dan didn't know what to say. He glanced aside at the hopeless, rainy autumn day. His eyes roved over the damp street, the withered grass and mud by the sidewalk across the street, the three-story apartment buildings, and at the sky which dumped down top-heavily behind the buildings.

"Yeah, you're goofy! You're goofy!" Dick sneered.

"Then so are you," Dan countered.

"Am I?" Dick challenged.

"Yes!" Dan answered with determination.

"Am I goofy?"

"If you say I am, then you're a goof, too!"

Dan hoped nothing would happen. He knew how, if he lost a fight when he was still new in the neighborhood, everybody would start taking picks on him, bullying him, making a dope out of him, and kidding him all the time because he had been licked. He hoped that he wouldn't be forced into a fight with Dick, who was about ten pounds heavier than he was. But he pretended that he was fighting Dick, beating hell out of him. He pretended that he slugged Dick in the face, and saw the blood spurt from his big nose. He slugged Dick, until Dick was bloody and winded and said quits, and a crowd of guys and girls watching the fight cheered and said that Dan was certainly a fine fighter, and then he pretended that Helen Scanlan came up to him and told him she was so glad.

But he'd already had his chance with her. She had seemed to like him, but he'd been too damn bashful. Once, he could have held her hand and kissed her, and they could have gone over to the park, and kissed some more, if he only hadn't been so bashful. She had even said that she liked him.

They were standing right in front of the parlor window of the Scanlan house. He thought again of himself slamming Dick around, with Helen in the window watching him. Red-haired Helen Scanlan, he loved her. He said to himself:

Helen, I love you!

"Why don't you pull in your ears? Huh?" said Dick.

"Aw, freeze your teeth and give your tongue a sleighride," Dan said.

He wished Dick would go away, because he wanted to walk around alone, and maybe go over to the park, where it would be all quiet except for the wind, and where the leaves would be wet and yellow, and it would be easy to think of Helen. He could walk around, and think and be a little happy-sad, and think about Helen. And here was Dick before him, and Dick was supposed to be one of the best scrappers in the neighborhood, and he seemed to want to pick a fight, and right here, too, outside of Helen's window. And maybe Dick would win, with Helen there to watch it all.

Dan wanted Dick to go away. He told himself that he loved Helen. He told himself that he was awfully in love with curly, red-haired Helen. He remembered last summer, when he had peddled bills for half a dollar, putting them in mail boxes all over the neighborhood. The day after, they had gone riding on the tail-gate of hump-backed George's grocery wagon, and it had been fun, himself and Helen sitting there on the back of the wagon, holding hands as they bounced through the alleys, and while they waited for George to deliver his orders. And he had spent all his money on her. He told himself that he loved her.

He remembered how, after riding on the wagon, he had gone home, and they had bawled him out because he had worn the soles on his shoes out delivering the bills, and then had gone and spent the money so foolishly, with nothing to show for it. There had been a big scrap, and he had answered them back, and got so sore that he had bawled like a cry-baby. Afterwards, he'd sat in the parlor, crying and cursing, because he was sore. He'd had such a swell time that afternoon, too. And the family just hadn't understood it at all. And then Helen had come around, because all the kids in the neighborhood used to come around to his front steps at night to play and talk. Somebody had called to tell him she was there. He hadn't known what he was doing, and he'd answered that he didn't care if she was there or not.

After that Helen hadn't paid any attention to him.
He told himself:
Helen, I love you!

II

"If I was as goofy as you, I'd do something about it," Dick said.

"Yeh. Well, I ain't got nothing on you."

"No? Well, look at it, your stockings are falling down. You can't even keep your stockings up," said Dick.

"Well, you're sniffin' and don't even know enough to blow your nose."

"Don't talk to me like that!" Dick said.

"Well, don't talk to me like that, either!"

"I ain't afraid of you!" Dick said.

"And I ain't afraid of you, either!" said Dan.

"Wanna fight?" asked Dick.

"If you do, I do!" said Dan.

"Well, start something," said Dick.

"You start something," said Dan.

"But maybe you won't, because you're yellow," said Dick.

"No, I ain't, neither. I ain't afraid of you."

Dick smiled sarcastically at Dan.

"I don't know whether to kiss you or kill you," he said with exaggerated sweetness.

"Yeh, you heard Red Kelly make that crack, and you're just copying it from him. You ain't funny," Dan said.

"That's all you know about it! Well, I made it up and Red heard me say it. That's where he got it. How you like that?"

"Tie your bull in somebody else's alley," Dan said.

Dick tried to out-stare Dan. Dan frowned back at him.

"And today in school, when Sister Cyrilla called on you, you didn't even know enough how to divide fractions. You're goofy," Dick said.

"Well, if I'm goofy, I don't know what you ain't," Dan said.

Dan again pretended that they were fighting, and that he was kicking the hell out of Dick with Helen watching. And he remembered how last summer when he had gotten those hats advertising Cracker Jack, he had given one to her. He had felt good that day, because she had worn the hat he gave her. And every night they had all played tin-tin, or run-sheep-run, or chase-one-chase-all, or eeny-meeny-miny-mo. He had just moved around then, and he had thought that it was such a good neighborhood, and now, if Dick went picking a fight with him and beat him, well, he just wouldn't be able to show his face any more and would just about have to sneak down alleys and everything.

But if he beat Dick up and Helen saw him, he would be her hero, and he would be one of the leaders of their gang, and then maybe she would like him again, and twice as much, and everything would be all so swell, just like it was at the end of the stories he sometimes read in *The Saturday Evening Post*.

Last summer, too, he had read *Penrod*, and he had thought of Helen because she was like Marjorie Jones in the book, only more so, and prettier, and nicer, and she had nicer hair, because the book said Marjorie Jones's hair was black, and Helen's was red, and red hair was nicer than black hair.

"One thing I wouldn't be called is yellow," Dick sneered.

"I ain't yellow," Dan said.

"I wouldn't be yellow," Dick said.

"And I wouldn't be a sniffer, and not have enough sense to blow my nose," said Dan.

"Who's a sniffer?" demanded Dick.

"Well, why don't you blow your nose?"

"Why doncha not be so goofy?" demanded Dick.

"I ain't no goofier than you."

"If I was as goofy as you, I'd quit living," Dick said.

"Yeh, and if I was like you, I'd drown myself."

"You better do it then, because you're goofier than anybody I know," Dick said.

"Yeh?"

"Yeh!"

"Yeh!"

"And let me tell you, I ain't afraid of nobody like you," Dick said.

"I ain't, neither. Just start something, and see!"

"I would, only I don't wanna get my hands dirty, picking on a goof. If you wasn't afraid of me, you wouldn't stand there, letting me say you're goofy."

"Well, I'm here saying you're just as goofy."

"I couldn't be like you."

"And I couldn't be as dumb as you," Dan said.

"You're so goofy, I wouldn't be seen with you."

"Don't, then!" said Dan.

"I ain't! I was here first!"

"I live on this street."

"I lived in this neighborhood longer than you," said Dick.

"I live on this street, and you can beat it if you don't like it."

"You're so goofy you belong in the Kankakee nut house. Your whole family's goofy. My old man says I shouldn't have nothing to do with you because of all the goofiness in your family."

"Well, my old man and my uncle don't think nothing of your old man," Dan said.

"Well, don't let my old man hear them sayin' it, because if he does, he's liable to bat their snoots off," said Dick.

"Let him try! My old man ain't afraid of nothing!"

"Yeh? Don't never think so. My old man could take your old man on blindfolded."

"Yeh? My old man could trim your old man with his little finger, and it's cut off," said Dan.

"Say, if my old man's hands were tied behind his back, and he said 'Boo,' your old man would take to his heels lickety-split down the streets, afraid."

"Let him start something and see, then!"

"If he ever does, I'd feel sorry for your old man," said Dick.

"You don't need to be."

"My old man's strong, and he says I take after him, and when I grow up, I'll be like him, a lineman climbing telephone poles for the telephone company," said Dick.

"Yeh?" said Dan.

"Yeh!" said Dick.

"Yeh?" said Dan.

"Baloney," said Dick.

"Bouswah," said Dan.

"B.S.," said Dick.

They sneered toughly at one another.

"That for you!" Dick said, snapping his fingers in Dan's face.

"That for you!" Dan said, screwing up his lips and twitching his nose.

"If this is the street you live on, I won't hang around it no more, because it smells just as bad as you do," said Dick.

"That's because you're on it."

"I'm going, because I don't want nobody to know that I'm even acquainted with anyone as goofy as you."

"Good riddance to bad rubbage," said Dan.

"If you weren't such a clown, I'd break you with my little finger!" said Dick.

"And I'd blow you over with my breath!" said Dan.

III

Dan watched Dick walk away, without looking back. He sat on the iron fence around the grass plot, feeling good because he had proven to himself that he wasn't afraid of Dick. He said to himself:

Helen, I love you!

He sat.

He sat through slow, oblivious minutes. He arose and decided to take a walk. Wishing that he could see Helen, he strolled down to Fifty-eighth Street, and bought five cents' worth of candy. He returned and sat on the iron fence in front of her house, and for about twenty-five minutes he nibbled at his candy, hoping that she would come along, wondering where she was, wishing he could give her some of his candy. He told himself:

Helen, I love you!

He thought of how he had held her hand that day on the grocery wagon. He imagined her watching him while he cleaned the stuffings out of Dick Buckford.

The day was sad. He wished that it had some sun. The day wouldn't be sad, though, if she came along and talked to him.

He walked over to Washington Park. It was lonely, and he didn't see anybody in the park. The wind kept beating against the trees and bushes, and sometimes, when he listened closely, it seemed to him like an unhappy person, crying. He walked on and on, wetting his feet, but he didn't care. He stopped to stand by the lagoon. There were small waves on it, and it looked dark, and black, and mean. He said to himself:

Helen, I love you!

He continued gazing at the lagoon. Then, he strolled on.

Yes, if Dick had started something, he would have cleaned the guts out of him. Dick would have rushed him, and he would have biffed Dick, giving him a pretty shiner. Dick would have rushed him again, and he would have biffed Dick a second time, and Dick would have had a bloody nose. He would have stood back and led with a left to the solar plexus, and Dick would have doubled up, and he would have smashed Dick with a right, and Dick would have fallen down with another black eye. Dick would have yelled quits, and Helen, who would have been watching it all, would have yelled for him, and maybe she would have said:

Dan, I want to be your girl!

He walked. He looked all around him at the park stretching away in wet, darkened, dying grass, with shadows falling down over it. The light was going out of the sky, and he said good-bye to Mr. Day. He felt all alone, and thought how nice it would be if he only had someone to talk to. Maybe Helen. Maybe himself and Helen walking in the wet grass. Maybe some man would try to kidnap her. The man would run away with her under his arm crying for help. And he would pick up a rock and fling at the guy, and it would smack the guy in the skull, and he would drop down unconscious, but Helen wouldn't be hurt. And he would rush up, hit the guy with another rock so that he would be out colder than if he had been hit by Ruby Bob Fitzsimmons in his prime. Police would come, and he would have his picture in the papers, and he would be a real hero, and Helen would say to him:

Dan, I love you, and I'll always love you.

He walked. It was almost dark, and the wind sounds seemed worse than the voices of ghosts. He wished he wasn't so all alone. He had strange feelings. He wondered what he ought to do, and it seemed like there were people behind every tree. The park was too lonely to be in, and he decided that he'd better go home. And it was getting to be supper time.

The wind was awfully sad. There wasn't any moon or stars in the sky yet.

He didn't know what he was afraid of, but he was awfully afraid.

And it would have been so nice, and so different, if he was only with Helen. She would be afraid, too, and he would be protecting her.

He started back toward home, thinking what he would have done to Dick if Dick had really started a fight. Yes, sir, he would have made Dick sorry.

Helen, I love you!

1930.

The Scarecrow

There, little girl, don't cry!
They have broken your heart, I know;
And the rainbow gleams
Of your youthful dreams
Are things of the long ago;
But Heaven holds all for which you sigh—
There, little girl, don't cry!
               JAMES WHITCOMB RILEY

I

"EITHER you be home when I get here tonight, or . . . never darken my door as long as you live! This time *it's final!*"

"But mother . . . it's . . . Hallowe'en."

"When I say final . . . I mean *final!*"

The Scarecrow was scrawny, and with her thin features and bony, angular body, she resembled her mother.

"You've been a disgrace long enough. It's all right to have a good time, but it's positively the limit when a fourteen-year-old girl like you makes a cheap whore out of herself for every little tramp and highschool bum that comes along. Young lady, while you live under my roof and eat my hard-earned bread, you'll not carry on like a harlot. Here I am, an old woman, slaving for you. It's not fair, and I'm not going on with it. What are you? . . . What are you? A slut! *Slut!* God knows I tried to be a good mother to you. But what does it get me? What have you done in gratitude? It's no use. Goodness just ain't in you. You've got your father's blood. You're like him. I tried with all my power to make a good girl out of you, but it's no use. I'm through!"

The mother fell dramatically into a chair. The daughter, after gawking after her mother, moved toward the door and tripped over her own feet.

"Gee!" she exclaimed, sitting on the floor.

"Ox! Cancha even walk straight! Cow!"

The daughter arose and stared vacantly at her mother. Timidly, she took a chair.

"I don't know what they can see in you. You're ugly, and a bag of bones. You got his ugly cheekbones, and his consumptive pallor and chest. No figure. You're nothing but a homely, bow-legged little beast. But then, I suppose pretty girls don't have to make whores out of themselves for every little bum that comes along the street."

The Scarecrow gawked at her mother.

"Well, *madam,* are you coming home tonight, or are you sleeping with some little cur? And, *madam,* shall I have your bawth ready? And perhaps you'd like to bring your little *gentleman* home and use my bed!"

The girl sat on the edge of the chair. The mother arose, and violently crossed the floor.

"Answer me! Answer me!" the mother screamed, continuing, "you're no daughter of mine. You take after that bastard father of yours. I wish to Christ he had taken you along when he cleared out. I didn't want him, and I don't want his dirty little bitch of a daughter. You're not my flesh and blood, you filthy little whore!"

The mother dropped to her knees in the center of the room and lowered her head. The daughter continued to sit in speechless fear.

"Oh, God! Oh, God! God, why must I bear this cross!"

The mother sat on the floor, and her raggedy hair splattered down her angular back. The Scarecrow's face broke into a weak slow-motion smile. Lifting her head, the mother perceived the smile on her daughter's face. She leaped at the girl.

"Go ahead now, cry! Cry, you dirty whore!" The mother's pathetic face contorted with pain and ecstasy as she beat the girl, who cowered from the chair onto the floor. "Cry! Cry! Cry! Cry! Cry, you slut! God knows you broke my poor mother's heart without shedding tears. Goddamn you, cry!"

Breathless, the mother ceased beating her daughter.

"You didn't cry, though . . . oh, no . . . you didn't cry that night I caught you with a little grammar-school bum in my bed. You didn't, neither, when you went into the boys' toilet at the Edmonds school. Well, cry now, you pig!"

The mother slumped back into a Morris chair. The girl sniffled on the floor, and, red-eyed, gazed out at the awfully sad day.

"You got his face, and his dirty eyes. You look like him and I hate you!" the mother screamed, leaping at, and again striking, the girl.

The Scarecrow arose to flee. The mother caught her and roughly flung her into a corner. She took a slice of rubber hosing from the sideboard, and battered the girl to her knees.

"That for your bastard father! . . . And that! . . . And that!"

Exhausted from the effort, the mother turned and sat down. Through tear-glazed eyes she watched her daughter trembling like one shivering with the cold. She buried her head and moaned:

"George! George! I've suffered loneliness! I've been lonely, George! Please come back to this aching heart! Please! I'll forgive and forget everything. I'll work, I'll work the skin off my hands for you . . . God, oh, please, God, send my husband back to me, my husband, my sweetheart, my lover! . . . God, oh, God, must I go on wearing myself out, carrying the heavy cross of a poor, helpless, lonely old woman! God, please send him back to me before it's too late. God, have you given any woman a cross as heavy as mine! God, if I was only dead! God!"

The mother gradually subsided and retired to her bedroom. A few sobs were heard, and then quiet wreathed the house. The daughter, still on the floor, broke the silence with hysterical laughter. Her bruised back throbbed like an over-stimulated pulse. She went to her cot. Her tears slowly dried. Half-asleep, she dreamed that she was the beautiful wife of a handsome millionaire, and he gave her beautiful clothes, beautiful yachts, beautiful airplanes, beautiful beach pyjamas, beautiful automobiles, beautiful everythings. She dreamed that she was a beautiful queen in a beautiful palace, wearing a beautiful dress of beautiful purple velvet, with a beautiful train, and that she was arising from a beautiful throne, surrounded by beautiful servants, and she stood in all her beautiful majesty, sentencing her mother to horrible tortures, because she was a mean old witch and a cruel thing. She dreamed that she was Cleopatra, dancing the dance of the seven veils, while all her marcelled generals, as handsome as Wayne, watched her with love for her in their beautiful eyes.

The Scarecrow was still asleep, her beaten, ugly little body thrilling with dreams, when the mother, who was a ticket-taker in an Illinois Central Suburban station, departed for work. Before the mother slammed the door, she shouted back a final unheard warning.

It was dark and windy outside when the Scarecrow awakened. Sitting up on her cot, she rubbed sleepy eyes, and thought about how nice it would be if she could sleep all night with Wayne. Last night, Kenneth had had such cold feet. She laughed over the way she had fooled her mother. Her mother had come home sick last night, and had gone straight to bed without looking to see if she was home. And she had snuck in the house and gone to her cot at about seven in the morning, and her old thing of a mother had not known the difference. The old fool! Ha! Ha!

When Wayne rang the doorbell, the Scarecrow answered in her greasy kimono. She told him he could wait for her in the parlor, but he answered that he'd like to sit and watch her dress. She said that gentlemen didn't watch ladies dress for the ball in their boudoir. He followed her. He laughed when she dropped her kimono and faced the mirror in her soiled under-clothing. She giggled. He told her that she was plug-ugly. He became excited, and kissed her all over and said crazy-nice things to her, using the nicest grammar. Afterward, he waited in the parlor, urging her to hurry. She combed her stringy hair, layered her face with cheap cosmetics, and fussed around putting on and taking off her ten-dollar black dress until she was finally satisfied that she looked like a society lady.

They were late and Wayne took a taxicab. He felt like a man-of-the-world. Even though she was ugly and not all there in the top story, she was another notch in his belt, and he could tell the boys at Tower Tech about it during lunch hours next week.

II

The party was being held at Ray's. Ray was a good guy. He made dough selling wholesale groceries. He was thick with Bill's old man, and like a kindly uncle to Bill. Whenever Bill and the gang wanted to throw a party, they called him up and told him. He usually said O.K. He was well stocked with food and liquor, and didn't care what they did, as long as they didn't break up the furniture and cleared out before he arrived home with his lady-friend.

Bill opened the door for them, and, staggering before Wayne, hurried their entrance, bragging of the liquor they had all drunk. Wayne hastily deposited his wraps in a closet, and appeared in the parlor. Above the clamor of the greetings, Bill insisted that they had all poured plenty down the old swivel, and that Wayne had to do some quick and fancy drinking if he wanted to catch up with them.

"I'm old Kid Lightning," Wayne said.

"Well, you got lots of territory to cover," Bill said.

The girls laughed at the humor, and gave Wayne the eye, observing his handsome face and blond hair.

"Lookat that! Ain't she a sight for the sisters who teach her Christian Doctrine!" George said to Wayne, pointing at Lois, who lay, as if soddenly unconscious, on a couch, a cigarette dying in her hand, wisps of bobbed light hair falling over her flapper's face. They laughed boisterously, and her face twitched.

"Hello, Scarecrow!" Bill said, as the Scarecrow minced into the room imitating movie actresses she had seen in pictures.

"Hello, Nickel Nose!" George said in greeting.

The girls smiled at her, distantly. George grabbed her arm and led her to the center of the room.

"Ladies and Gents!" he called, gesturing profusely.

Bill asked where the ladies were because he, for one, could not see any. Joe asked did George think he was funny or what, calling the Scarecrow a lady. They were amused.

"Think of your mother!" George said in an exaggerated voice; they laughed; the Scarecrow picked her nose.

"Well, Bill, I certainly like your nerve!" little Marge said, babyishly elevating her pug nose in a gesture of mock indignation. She continued that there were ladies present, but that she could not see anything that would serve as a model even for an imitation of a gentleman.

"Aw, Hot Monkey, Vomit!" Bill snapped, causing little Marge to throw a shocked look at him.

"Ladies and Bums!" George megaphoned through his hands, while the Scarecrow stood with a silly grin on her face, pleased to be the center of attention. "Ladies and No-dough Bums!"

Joe asked George why he didn't marry the girl, and George retorted that it would be foolish because the wench doled out the marriageable goods gratis.

"Ladies and Bums, I have here . . ."

"Doesn't he look like Harold Teen?" the Scarecrow tittered in interruption.

George blushed and sputtered incoherently as they gave him the razzberry. He held the Scarecrow's upper arm tightly, squeezing until she winced.

"Ladies and Dopes! Allow me to introduce you to a real, unadulterated celebrity. . . . I have here with us tonight none other than

Miss Nickel Nose, the best known virgin in all the grammar schools of Chicago."

"Razzberries," Wayne said.

"Put him out of misery," Bill said.

"See if tickling the boy's funny-bone will make him amusing," Mary Jane said, blasé.

The Scarecrow gawked at them. Jack, a bath towel flung over his left arm, entered with a tray of filled wine glasses.

"Garçon," little Marge said in her best high-school French accent.

"Now you found your speed, being a bartender," the Scarecrow said, hoping they would laugh at her remark.

"Listen, Nickel Nose!" Jack hissed.

They scrambled for the wine, spilling some on the carpet. George proposed a toast to God's Guts. Lois, coming to, grabbed the last glass from the tray, leaped onto the divan, and told George that he should be more scientific and say God's alimentary canal. Little Marge expressed shock that Lois, a Catholic high-school girl, should speak like that. Lois proposed her substitute toast. Marge persisted in being shocked.

"Hey, wench, put a padlock on your buccal cavity!" Bill said.

"Well, of all the nerve!" little Marge said.

Mary Jane and Frances said they were totally disgusting and unregenerate. They sipped to the toast.

The Scarecrow planked herself down beside Wayne, considering her action to have been done in the queenly manner. She whispered to him that he had nice hair.

"Save it," he told her coldly.

Little Marge made room on her chair, and called Wayne to come and sit by her so that she could tell him a secret. George said that every time Marge got a yen for a guy, she had secrets to tell him. She told George that he was disgusting and insulting. Wayne sat by Marge. Lois immediately jumped on Wayne's lap and commenced to finger his tie.

"He's my man," Marge protested feebly, squashed under their combined weight.

"Hello, Handsome!" Lois said.

Wayne blushed. Marge protested until they both arose and gravitated to a corner. Marge frowned after them. The Scarecrow, viewing this by-play, seemed on the verge of tears. She asked for a drink. Jack told her that she was not a cripple. She hastened to the kitchen. She poured a glass of wine and sat down at the kitchen table. Crying, she drank a toast to herself, and thought of some tall, handsome, awfully rich millionaire's son who would come and marry her and make her his beautiful happy wife with all kinds of beautiful things and beautiful clothes of her own. Then, wouldn't these mean old girls at the party turn every color and green wishing they were her. She drank a toast to the handsome, awfully rich millionaire's son who was going to appear like in the story of *Cinderella* and marry her.

She arose, telling herself that a lady must always look her best. She went to the bathroom and smeared powder on her face and dabbed her lips with carmined rouge. She returned to the parlor while George told a joke about how fleas got in the preacher's soup. The fellows guffawed; Mary Jane protested that it was a vile joke.

"We tell much better ones than that down at Tower Tech," George bragged.

The Scarecrow laughed stupidly, and announced that she knew a joke that had nothing to do with you-know. She told it. Two men were lost and starving in the desert. The poor men were really awful hungry, because they had been traveling in the desert for days and days without anything to eat, and they were really almost dead from being hungry. They finally were beginning to get awful afraid that they would die of starving on account of their having had nothing to eat for all these days and weeks that they were traveling in the desert, and they didn't think that they could go even one more step unless they got something to eat. Just then, one of the men saw a dead horse that had been dead a long time, because he could see maggots all over the dead horse, crawling over it like ants. One of the men asked the other if he wanted to eat part of the horse, but his friend didn't want to, so the other man ate the whole horse. They walked along and soon the man who ate the horse vomited. The other man jumped up and down because he was so happy, and he said:

"Good, I knew I'd get a hot meal."

"Ugh!" Lois exclaimed.

"Somebody please chloroform the woman," Marge said.

"No, fumigate her," Mary Jane said.

"Say, I told you that joke, Scarecrow," George said.

"Well, I wouldn't brag about it," Lois said.

"See, wench, they all know you're vacant in the attic," Bill told the Scarecrow.

THE SCARECROW

There was a round of smutty jokes, and Bill got a big laugh by saying that the dirtiest joke he had ever known of was the Scarecrow.

"Say, that reminds me," George interrupted.

"What?" asked Bill.

"The granary," George answered.

They rushed to the kitchen. Food and beer was taken from the icebox. Several of them grabbed for items at the same time and some of the food was slopped onto the floor. The Scarecrow stood isolated by the radiator, gnawing at a cold chicken leg. Marge warned her to be careful or she would break her teeth off. The Scarecrow answered that she wouldn't do that. Clucking in disgust, Mary Jane said that she acted just like a dog with a bone.

"I'll bet her mater kicked her out again," George said, tapping Bill's shoulder.

"Hey, Scarecrow!" Bill hollered.

She looked at him with a grease-smudged face.

"Did the mater toss you out again into the crool, cold world?" Bill asked.

She cried.

"Yep, I told you so," Bill said.

"It ain't the first time," George said.

"Hell, no!" Bill said.

"Hey, Wayne, are you taking the Scarecrow home tonight?" George called, while she resumed her gnawing at the chicken leg.

Marge and Lois, hearing the remark, looked contemptuously at the Scarecrow.

"What you mean?" Wayne asked, irritated.

"Ain't you her boy-friend of the moment?" Jack said.

"I managed that business with her before I came," Wayne smirked.

"Jesus, fellows, look at her. She's flowing again," George said.

"I hate my mother!" the Scarecrow sobbed.

"Well, that's no reason for not wiping your nose," Bill said.

"Scarecrow, it looks to me like it's mutual. And anyway, whether the mater likes you or not, she certainly doesn't waste any time feeding you. Boy, I never saw a wench stow away the grub like you do. Better be careful or you'll be getting fat," George said.

"Yes, Scarecrow, you don't want to go and get sick from overeating," Jack said.

"Hell with her troubles. Let's have a drink," Wayne said, talking with a mouth full of ham sandwich.

Jack prepared a round of drinks. George took a glass, mounted the table, and held his glass aloft.

"To the Scarecrow, may she find a bed . . . ump, a home!"

"Hell, she's just as used to alleys, garbage cans, and hallways for that. What the hell!" Jack said, gulping a drink, spilling some on his coat.

"You boys are horrid!" Mary Jane said, laying her glass on the sink.

Mary Jane walked over to the Scarecrow and told her not to cry. She listened to the Scarecrow's story sympathetically, and nodded an insincere agreement when the Scarecrow said that she couldn't see why her mean old mother should go beating her up for liking boys when she couldn't help liking them.

"But what's it like?" Mary Jane interrupted.

"Huh? What?"

"You know. I mean when fellows and girls violate the sixth commandment?"

"Some boys, like Kenneth, have cold feet," the Scarecrow said, after giggling.

Mary Jane said that she always wondered how it was when you were just such a naturally frigid person that your icy blood froze your heart.

The doorbell rang. The party answered the ring ensemble. It was Caroline and Mike. Caroline was a tall, handsome girl of sixteen, who looked to be at least twenty. She had milky skin, expressive blue eyes, and a wealth of lovely chestnut hair. Wearing a long, black satin panelled dress which emphasized her hips, she was alluring. While the fellows were stupid in their attempt to greet her wittily, and the girls were formal, Marge flung her arms around her classmate, and they kissed.

"Carrie, dear, you look just ducky," Marge exclaimed.

George repeated Marge's words, and embraced Caroline. They were amused. Jack and Bill scrambled to procure her a drink. Her wraps removed, she vamped into the parlor, swinging her hips effectively. She accepted the glass Jack offered her, and drank it in one gulp.

"We learn to take our drinks at St. Paul's," she said in a stagey amateur-theatrical voice.

During a round of dancing, the Scarecrow sat alone in a corner of the floor. Lois, with a coated smile and sweetness of voice, asked Caroline how she attracted all the men. Caroline arched her eyebrows.

"You maybe don't know how," the Scarecrow said to Lois, giggling.

"I hate you, you dirty old . . . Nickel Nose," Lois said.

Caroline and Wayne danced through three successive jazz pieces. Then Marge cut in on her. Caroline majestically retired to the kitchen, and consumed a full jar of stuffed olives. The Scarecrow followed her, and sat down at the opposite end of the kitchen table. In tears, she told her story. Caroline listened until Lois, with a challengingly possessive manner, appeared on Wayne's arm. Caroline eyed Wayne and offered him a sip of a drink she had just poured herself. The Scarecrow said to Wayne that he was her partner at the party and that he had not danced with her once.

"Why don't you eat while you have the chance, and not bother? You'll find someone to sleep with you tonight," Lois said spitefully.

Caroline purposefully broke her beads, and asked Wayne to fix them. She walked back to the front with Wayne, bumping Lois with her hip in passing.

"I always thought that that big can of hers was good for something!" Lois said, watching them go down the hall.

Caroline and Wayne talked in the parlor, oblivious of the others. The Scarecrow came in lost-eyed, and sat beside them. Caroline turned to her and said that the seat she had taken belonged to someone else. The Scarecrow meekly arose and took a place in a corner of the floor.

"Well, all I say is that when Ray comes home, he'll get a nice surprise," Bill said.

"He'll be bringing his latest damsel home to this mess. And you know, when he brings a damsel home, he keeps her for breakfast, dinner, and supper," George said, emphasizing his last words.

"No man ever knows how to treat a woman right," Marge said apropos of no previous remark.

"Sure he does. Whip 'em! Treat 'em rough!" Wayne said, inclining his head toward her.

"Say, big boy!" Caroline challenged.

"I didn't mean you, darling. You're different, a queen. You're a beautiful empress of a glorious empire of Love and Dreams that no mere mortal can attain. You're an angel with orbs like stars, and skin as beautiful as the milky ways, and to compare you, an ineffable creature, with any of the profane, mundane beauties of this mundane terrestrial spinning globe is a sacrilege. Why, a miserable homo sap like myself is not worthy to kiss the hem of your garment, or the sole of your dainty slippers," Wayne said in his most polished and sophisticated high-school fraternity manner.

"Hey, Wayne, there's a word for all that," Jack said.

Oh, I wish I were a ring, upon my Lulu's hand,

George sang.

"What have you been feeding the man?" Caroline asked.

"Why, he tol' me all those things tonight when . . ." the Scarecrow tittered.

"She's your speed, Wayne," Caroline haughtily said, pointing derisively at the Scarecrow and leaving him.

Wayne was laughed at. He sulked to the kitchen for a drink. Several fellows crowded upon Caroline.

"See her! Ain't she a comely wench!" Mike said, pointing at Caroline, and toppling about with a half-filled glass in his hand.

Mary Jane inclined an elevated nose in Mike's direction.

"Yes, she's a comely wench. And I brought her here, see! I'm the guy that brought her to this party. I am. Hey, wench! Hey, Caroline! . . . Didn't you make Wayne yet?"

"Mike, you're perfectly despicable. You're too unspeakable for words, and if you utter another sound, I'll never speak to you again," Caroline said.

"O.K., wench!" Mike said, with a salute.

Jack, followed by Wayne, appeared with a new tray of drinks. The Scarecrow took one and drank it down. It warmed her insides, and made her laugh. She forgot that Wayne had ignored her, and that her mother had beaten and cursed her. She sat on the floor in an exhilarating state of animal comfort. She giggled. She twisted her right foot, watching it with keen curiosity. A look of surprise lit her face, and she giggled again. She stared dazedly about the room. Suddenly, she was awful sad. She arose with tears flowing, looked at Wayne with dumb, meek admiration, and sang in droning drunkenness:

> *My man, I love him so!*
> *My man, I love him so!*
> *My man, I love him so!*

"Put a nickel on the drum," George said.

"She's maudlin," Caroline said.

"Go ahead, Wayne, be a man, and satisfy the wench," said Mike.

The Scarecrow, imitating her mother, swooned onto the floor, and sat heaped like a scared, lost child.

"Another shower bath," Mike said.

"Christ, doesn't she ever stop flowing?" George said.

"I ain't got no home," she sobbed.

"Hey, Scarecrow, I got an idea," George said.

"Spill it before it expires of Siberian loneliness," Jack said.

"Pipe down there, wise guy! . . . Hey, Scarecrow, you'll be safe in the park now; it's too cold for the squirrels," George said.

"I'll bet she's already slept there," Mike said.

She looked sheep-eyed from person to person, her face splotched from tears. Her thin hair tumbled down her back.

"I ain't got no place to go. If I go home, my mother will beat me 'n' call me bad names. She beat me today with a rubber hose she keeps for beating me 'n' she made my back all sore and red, and put lumps on it. I ain't got no home, and ou, it's cold out tonight," she sobbed.

"You got pounded full of lumps, huh, Scarecrow?" George said.

"George, you don't need to be vicious," Caroline said.

"God's guts, she's used to it," George said.

George gave her a drink, and she gulped it.

"What'll I do? It's so cold out. *Ou!*"

"What I want to know is where did the Scarecrow get that hair?" Jack said.

"Yeh, it is awful. It falls down her back just like the rain," George said; they laughed.

"I got black-'n'-blue marks all over my back," the Scarecrow sobbed.

"Let's see 'em," Mike said.

She arose and quickly pulled off her dress. She stepped out of it on the floor, and stood before them in her soiled underwear. She gulped down another drink, and they examined the welts on her back. She raised her legs, one by one, to reveal the welts on the inside of her thighs. She showed them a bruise between the pathetic little knobs of her breasts. The fellows revealed curiosity.

"Well, where are you going tonight?" Caroline asked her.

She accepted another drink, and swayed about the room, kicking her dress into a corner.

"Can't you go back to Kenneth's?" Wayne asked.

"Last night I didn't like him so much because his feet were so cold and I couldn't make them warm. Oh, they were almost like ice," she said; they laughed.

"Who's Kenneth?" Caroline asked.

"Oh, a boy-friend. His family are all nomads. They're never home. The pater is a beer-runner, and the mater and sister, they're nomads and are never home. Kenneth and his brother generally have an eight-room apartment to themselves, and the brother is always too busy with his own damsels to bother about Kenneth's," Bill said.

"Well, Scarecrow, are you going back to Ken's?" asked George.

"His feet are so cold in bed," she replied, looking plaintively at Wayne.

"Well, where are you going?" asked Marge.

She stood in their midst, sheepish.

"My God, what a frau!" Caroline exclaimed.

"She's so dumb, she's been in the seventh grade for three years now," George said.

"I wonder if I could bring her home with me?" Caroline said to Marge.

"I tried that once. You'll never get her out. She'll just squat on you, and she'll be making eyes at the janitor and peddlers. And then her old witch of a mother will come around and throw a scene. I took her home out of kindness of heart, and that's what happened to me," Marge said.

Bill suddenly remarked that it was getting time for them to be blowing before Ray came home with his lady-friend. The Scarecrow was neglected in a flurry of straightening up, furniture moving, and bed-making. She staggered about getting in everyone's way. When they left, she threw her coat on over her underwear, forgetting her dress, and tagged out after them. They stood before the building, half seriously, and half humorously, discussing her plight.

"I'd go to Kenneth's, only he has such cold feet."

The group gradually thinned down. Caroline and Mike, the last to leave, departed in a Yellow Cab. They looked back through the cab window and saw her, unsteady of foot, shivering in front of the building.

1930.

Looking 'Em Over

I

Don scrutinized the mirror, and saw the reflection of Don Bryan, looking just about as well as Don Bryan could look. He was an angular young man in the very early twenties, with a vertical face, slightly pocked and marred by pimples, and ratty greenish eyes. His light hair, gradually darkening from the frequent administration of hair oils, was brilliantined and meticulously split in the center. He guessed that his appearance was O.K. If he had more of the appearance of an athlete, with burly, football shoulders, a darkling aspect of eyes and brown, naturally curly hair, he would have been more pleased with himself. But he did the best that he could with a bony and skinny frame, and thanks to budget plan collegiate clothing—purchased at the store of Sankey, Hatfield, and Cohen—polo shirts, nobby ties, and patent-leather pumps, he was prepared to cut some figure. He stepped backward to achieve a more complete survey of himself; then he came forward to observe his face close up and to determine whether or not he had put too much powder on his cheeks. He passed satisfactory judgment upon himself, having worked wonders with limited possibilities.

Giving a final scrupulous part to his hair, he left his bedroom, and in the parlor, his mother examined him approvingly.

"Yessir! Um, the girl will be proud of her tall, handsome cake-eater today," his father said, distracted from his *Sunday Questioner*.

"I ain't got any girl. I'm just going to walk down to the beach and see the fellows," Don protested.

"Old stuff!" Mr. Bryan snorted.

"No kiddin'," Don said.

"Now, Donald, do be careful, because these girls nowadays, they just are looking for husbands. And I won't stand for none of these fast, cigarette-smoking immoral girls stealing my son from me," Mrs. Bryan said.

She disconcerted him with a kiss.

"I was young myself once, lad, I know. You're going to see your girl, and don't try to kid an old duck like myself," Mr. Bryan said good-naturedly.

"No kiddin', I ain't got a girl," Don said.

"That's splendid, Donald. You listen to your mother, and don't let any of these here fast-living, cabareting girls get their hands on you. You're too young."

Don did not appreciate his mother's sentiments. He stated, in a disgruntled voice, that he had no girl. Withal, he liked the old man intimating that he had. It gave him a feeling of expansive and justified maleness.

"Now I told you, don't try and deceive an old duck like myself," the father said, chortling.

"No kiddin'. It's just that . . . well, that I'm a lone wolf."

Don departed, ruffled at the way his mother tried to baby him. But mothers were mothers, and he had learned plenty of times, through sad experience, that he couldn't talk sensibly to his mother.

He strode through a section of lazy streets. The day was good, full of sun, and warm, with a slight hot wind blowing. He was glad for the freedom of Sunday, and hoped that he would be able to make the most of it. He gave attention to the many automobiles lining the curbs, and those which shot through the streets. He spotted a pearl gray Stutz; bitchey roadster, all right. A dark, flannelled Jewish young man, a roadster personality, drove it, and beside him sat a blonde girl who looked like hot stuff.

"Oh, daddy, buy me a bow wow!" he said half-aloud.

He commenced to sing in a dragging, heavy voice which falsely accentuated the words and tune.

> *Blue heaven and you and I*
> *And sand kissing a moonlit sky;*
> *A desert breeze whispering a lull-a-by.*
> *Only stars above you*
> *To say I love you.*

He started supposing that his father owned a car. It would be the nuts. And suppose, too, that he was a big-shot instead of just a twenty-five-dollar-a-week clerk.

It was nice to walk, as long as he did not have to do much of it. But how much nicer wouldn't it be to loll in a keen sporty roadster, say a Marmon, or a Stutz like the one he'd just seen! Nowadays to get yourself a first-class girl, a fellow had to have a car. If he only had any kind of a one, a Ford, Chevey, even an Essex. And if he or his old man were only filthy with money!

Coming in his direction was a mincing girl. Something not to be sniffed at, and yessir, it could park its itull shoosy-woosies under his beddy any old time, he decided. Keen! H'lo, baby, let's you and me cooperate! H'lo, baby, for you I faw down! He eyed her as she approached. He could not complain about the figure as it grew toward him into the life-size tantalizing flesh of a young female with Irish eyes, dark brows, black hair, Irish face, and just the nicest little figure, and the cutest little bouncing. . . . Slender, too, but just enough meat in the right places. And she was dressed just perfect, in a silver-gray, caped suit, with stockings and shoes to match. He wished she'd give him a tumble, or that he could snap out a wisecrack. All he was able to do to attract her attention was to express surprise and elation by whistles. She passed him cold as ice. He gaped after her, observing that she had the fetchingest little wriggle.

He proceeded, supposing that he had picked her up. He held snappy imaginary dialogues between her and himself, and all kinds of bright sayings came to his mind. He hoped that at the beach he could pick up something as sweet as she was. But generally, he was not the one who picked up the swell ones. Now and then, he made the grade with one of the tramps that the boys would dig out somewhere or other, but he'd never been speedy enough for a rich, virtuous girl who rated. He supposed himself having a romance with the girl who had just passed him. Perhaps she was the daughter of a Savings' Bank, with a car of her own, and plenty of crisp greenbacks. Romance, kisses in the moonlight, dances in dimmed rooms to the graceful strains of sentimental waltzes, days on white-sanded beaches, parties at which he showed her off to the fellows, boat trips, golf at the exclusive country clubs, weekends at that ritzy resort, Grand Beach and. . . . Wouldn't that be jake, and wouldn't that knock the boys for a row or two!

Don Bryan walked along, smoking a Lucky Strike, wishing that it were a Pall Mall.

II

People flooded the beach at Seventy-fourth Street. It was a miserable beach, irregular, and with cramped space. The sandy portion had been fenced off and made into a private beach by a parvenu club, and the remainder was more rock than sand. The lake looked insensate, dirty. Waves slapped the shore. But the people were in a laughing picnic mood. There was much loud talking and high-pitched laughter. Beach games were in progress, and one group was playing blue-my-black-berry. Many collected to watch it, it was so screaming. A Jewish girl, with extended buttocks, was down, and the lad guarding her made only feeble attempts to tag those who came in to slap her. The spectators were splitting with laughter, as one after another of the players shoved the guard over and cracked her on the buttocks. The beach was colorful with the many hues of bathing suits, sensuous with female flesh. There were no lockers, and the sidewalk of Seventy-fourth Street broke off abruptly and the sand and rocks sloped downward.

Don stood at the sidewalk edge and surveyed this scene, attempting to stand in a loosely confident manner like a young man who was somebody, who had gone places and done things, who rated. He spied a girl by the wire fencing of the club premises, and he judged her a pip, admiring her curving line of hips. She wore a tight, powdery blue suit, her legs were long and thin, her breasts small and round, her body bronzed. He watched her, wishing that he knew her, sagaciously proclaiming to himself that he would not throw her out of bed. H'lo, baby! Watcha say, kid! He hoped and determined, but then perceived that she was accompanied. The fellow with her familiarly slapped her in the rear. He wondered if that meant anything, because generally a girl who permitted a fellow to slap her in that part was not so very innocent. Often, he guessed, such girls would go the limit. He watched, supposing that she ditched her friend, and picked him up. And she would turn out to be the only daughter of a Beef Trust, a Corner on the Wheat Market, or a City Haul racket. He imagined himself and her falling in love, a whirlwind, happy and frenzied courtship, preliminary to a wedding in the Holy Name Cathedral at high noon.

"Hello, Don!"
"Hello, Paul!"
"What are you doing out here?"
"Oh, Paul, I'm just looking 'em over."
"Lookin' 'em over, huh?"
"Yeh, I'm lookin' 'em over."
"Plenty of nice stuff out here."

"And then some."

"I like that in brown, don't you, Don?"

"Me, too."

"I sa-ay there, Buster Brownie. Hum, I sa-ay."

"Yeh, I sa-ay there," Don parroted.

"Stuck up! I'll bet she's lace-curtain Irish."

"Yeh, ritzy now, and probably used to be nothing but pig-in-the-parlor Irish, that's what I'll venture," said Don.

"Well, there's a lot of good stuff out here," Paul said.

"Damn tootin'," said Don.

"Guess I'll mosey along and look 'em over myself. See you later."

Don remained in his strategic spot, smoking a cigarette. It occurred to him that the world was full of girls. He attempted to calculate the number of them that there might be in the world. There was little excuse for a fellow not getting all that he wanted. Hell, the dance halls were full of them, waiting to be picked up, and prepared to go to the limit. And he always argued that any of them will say yes if the right guy comes along and uses the right technique at the right time. He had been hearing plenty about girls from rich or well-to-do Catholic homes, girls you would think of only as decent girls, who were losing their cherries, one right after the other. He didn't get any of that luck. He generally had to take pushovers, or do like he did last night, pay for it.

He eyed a girl near him, who was wearing Chinese beach pyjamas. His mind drifted and he ecstatically thought of how it would be the nuts if all girls went swimming naked. He saw another, in a tan suit and shoes to match. Nice legs, narrow hips, pretty. A tuft of wind blew her dress up. No pants, cute little pink thighs. Just what he liked. I say, baby, h'lo! Why in hell didn't he have a ready line? Have to learn one. I sa-ay there, ba-bee! I sa-ay. . . . There's danger in your eyes, Cherie, I sa-ay, ain't we met before? . . . He wondered about approaching her. And there was another, Irish, too. Nothing like Irish girls. The dark-haired, dark-eyed ones were the prettiest in the world. And once they go, they go plenty far. Hot! She was wearing a white plaited skirt, and a golden-colored sweater in a broken pattern, and she was a proper handful. Gee, if only a rich broad would come along and give him a tumble. Another one, wearing sport shoes. But anyway, it was the fundamentals that counted, not the clothes. That was one he would have to remember and spring when some of the boys were around.

"Don! What you doing out here today?"

"Oh, Larry, I'm just lookin' 'em over."

"Well, there's no shortage of 'em."

"Enough out here today for all tastes."

"Now take that in red. She's what I call cosy," Larry said.

"You said it," Don agreed.

"Anyway, I think I'll scrootch around and look 'em over myself. So long, Don."

"Don't get strained eyes, Larry."

"There's plenty of reason to," Larry called back.

Don sang, low and in a mumble:

> *There's danger in your eyes, Cherie!*
> *There's danger in your eyes, Cherie!*

He could not remember the remaining lines; he lit a cigarette, and stood, posing.

III

Don leaned against the thrown-together red hot stand, munching at a hot-dog sandwich. A dab of mustard splashed on his thumb, and he cursed with annoyance as he wiped it off with a clean, neatly ironed handkerchief. He perceived the automobiles, tightly lined along both curbs. A blue, low-lined Buick fascinated him. The tan, winged Chrysler, three cars down from it, was a better choice. Beside the Chrysler there was a Cadillac that was the real ticket. He supposed that he owned it.

"Here's Don Bryan."

"Hello, Jack."

"Looking 'em over?"

"Yes, Jack, I'm looking 'em over," Don said weightily.

"Well, they're here to be seen. Now, look at tha-at! I like it!" Jack said.

Tha-at was a tall blonde girl, lecherous in blue-and-orange beach pyjamas. They stared at her, their eyes swelling lust.

"Whizzz!" Jack exclaimed.

"Wheeee!" Don exclaimed.

"Yoo-hoo," Jack called.

"What do yuh say, baby!" Don said.

Tha-at flung her head around, glared, elevated her aquiline nose, and shook herself along.

"Swell stuff, we are!" Jack called.

"We're swell stuff," Don shouted.

"Yeah, we're real swell!" Jack brayed.

Tha-at again about-faced, snapped her fingers disdainfully and mumbled; the only words they heard were "small change."

"Stuck up or not, she could blow her nose in my soup any time she wanted to," Jack said.

"I'll say this much for her; she's got something to feel stuck up about that plenty of broads ain't got," Don added.

They crossed the sidewalk to stand in front of a new Ford. The space to its left was vacant, and a Chrysler, driven by a tall, burning blonde in purple, was driven into it. She sat by the wheel, powdering her nose. Replacing the powder puff in her bag, she lit a cigarette with a nickel cigarette-lighter.

"She's got what I call meat," Jack said, surreptitiously back-glancing at her.

"And class," Don said.

"It's just meat!"

"She makes most of them out here today look like pikers," Don said.

A dark-haired girl in a black bathing suit strode boyishly by them. She was long, supple, and tanned; her thighs were narrow, and she was flat-chested.

"Oh! Oh!" exclaimed Don.

"She's jail bait," Jack said.

"Know her?"

"I know who she is. She goes to St. Paul's. All the boys around the beach here have a feel-day with her, and she doesn't mind it."

"Piggly-wiggly girl, huh?" Don said, his mind inflamed.

"Well, now, I think that Monk Sweeney made the grade with her over on the Jackson Park golf course one night. I wouldn't say for sure, but that's my suspicion."

"Ummmm!" Don meditatively exclaimed.

"She's not hard on the eyes, but she's jail bait."

"Well, you can see that there's something to be said in her favor."

"By the way, she was with some cake last night at the Neapolitan Room of the Westgate Hotel."

"How is that place these days?"

"Same as ever. Pretty hot orchestra. Good crowd. All the old bunch that used to be up at the Grove when it was the place to go, are usually up there now. Lots of guys who rate, and broads from sororities like *Alpha* go there."

"I was at Shannon's last night," Don said.

"Have they got any new girls?"

"I had one. She's swell."

"What she look like?"

"Big, but knows her movements. After all, it's not the looks, but the fundamentals that count. And she has them. She gives you your money's worth."

"But me, I'd prefer something like that in the Chrysler behind us."

"Wouldn't I!"

"And take a squint at what's coming along," said Jack.

"She turned off. Well, anyway, she was nice."

"Edge a little closer to the Chrysler. I think the broad in it is waiting to be picked up," Don said.

Dear heart, Romance is ended ...

The girl singing needed only a stick of gum to complete the picture she made. She was a bushy-headed brunette, with thick solid legs, and her blue dress was outlandishly bright.

"Hello Sophie!" Jack said.

"Hello baby, what do you say!" she sing-songed.

"Well, if I said what I think, I'd burn you up," Don said.

"Not me. I'm asbestos," she retorted.

Shaking her shoulders, she sang staccato.

> *We'll be so happy, we'll always sing,*
> *If we remember one little thing,*
> *A little kiss each morning, a little kiss each night,*
> *Who cares if hard luck may be ahead?*

"Going fishing?" asked Jack.

"Sa-ay, don't be a mud turtle," she said.

"That your swimming suit?" Jack asked, pointing at her dress.

"You wouldn't kid any one, would you?" she said, cynically.

"Me, I just asked was that your swimming suit?"
"He wants to know if you think it'll rain tonight," Don said.
"Say, don't be a mud turtle," she said.
She performed several Charleston steps, and sang:

> *Where is the song I had in my heart*
> *That harmonizes with the pines?*
> *Anybody can see what's troublin' me,*
> *I'm cryin' for the Carolines.*

She cut short her song, and winked.
"Ain't I seen you before?" Don said.
"Say, big boy, whatcha think I am?"
"Well, you know, there's girls and girls," Jack said.
"Say, what's your meaning?" she asked in a harsh voice.
Jack smiled fatuously at her.
"Take a sugar cookie and snookie cookie," Jack sing-songed.
"Take a great big papa," she sing-songed in reply.
"Listen, don't kid me now, ain't I seen you some place before?" Don said.
"Sa-ay, I seen your kind before hanging around with your tongues lopping out. Don't kid me, big boy! I know tings. I go aroun', see," she said, flustering Don.
"Well, I know I seen you before," Jack said, more possessed than Don.
"Don't you hang around at The Bourbon Palace?" Don said, still flustered.
"Sa-ay, where you get that way? Me hang around a joint like that! Wrong number. Ring again!"
"What do you do, lay down, instead of hang out?" Jack asked.
"Don't get fresh, see!"
"Anyway, baby, what do you say?" Jack asked.
She ogled suggestively.
"I don't catch your meanings," she said.
"Oh, I only mean, think you'll go fishing?" Jack said, superciliously.
"Come on now, don't be a mud turtle."
"But listen, where have I seen you before?" Don asked insistently.
"Say, Skinny, how about a new tune? You been singing that one pretty regular, haven't you?"

Don was hurt at being called Skinny, and decided that she was only a goddamn Polack anyway, and she looked worse than a beer truck.

"You go to colledge?" she asked Don.

"Sure. I'm president of the intra-fraternity council down at the U," Don answered.

"Y'are? Say, I got a boy fren down there in a frat named Jack Von Williams. Ain't that a name?"

"I think I know who he is," Jack said.

"He's a blond and good-looking, and does he dress!"

"Yeh, he's a classy dresser," Jack said.

"He's a funny guy. You know, he uses words a yard long. I never know what he's talking about half the time," she said.

Jack got a telephone number out of her, and they watched her plunge through the crowded beach, singing jazz songs.

"She's dumb," Don said.

"A Polack, but what the hell! Some night when I got nothing to do, I'll ring her up. She ought to be worth a night's investment," Jack said.

"I'd like that in the Chrysler for a night's investment," said Don.

"Might be hard, making the grade with her. She looks pretty high-hat," Jack said.

"Hello, kid, what do you say?" Jack said to Kenny.

"What are you fellows doing, looking 'em over?" Kenny said.

"Yeh, Kenny, we're looking 'em over," Don said.

"Any luck?"

"I just got lined up with a Polack, and I'll get myself fixed up with her some night when I got nothing more important to do," Jack said.

"South Chicago?" asked Kenny.

Jack nodded.

"Those broads out there are like rabbits," Kenny said.

"But they're ice. I had one who calmly picked blackheads off my forehead," Don said.

"There's something neat behind us," Jack said.

"Sa-ay, I like tha-at. That's perfection," Kenny said, seeing the girl in the Chrysler.

IV

"Jesus, he's made the grade," Jack said; he and Don watched Kenny, who sat beside the girl in the Chrysler and talked familiarly with her. When she laughed in animation, they stared with envy.

"Now how in the hell did he pull that stunt off so quick?" Don said.

"Say, look at the way that boy's jaw is working. You got to give him credit. Credit, I say! When he starts jawing he could sell real estate right out in the middle of the lake."

"Yeh!" Don exclaimed with mounting envy.

"When he starts pumping that line of his into a broad, she's as good as made. Once I was with him and he picked a broad up at a street carnival, and took her over to Jackson Park, and she just said to him 'Daddy, I never did this before, but I'm sure going to now!' And she did. When he cranks his jaw, the story's ended," Jack said.

"He's lucky," Don said.

"Luck, hell, it's art. He's an artist in that line."

"He gets swell ones, too," Don said.

"Listen, I'll bet he ain't stringing that one along nohow! No, he's not stringing her!" Jack exclaimed.

"We should have tried something ourselves," Don said.

A girl in a two-piece bathing suit without brassière walked by them.

"Oh, baby, you can make me so happy!" Don sing-songed.

"Neat!" Jack appraised.

"Keen!"

"I sa-ay!" Jack exclaimed while she re-passed them, daintily biting into a red-hot sandwich.

"I sa-ay!" Don said.

"Don't!" the girl snapped at him.

"How's the water?" Don asked.

"Cold," she answered.

"I know where it's warm," Jack leered.

"I know where it's like a refrigerator," she said, passing out of hearing.

"Well, it's plenty thick with them today, isn't it, boys?" Eddie said, coming along with Dapper Dan O'Doul.

"Get a load of that in the Chrysler," Jack said.

"Kenny's making the grade with her," Don said.

"Plenty keen if you ask me," Eddie said.

"Bo-oy!" Dapper Dan said.

"Watch O'Doul's buttons," said Jack.

"Did you seen what I just seen?" Eddie said, referring to the sight he had viewed when a girl in a black dress bent over to retrieve a dropped handkerchief.

They blocked the sidewalk debating why seeing a thigh under a dress had more effect on a fellow than seeing the same girl in a scrimpy bathing suit would. Don forgot their conversation, and supposed about the rich girl he hoped some day to meet and marry.

V

The hot glory of the summer evening spilled over the corner of Sixty-seventh and Stony Island Avenue. Many people were out walking, and in automobiles. Don and his group clogged the sidewalk in front of the Walgreen drug store on the southeast corner, and Don continued supposing about rich girls.

"What are we going to do?" Jack asked.

"What?" asked Kenny, fresh from a drive with the girl in purple. She had invited him to come on next Wednesday night for a parlor date, and she'd added that no one would be home.

"How about a show?" Eddie asked.

"Too hot," Jack said.

"We might go up to The Bourbon Palace, and jig a little," said Eddie.

"It's too hot to shimmy with Polacks," Pat said.

"Shannon's?" asked Jack.

"Last night was enough for me," said Don.

"Reformed, Don?" asked Pat.

"Hell, you never get your money's worth in those joints," Eddie said.

"But what'll we do?"

"Yeah, what?"

"That's what I like to know."

They went to Shannon's brothel. Don stayed behind because he was too low in finances. He stood on the corner staring at passers-by. At eleven o'clock, he drank a chocolate malted milk, and purchased an evening's copy of the following day's *Chicago Questioner*. He wished that he didn't have to work in the morning.

"Well, son, you're home early," the father said when Don entered the flat.

"I got tired," he said, lackadaisically.

"She sent you home early. Ha! Ha!"

Don yawned. His father was a fool. He went upstairs, read his paper, and turned in, still supposing about a rich girl whom he would love and marry. It was a hot night and he tossed in his sleep.

The alarm clock knelled the end of Sunday's freedom, and he arose sleepily, hating the very idea of going down to that office. While shaving, he supposed.

1930.

The Buddies

JACK and Smitty drove wagons out of the South End barns for the Continental Express Company. They were clean-cut twenty-one-year-old kids. Nobody could say that they were company men, and they were frank, friendly, and hard-workers. They each had only a grammar-school education, and their hopes of getting ahead were day-dreams rather than ambitions. They wanted to end up as something better than teamsters, and occasionally they imagined and spoke of how they might make a killing on the baseball pools and get a stake so that they could make some kind of a start in life. They were healthy with plenty of animal spirits, and they liked their good times; but some day they figured that they would settle down, marry a decent girl, have kids and give the kids a better chance than they had, pay down installments on their own homes, and buy a Ford or second-hand Buick. They had quickly become well-rooted in the service of Long John Continental, and they would most likely continue on his vehicles until they had passed their days of usefulness.

They generally ate their lunch at a little restaurant near the South End barns, which all the men called Nelly's Greasy Spoon. One day, while at the counter, they happened to get talking about an idea which interested them enough to take precedence over kidding with Nelly, ragging each other, or arguing about baseball. They got to feeling how swell it would be to get all the fellows from their stables organized into some sort of a club in which they could do things together outside of working hours, where they could get to know each other better, and where they could have some really good times. They figured that such a club could run regular dances and picnics, and athletic teams that might compete with teams from other stables and company garages. They thought that they might even get an inter-stable and garage baseball league going. It was a dandy idea, so good that they feared it could never be worked out. If it did, it would make for more friendliness and sociability among all the lads from their stable, and it would give them mutual interests. While the idea remained only as a hazy and hoped-for dream, they discussed it, and soon they had other wagonmen interested. It was expanded to include a sinking fund for sick benefits, and probably for death insurance also.

The plan spread contagiously, and a meeting was held and enthusiastically attended. A constitution was drawn up and officers elected. Smitty was elected president, Jack treasurer, and Old Billy McGee secretary. Billy was one of the old-timers, liked by every one in the Wagon Department from the superintendent, Patsy McLoughlin, on down, and his election was a very popular choice. There was a lengthy debate over naming the organization, but it was finally titled *The Buddies*. Smitty appointed an entertainment committee of three, and they immediately commenced outlining plans for a picnic. They prepared raffle tickets, and conducted the raffle on the square. Jim Bates, considered by most of the wagonmen as a goddamn company stool pigeon, won the ten-dollar gold piece. In less than a month after the initial meeting, four hundred men from the five hundred odd number working out of the South End stables had joined *The Buddies*, paying their first monthly dues of a dollar.

The picnic was held out at the Forest Preserve, and there were games, dancing, and odd races, with prizes for the winners. Several kegs of beer, supplied by Jerry Looney the bootlegger who had once driven a single wagon for the old Continental before the war, were on hand, and nobody complained of thirst. Many of the younger men brought girls, and they danced, or strolled off in the woods. Smitty had his girl there, and he took her off in the woods, and she was very willing in the soft grasses under a tree where it was very nice. A few lads got drunk, but there were no fights. And the old-timers had a good time, sitting under the trees, retailing anecdotes of the old days and drinking beer.

The first picnic was so successful that they immediately planned a second one; and it also went off to their satisfaction. The men all felt that *The Buddies* was going good, and that there was no danger of its breaking up. They realized that they were getting along better together, and that it was making their work more interesting. They had mutual affairs to·talk about, an organization which was theirs, planned for their mutual and collective benefit. They discussed plans for the winter, and Smitty and Jack labored, preparing a winter program. They also began practicing baseball, hoping that for the following summer they could put a good team on the diamond. And about fifty fellows all bragged that they would win the bowling tournament planned for the late autumn. They even talked of some day building their own club-house.

For three months, *The Buddies* functioned smoothly. Several drivers and helpers were laid up sick or injured, and they received sick benefits of twenty dollars a week. The meetings were well attended, and most of the men were anxious not to miss them. Dues were paid regularly, without the use of pressure and force that was necessary in the case of the regular wagonmen's union. It, on every pay day, stationed sluggers at each stable and garage, and dues were paid up immediately. Otherwise, men would have been pulled right off their trucks and wagons. *The Buddies* was quite different from the union. It belonged to the men. They knew that the union was not theirs. It was a racket for Joey Murtry, the ex-teameo, and a few of his gangster sluggers. And the men knew, also, that Joey was always going up to sit on the laps of Charley Leonard and the other bosses and assistant superintendents. They hated Joey because they knew that at one time he had been nothing but a common ordinary manure whaler like themselves, and that now he was putting on the dog, and getting high-hat. He wore loud and expensive clothes, flashed a diamond, lived like a king in a home out on Washington Boulevard, and drove about in a Lincoln on "union business." They knew that Joey would sell them out whenever there was an opportunity. They had to pay their union dues because they wanted their jobs, and they knew that if they squawked or tried to oust Joey from his control, they would be terrorized by Joey's hired sluggers. If they tried to get radical, they would be fired, and Joey would not go on the carpet for them, because he was working hand and fist with Long John Continental. And after all, their jobs did pay them better than they would have gotten working as teamsters and helpers for practically any other establishment in the city. The union dues were only two dollars a month, with perhaps an added dollar or two a month in special assessments for sick members, and deaths, because the union treasury was usually empty. Even with the union as crooked as it was, they could do much worse for some other company, although they had their many complaints and grumblings against Long John Continental.

But *The Buddies* was their own, different from the union. And the insurance plan of *The Buddies* paid a higher sick benefit than the company's insurance plan. The latter charged a sliding scale of rates, and paid out five hundred dollars at death, or at the end of twenty years. It also provided sick benefits if the accidents were not due to personal negligence.

One day in the fourth month of the existence of *The Buddies*, Old Billy McGee told Jack and Smitty that he had to resign because the organization was taking up too much of his time, and he was getting along in years. His excuse seemed lame, and they smelled something in the air. They talked it over, and decided that nobody could do anything to them, because they were running things honestly, and not forcing men out of the union or the insurance plan. They were within their rights, and the company couldn't fire them. But still, they knew that there was something queer, because Old Billy was a square-shooter, and his resignation was funny. Finally, they decided that Billy was old now, with a wife and three kids, and that he was getting cold feet because he wanted to feel absolutely safe on the job.

A few days later, they were both called up to the general office of the Wagon Department to see their assistant superintendent, Charley Leonard. Charley was a long-nosed, falsely jovial man, and most of his men called him a rat. They knew that behind his jokes, and his air of democracy, there was a plain face and soul of a snooper who did not mean any good for them. When Jack and Smitty approached his desk in the large office, he smiled pleasantly, and cracked a joke. He laughed so enthusiastically at his own joke that all the stenographers and girls working on loading tickets in the office turned to glance at him. In his oiliest manner, and with bowing regrets to the rigors of outright necessity, he told them that the wagonmen had their union, and that the company had a well-organized insurance plan, and that, therefore, *The Buddies* was totally unnecessary. He did not blame them for having started such an organization, because they had done it evidently without thinking, and he was not going to hold their efforts in its behalf against them. But he would have to ask them to disband it immediately.

They had no choice. They walked away after Leonard had patted them on the back. They went to the Wagon Call Department to see Heinie Mueller, one of the Wagon Dispatchers in that department. They always liked to say hello to Heinie Mueller, because he was a funny Dutchman, and he was white. They wished they were working under Heinie instead of their own boss, Mike Mulrooney, the route inspector. But Mike was not as bad as many of the other route inspectors, like Emmett Carr. Outside, they cursed, and squawked. Their disappointment cut deep because *The Buddies* was their own creation, and they had been betrayed. When they told the other men at the stables, there was more kicking. But they all knew that these gestures would get them nowhere. If they tried to pull a strike, they would simply be S. O. L., and they would see others on their wagons. *The Buddies* was disbanded. Jack paid all its debts from the treasury funds, and divided up the remaining funds equally among the members, totalling one dollar for each of them. Privately, Charley Leonard was called a pretty lousy sonofabitch. They still wondered why they could not keep their organization going. But that was hopeless.

Two weeks after *The Buddies* was disbanded, Jack and Smitty were walking from the stables to the streetcar line. The rankling from their betrayal still persisted, and they walked along gloomy and silent. Joe Murtry suddenly accosted them, and four husky fellows with padded shoulders stepped out of an entrance way. Joe said:

"These two guys!"

Two of the sluggers cornered Smitty, and the other two took care of Jack. Before he was able to defend himself, Smitty was punched in the eye and the jaw. Jack was knocked down with three simultaneous belts in the face. Smitty was knocked on top of Jack. They were jerked to their feet, and knocked down again. Smitty's nose streamed with blood, and his face began to swell and discolor. Jack was punched in the mouth, and the sharp pain made him realize that one or two of his teeth had been broken. As he bent his head down to spit out the broken pieces of teeth, he received a terrific uppercut. Both of them lay on the curb, bleeding, punched into helplessness. They were kicked in the ribs for good measure. Joey Murtry leaned over their semi-prostrate forms, and told them that the next time they had better think twice before starting any of their rackets to demoralize the union.

Thus ended *The Buddies*.

Jack and Smitty were both laid up for several days, and they lost that much pay. When they returned to the stables they told the men what had happened to them. There was a general and spontaneous age. Many talked retaliation, and of starting a movement to take the union away from Murtry. But beneath this rage and talk, most of them were cowed, and rather glad that they had not been the victims.

A month later, a special union meeting was called for a vote on a proposed special assessment to be levied in order that Joey Murtry could buy a new Lincoln which was, he explained, absolutely needed for the conducting of "union business." He also delivered a long speech, full of salve, in which he defended his work, and told them that he was always at their service. He asked the men if they had any complaints against the manner in which he was rendering his stewardship. A few chauffeurs and drivers glanced around the hall, and saw Joey's sluggers. There were no complaints. The vote was taken. Most of the men at the South End stables had determined to vote against the assessment. Jack and Smitty had kept their mouths closed, and had not attended the meeting. They later learned that there were only five votes against the special assessment.

1931.

A Front-page Story

THE undertaking parlor seemed oppressively formal and impersonal, with its subdued lights, its dull green carpet, waxed flooring, scrupulously polished but stiff-backed chairs, weighty sofas, and potted green plants set upon marble-topped tables. And shadowed toward the rear of this room of artificial sublimity Ruth Summer was laid out in a sleeveless pink taffeta dress with a shoulder corsage. She had been a short dumpy girl with thin, stringy, blonde hair, and a commonplace oval face. Now, she was a blue and bloated corpse, and her fatty bloodless arms gave one the impression of semi-nudity. The dress had evidently been her best party frock, purchased after stinting sacrifices, and lovingly doted over. It had been saved and preserved for those parties and affairs which she had been only infrequently able to attend, and when she had worn it in life, it must have hung like a sack on her squat figure, the inappropriate type of dress that just such a monotonous and uninspired girl would wear. In death, it draped her like a last treachery.

The young campus reporter for *The Chicago Questioner* studied this twenty-one-year-old corpse, feeling like an impostor. Near him stood a small and repressed group which spoke in semi-articulate whispers. In its center was Ruth Summer's father, a tall, homespun man with unpressed clothes, lop-sided shoulders, and a genial but rutted visage. He had just arrived by train to send his daughter's body back home to Iowa for burial, and he was speaking with Ruth's tall, homely cousin, the woman at whose house Ruth had boarded. The cousin was explaining that if Ruth had only taken her into confidence, such foolhardiness might have been prevented. Three of Ruth's student friends, bucolic carbon copies of the dead girl's own personality, completed the group. As they listened to the conversation between the father and the cousin, their faces were intent and bewildered. The young campus reporter continued staring at the corpse, surreptitiously straining to hear and remember every word of the conversation. He recalled the statement which the tall, homely cousin had inadvertently made, prior to the father's arrival:

"It was literal suicide."

He approached the group, his presence causing an additional awkwardness among them. Replying to the question of one of the student friends, he re-explained that he had been in several classes with Ruth. The confused father drew a frayed newspaper clipping from his worn wallet and, without comment, handed it around. The young reporter read it last, and as he read slowly, he forced himself in the effort of remembering as much of it, verbatim, as he could. It recorded that Ruth Summer, honor student and valedictory orator at the town high school, was leaving to attend the University, and that all her many friends, admirers, and classmates predicted for her a brilliant academic career at this famous Temple of Truth. After having read the clipping twice, he returned it to the father, and shook his head with sad expressiveness. No one spoke. No one looked at anyone else. The young reporter, after shuffling his feet nervously and turning his face aside to blow his nose, stated that he would be going. The father thanked him for having remembered his daughter, and the tall cousin reiterated this expression of gratitude. The three student friends stared after him with puzzled suspicion. After a final glance at the dead girl, in her sleeveless frock, he departed.

Outside on the Midway he paused to jot down as much as he could remember from the clipping the father had shown him. He perceived that he was using, for his notes, the blank sides of an official release from the Department of Public Relations. He knew what the release contained: a eulogistic description of the commencement exercises, six and a half mimeographed pages of sugared words reflecting praise upon the University. That he should be using this release for his notes was, like the dress, another accidental irony. Even after her death this simple, betrayed girl must be humiliated. He stuffed the papers back in his pocket, lit a cigarette, and, walking toward the line of Gothic University Towers, attempted to think of other subjects. The Midway, and the buildings in the distance of several blocks, glowed and were mellow under a spreading June twilight, and the sky was calm. All about him were the heedless echoes of living people, children playing on the shaven grass in the center of the Midway, strolling pedestrians, a succession of whizzing automobiles, a jazz song audible from a radio within an opened window, an Illinois Central Suburban electric train, drawing into and out of the Midway station, an airplane rumbling overhead, causing people to pause and gape skyward with dreamy oblivious eyes and opened mouths.

He crossed over to the north side of the Midway and passed the white-stoned million-dollar Gothic chapel in which, on the previous day, the graduation exercises had been conducted, and he briefly glanced upward at the high and serene white-stoned tower. He entered a long, low and ornate hall dedicated to the recreation and social life of the female students. It was here that Ruth Summer had worked for two years as a checkroom girl. And it was from a garrulous elderly woman in this building that he had indirectly received the tip on the story. He nodded and smiled at the blue-uniformed guard who stood inside the door at the edge of the broad lobby, a rubicund jolly-faced man decrepit with age. Casually, he sauntered to the bulletin board, and paused as if he were interested in the few tacked-on announcements and notices. Copies of the University annual lay on a table which stood near the checkroom on his left, half-concealed by a post. Since he had to procure one immediately and he did not have the ten dollars to purchase it, a copy would have to be stolen. Once before he had had to steal one in the same manner. He glanced about the lobby, as if he were seeking some girl. He walked to the table, quickly snatched a copy, and proceeded around behind the checkroom where there were telephone booths and a cloister. In one of the telephone booths he concealed the annual under his jacket, holding it in place with a stiffened left arm. Coming out of the telephone booth, he sat

A FRONT-PAGE STORY

at the edge of the lobby for several moments, arose, and drifted toward the door, while the guard was answering questions.

A few paces down from the building he removed the annual and placed it under his left arm. He knew that it contained a photograph of Ruth Summer, but he had no curiosity to look at the picture.

He walked with a slackened pace. This one was a front-page scoop, and he experienced none of that quickening sense of keenness, that thrilling feeling of a dog on the hunt, which he should have. He harbored no illusions that he was more than a part-time campus reporter, whose principal duty was that of supplying *The Chicago Questioner* with a steady succession of leg pictures of prominent and attractive campus girls. And he had no ambitions of becoming a newspaper man, particularly one employed by *The Chicago Questioner* and working under Kelly Malloy, the triple-chinned editor. Withal, his work had permitted him to return to classes this last quarter. He desired to retain it, and to do so, he could not permit such stories to pass. If he did, they would be picked up by someone else, and then he would have to explain to Kelly Malloy why he was missing them.

As it was, Kelly was continuing his job largely on sufferance. Bobby Wallace, the ex-baseball writer who was now the University's Director of Public Relations, was tight on news, and barely deigned to recognize the existence of the campus reporter. Rather, he sent news in official releases, and whenever he needed a reporter or photographer, he telephoned the City Desk. He had countered Bobby's tactics by turning in as many ridiculous stories about the University as he could, and most of them had been printed. But it still seemed to puzzle Kelly Malloy that Bobby should always be telephoning for reporters and photographers. This story would settle all grudges with The Department of Public Relations. It was a sole measure of compensation for not having ignored the story, in the hope that no one else would have dug it up.

He sat on the steps of the main library building, smoking, shrinking from the moment when he would go inside to the phone booth and call up the City Desk. In quick, epitomizing mental pictures, he had a sense of Ruth Summer's whole university career. He could visualize this unostentatious, unsung, practically unknown small town girl against various familiar campus backgrounds. He could see her during that now forgotten freshman week of four years ago, when she had matriculated. He could sense that lost and lonely feeling that must have been hers as she stood in slow-moving lines, waiting to interview her dean, waiting to register for courses, waiting to apply for work at The Bureau of Vocational Guidance, waiting to pay her fees. He could see her sitting in chapel during that important first week, when deans and administrators officially welcomed the class of 1929, with lip-service to TRUTH, with clichés describing benefits and privileges which the University so altruistically placed at the disposal of its students, with stale stereotypes expressing the formal ideals of the institution. And he could see her attentively listening and literal-mindedly accepting their words, determining that she would make the most of her opportunity. Likewise could he see her in classrooms, with a loose-leaf notebook before her, diligently copying notes from lectures. And again in the library studying. She had majored in Education, and had planned to become a teacher, and he could see her poring over her assignments in one of her text-books, perhaps a text-book with some such title as *The Theory and Method of the Theory and Practice of Teaching High-School English*. He wondered how many hours she had stolen from sleep, from fun, from dreams, from her life, to devote to her courses in Education. How much of her short life had she given to such problems as the scientific method of grading high-school English papers, to drawing up reading lists for English courses in junior high schools, to the laborious listing of the titles of innocuous books which she herself had no time to read, to considerations of the quantity of fresh air to be permitted twenty-five students, to theoretical discussions of the value and efficacy of using the True and False method in conducting examinations. And again, he could see her on some rare evening of relaxation, when she would have been able to attend an International Club Dance—affairs generally considered freak shows by the prominent campus men and women—when she would have stood like a wall-flower, perhaps in her sleeveless pink taffeta dress, waiting for someone to ask her to dance, watching dance after dance without any invitation, or, if she were dancing, moving so woodenly and awkwardly that she became a trial to her partner. He could see her, again, emerging from the office of her doctor at the beginning of her junior year, pondering and brooding on the words she had just heard, knowing that she had such a very weak heart that she could not hope for a long life, and that any undue excitement or violent exercise would induce her death. He was forced, from this reflection, to admire her persistence and courage in continuing with full-time schedules and going on with her work as checkroom girl and waitress, despite the doctor's warning. He could see her, constantly tired, moving from classroom to library, to hasty meals, to work, and then home to her room for study until she dropped off into a sleep of physical exhaustion. He could see her, a plainly dressed girl, proceeding along a campus walk, moving by the lilac trees on a sunny spring day, just another grind driving herself toward her goal of an education and a degree, smothering impulse after impulse to dally and deviate from her purposes. He attempted to imagine how she must have felt on such occasions, when she would have passed some athlete or club girl who had sat near her in a class, and who passed her by outside without even a formal nod of recognition. He thought of this dead girl, and of her career, that had been so completely fruitless. All her work and study, the more than a thousand dollars which she had paid for tuition, the strain of her effort to obtain an education—all fruitless.

And yesterday, a cold and rainy day, she had gone out to the sand dunes with a newly found friend who had been ignorant of the condition of her heart. While the successful members of her class were in the million-dollar chapel, listening to oratory on the subject of TRUTH, EDUCATION, and CITIZENSHIP, and receiving their degrees, she was out on the sand dunes, her unattractive body clothed in a swimming suit. She had known what the consequences of her gesture would be.

"It was literal suicide."

She had known that if she ran about the dunes, and that if she risked plunging into the icy waters of Lake Michigan, she would not return alive. It had been with a final desperation, nursing a final disappointment, that she had gone on this expedition. Her friend had been first in the water. Ruth had run among the dunes, shouting. She had stopped for a moment to wave to her friend while the latter swam outward. Shouting and laughing, she had pitched down to the shore line. She had collapsed in shallow water, and a wave had washed over her and dragged her to the shore where she had lain, buffeted by the steady charge of waves until her friend, coming in unaware, had discovered her. She had been dead for over an hour when a doctor had examined the body, diagnosing heart failure as the cause of death.

The young campus reporter tossed aside a half-smoked cigarette butt, and stood up. Twilight had settled and it was almost completely dark. The Midway was wrapped in an atmosphere of loneliness, with its passing automobiles, its blinking traffic signals, and its sauntering pedestrians. He turned toward the door of the building. He had forgotten that it was closed, so he walked over to an open hall at the other end of the campus, to telephone.

The City Desk gave him a rewrite man. He stated the facts simply, one by one. She had come to the University with the reputation of being a brilliant student at her small town high school. She had worked her way through school as a waitress and checkroom girl. This June, she had expected to graduate. She had been too busy to have many friends, or much fun during her four years. A few days before graduation she had received a formal notice informing her that she would not be permitted to graduate because she lacked one grade point, and that her average, therefore, did not qualify her for a degree. She had told none of her friends of this development, and had proceeded with her graduation plans. She had paid for her cap and gown, and had sat with the graduating class for the official picture. She had attended the annual senior class breakfast, held one day before commencement exercises. Then on the day of graduation, she had gone out to the sand dunes in the rain, and had attempted to run and swim. For two years, she had been the victim of severe heart attacks, and was under the care of a doctor. She knew that her action would result in death. Now her father was in town, and in the morning she was being returned home in a coffin without the degree for which she had struggled.

The rewrite man asked how the facts had been gotten.

"By lying," the campus reporter answered.

"Come on, I'm busy. How did you get them?"

"I posed as a friend, and spoke with her cousin, her father, and some of her friends. And I saw her laid out in the undertaking parlor."

"Anything else?"

"Yes, she lived with her cousin, and the cousin stated that 'It was literal suicide.'"

"Sounds like it was. How about her picture?"

"It's in the latest annual. I got a copy, and I'm sending it down in a cab."

"Swell stuff, kid! That's good work. I'll have to remind Kelly about it tomorrow."

"And listen! Give her a break. It'll be the first one she ever had. Try and keep out too much of the sob stuff. If you make it too gooey, the story will be spoiled."

"Yeh, it's pretty sad. All right, and are you sure you got it all in now? Nothing else?"

"You got it."

"Well, listen while I repeat it for you."

After hanging up, the campus reporter telephoned for a taxi cab. Waiting for the cab he looked across the street at the gymnasium, which stood darkened and clothed in shadows. He gave the driver the annual, instructed him to get it down to the city desk of *The Chicago Questioner* as quickly as possible, and that he would be paid down there. He watched the cab shoot off. In the morning, his story and Ruth's picture would be on the front page, and the girl's body would be on the train, moving toward home. And the father, with the unpressed suit, the lop-sided shoulders, and the genial but rutted face, would be sitting by the train window, looking out, a bewildered man.

He walked eastward, reflecting on the final meanings of this girl's life. Bobby Wallace would read the story, and become furious. He would receive a telephone call from the office of the vice-president, and he would be called on the carpet to explain why such unfavorable news had gotten into the papers, and particularly at this time, following the commencement exercises, and all the favorable national publicity which the University had received following its recent surprising appointment of the new "boy president" from Yale. Bobby would have to say that he knew nothing about it. He would have to confess defeat. Then the dean of women would get him and demand an explanation. And even the chairman of the board of trustees, Morton G. Quick, the stockyards capitalist and power behind the University throne, would telephone Bobby and ask about the story. Bobby would telephone Kelly and brand the story as a lie, and the campus reporter as a liar. Kelly would chuckle to himself, his three chins moving, and answer ambiguously. Ruth Summer, who in life had merely been one undistinguished student out of about five thousand, a name on reports, a source of one hundred dollars tuition fees every quarter, a student employee with a name on payrolls, a student who must have a desk in various classrooms, and, finally, a member of the class of 1929 who had had to be formally notified that she lacked the prerequisites for graduation—in death, she would be an embarrassment to all the institution's officialdom. To the campus reporter, she was a scoop, a means of preserving his job, and the instrument of settling his grievances with The Department of Public Relations. To *The Chicago Questioner,* she was a front-page story, exciting the staff for the space of a few moments while the story was written and turned in. To the editors of the other papers, she would be a source of annoyance, something they had missed, and her story in *The Questioner* would be turned over to their rewrite men to be hashed up for their own editions. To a nameless taxi-driver, she was a long and easy haul from the University all the way downtown, with no passenger to watch whether or not he took a long route to jack up his fare.

And while she had become or was becoming all these various meanings, she lay in that oppressive undertaking parlor, blue and bloated in a sleeveless pink taffeta party frock, and all the fruitless dignity and courage of her life was betrayed, even after her death.

1934.

Just Boys

I

BABY FACE was blue. At the Public Health Institute, he had just received another shot. The doctor had told him that he was making slow progress toward a cure, and that it should take at least another year. He rode out on a Jackson Park Express elevated train, sorrowing as he gazed through the window. He smiled, recalling the man with whom he had ridden down on the building elevator after his treatment. He had been small, and disgustingly unattractive, and he had had a scabby, unshaven face. He'd been wearing a khaki shirt, and perhaps he had been an ex-soldier, but he was most certainly not the type of soldier boy whom Baby Face liked. But Baby Face continued to smile, recalling the man's ebullience, when he had said:

"Damn it, kid, I've been having Wassermann's taken for seven years, and this is the first goddamn one that's been negative."

Baby Face's delicate profile clouded, and he wondered when he would be able to show a negative reaction in a test. The train swept on, overhead the tumbling buildings of the Chicago black belt. Baby Face stared at them, twisting about like a jumpy awkward girl. He almost could have cried disgracefully, right out in public. He had a thin sensitive face, with deep blue eyes, a short nose, powdered cherry-red cheeks, and thin, artfully rouged lips. And he was blue. He told himself that he didn't care, he was just not going to be celibate like a nun until he was cured.

He thought of Kenneth, and his blues changed to an emotion which he described for himself as sheer fury. He would just like to scratch Kenneth's yellowish face until the blood poured from it like a river flooding over a dam. And he would like to rip Kenneth's eyes out, and just choke him until he fell gasping, and dead, and then he would stand over him and laugh, yes laugh hysterically. For Kenneth was nothing but a poaching black bitch, and Kenneth had had no right to take Caesar away from him. He thought of Caesar, a strong, husky, magnificent-looking coppery brown boy of twenty-one, with such a handsome innocent face, and such a manly torso. He remembered that scene with Caesar when Caesar had lost his temper and struck him. Baby Face visualized Caesar's face, just before he had punched; tense, sweating, contracted. And after that first punch, he had taunted Caesar, demanded that he be struck again and again, and he had screamed while Caesar had discolored his eyes and split his lips. Baby Face determined that he was going to write that poem he had been intending to write, describing his wild night with Caesar. And he would name it: *Purple Madness*. It made him furious, too, to think how those black bitches at the Princess Amy's would taunt and flaunt him because he had lost his big man to Kenneth, who was nothing but a disgraceful black trollop. And they would laugh at him for having contracted such a vile, perfectly disgusting, and obnoxious disease from that marine he had met at the Blue Eagle Cabaret on South State Street. If Kenneth had not stolen Caesar from him, he never would have gone there that night. Well, he did not care, he was not going to be celibate. The world had been unfair to him, and it had placed a tragic load upon his shoulders. He was going to repay the world. And Kenneth, too. He studied his thin, effeminate hands, with their tapering fingers, and long, polished finger nails. He imagined himself sticking the nail of his right index finger straight in Kenneth's eye.

He got off the elevated train at Fifty-eighth Street, and lightly pranced down the station steps to the street. He decided not to go to the Princess Amy's until he had found himself a big, husky black boy who would cause Kenneth to squirm with spite and envy. He turned his steps toward Washington Park. He had been cruising about the park when he had first met Caesar. He might have better luck on such a fine spring day as this one.

II

Sammy was a muscular and broad-shouldered Negro of about twenty. He was close to six feet tall, and his skin was dark and oily. He had high cheek-bones, large, even white teeth, and a pleasing smile. He strolled around the southern bend of the park lagoon, wistful and lonesome. He hoped that he would meet a girl, and his mind was choked with images of crude sex. Since he had split up with Annie Jones, he had not had any girls, and that had been at least a month ago. If he found a hot mama, he would feel more at peace with himself. He had also just lost his job, and he had very little money left. His room rent was paid up only until Saturday. After that, he did not know what he was going to do.

"Hello, there!" Baby Face lisped, falling into pace with Sammy, and rolling those well-practiced eyes of his.

"Hello!" Sammy abstractedly replied; he looked at the stranger, and immediately reflected that this flapper of a white boy was queer. He determined that he would have nothing to do with him.

Baby Face held out a package of perfumed Turkish cigarettes, and Sammy, tempted, accepted one. Baby Face lit it for Sammy. Sammy obliviously kicked his foot at the gravel walk. Baby Face held his puny shoulders back firmly, and swayed his narrow hips as he walked. He asked Sammy his name, and whether he lived in the vicinity. Not intending to reply, Sammy nevertheless answered.

"Well, I say, Sammy Lincoln, did you ever get your kitchen scrubbed?"

Sammy stared at Baby Face with open-mouthed bewilderment. The whites of his eyes showed. Baby Face laughed nervously. Sammy shook his head, and could not understand why this white boy asked such a peculiar question.

Sammy drawled that when he had been young, and living with his mammy, he had used to scrub the kitchen often while his mammy was out working for white folks. But that was a long time ago, and now, his mammy was dead, and his father was in jail. And he had never liked to scrub the kitchen because it was a wet job. Baby Face smiled. He questioned Sammy about sweet dark girls, and as they passed over the stone bridge, onto the wooded island, offered him a second perfumed cigarette. Sammy wanted to talk about girls, and about Annie Jones. He described her with simple eloquence. He sighed and said, with obvious and rather child-like regret, that Annie and he had gone and had a quarrel and split up, and that now, some white pimp down around Forty-third and Grand Boulevard had her working for him. Baby Face discreetly suggested that it was a poor policy to trust a girl. Sammy countered that he had been to blame in the quarrel. Baby Face asked Sammy if he worked. Sammy told him that he had been working, running an elevator in a building down on South Dearborn Street, but his boss had done gone and fired him because it was hard times. Now, he had no work, and he was tired of sitting around the pool room, so he had come for a walk in the park. Baby Face smiled coyly, and asked him if he were not out looking for a girl.

"Well . . ." Sammy drawled, commencing to answer.

Baby Face interrupted to tell him that girls were treacherous and lecherous bitches, who ruined clean-minded boys. As he spoke he laughed with a nervous subjective laugh that puzzled Sammy. Baby Face continued by advising Sammy that the only thing to do with girls was to put them on the block. Sammy did not understand this white boy's language. He thought of Annie, while Baby Face told him a story of how a black boy he had known had gone cruising around Washington Park, looking for a girl, and that he had found one. Five days later, he learned that he had contracted something that was perfectly disgusting.

"You like boys . . . too?" Baby Face asked, posing and posturing, rolling his eyes and concluding his pantomime with a suggestive wink.

Sammy wanted to say no. The words did not come out of his mouth. He thought that he knew what this queer white boy meant. His friend, Albert, always had bragged about the way such white boys chased after him, and how they gave him clothes and liquor, and took him out for good times at cabarets. He also thought of how he had lost his job, how he was almost without money, and how on Saturday when his room rent was due, he would not have it, and his landlady would probably tell him to clear out. Very soon that stomach of his was going to start tantalizing him, and ask him: Sammy, how about some pork chops? And Sammy would have to tell it: Stomach, we ain't gonna have no pork chops.

"Sammy, with me it's searing purple passions," Baby Face said, acting strangely, his voice jerky.

Sammy covertly observed Baby Face, liking the clothes he wore, particularly his purple tie.

"Well, white boy, that all . . . depends," Sammy said, speaking very slowly.

They sat on the bench, and after questioning Sammy further, Baby Face learned that he was jobless and broke. He told Sammy that he might be able to help him. It commenced to grow dark, and Baby Face took Sammy down to the Golden Lily on Garfield Boulevard for supper. After they had eaten, Baby Face asked Sammy if he would like to walk over to his room, and look at some of his ties.

They crossed the park toward Cottage Grove Avenue, and went to Baby Face's room in a run-down apartment hotel near the University, where Baby Face had been a student until he had been flunked out. Sammy was suddenly struck by the whiteness and rosiness of Baby Face's complexion. He was as pretty as a girl, with skin as tender. And he might take care of Sammy.

III

On the following Saturday evening, Baby Face brought Sammy to a party at the Princess Amy's. Baby Face wore a blue flannel shirt, with brilliantly flaming red cravat, crystal earrings, and two imitation diamond rings from a five-and-ten-cent store. Sammy wore a purple tie which Baby Face had given him.

The Princess Amy had an apartment in a three-story building, a few doors north of the Prairie Theatre at Fifty-eighth and Prairie. The Princess was in his thirties, a coal black, corpulent, perspiring Negro, with small fat bags of flesh under his eyes. For his Saturday evening party, he was wearing a trailing green formal dress and artificial breasts.

There was a Negro group already gathered in the parlor when Baby Face and Sammy arrived. The parlor was rectangular, with shaded lamps, a plush carpet wine red in the lighting, a large overstuffed divan, several wing chairs with leather seats and claw feet, an electric victrola, and red satin pillows that had been scattered indiscriminately about the floor. The room was odored with incense, and with the perfumes which most of those present had applied to their persons. The only female in the group was Louise, a washed-out Negro prostitute with a drawn mulatto face. She was attempting to reform Kenneth, and sat on a pillow near the victrola, frowning while Kenneth, a wiry twenty-one year old Negro with blue velvet coat, a red-and-black checkered lumberman's shirt, and an orange tie, danced with the Princess.

Baby Face's entrance heralded giddy greetings, and several references to his disease. Sammy Lincoln was introduced around, and appraised by the various and effeminate black boys. Baby Face immediately asked why they did not have candles lit instead of lights. The Princess Amy touched the electric button, and the room was in darkness. Those present made various smacking noises with their lips, shouted and laughed, and jovially complained of wandering hands. Soon there were several candles lit, and the Princess Amy waddled about the room, lighting and arranging additional ones. Kenneth started a victrola record going, and the room was filled with the sounds of hot Negro jazz. The Princess and Kenneth shimmied in the center of the floor, scarcely moving their feet. Louise frowned at them. One of the boys pointed to them and loudly smacked his lips.

Sammy sat next to Baby Face on the divan, casting his eyes around the room, looking frequently and questioningly at Louise, lost. He could not understand the others in the room, but he was slightly complimented by the attention he received from them. Baby Face danced with Sammy, and several other boys succeeded Baby Face. Princess Amy, sitting in a winged armchair as if it were a throne, suggested that Kenneth dance with Sammy, and there was responsive laughter. Kenneth said that he didn't care to, if Baby Face had gotten to him first. Baby Face wasted a hateful look on Kenneth, who turned his back, and spoke with Caesar. Sammy next danced with a mulatto boy who was called Marie; he was wearing wide bell-bottom trousers, with a red patch of flannel and pearl buttons just above the pants cuffs. Sammy was relieved when the record was ended. He quickly approached Louise and asked her to dance. She seemed bored, and in the dance did not give him a tumble. Baby Face and Princess Amy kept ragging at her, telling her that she had no right to go hustling now, scabbing on them.

Drinks were served. The atmosphere of the room thickened. The perfume odors commenced to stale, and they mingled with the odors of incense, gin, and perspiration. The room was clouded in unwholesomely thick curtains of cigarette smoke. A number of the guests started clamoring for a game of *Truth*. Kenneth fetched a leather-covered Bible, and commenced to pass it from person to person, each one improvising a mock oath, swearing to tell the truth to all questions asked him in the game. The Bible passed around the room very slowly, because the oaths were made an occasion of wit, and each occasion of wit produced additional wit and high-pitched laughter. In the midst of the mock oath-taking, two boys arose from pillows, and, arm in arm, crossed toward the hallway. They could not be persuaded to remain for the game, and while they stood at the entrance way of the room, bandying jokes, Kenneth rushed to the rear of the house, and quickly reappeared with a knife, fork, and plate. He handed the implements to the two boys who were bent on leaving, and the room was convulsed. Sammy sat scratching his head, trying vainly to understand the joke. The boys went down the hallway toward another part of the apartment. The oath-taking finally was concluded. Kenneth stood at one end of the room, and opened the questioning.

"Marie?" he asked of the boy with the pearl button sewn in his trousers, "Marie, what was you and the Princess doing on the back porch, just before Baby Face and Sammy came?"

There was more laughter.

"Well, you see, it was thissaway . . ."

Another outburst of laughter interrupted him.

"I done stood up and . . ."

They laughed so loudly and interpolated so many comments that the answer went unheard.

"Sammy," Kenneth continued when there was enough quiet to permit speaking, "how many fish has you on the block?"

"What? . . . What's 'at?" Sammy asked, slowly shaking a troublingly confused head from side to side.

"He's asking you how many women you have working for you?" Baby Face whispered.

"Why, me . . . ah . . . no one. Ah ain't even got a job for myself," Sammy said, much to their amusement.

"Baby Face, has you all told Sammy Lincoln what you has got wrong with that hot blood of yours?" Kenneth asked with unmasked malice.

As they laughed, Baby Face dabbed aside a tear, leaped to his feet, and said tensely:

"Kenneth, you're just a jealous, viperish no-account lying bitch."

"Is I?"

"I'm as pure and as white as a lily," Baby Face hastily said before

Kenneth could say more, and the laughter and comments drowned out Kenneth's words.

"What's at? What's he mean?" Sammy quietly asked Baby Face. Baby Face answered that Kenneth was just trying to insinuate lies out of jealousy. Sammy scratched the poll of his kinky head. He was sorry he was present with these people.

"Clara, what kind does you prefer the most?" Kenneth asked, continuing the Truth game.

"Whatever my big man says," Clara, a frail dark boy in a gray suit replied, and they went into fresh paroxysms.

The Truth game proceeded until Kenneth finally got them to change to a game of kiss-the-pillow. Baby Face frowned at Kenneth, arose, and left the room in an angry flounce. He went out to the back porch to have a good cry by himself. He drooled tears. In the parlor, Kenneth postured in the center of the room, holding one of the red pillows in his hands, while he audibly wondered where he should drop it. He exclaimed, to their amusement, that Baby Face should be paged, and the pillow dropped at Sammy's feet. Sammy pointed his finger against his chest, and asked if it meant that he was supposed to do something. Kenneth knelt on the pillow and smiled up at him. He was told to kneel on the pillow, and he complied. Kenneth embraced him, and planted a long, wet, slobbering kiss on his lips, much to everyone's amusement. Sammy arose startled, and Kenneth placed the pillow in his hands. Sammy was told to close his eyes, twirl around and drop the pillow. It fell before Louise, and she knelt and kissed him casually. The game of kiss-the-pillow was punctuated with prolonged, salivary, sometimes smacking, and sometimes sloppy, osculations. It broke up when Princess Amy bestirred himself to produce a tray full of highballs. They drank slowly, discussed their lives, likes, inclinations and problems, and cordially teased and insulted one another. Every insult, every smutty joke, every sexual reference was a source of delight. More drinks were furnished. Slowly, some of them commenced getting drunk.

Baby Face went to the bathroom and studied his red-eyed face in the key of tragedy. He made his face up, and then quietly sneaked into the Princess Amy's bedroom. He donned one of the Princess' red silk dresses, and his appearance in the parlor occasioned hilarity. He and the Princess shimmy-danced while the hilarity persisted.

"Baby Face, if you all wasn't a diseased bitch, I could kiss you and make up," Kenneth said, mischievously.

Baby Face emitted a hysteric scream, and sprang for Kenneth, sinking his nails into Kenneth's cheeks. Princess Amy, fearful of his dress, separated Baby Face from Kenneth. Kenneth, in tears, applied a silk handkerchief to his scratched, bleeding face. Baby Face raved ignoring all consolation, and refusing the drink which the Princess offered him.

"Kenneth, as long as I live, I'll never forgive you!" Baby Face declared, his voice cracked, tense.

Caesar led Kenneth to the rear of the apartment.

Sammy, in mounting perplexity, arose from the divan.

"Tell me, white boy, has you all got one of them diseases?" he asked haltingly, over-emphasizing the final word of his question.

"He's just a lying, jealous bitch," Baby Face said.

Princess Amy placed a fat, restraining hand on Sammy's shoulder. Sammy shook it off.

"Tell me, white boy, has you?"

Baby Face crumpled himself on the divan, sobbed. Sammy, the center of attention in the suddenly excited room, stood over him, his face hard and determined.

"Has you all got a disease, and gone and given it to me?"

Sammy did not know much about diseases, but he knew that they were quite terrible, and that getting one cost a lot of money.

He jerked Baby Face to his feet, gripped his throat, and stared into his watering eyes. Baby Face went limp. His arms flung above his head, and he fell into Sammy's arms in a faint. Princess Amy revived him with smelling salts. He asked, his voice throbbing, to speak alone with Sammy. Sammy followed him into Princess Amy's bedroom, pushing the button to switch on the electricity. Baby Face asked for darkness, but Sammy ignored his request. Baby Face fell into Sammy's arms.

"Sammy, I can't live without you."

In a firm but slowly deliberate manner, Sammy removed Baby Face's arms from his own neck. He held him off at arm's length, and stared at him intently.

"Look me in de eye, white boy, and tell me, has you all given me one of them diseases?"

"No!" Baby Face whimpered.

Sammy shoved Baby Face, who, losing his equilibrium, tumbled back onto Princess Amy's high-poster bed. Sammy left the room, and searched for Kenneth. He found him on the back porch in Caesar's arms. Kenneth told Sammy that Baby Face was diseased, and described how it had been contracted. Caesar confirmed Kenneth's statement.

Sammy seemed to petrify on the spot. He blew instead of breathed. He was a simple and ignorant young Negro boy, with little education, and with only crude experiences in living. Back of him were whirlpools of superstition and fear, and they cluttered his consciousness like a sudden rush of blood to the head, focusing themselves through his sudden discovery. He slowly returned to the bedroom, where Baby Face lay, head downward, in tears.

Methodically, he dragged Baby Face to his feet by the neck of Princess Amy's dress. The silk split and ripped. With equal methodicalness, he knocked Baby Face down with a calculated, timed punch in the jaw. An insane ecstatic gleam lit in Baby Face's eyes. He crawled on his hands and knees to Sammy, and tightly clutched him below the knees. Looking up insanely, he screamed:

"Hit me! Hit me again!"

He jumped to his feet, and thrust his face forward.

"Hit me! Beat me! Kill me!"

"White boy, has you all gone and . . . diseased me?"

"Kill me! Kill me for it!" Baby Face shouted, emitting saliva which struck Sammy's cheek.

All awareness of the situation was gone from Sammy. He saw, like an object in a dream, the tender face and soft white neck of Baby Face. He was an automaton driven on by a whole heredity of superstitions and ignorance, which caused him to be almost paralyzed with fear. In an unwitting trice, and fighting with this fear, he flashed a razor, and with one stroke, slit Baby Face's throat. Blood spurted onto Sammy's clothes, as if from a pump. Baby Face's head, half-severed, unsupportedly dropped forward, chin striking chest, and he fell to the floor. His blood pooled over the carpet, soaked in.

Sammy stood over him without any realization of what had happened; tightly grasped the handle of his now bloodied razor. His head was in a sweltering circle of confusion. His motor centers seemed unable to function. Perspiration arose in great beads upon his forehead. He sat on the bed like a somnambulist, and stared at the green lizards painted over the wall paper. Princess Amy appeared in the doorway, screamed, and fell in a hefty heap on the floor. Others appeared, and by the time Princess Amy was revived, the room was in an uproar of shrieks, outcries, and fainting boys. Sammy continued to sit ghost-

earning seventy-five dollars a week in a bond house, and his employers assured him that they were watching his work and planning a future for him. They circulated in a gay, happy young married set, including many young people who had—connections. Their social life was a round of joy and entertainment which afforded them the best fruits of living. They attended formal dances at country clubs, and exclusive clubs and hotels in the city. They went to shows and parties, and their group maintained a regular bridge circuit. Young people envied them their success and happiness. The fellows with whom Bill had palled before his marriage looked upon his life, success, and prospects as ideal. His position was a standard for many of them, and whenever one of them secured promising employment, he would brag that he would soon have a job as good as Bill Mahoney's. Every Sunday, at mass, people, even elderly strangers, pointed out Bill and Catherine, stating, almost lyrically, that there was a fortunate and happy, even a brilliant, married couple. They represented the best and finest of young Catholic manhood and womanhood at one of the richest parishes on the south side of the city.

Their prospects were so glowing and so certain that they saved relatively little. They lived according to a strict rule of never going into debt, but still they were able to give themselves a sufficiency of comforts, good clothes, and amusements. The smallness of their bank account never distressed them. They were happy and lucky, and Bill's employer, Mr. Steinfeld, would soon be giving him a raise.

Sometimes, the days would grow dull for Catherine. But dullness was part of her station in life. Working would have been a disgrace and humiliation to Bill, and in her *milieu* people frowned on activities like social work as an outlet for the excess time and energies of a young wife. She busied herself now and then with arrangements for card parties in the parish, but these were not very frequent. Her housework was negligible. She used up much time munching chocolates, reading sophisticated novels and mystery stories, attending motion pictures, and gossiping about feminine troubles with her married girl friends. And whenever she became too bored, she would stretch herself out on the expensive couch, built like an armory, and in animal comfort dream sweet dreams of the time when Bill would be rich and she would be a smart and beautiful young matron, creating a stir in the best circles. She would picture herself engrossed in swirls of social activities, all of which would be duly recounted in the society pages of the daily newspapers. She would image this glorious future life in detail, even down to harmless but gratifying flirtations which she would never permit to go beyond furtively stolen little kisses. Because she loved great big Bill, oh, so much! And her great big strong Bill loved her, and kissed her, and played with her. Often, they played bear. She would be the mother bear, and Bill the little baby cub. And after a few minutes, the baby bear would grow up, and become the husband bear, and then, they would play differently. When Bill left for work in the morning, he kissed her and kissed her, because she was always sad to see him leave her, and feared lest something happen to him before he returned, when she would have little surprises prepared for his supper. All day, they telephoned each other. And when Bill came home for supper, he kissed her, and kissed her, and often at night he played bear with her.

Sometimes, in their rose-hued future, Bill and Catherine planned to have two lovely, perfect children. First, they would have their fun alone. And the case of Bill's friend, Tommy Collins, served as an added incentive to delay child-rearing. Bill and Tommy had grown up together, attended the same schools, belonged to the same high-school fraternity. He had married two years ahead of Bill. Tommy and his wife had believed that they should perform their duty to society and get their children born and raised early. Then they believed that later on they would have their children raised, and they would be free and unhampered before reaching old age. They had had two children, and now Tommy and his wife were chained and saddled, and the daily grindstone was scraping Tommy raw. He was a manager of one of the chain grocery stores owned by The Peoples' Stores, Incorporated, and he was barely able to carry his family along on his salary of forty-five dollars a week. His hours were long, and his work and its responsibilities were nerve-straining. In the evening, he was generally too worn and tired to do anything but sit down and read his paper, before going to bed. Whenever Bill met him, Tommy seemed to feel hopeless. And after their second child, Tommy's wife was getting fat, losing her figure and her looks. Bill and Catherine were determined that they would never be as foolish as the Collinses had been. They would have their fun, maintain their present standard of living, and be just alone with each other for a while. Later on, they would have their children, when the darlings would be a luxury they could properly maintain, and not a necessity robbing them of their precious fun and luxuries.

However, their methods of contraception were spasmodic and ineffective. Sometimes, they did nothing, trusting to the friendly fortune which had seemed to follow both their lives like a good fairy in a child's tale. Sometimes, they used devices which Catherine had found advertised in a magazine about motion picture stars. Shortly after their wedding, Catherine had become pregnant, and though they had gone through fear and terror, Catherine had had an abortion performed. Before they had taken this step they had been almost completely panic-stricken. A feminine doctor downtown had performed the operation, charging Bill three hundred dollars. It had been completely successful, and there had been no deleterious after-effects, except that occasionally Catherine would be sorely disturbed with fears, and she would repeat the operation in imagination. While Catherine had been under the ether, Bill had paced the sidewalks adjacent to the building, like a person in a coma, and he had almost walked directly into the path of a moving automobile. Catherine had also had several fortunate miscarriages. Three of these had been so close to her regular menstrual period that they had gone unrecognized. But there had been one very painful miscarriage in the second month which had almost necessitated a curettement, and it had kept her confined for two weeks. On a number of occasions, she had been worried about not coming around, and she had taken overdoses of a drug recommended by a girl friend who was the mother of three unwanted children, coupling it with physics and old wives' contortionings. Her religion forbade such practices, but she easily calmed and quieted the voice of conscience, convincing herself that it was her own personal business, and no one else's, and that God was too kind and good a friend of hers to demand that she admit such private and intimately embarrassing matters in confession to an old priest. And even if it were wrong, she could explain it all to God, and He would understand and forgive her. She had reasoned similarly after she had pantingly succumbed to Bill in her own hallway before their marriage. Her married girl friends were completely awed by her luck in bringing herself around after she would get caught, and they nicknamed her, among themselves, The Miracle Woman.

For Bill and Catherine were young and in love, and in their fun and intense absorption in each other they forgot such things as unpleasant consequences. They lived in a world too full of movement, of hope, and of their own mutual love for them to be uncomfortable. They had never known sorrow, the inexplicable cruelties of life, the brutal inhumanity in the working of natural laws. Life was a dream, and the future was a great bank of success and happiness upon which they could draw and over-draw with no fear or compunction. To them, their every word, deed, thought, and action was dramatic and important, doubly so because of their mutual love and affection. Bill's work was a fight, a struggle, a battle for Fame and Fortune. Whenever they met a rich snob, it was, in Catherine's terminology, a Triumph. Even their petty little domestic squabbles were fought and settled in emotional exaggerations. When they quarreled over some triviality, Catherine would quiver in a tearful heap, and Bill would sternly pace the floor, chin in hand, as if he were thinking as ponderously as Rodin's Thinker or presenting a Hollywood interpretation of Abe Lincoln on the screen. But these misunderstandings were always concluded in kisses and hot-breathed love, which they imaged and expressed as a union of their own superior souls in some beautiful mystery.

Bill and Catherine were sitting on top of the world, and their future was an undrawn check on happiness.

II

Bill arrived home at the usual hour, hung his derby in the closet, took his darling little love-cake of a wife in his arms, and kissed her ardently. He sat down to read the newspaper while she rushed excitedly into their cubby-hole of a kitchen to complete the preparation of supper.

While they were eating, with their knees touching and rubbing under the table, she said:

"Didn't your little piggy of a wife cook you a beautiful supper?"

"Yes, it's lovely, honey bunch."

"And what does your little piggy of a wife get for working, oh, so hard?"

He arose and stood over her, while she gazed up at him with love-wide eyes. He smiled, his face love-soft. He kissed her. He kissed her. He kissed her again. She kissed him. Tightly clasped in his arms, she sighed, and said that he was not showing off his nice table manners. They kissed, and resumed eating their supper.

"Anything happen today?" he asked.

"No, honey!"

"Well, we needn't worry yet."

"No, dear."

"It's only the second day overdue. You can take a hot bath, and maybe tonight we'll . . . play bear . . . because I hear that it sometimes brings things on."

She blushed.

"And you can take some good strenuous exercise," he said in the manner of a doctor confidently prescribing for a patient.

"We'll dance," she said with a rush of excitement and enthusiasm.

"All right."

"But, honey, I don't think there's anything wrong. You see, my periods are not always very regular," she assured him.

They completed their supper, several times interrupting to kiss each other.

A slight rash had broken out on her face, and she had a mouth sore which worried her. She asked him if he believed that it was anything serious, and he remarked that the mouth sore was probably from indigestion and that she could take some Ex-Lax, or, even better, some castor oil. And the rash would probably clear up after her period had arrived.

She washed the supper dishes, and he dried them with an apron strung about him. He telephoned friends, but could get no one to accompany them dancing. They went alone to the Bourbon Palace dance hall. Journeying there on the street car, she suggested that they have a little game of pretense. He pretended that he was taking her out on a first date—and they had fun, talking to each other as if they were almost strangers who were flirtatiously attempting to make an impression on one another. He told her that she made him jealous because she flirted too well, and she laughed so loudly that many passengers in the car turned to stare at them. Bill flushed.

The Bourbon Palace was a huge public dance hall. The entrance floor was tiled and contained checkrooms and super-sanitary lavatories that were scented with perfumed chlorine. A stairway, ornately banistered and carpeted with midnight blue, led to a landing which was dominated by an imitation French neo-Classic painting. Just above it was the lounge, a long rectangular room. It was lit from huge hanging crystal chandeliers. The carpets were pale blue, and the chairs were modeled after the style of Louis Quatorze, larger than required to fit the size of the human body, with tapestry seats and backs in pale pink and weak, almost greenish, blue. The dance floor, flanking the lounge, was a large oval of polished parquet, with a capacity for three thou-

and couples. It was surrounded by a wide and lavishly upholstered promenade, while above it there was a spacious balcony. The establishment was not as crowded as usual, and Bill and Catherine found dancing to be a pleasure because they were not constantly colliding with other couples. They danced with histrionic grace. Bill taking long and slow gliding strides, and Catherine following him so lightly that he imagined himself to be dancing with some winged and airy creature. As they moved about the smoothly polished and slippery dance floor, they continued their game of pretense. Bill strung out a line of conversation which caused her to shake with giggling. He described himself as a big shot with a seat on the stock exchange, and a partnership in one of the most prosperous and popular bond houses on La Salle Street. He mentioned the names of many Chicago rich people as his customers, calling them by their first names as if they were his personal friends. She replied that she was a co-ed from the University of Chicago who had escaped for a night from the wearisome round of dates with fraternity boys, and that she was here because it was such a gay lark, and because she was anxious to get material for an English composition theme. It was fun, carrying on this make-believe, and they danced repeatedly.

Swinging her around the floor, Bill's excessive pride was seemingly expressed by the slanting angle at which he elevated his nose. He observed the motley crowd and enjoyed the enormous sense of superiority which he felt toward them, particularly toward the many creatures with Slavic faces who gyrated and gyroscoped in ugly, twisting and hopping dances. And he compared Catherine with many of the girls present. He noticed a large number who obviously were working girls from factories, restaurants, offices, and the homes of rich people. They were dressed in cheap, and over-stylish or over-stylized dresses, their faces were crusted with cosmetics, and they looked tinselled, gaudy, unrefined. Many of them had crude faces, high cheekbones, or large pipe-organ legs and barrel-shaped figures. Others were thin girls, shrunken and pinched-looking travesties of the female species, who sought compensation for their starved lives by sexual dancing. Along the sides of the dance floor, sitting and standing, awaiting the invitations to dance that came so rarely, were many females with cow-faces; with the ineradicable marks of middle age planted in small, creeping first wrinkles; bagginess under the eyes; developing chins; the first appearances of the distortion of features by fat; with skinny frames that made them seem like creaking poles of flesh garbed in loose dresses. They looked ridiculous, comical, grotesque. Bill knew the type from his visits to public dance halls in the days before his marriage. They were born wall-flowers, who came to such establishments and stood along the sides of the dance floor with wistful, dreamy, self-absorbed expressions, waiting for the slightest notice from anything in pants, and if they received that notice, most of them were prepared to go to any limit. Seeing them again, Bill sneered. He noticed the prettier girls, too, the ones who looked hot, who danced every dance with the sleek, greasy-headed dance hall sheiks. Among their number were many tall, fleshily slender girls, flaming blondes in bright clothes, the personification of the mean-mean mamas of the hot jazz songs. When Bill saw many of them dancing in such a manner that their abdomens were their centers of gravity, he had to quench vagrant desires. He thought that none of these *creatures* was like his lovely little Catherine, his blonde, baby-faced, dimple-chinned wife who loved and respected him so much. Most of them were just pickups, and if they were not downright hustlers, they were at least amateur pushovers. The kind with which a fellow sowed his wild oats. They had no breeding, no manners, no real social station or talents, no high ambitions, no modesty and decency, no self-respect. Their fondest dream was to be picked up by a black-haired sheik with sideburns and wide, flopping trousers and to be laid in a taxicab, hallway, or on a park bench; or else to find and gold-dig some chump for all he was worth. Yes, after Bill quenched the desires which these girls caused in him, that was what he thought of them, and, compared with such vulgar things, how pure, fine, noble, refined, well-mannered, spotless, and virtuous his Catherine was! She had dignity and self-respect, charm, intelligence, grace, *superiority,* and she was not—like they—just lower class. In his high-school fraternity days, they had had a name for such girls—*pigs*. And they would never even speak of them in the presence of girls like Catherine. He thought of how Catherine loved him, and of how he could never truly be worthy of that love, and his pride assumed monstrous proportions. He swept her around the floor with such decisive grace and precision that he felt everyone in the hall must be enviously watching and admiring them.

People would be forced to see that they were not just the regular type of customer to be found at a public dance hall, and that they were not descended from the lower strata of society. For there was one characteristic which both he and Catherine possessed to a remarkable degree: they never acted—*common*.

They danced until both of them were ready to sag with tiredness. With aching muscles, they danced gallantly on, stiffeningly suffering to preserve their erect postures and their form. They were drooping, but they still danced, because they hoped the exercise would bring her around. And they talked steadily with each other, and of various things, of their love, of the mob at the dance hall, of events, affairs and personalities at Bill's office, of the difference between their own friends, and the kind of people they saw dancing about them, of jazzbands. Suddenly, between dances, Bill flared with anger, commenting on how it was such a downright shame that as beautiful a ballroom as this one should be spoiled by the low class of people who patronized it. Its dance floor was so smooth, its decorations and architecture were so beautiful, and the music was so soul-stirring. Then another dance started, the orchestra slowly played *The Rose of Picardy*, and dim orange, red, and violet lights were sprayed over the moving couples. For both of them, it was beautiful, more beautiful than words—ineffable. Catherine said that it was just heavenly. And that caused Bill to boil and he said that the place was just like a community center for foreigners from the districts around the steel mills in South Chicago and in back of the stockyards. All the management needed to do to complete the job of ruining and defiling all this beauty was to admit niggers.

They danced until the orchestra drooled out *Home Sweet Home*.

Dog-tired, they taxied home. Catherine took a hot bath, and called in Bill to wash her back. They kissed, and became excited, and played bear in the bathtub. She continued to sit lassitudinously in the tub of steaming water while Bill made her a hot toddy. As they were tumbling into a heavy sleep, Bill muttered:

"I'm sure you'll come around, honey."

III

Three evenings later, they sat in their combination bedroom and parlor, Bill in the red-plushed monstrosity near the radio, Catherine curled up on the small couch.

"Bearkin, come here and hol' me tight," she suddenly said, with pleading, teary eyes.

He folded her tight in a manly pair of arms until she gasped for breath.

"Honey, I don't want to have a baby now. I don't, dear, because I don't want there to be any extra expense on you, and I know you want things, and want to get ahead, and want nice things, and nice clothes for yourself and me, and want a roadster. And, dear, I don't want a baby now. I just want you and me to be together, and be just us for a while."

He kissed her, his being expanding with soft and complicated emotions. He felt paternal, big-brotherly and protective, as well as husbandly. He was proud of the child in his arms, who loved and trusted him so, proud that he was able to care for her. He told himself that he loved her intensely, and that he wanted to do things for her, and for himself. He wanted to be a success, to have money with which he would be enabled to buy her the most expensive of clothes and jewels, to take her into the highest social circles, to give her all the comforts and *beautiful* things of life. That was his ideal, and that, he believed, was why he lived and worked, and had plans, and dreams, and ambitions. Thinking of these things, and his wife who was the center of them all, he softened, grew moony, and assured and reassured himself that he loved her, his use of the word love embracing intermingled feelings, hopes, desires, and memories for which he did not have specific words. He told her that he loved her, and they kissed.

"We don't have to worry yet. It's only five days, and you've been this long overdue before. You keep taking those exercises and hot baths, and before you go to bed, I'll give you a good stiff drink of the stuff I brought home the other night. And dear . . . take . . . another . . . physic."

She kissed him and nestled against his shoulder. He brushed her short blonde hair with his lips, ran his fingers through it slowly and caressingly, gazed at it studiously. They sat down and listened to the crooning and sickly sweet love songs of Rudy Vallee. The music expressed and represented feelings and emotions for them, and they were very happy.

She broke a meaningful mood of silence between them by asking if she could take some stuff sold at drug stores.

"No, dear! I'm afraid. I don't like trying it. You know it's a drug, and anyway, dear, things might turn out all right."

"But suppose they don't?"

"Well, if they don't . . . other people have babies," he answered, after a pause.

"Yes, but, honey, I don't want that—well, I don't want any added expense on you, and I don't want that, well, I don't want it that we'll have to sit home and mind a baby."

"Dear, life is a fight, and we all got our battles, and we got to face them, and fight it out. And, dear, you and I can fight it out together, can't we?"

Her answer was a long kiss.

"But, dear, maybe it will hurt me, *awful?*" she said.

"Yes, but if we have to have it, we have to."

"I love you," she said.

He lit a cigarette, and they puffed on it by turn.

"Yes, dear, we love each other, and if we have a baby, I want it to be a boy, and to have blue eyes, and light, soft, curly hair like you've got. I don't want it to look like me. I want it to be like you, big, and strong, and manly, and to have lips like you have. Dear, the first thing I loved about you was your lips, and I'll want our baby to have lips like yours, because it is going to be your baby."

"It will be yours, too."

"But I'm part of you."

They kissed.

"But dear . . . what will we name it?" she asked.

He didn't know, and she questioned him with persistence, suggesting various names, but returning continually to her decision that it be named William Mahoney, Junior. He was inclined to give it a classier name, like Garnet, or Cornelius, and said that he'd have to find out if there were any saints with those names, so that when they had it baptized it could be called Garnet or Cornelius. If not, then they could call it William Garnet, or William Cornelius, and later drop the William. She replied that William was a beautiful name.

They talked of what the baby would be like, and of how they would play with it, and train it, and raise it to be a very superior and very intelligent child. She was happy with a budding woman's dreams and expectations of maternity. They talked on, but finally grew bored, and rushed out to make the last show at a neighborhood theater. They saw, and thoroughly enjoyed, Greta Garbo in *Inspiration*.

Finally they calmed, and ate a cold supper.

They remained home, and after doing the dishes, they sat in the parlor, he, comfortably smoking, allowing sugar-jazz from the radio to dissolve his worries. He meditated and day-dreamed, a succession of saccharine happy thoughts traipsing about his mind like angels bearing news of good omen. She read an article from a movie magazine, telling which actress had the most beautiful figure in Hollywood.

"Dear . . . do you like my figure?" she asked with sudden and unexpected coyness, and he answered affirmatively.

"When you take me to the talkies, you don't watch the actresses and think that they have a better figure than me?"

He smiled, called her silly, and avowed his love for her.

"And you don't think less of me or not love me as much when you see Dolores Del Rio in a picture?"

"Don't talk silly."

"But I'm not. This is awful important."

He kissed her, resumed sitting, smoked, listened to the radio music. She read.

"Dear . . . I want to ask you something," she said after several non-talkative minutes.

He looked at her, quizzically.

"You won't be angry?"

"Why should I?"

"Promise me?"

"Promise."

"I'm afraid to ask you," she said; she continued to wheedle him.

"All right, dear, what is it?" he asked with nervous curiosity.

"Can I have another . . . another abortion?"

He checked an impulse to be impatient and exclaimed that he was afraid to have her take another chance. He calculated the cost, and it furnished an added deterrent. He recollected how he had worried over the previous abortion, and these memories re-enforced his decision, because he feared the necessity of again undergoing such a nervous strain of fear and anxiety, again pacing the streets with his mind almost a blank, again frantically and half-coherently praying to God that she be spared. No, he couldn't do it again. He realized how they had been so completely foolish, damn fools, for not having been more careful. He assured himself firmly that she should not undergo any more such operations, and reflected that it was sinful, and might bring down upon their heads the wrath and punishment of God. He told her they hadn't better take another chance. She kissed him meekly, answering with a yes. They kissed, and, strung by morbid thoughts, they prepared for bed.

V

Bill and Catherine had invited their parents over for dinner, and for an evening of conversation and bridge. She told them that she was going to have a baby, and this surprising but over-welcome news brightened the evening, giving the old folks something to talk about and thereby relieving the monosyllabic dullness customary to their visits. Both of the fathers had been gloomy because of the depression and the inroads it had made and was still making upon their incomes. The announcement had changed them into smiling granddaddies-to-be, and they had become verbose. Mr. Bell had been particularly and unusually talkative, and had, in fact, seemed almost queer, and not himself. He had spoken exaggeratedly and grandiloquently of himself and of the Bells. He had traced the lineage of his family, repeatedly speaking of it as a noble one. All present had looked at him curiously. He was only forty-nine, too young for a senile second childhood, and yet he had not seemed like himself. It had been, however, a pleasing and happy evening, despite Mr. Bell, and despite an under-the-surface jealousy that he had almost brought to the top with his reiterative and gratuitous talk of the Bell characteristics. Also, both sets of parents had wondered whether the child would be a Bell or a Mahoney. Both had invited the young people to close up housekeeping and join them until after the confinement, but Bill and Catherine were too happy by themselves. And there was a prolonged discussion of doctors, while they had sat long over the supper which Catherine had cooked, and which all had pronounced excellent in order not to hurt the young wife's feelings. Mrs. Bell had advised them to have old Doctor Jones, who had delivered Catherine. Mr. Bell had rubbed his paunch, and declared that Doctor Jones was old-fashioned, and that what the young folks needed was a bright young doctor who was up with the times and all the latest things in medicine. He said that these old medicoes were fogies. And with each reiteration, he had added a peroration on keeping up with the times, illustrating how, from ages immemorial, the noble line of Bell had always kept up with the times. The Mahoneys had advised getting their family doctor. But the young people had tactfully settled this stream of mongered advice by speaking of their doctor, Doctor Johnson. He was kindly, understanding, and middle-aged, and he had indicated that he knew his profession well when he had attended Catherine during her miscarriage. Other aspects of the coming nativity were also discussed, and both Mrs. Bell and the older Mrs. Mahoney delivered long eulogies on the merits of Carter's Woolen Undershirts. They considered the naming of the child, the selection of a godfather and a godmother, its career, and its education. And Catherine remained in the kitchen while the two mothers washed and dried the dishes, which they would not permit her to touch. They regaled her with advice, knowledge, hints, and old wives' tales garnered from their own past and its superstitions. Afterward, there was bridge, and every time Mr. Bell won, he boasted of the noble lineage of his ancestors. The old folks even remained an hour later than usual, and they had departed with enthusiastic faces. The prospects of becoming grandparents had stirred new interests to blast out the monotony of their fading and atrophied lives. It made them excessively happy and expectant.

When they had gone, Bill and Catherine sat on the edge of their bed, and she wondered aloud about naming the baby, insisting that it had to be a boy, because she did not want to have a girl—yet. She wanted a beautiful boy like her husband, a beautiful new William. And she insisted that it would resemble its daddy, and she would love it, but, of course, she would not love it quite as much as she loved Bill, and after it was born, Bill would, just the same as now, be first in her heart. Bill listened to her chatter with a sense of gratification, thinking how cute and fine she was, and how he had such a right to be proud of her.

She rambled on gaily, explaining how she desired the child to be healthy, and to have the very best education. Why, when it grew up, it might even be president, or at least a senator, or anyway a judge like Judge Dennis Gorman, or Judge Joseph O'Reilley, who were such good friends of Bill's father. Bill ceased listening, and gazed at her, reflecting that she looked closer to sixteen than twenty-one, and that her approaching maternity seemed preposterous. And himself, a father! But then, he was a responsible, promising young man with a future. The prospect of paternity fed that sense of responsibility, made him feel completely mature.

"Wasn't father queer tonight?" she suddenly said.

He only shook his head, not wanting to say anything that would hurt her feelings. Then, he added:

"Probably worry over the depression. But things are going to pick up. And we'll be more prosperous than ever. This is too rich a country, with too many fine business brains, to allow it to sink like Russia or Europe."

"Yes, but father was like an old frog, and the way he talked, it was funny. He sounded like he wasn't all there."

"Probably worry over business."

"I wish we weren't going to have this old baby . . . but . . . but . . . anyway I'll love it and be good to it, because it will be your baby," she said, commencing to undress.

He kissed her, and she curled against him, saying in a manner which he regarded as cute:

"Dear!"

"Yes."

"I love you."

After their embrace, they continued undressing, and she said:

"Dear?"

"Yes."

"After I have the baby, you'll love me, still?"

"Why, you know I will. You shouldn't have such foolish thoughts."

"Even if it makes me swell out, and look ugly, and leaves me with marks on my body like mother got?"

"I'll always love you!"

"It's me you love, and not that you love me just for—that other thing."

He kissed her, spoke with romantic triteness about her eyes, her soul, her whole pure self. He believed his own words, implicitly. They kissed.

"And when we have our baby, you'll take care of it, and of me, and you'll love it, and you'll love me?"

"Yes."

She flung herself on him. She smiled up at him, insipidly, and he thought that it was all charming and beautiful, and his emotions seemed to melt. He uttered more romantic triteness about her eyes, her soul, her whole pure self.

"Dear, if you would, if you'd love the baby more than you do me,

I'd be frightfully jealous, and mean to it, and I'd let it get dirty, and not take care of it."

Silence, and she took off her undergarments, and stood before him, shy in her nakedness.

"And I won't have to feed it from my breasts, so that they'll get big and ugly?"

"Why, no."

"And you'll give it a real good education, and not let it have any suppressions or things like that that people have in novels?"

He assured her.

"And later on, we'll get our car, and all the nice things we want anyway?"

"You bet! I'm going to fight to be a success, and this is going to spur me on to fight with more determination and . . . stick-to-it-iveness, and I'm going to fight, just like Notre Dame fights all the harder when the going gets rough."

He wanted to say more. He wanted to tell her how he felt that he was a son of destiny, like Napoleon or John D. Rockefeller, and how nothing, absolutely nothing, no obstacle could stop or block his striving, his climbing and battling up to the very topmost pinnacles of success . . . because . . . he was a . . . son of destiny.

"Dear, why, I have all kinds of, why, I have gobs of faith in you."

His vanity was warmed, stimulated. He smiled fatuously, enjoying his own large thoughts of himself, and he envisioned his future optimistically as a long series of conquests and victories.

"Bill . . . but I'm afraid . . . I'm afraid," she said, interrupting his reverie.

So was he, as he stepped into his pyjamas, and looked at her in her pink nightgown, but he tried to retain calmness. He told her that all kinds of women have babies, and that having babies was the main purpose God had in mind when He created Eve.

"But some die."

"There won't be any danger. We'll be careful, and Johnson is a good doctor."

"Promise me that you'll pray every day that there won't be any danger, and that I'll not die!"

"Promise."

"And if I do die, you'll be good to the baby?"

He said yes, adding that she would not die.

"And if I die, you won't run off right away and marry some other girl?" she said, wiping away a tear with the back of her hand.

He assured her.

"And if I don't, you'll always love only me, and never anyone else?"

He embraced her, and she said she loved him. Suddenly, she peeled off her nightgown, and stood before the mirror, her shyness absent. She studied her body closely to note if there were any swelling, and asked him if he perceived any. He could not observe more than a slight expansion, and a scarcely noticeable swelling of her small breasts.

"Well, it isn't going to happen right away, and for a little while longer I won't be fat or ugly, will I?"

They went to bed, and she cried and was afraid. She forgot her fear by playing bear.

VI

The days seemed to drift slowly. Her initial fears abated, except for sporadic periods when she would experience brief and moody moments. She was commencing to anticipate her maternity with pride and hope, and she was becoming accustomed to the slow swelling of her womb. She spoke of her pregnancy with her girl friends, her mother, and her mother-in-law, even to herself. She commenced to wear it like a badge of distinction. It always enabled her to become the focus of attention, and she could keep the talk about it going interminably, detailing her condition, her future child, what it would wear. And it made her feel grown, mature, a full woman. Vaguely, almost unconsciously, she enjoyed a sense of shared experience with the mothers of the world. She was very contented, and she often sang by herself.

And Bill was even more proud and satisfied. His success in quashing her talk of an abortion ministered to his already well-formed feelings of self-righteousness. Having a child would make him more responsible, more upright, settled, a steady and stern member of society. Daily he told his fellow employees at the office about it. They nicknamed him Daddy Mahoney, and showered him with lascivious jokes and innuendoes. One day, one of the lesser paid clerks tried to kid Bill by telling him that maybe the baby would not be his, but some iceman's kid. There was almost a fight. The seed of worry and jealousy dropped in his mind, and it grew, deviously and disguised. He developed the habit of questioning his wife persistently, speaking to her ambiguously in double entendres. She could not understand what he was driving at, and worried herself into constant tears, fearing that he did not want the child.

The days drifted on. She was swelling slowly, and had occasional fits of nausea and morning sickness. But Doctor Johnson found no cause for worry.

They were completely habituated to the prospect of becoming parents, and at times they even anticipated it with eagerness. On many evenings, they sat side by side, and talked about it and its future, the buggy it would have, the way it would play and smile and coo.

One day when Bill came home from the office, she lay on the sofa, pale and lethargic in a post-natal lassitude. She acted very weak and tired, and her eyes were drawn. She could move only with difficulty. In a low, wearied tone, she said that she had had another miscarriage. Luckily, it had come while she was at home. She had just been preparing to leave for a matinée at the neighborhood movie house when the pains had gripped her. They had cut and pressed, seemingly threatening to break her back. She had screamed, and felt something awful pressing out of her. She had run to the bathroom, screamed again, and it had happened. No one had heard her scream, and she had dragged herself weakly to the couch, and waited for him to come home, lying there, dozing off, waiting and feeling so afraid and lonesome, waiting for him. Now, she was just tired, and she felt that nothing would happen to her, if she remained quiet so as to prevent a hemorrhage. Bill telephoned Doctor Johnson, and then performed the distasteful task of cleaning up the bathroom. He also phoned his and her mothers, but neither of them was at home. He sat by her side, and she drowsily told him that she was glad it had happened, because now they could get on better, and have the things they wanted, and he wouldn't have that added expense on his shoulders. He, too, was relieved.

She commenced to cry, and exclaimed that she loved him, and was sorry that it had happened. It had been awful funny-looking when it had come out of her, like something being ripped out, but she had loved it just the same. She cried, and then dozed off.

Doctor Johnson arrived. She was without fever and her pulse was normal. There was probably no danger. She could not recall if the after-birth had also come out, or not, but she believed that it had. Judging from her lack of fever and her pulse, the doctor decided that it had, and that she was in no extraordinary danger. If she rested for a few days or a week, she would probably be all right again.

Suddenly, he recalled her first miscarriage, and he pursed his lips reflectively. He decided to take a blood test. But he did not want to worry them until his suspicions were either confirmed or disproven. They were already sufficiently frightened and confused. They did not question him, or consider it curious and unusual when he said that he wanted to take a blood count to determine if Catherine, a healthy red-cheeked girl, had pernicious anemia. He merely explained that he was anxious to ascertain the precise cause of the miscarriage. They let it go at that. The doctor hurried home, and while they awaited his return, Bill had a chicken supper sent up from a nearby restaurant. The doctor returned with his needle and drew blood out of Catherine's arm. They finished supper.

Two days passed, and in the evening, Doctor Johnson returned. Catherine was able to sit up, and even to move around a little, although the flow was still heavy, causing slight fear lest there be a hemorrhage.

The doctor looked worried. He sat talking with them, rubbing his hands, looking at them in a soft and sympathetic manner, staring off at the walls, tightening his lips. He obviously had unhappy information to give them, and he was striving to find a way to tell it. He explained, slowly and at length, that whenever women had miscarriages as easily as Catherine had had one, and particularly when they recurred, there was cause for wonder. Some women went through unbelievable tortures and took dangerous and ineffective drugs to accomplish what had happened to Catherine with no effort. And still with all their abnormal efforts, they were unable to induce abortions. Hence a doctor always tried to determine the cause of such a facile miscarriage.

He paused, and delayed lighting a cigarette. He stated that in Catherine's case he had wondered, and that was why he had taken the blood test. He had sent the specimen to a perfectly reliable laboratory for analysis. The result was unhappy, but it was his professional duty to inform them.

He paused. He looked at them as a father looking on his children. He told them the actual nature and purpose of the test, and added that the laboratory finding showed a strong positive reaction.

Her face wrung into an expression of uncomprehending fear,

Catherine asked what that meant. Bill patted her head, kissed her tenderly.

The doctor gazed away. He paused. He made several false starts, and stopped. There was a moment of undue tenseness.

"A strong positive reaction on a Wassermann probably means . . . syphilis."

"Oh!" she murmured.

There was a lump in Bill's throat. He tried to explain that it was impossible because neither of them had been exposed, and his words collided with each other, and tripped over themselves.

Doctor Johnson told them that in Catherine's case the strong positive reaction was pretty good evidence, that, in fact, it practically constituted proof. He told them that the disease could be contracted in various ways, and that it could be hereditary, which meant that it could be contracted in the womb before birth. Bill stuttered that it was unbelievable.

Catherine cried. The doctor attempted to explain that they should view the situation neither as a tragedy nor a disgrace. It was a misfortune which they should attempt to right as soon as possible. If they were diligent in taking precautions, and if they were conscientious in their treatments, there was a possibility of their being cured. He told them that consumption, pernicious anemia, or cancer could all be more dangerous or fatal diseases than syphilis. The doctor added that the disease was probably in the secondary stage, whereas Bill told of having had a negative Wassermann about three weeks before his marriage. Doctor Johnson drew blood from Bill's arm for a test, and arranged for them to visit his office in a few days for skin tests. They sat, unable to speak. He reassured them that syphilis was curable; but did not add, for reasons of tact, that if his surmise were correct that the disease was probably hereditary with Catherine, it would be extremely difficult to cure. They were sufficiently worried already. Catherine was sobbing. Bill appeared as if he wanted to cry.

"And now I can't have a baby, never," she lamented.

"That, Catherine, depends on how you respond to treatment," the doctor said.

She continued to sob and lament. Bill slumped back in his chair. The doctor bid them a cheerful good-bye and departed for another patient. He shrugged his shoulders. He came upon such situations all the time, and he had to consider them professionally. Going down to his car, he shook his head. Now, he had to call on an old man who was dying from cancer of the intestines.

VII

Catherine was lying on the couch. Bill sat beside her. He dismissed an impulse to grow angry and to blame her. He knew that she was an innocent victim, possibly of himself. He figured that he might have contracted the disease somewhere through an open cut, or possibly from his own parents. Her father, the last time they had visited him and Catherine, had sounded like something was wrong. Or she might have been infected by some unknown syphilitic, through a drinking glass or in some such way. It was a predicament in which he could not believe, let alone fathom. . . . Nor did he know how he could face it. He glanced around their apartment, the background of two married years. It was bleak and comfortless now. All hope had gone out of it, out of his life. They talked the matter over, but did not know and could not decide what was the cause of this unexpected affliction. They were loath to believe it hereditary. Their parents were good people, and they came from good families. It seemed impossible, too, to believe that his or her parents could have such a disease. They were good people. They lived good lives, and they fulfilled their religious duties conscientiously. They were good people. . . . But if it was hereditary, how could they tell their parents? Thinking of this, Catherine sobbed anew. Bill lit a cigarette, took one puff from it, and squashed it on the floor. He lit another cigarette. He sat and looked at the designs of the wallpaper. Their world was a crumbled heap, and they must face a black and danger-ridden future, at the end of which might be decay, death from insanity, blindness, rotting, wasting flesh, paralysis. Syphilis was not merely a disease to them. It was a horror, an almost mystical nightmare, like the leprosy they had read of in their bible histories back in grammar school. It hovered over them like a monstrous, rapacious and huge pre-historic animal. They both cried. He kissed her. She tried to warn him away, saying that possibly he was not infected. He kissed her protests away, and she was curled and silent in his arms. She sobbed like a frightened little child, and she muttered, almost incoherently, that she would give him a divorce, because she was probably to blame, and she did not want to ruin his life. He kissed her tenderly.

Then they were silent. The night, plastered against their window, was black, and the moon beyond it was feeble. A wind rattled the panes. They were alone, surrounded by that dark world.

She lay back on the couch, and he sat on the edge, stroking her forehead, fighting back his own tears.

She sobbed and said that maybe they ought to commit suicide. They were silent, and both of them entertained thoughts of suicide with melodramatically youthful pretense. The silent room, and the boy and the girl alone in it, with night plastered black against their window panes, and a feeble moon beyond.

He wiped her tears away and kissed her.

"Honey, we'll stick this out," he said with a strong effort to be brave and determined.

"No, dear, I won't hold you down. Maybe it's my fault," she sobbed.

"Honey, we'll stick and fight it through!"

"I love you, Bill. Oh!"

"We have each other. We'll stick," he said chokingly.

He shook his fist randomly, in bravado and defiance.

"We'll fight it, honey!" he said.

She dried her tears, and he kissed her. She moved closer to the wall, and he stretched out beside her, and they lay side by side, embraced, trying to find heart and courage by speaking brave words to each other. It would turn out all right. They would be cured, they would again be healthy and happy, and they would have children, and be normal and strong. They would stick and fight their way back to health.

Brave words that were like the shades children pull down to ward off the lonely midnight darkness which scares them. Big words! Brave words! Honey, we got each other. Darling, we love each other, and we'll stick. Oh, god, jesusmaryandjoseph, jesus, god, ohmarymotherofthecrucified savior, ohbleedingheartofjesus, oh mary, oh mother of god, help us, cure us. . . . Prayers for help flung through the godless mechanisms of the universe, flung through the black night with the feeble moon behind it. Impotent prayers giving their only measure of consolation a frantic hope born of fear.

They lay there. The world was a massed and lonely silence towering down upon them. They lay there in silence, hearing nothing but their own rapid breathing, the rattle of the wind on the pane, and then, an automobile starting outside and footsteps in the hall outside their door. They lay, clinging together, thinking big, brave words.

"Darling, play the radio. I can't stand this any more," she finally said.

He turned on the radio, and he heard a jazzband braying *The King's Horses*.

1931.

A Casual Incident

THE kid stood at the edge of a small, nondescript crowd at State and Quincy Streets, listening while a sleek Greek conducted a Come-to-Jesus meeting. With appropriate showmanship, the fellow introduced presentable females who stood on a soap box and gave testimony. One of them was a mother, and after she had luridly described her sinful past and the joys and satisfactions of being washed from sin in the Blood of the Lamb, she put her seven-year-old girl on the box, because the girl had been living with Jesus inside of her for two years. The mother and the Greek tenderly instructed the girl to explain just how Jesus had come to her, as quick as a snap of the fingers, and just how nice and good and holy and happy it felt when you had kindly Jesus right inside of your breast. The child stood on the soap box, fidgeting, shyly dropping her eyes, saying nothing. The crowd laughed good-naturedly at her cute gestures. All coaxing failed, and the Greek lifted her down. He declared that anyway she loved Jesus, and loving Jesus was all that counted in this dark world of sin.

"Jesus got tongue-tied that time," the kid said to a burly Pole on his right.

"Dey all queer here," the stolid Pole answered, pursing his lips.

"Yeh, and it's funny the way Jesus got tongue-tied that time," the kid said.

"Yeh," the Pole said, smiling.

"I think it's damn funny. Here they say Jesus has been inside the kid for a couple of years, and then when they ask Him to speak, He gets tongue-tied."

The meeting concluded in song and the crowd dispersed. The kid and the Pole leaned against the window of an Owl Drug Store that was jumbled and confusedly decorated and placarded. They talked, and the kid noted that the Pole was a giant, with a heavy, planed face, and a deep bass voice. He had ox eyes, and looked very masculine.

"You know, dese religious people, dey all a little queer in de head," the Pole said.

"They're nuts. But it was funny, the way Jesus got tongue-tied," the kid said.

The Pole surveyed the kid. He was about twenty, with cleanly carved features, and he was carrying several books.

"Religious guys always like de ladies, doh," said the Pole.

"Yeh, they get themselves hooked up with a skirt every time."

"I was in Seattle one time, and dey had a big big place. It was a great big tent, and dere were crowds evry night. It was dat religion, what you callum? You know? Dat religion, oh, gee, I know de name well. Dat religion, you know, where dey all roll round, all crazy in de head?"

"Holy Rollers."

"Yeh, dat's it, de Holy Rollers."

"Yeh," the kid said.

"Dey had a big big tent, and so big a place, and dey had big crowds evry night, and dey made all kindsa money, too. Well, de guy what was de preacher, he liked de wimmin . . . you know what I mean?"

The Pole smiled, and pursed his lips. He described how the preacher had seduced the choir master's wife and several girls in the congregation. He had finally eloped with the former, taking along the congregation funds. There had been a story about it on the front pages of the papers. The kid considered the account to be pointless, but listened, because he had nothing to do.

"Wimmin, dey all dangerous," the Pole said, pursing his lips.

He talked on, describing his life. At the age of twelve, he had run away from his native Polish village because of the poverty of his family. He had followed the sea, going to all parts of the world, and he had had adventures on many a waterfront.

"When a young fellow goes on his own, tings happen to him. You know . . . well, tings happen to him," the Pole said.

"I know."

"A young fellow, he goes on his own, and he don't know nottin', and well . . . tings happen to him."

"You have to take your chances, and if you can't swim, you sink. It's just your tough tiddy, then," the kid said.

"Yes, but tings happen."

A CASUAL INCIDENT

The Pole recounted more of his experiences, interrupting his tales to remark:

"I got a nice place now, wid a fren. We have nice big place 'n' we bring anyone we want dere. No one to bodder us."

"That's pretty nice. You can bring your women there."

"Wimmin. . . . No, dey're dangerous," the Pole said, pursing his lips.

"Yes, I guess they can get to be a nuisance."

"Where you live? . . . At home?"

"Me, I live in an undertaking parlor."

The Pole laughed. The kid explained that he was paid three dollars a week, and received a bed for hanging around, answering telephone calls and sometimes going out on the ambulance. This was his evening off. The Pole again laughed, pursing his lips and exclaiming that it was funny.

"You bring girls dere, too?"

"Hell, no! We got six religious Irishmen there, and if I brought a girl around, sure as hell there would be a gang rape."

"Well, wimmin, dey're dangerous," the Pole said, laughing.

The kid leaned back against the window, and watched the sleepy-eyed parade of people along State Street. He heard the traffic sounds and sudden jets of conversation.

"Wanna see my place?"

"Not tonight, thanks. I feel pretty tired," the kid answered.

The Pole seemed to become confused, and, to mask his confusion, he quickly asked the kid about the books he had under his arm. The kid casually answered that they were story books. The Pole talked about the sea, and then asked the kid if he had ever been on the road. The kid nodded, and told about how he had once gotten blind drunk in Hoboken.

"Well, as I say, tings happen to young fellows."

"Yeh," the kid yawned.

"You out now, lookin' for girls?"

"Not particularly. I feel pretty tired."

"I was just wonderin'," the Pole said, shrugging his broad shoulders; he pursed his lips.

"I don't like can houses," the kid said.

"A young fellow, he got a have girls."

"Yeh, I guess he does," the kid said.

The kid yawned, said he was getting pretty tired, and guessed that he would be getting back to the undertaking parlor.

"Come up 'n' see my place?" the Pole said.

"No, thanks, I feel too tired."

The Pole smiled, and gave the kid his address. He told him that any time he was broke, or needed a place to sleep, to come up. He pursed his lips, and looked at the kid.

"Come up 'n' see my place," he said, his voice suddenly strained.

"I feel too tired. . . . Say, there's a saloon called Reilley's in Hoboken, right off the Fourteenth Street ferry. Ever been there?"

The Pole eyed the kid queerly as the kid went on to talk about the beer at Reilley's, fifteen cents a glass with the headache guaranteed. The Pole said he guessed he would be going home.

"And I guess I'll be blowing this town again pretty damn quick," the kid said.

"Chicago's a nice town. Lotsa girls here," the Pole said.

He pursed his lips.

"Nice girls are everywhere. They grow like apples on trees."

The Pole laughed, and said nice girls were very dangerous. The kid said anyway the idea about life was to live dangerously, on a volcano.

"Girls dat are nice, sometimes dey give you . . . you know . . . dose," the Pole said.

"Well, you got to take your chances," the kid said.

"But dere's a way ob not taking chances," the Pole said in a tense voice.

"What do you think of Cleveland as a town?" the kid asked.

The Pole was uninterested while the kid talked of Cleveland, comparing it with Chicago and New York.

"You got nice girl, ob your own?" asked the Pole.

"No, I don't believe in dragging nuisances around with me."

"But you like de girls?"

"Yeh, sometimes."

"Tonight?"

"No."

"You goin' back to de undertaker's and read?"

"Yes."

"Oh, gee, ain't it spooky?" the Pole asked, laughing; he pursed his lips, and he concentrated his ox eyes intensely on the kid.

"I got nice place. You come on up?"

"I'm pretty busy. I'm writing a book," the kid said.

"About de girls?"

"Not particularly."

"It must be nice to write books?"

He told the kid if he'd visit him, that he would tell him lots of things to put into the book, things about geisha girls, and Asiatic beachcombers, and sailors, and towns in all parts of the world.

"I'm pretty tired. Guess I'll blow," the kid said.

"Got my address?"

"Yes, but I'm pretty busy," the kid said.

"But ain't it spooky, out dere wid de corpses?"

"I don't mind it."

"It's funny," the Pole said, laughing hoarsely.

"Yep, I guess I'll be blowing," the kid said.

"Dat's funny, livin' at de undertaker's."

"It's better than sleeping in the parks," the kid said.

"You sure you wouldn't like to come to my place a little while?" the Pole asked, pursing his lips.

"No thanks," the kid answered, yawning.

"Sure?"

"Yes."

"But you got to be careful ob de girls. Dere dangerous."

"Yeh," the kid said yawning, again stating that he was going.

"So long," the kid said.

"So long, kid . . ."

"I'm going to the I. C. station at Van Buren Street."

"So long, kid . . . but I got a nice place."

1929.

Clyde

I

CLYDE, with his reddish cheeks, had a boyish appearance. He had clear blue eyes, and blond hair which tended to jut upward spikily. His wistful lips lent an innocence to his expression.

He worked behind the soda fountain of a chain drug store near the University, and he was alert and conscientious. His partner, Clement, was a droll fellow from the south. Clement was fond of Clyde, anxious to help Clyde lose his virginity, and thereby, as Clement believed, make a man of him. Clement often strutted before Clyde, assuring him that he did not know life. Clyde was his audience, and daily Clement described his dissipations, his drinking and gambling parties, and the various techniques and approaches he used on women. After these descriptions, Clement would always invite Clyde to come along the next time he went on a party. Often, he had even offered to pay Clyde's expenses, if Clyde would accompany him to a brothel. Clyde always blushed and declined such invitation. Clement's pat reply to Clyde's refusal was that some day, a baby-face would pick the lock of the refrigerator where Clyde was trying to keep a pickled cherry.

"You don't seem to care foh women," Clement said one day behind the counter while there was a lull in trade.

Clyde answered that it was not a lack of caring as much as it was something else. Women and girls were sometimes nice and pretty, but then, there were others who were just low, and a disgrace to everybody's mother and sisters. But it was still another reason which kept him from women. Clement asked for that precise reason. Speaking slowly, Clyde tried to explain his belief that women liked to make a fool out of a fellow, and that all they cared to do was to spend his money and waste his time. He was too poor, and he had ambitions which did not permit him to be extravagant with his money. He was saving up to go to college, and an education meant more to him than some chance female and the passing pleasures she could give, if pleasures they be.

"Well, I suah want to know things; but not if ah had to give up my honey. No, sir, ah couldn't go without getting mahself a piece of honey now and then," Clement said.

"Now and then?" Clyde retorted.

"Son, let me tell you this much: Let me say that women is one of life's sweet delights."

"And one of life's headaches," Clyde said.

"Well, son, it's thissaway. Now it's all in the way you take 'em. Me, now, ah never commit mahself, and then, you see, they got nothin' on me. Get it! This here gentleman never lets them get any goods on him. It's all in the way you-all take them," Clement drawled.

Clement then proceeded to describe how he had met a little blonde girl at a public dance hall only a week ago, and how, by using a delicate and gradual approach, he had already been the first fellow to succeed with her, although plenty had tried. He could tell that from her elaborate defenses.

"What you say can all be true, but if you want to get anywhere, you got to save and work," Clyde said.

"Suah. Ah knows all that. A fellah works and works the Jesus out of himself. Then he becomes, if he's riding in high luck, a rich old sonofabitch without a belly foh food, and caint eat anything but dog's milk. Suah, ah understands that idea. And after you all has become rich, and haven't got any belly left, you all laps up dog milk, and pays some young gal to let her have you become her lap dog. Ah knows that story from *a* to *z*."

"Well, I don't agree with you," Clyde said.

"Well, I suah want to know things; but not if ah had to this much. Git all the fun you can out of life while the gittin' is good and you're young. And nevah, under any circumstances, turn down a piece of honey that drifts your way," Clement drawled, smacking his lips, enjoying his philosophy of life to the utmost.

Clyde blushed, and busied himself polishing the nickelware which already shone with a dazzling surface.

Clement stood pondering, his heavy hand pressed against a beefy chin. He soliloquized:

"Ah know. You is just one of those there bashful guys. That's it. You're a bashful guy, that's all, so you got your cherry pickled in an ice box. Well, son, let me give you some advice. Keeping your cherry on ice is what gets plenty of those guys put in the booby hatch. I know that. Daown home, now, they was a jellybean who was a bashful guy, and he couldn't git up the courage to find himself a piece of honey. So he goes along whipping the dummy, until he went plumb crazy. You should have seen him. He was all pimply in the fohead, and he was plain bugs, as you say here up north. Why, when you told him a joke, he looked at you, bewildered, and five minutes later he laughed like he was going to split. Clyde, take the advice of a fellow who knows. Git yourself a piece of honey that's plump and willing and nice, and don't evah let it bother you. Because it's only natural."

Clyde was grateful for a sudden rush of customers.

to another. Reading, he devoured anatomical details and biological suggestions, his mind gulping them down like a starving man gorging food. Reading, he would be swept from sexual vision to sexual vision, heedless of plot threads. And he sat in motion picture theaters with features for adults only, visioning, against his will and his intelligence, the heroine nude and lying beneath him. Once, he sat close to the stage in a burlesque show at State and Congress Streets, his senses overstimulated with the sights of fleshy dancing girls and of jokes with crude explicit innuendoes. The entertainment climaxed when a fattening peroxide blonde leading-lady in her thirties, purple-veiled, varicose-veined, shrill-voiced, appeared for a solo belly dance. She wheezed a baby-daddy song, and the orchestra jerked off-key in a simple, tricky rhythm. Her veils were slowly shed, and she faced them with a projecting abdomen, clothed in a slab of thin shrunken purple tights, above which an operation scar was visible. There was also a strip of similarly colored cloth over her bulging breasts. Her movements oscillated between fast and emphatically jerky movements and slow, tantalizing stomach rollings. The audience, almost exclusively male, watched her thirsty-eyed, sex-stricken, and they applauded, and cheered, and encouraged her to give them more, and to strip off the meager cloths that saved her from complete nudity. Clyde watched her with rigid attention, his being too absorbed and fevered to heed the conscience which feebly told him that he should be disgusted. He became part of the unity of thought and desire in the audience. Stimulated by their applause, she stepped down from the stage onto the top of the piano, and offered an encore, wheezing out another daddy song, and repeating her simple and crude twisting abdominal movements. Clyde returned to his furnished room almost ill with flesh frustrations.

Clyde had willingly rushed into the alienness of the enormous city, sentimentalizing his determination to fight out its loneliness. He had changed. In the city, he had been baffled by a sense of hugeness and strangeness. It had been empty of the human associations for which he yearned. The unconcern of the crowds, the impermanence of the acquaintanceships he formed, the crushing noises, the shouts of a ceaseless, merciless dollar struggle, all attacked his dazed nerves and his bucolic naïveté. In the ugly, dusty city streets he felt a lost and poignant homelessness. Nothing in the swiftly pacing current of life, no promises or hopes or dreams of future success and power could compensate for the feeling of belonging and the assurance of being in a group that he had lost when he had gone away from that lazy, dead, Indiana village. His memory pained for home. His imagination repeatedly fixed and caressed images of his beloved Indiana earth, beloved earth and foliage and woods withering through remembered but dimming distances. At home there, life, the universe, all those images, objects, associations and events which adolescence links into the abstraction called life, had seemed friendly, saturated with amiability. Back in Indiana, everything, even stray stones, seemed to have had personality to the young man, Clyde, as he recalled them in his urban isolation. The city was cold, mechanical, forbidding, bare. Many times he walked along its strange and dirty streets, gazing at the crowd of work-worn, tired people, pausing to stare at aloof buildings which screeched almost to the clouds. He experienced intense feelings of severance from all this life, this effort, this pounding motion and momentum. It was all a puppet show, a macabre automatic dance. It was foreign. He surveyed the faces in this new, steel-stone world, and vainly wished for, sought out, some understanding face, some face gentle with the promise of friendship. In vain. He was jerky, and twitchy, and nervous, forced to live locked within his own being. His personality was crushed and cabined by a cruel and steady conviction of uncertainty. Loneliness! He met none of his kind, no fellow, no comrade. He walked among and talked with strangers. He was . . . hurt.

Through the future he visioned college, assuring himself that after he had entered the University, he would be more happy. Then, he would know people, and his personality could bloom and expand from the soil of a rich, and even a gay, social life. He would meet girls who were fine . . . the right kind. He sloughed on from day to day, entertaining unreal dreams of what the University would give him in friendships, love, and in that knowledge and power which would enable him to win out in what he called—The Battle of Life. The University rose before him in imagination, an Arcadia of superior people, with eyes turned inward, away from trivial little dust-ridden delights. The University! And at it, the girl he would meet, the girl who would fill up all those little holes and crevices in his world caused by the bruising loss of Eileen! The girl who would be all that she— he called her still his Eileen—should have been. He lived on in faith-accepted expectancies, and they chipped aside some of the hard small crusts of experience that were in his daily path. On several occasions, he visited the peaceful University campus, with its churchly, ivied Gothic. He sat on quaint benches, rapturously watching the parade of passing students, looking with an intent, questing, abstracted gaze at the towering, sentimental stone edifices. The calmness of the campus seemed to enter him, and he gave way to slow, comfortable daydreams. It was life, he told himself. He was hungry for it. He devoured everything about it that he saw: the lilac trees, the girls, the carefree students, the buildings. And he was confident that soon he would be a part of this fine life. He sat, unbothered by the hot tensions and stress of sex. He was hoping.

IV

Clyde had often debated with himself about visiting a brothel and getting that first experience over with. Then, he might have more peace. He might be free from those crude, ugly fantasies that turned every object before his mind into the twisting nude body of a woman. He knew that the city was full of brothels. Several times, he had taken walks along South State Street; and once, he had been approached by a pimply fellow, who had asked him if he wanted to make love to one of the girlies. He had wanted to answer yes, but an inhibiting compulsion had choked his tongue into silence, and he had walked on his way, excruciatingly miserable. On other occasions, hawk-nosed, painted prostitutes had accosted him, but with similar results. He feared sex, that strange, weird mystery which blew such hot disgusting breaths through him, like a simoom. He was afraid of the diseases frequently contracted in indiscriminate relationships. The exaggerated and only semi-precise tales of the horror of venereal diseases, which he had heard, made him shake and shudder when the fear came upon him. The fear of sex and the fear of disease seemed to drive upon him in a united effort. At times, he rationalized these fears, and convinced himself that he was pure because sex, unless it was beautified by love and marriage between two virgins, was dirty and vulgar—filthy. Often, he stood gazing out of his boarding-house window at the far and fragile moon, nobly praising himself, because he had kept himself unsoiled of the mess and dust. He would stand there, informing himself that most women were dirty and ugly, that they stank. He would think of prostitutes, and envision them writhing in mud. Only now and then in the mall of living, he would tell himself, did one find a rare, clean, pure woman, who was capable of the highest love, of that high, ethereal yearning which he so ardently wanted to carry with him to the altar as his matrimonial credentials. He would stand, staring out at evenings which were tender and delicate, unfriendly with a rare fragility that repulses human blundering, and he would hold dialogues with himself, proving that he could not tolerate cheap, vulgar, commercial love. And he would sigh quietly because human beings were not sexless, because women were not pure and bodiless, like flames, or air, or summer skies, or horizontal mists.

Sometimes he would look down upon the moon-touched and night-shadowed pavement. Sometimes he would see a trim, silk-stockinged young woman, and his romantic yearnings would be scattered. He would again go through his cycles of powerful and unfulfilled desires.

V

After six tense, hard-working months at the soda fountain, Clyde was able to enter the University. He had his credits accepted, and on the sunny September morning that was the beginning of freshman week, he became a student. He was able to work nights at the fountain, and his earnings provided for his expenses and enabled him to save a small sum. Work and study, he felt, would keep him completely occupied and free of sex torments. And now, he would find the right kind of friendships. He was expectant, and he braced himself for grinding study. He enjoyed and thrilled, telling himself that now he was moving down the straight and steady road to success to that someday which would see the realization of all the vague wants that stirred within him. But that someday of his hopes was tricky. It receded from vision like will-o'-the-wisps. The University, like the crushing city, was an impersonal machine. At it, only the other fellow had fun and good times. Clyde did not conquer his bashfulness, and he made no friends. He hardly made acquaintances, except for a few bucolic individuals like himself. They were as lonely as he, and sometimes they talked of their problems. They talked and talked, once they were started; and they were so concerned with their own loneliness that Clyde would have spoken to deaf ears had he been able to describe to them how he was personally troubled. There was one chap from Iowa, who was forced to work eight hours a day, and who was worried because of heart trouble. He did not know how he could keep on. But he was determined. Over and over again, he reiterated that he was determined. And the fellows Clyde got to talking with always gravitated to sex. They would point girls out on the campus, and describe their sexual desirability in language that made him wince. Such conversations and remarks only intensified his own problem. He had never imagined that there could be such loneliness on a campus, that amidst such youth and bubbling energy there could be so many unexpressed, unobserved little human tragedies of adolescence. There were many —athletes, fraternity men, the girls who belonged to exclusive and snobbish clubs—who seemed to have a grand time, with extra-curricular activities, dances, dates, parties, social occasions. But such people seemed like a minor sect with all its own mysterious rites, and they wasted no time even to greet a hick like Clyde. When he sat next to them in classes, they were distant. Outside of the classrooms, they did not even know him. And the instructors, whom he had, tended to be formal. Most of them were working for doctor's degrees, and they were unconcerned with the freshmen and sophomores whom they were compelled, from necessity, to teach. They treated their students as nurslings. At conferences, they were brief, informally precise. Clyde grew to look like the others he had met, a young person with life dulling on his almost beardless features.

College, his dreamed-of life, left him more, instead of less, frustrated. He had gone to college because he had wanted to make something of himself. But he was still a nobody, a nobody amid happy young people who were principally bent on good times and the fun he had never had. Day after day, he attended his classes, expecting, hoping that things would change, that he would meet the right girl, that he would form a deep and genuine friendship. And the school year passed.

VI

Clyde's scholastic work was steady, satisfactory and uninspired. He displayed none of the brilliance which he dreamed of and conceived in those days behind the soda fountain when he was hoping and saving his money for tuition fees. The day of his last examination, concluding his freshman year, found him tired, excessively relieved that the grind was over until autumn, happily looking forward to a breathing spell of freedom. After turning in the neatly written yellow examination book, he was ready to droop and wilt. It was his day off from work, and he could amuse himself as he pleased. He was too fatigued to do anything. He sat on campus grass, and sang aimless snatches from the songs which Clement always sang at work. He thought, with melodramatic pride, of how he was one year closer to his goal of success. Yet he was still left frustrate. He was centering all of his hopes and thoughts upon his goal. He could not enjoy working as others seemed to. It was hard work, demanding brutal concentration. Other students could receive higher grades than he did, and yet not become classroom automata. They could have their fun. Self-pity rushed to his defence. He relaxed into a brief, tired sleep. He awoke drowsy and weak, and gazed about him, wistfully enjoying the passing noon-hour scenes when the campus was flooded with girls. One girl passed on the walk close to him, a white, slender creature in a white voile dress; she was chic and lithe. He watched her free, easy movements, and numberless urges and desires conglomerated within him. He imagined himself knowing her, having her. He revolted in self-disgust, because every time he saw or thought of a girl that thought came like an accompaniment.

The campus chimes stridently tolled *Nearer My God to Thee,* and she passed out of sight. The campus seemed unreal, so blessed was it with peace and serenity. It impressed him as being medieval and changeless. He sat in vague and satisfying melancholy. He heard the engine beats of a sputtering automobile, and the noise was an interruption blasting his mood. He realized that he was hungry, and had luncheon at the University Commons, eating alone, wishing that he were sitting with a friend to whom he might talk.

VII

At ten o'clock that evening, he sat in his narrow room. Though tired, he was nervous and fidgety, and was unable to concentrate upon the novel he was reading. He thought of an "adults' only" picture he had recently seen at a theater downtown. It released the sex tensions within him. He wished that he had a woman. He counted the flowers in the unimaginative rose-patterned wallpaper. He stared vacantly at the ceiling. He looked out of the window, up at the placid June sky. He paced the floor, flung himself on his bed, lay head down, his body tautening and perspiring under the influence of wild dreams and desires that had gathered like a boil coming to a head of pus. Suddenly, without will, he leaped to his feet, snatched his hat, and fled to the streets. It was slightly cool, and the wind touched his hot brow until it felt like soothing maiden fingers. Unthinkingly he hailed a passing taxicab, and asked the driver to take him to a brothel. He leaned back, as the cab rocked along, retrieving a measure of calmness which caused him to regret his impulsiveness. He desired to leap out, to run, to halt the cab, to go back to his room, and he was impelled not to act on these new impulses by some nameless inhibition, and lest he seem ridiculous to the driver. He was in misery, and suddenly began to feel that at the moment he hailed the taxicab, the driver had seen through and understood his intentions, and that he was now quietly laughing at him. His weight of dread and uncertainty grew heavier. He tried to force composure upon himself, and meaninglessly he told himself that what he was doing was not unusual, that thousands of men did the same thing nightly. He glanced out of the cab window at the passing buildings and the cab sped northward along Michigan Boulevard. Many of the houses, jumping across his field of vision, appeared like dark and strange structures. He wished that he had never been born, that he had never left home, that he was going regularly with a sweet girl of the right kind, that he was decently married and happy, that he had his Eileen, pure and undefiled. He gazed vacantly at the jumping succession of buildings. The cab halted at Twenty-second and State Streets, and he had a hasty impression that this section of old and infirm buildings and low lights was tough, mysterious, a glaring combination of the dives of Shanghai and the Bowery as reflected through a Hollywood motion picture. He absent-mindedly paid his fare and opened the cab door to emerge from it. He intended immediately to flee the neighborhood. A husky-voiced individual, with broad, padded shoulders, stood beside the cab, and Clyde's fear became so pronounced that he lost all self-possession. He heard the driver tell the individual to take care of him, and check it up, and saw the individual hastily scrawl into a small notebook. The taxicab drove off, and Clyde stood beside this stranger.

"Come along, kid. I'll fix you up," the stranger said out of the side of his mouth.

Clyde was led through a dismantled saloon, where a ratty-faced, thin-shouldered man directed him toward a side door. He found himself standing in a meagerly lighted splotchy-walled hallway, with carpetless stairs. From the floor above him, he heard jazz music and female voices. At the head of the stairway, and behind a counter, he saw a stout Negress who looked as if she might have just walked out of a mammy photograph. Behind her, there were shelves of towels. The stairs squeaked as he ascended, step by hesitant step. He felt as if glaring eyes and vile faces peered at him from every side. As he passed the Negress, she asked him if he came for love, and smiled. He found himself in a large room unfurnished except for camp chairs and a player piano in a corner. It was bright with electricity, and populated by girls in undress with painted faces who sat in a row on the chairs. They blurred before his eyes as they arose with his entrance. He knew that he must be blushing furiously, because several of the girls tittered at him. He stood before them, hopelessly ill at ease. He had a vague impression of female flesh, of washed-out faces, of colored teddy bears, and of hefty hips and lumber legs. A vision of Eileen came to him, and he wondered was she like these girls. He watched them, his heart pounding like a powerful machine. A small dimpled girl winked at him. A broad woman with Slavic features placed a nickel in the player piano and contorted before him as the dancer in the burlesque show had done. He watched, and the girls sat down. More men entered, and the girls arose again. One of the men smiled at him. They quickly selected girls and disappeared.

"Want to play in my garden?" a woman with a crooked nose and Jewish features asked him.

He wanted to run. Stabbing out with his right hand, he pointed at a Slavic-faced girl who was small but burly and bow-legged. She smiled mechanically, and as they passed the counter, she collected a towel.

"Have a good time, chillen," the Negress called after them.

He followed her upstairs, hearing footsteps and jazz music behind him.

They entered a small bedroom, with sooty, daisy-patterned wall paper. The bed was in a corner, its sheets gray from the boots of many men, and opposite was a bare enamel-topped dresser without mirror. The prostitute disappeared and quickly reappeared with a basin of tepid water. She discovered Clyde removing his shirt, and told him that was unnecessary. He faced her, barefooted, and without his shirt, wishing he were elsewhere, afraid. She looked at him and cooed out the question if he were ready. He shook his head.

"Well, gimme the dough . . . dearie!" she said, softening her voice on the last word.

Artlessly, he pulled out an impressive-looking roll of fifteen one-dollar bills. He handed her three dollars. She snuggled against him.

"Dearie! How about being a good guy and adding a little extra. Come on, dearie, be a good guy! If you do, and show me you're a sport, you'll get your loving!"

Not knowing what he did, he handed her another dollar. She pressed herself to him, and coaxed:

"Come on, dearie, make it five, like a real sport!"

He handed her an additional dollar. He started to remove his remaining clothes, and she charged him a dollar more. Calling him dearie, she gave him the works.

VIII

After his experience, the air seemed fine and cool. He hurried eastward along Twenty-second Street, tired, with pains in his groin, frazzled, sick with self-disgust. He told himself that he was unclean. Fears of disease assailed him, and he became convinced that his hands were dirty. He paused at a drug store and purchased a bottle of iodine. At a filling-station lavatory, he administered it to himself, and it burned severely. He washed his hands. He walked south along Michigan Boulevard, still obsessed with the feeling that his hands were dirty. He thought of what he had done, and he was ashamed of himself. He remembered the bed, and it grew into a strange object, like one in a terrorizing nightmare. His hands still seemed dirty. He walked at a doubled pace. He paused where wind tipped the branches of a lone tree. He looked upward, pained by the calmness of the sky and the clarity of the moon and shining stars. He listened to the winds, wishing that he were bodiless and clean like them. At Forty-second Street, he again washed his hands at a filling-station lavatory. He walked all the way home, in dejection. He tumbled into bed, and dreamed of prostitutes, and of himself pawing the winds with soiled hands.

IX

On the following morning, he was sluggish. He drowsed about restlessly until it was time to leave for work. At the store, he was so listless that Clement prescribed a woman for him. For several days, he remained in a dragging mood.

Then, he returned to the brothel. All summer, he visited it, and while it seemed evil, his nervousness lessened. When he resumed studies in the fall, he was less tormented with loneliness. He walked and carried himself with an added conviction of personality. He continued to yearn for a girl like his dreamed-of Eileen, but he had solved the mystery of girls. He viewed them critically, and made appraisals of their bodies. At work, Clement continued to kid him as an innocent. One day, when Clement was at him, he nonchalantly remarked that on the previous evening he had had a pretty good girl. Clement shook hands with him in congratulation. That evening, after work, they went down to Twenty-second Street together. Going upstairs with the ebullient Clement, Clyde felt like a sophisticated man of experience. Suddenly, a memory of Eileen struck him like a sharp, swift, and unexpected blow. She might be a . . . An old feeling of revulsion came upon him. He became nostalgic, and thought of brown clumps of Indiana earth. He thought of success, of fame, of a decent girl. He clenched his fists, determined to win these things for himself. He pitied himself. He and Clement stood in the bare room full of prostitutes, who waited like worn-out machines of pleasure. They each selected a girl.

Eileen, and brown clumps of Indiana earth, and the damp odors of sylvan foliage, and the songs of short-lived insects and clear brilliant starlight and moonlight, and deep, full shadows of aged oaks, and clean winds. He thought of these things, and followed a prostitute upstairs to a dingy bedroom with a bed on which there were sheets filthy from the shoes of many men, who were lonely like himself.

1930.

Jim O'Neill

LIZZ had closed the window, and when he awakened, the bedroom air was stale and musty. He lay awake, very tired, and glancing idly at the drawn shade around which there were cracks of daylight and the yellowing afternoon sun. He rubbed his right fist and wondered how long he would last. Then he swung himself up to sit on the side of the rumpled bed in the long drawers in which he had slept. From the vacant lot outside his window, he could hear the shouts and arguments of a boys' game of indoor ball. His son Bob was playing in it. Jim made a pass at the air with his right fist, and then rubbed the knuckles of that hand. Sure he was all right. He was over that stroke. Everything was all right. Sure. He remained seated, listening to noises from the ball playing outside.

With that recurrent feeling of pride, he pulled the chain turning on the electric light. For it was the first time in his life that he had lived in a flat of his own with electricity in it. And it was only two years now since he had moved into this building on Calumet Avenue. Well, the war had not been good for a number of men, but it had for him. Except for the war, he probably never would have been promoted to Wagon Dispatcher at the Continental Express Company. It was getting somewhere to be promoted to the supervision with a salary of one hundred and eighty-five a month, and now, with this new raise, he would be earning two hundred and twenty-five a month. That would mean many things for his family.

He touched his hand again. Not any too much feeling in it, and he grew worried. He clenched his fists, and gritted his teeth, determining not to worry. He had, goddamn them all, supported his family with his hands and his back for years, and now he was better off then he had ever been, he had come through, and nothing was going to take that away from him. He was in a position to give his kids a better start in the world than he had had. They wouldn't have to teach themselves how to read and write, after they had become grown men. And goddamn them all, they couldn't say that he wasn't an honest man.

He remembered that time, back in the days when his cousin, Joe O'Reilley, the lawyer, had been coming up in politics, and he and Joe had been together in the loop. They had accidentally met Bart Gallivan, the Democratic boss of Cook County.

"Bart, I want to introduce you to my cousin, Jim O'Neill."

"Pleased to meet you, Jim," Bart had said with that put-on friendliness of the politician, extending that glad hand of his.

"There's at least one man in the city of Chicago who won't shake hands with a crook."

And he had walked away. Well, he was proud to be an honest man, and to have turned down that political job which Joe had offered to get him at the City Hall.

And now he was all set. He squeezed and patted that hand, stimulating the circulation.

He drew on his trousers, and looked into the mirror, rubbing the whiskers on his long, rough, leathery face.

"Oh, Lizz, get me something to eat!" he called loudly.

There was no answer.

"Oh, Lizz!"

He walked through the narrow dark hallway and stood at the entrance to the small, square dining-room, seeing rags, paper, dirt and confusion, an opened loaf of bread on the table, butter and sugar attracting buzzing flies, dirt.

"Lizz!" he called surlily.

He walked through to the kitchen. Dirtier! That goddamn woman. Always praying at church. It was all right to go to church and pray, but a wife and a mother had some duties to her family, and order was heaven's first law, and cleanliness is next to godliness. He tightened his lips in inarticulate and impotent anger.

He re-entered the dining-room, and paused by the window, to watch Bob, his youngest son, who was at bat. The other boys all were shouting at him, and he seemed to be giving them back their talk in kind. A sassy kid, and Jim didn't like the sass in him. He watched, hoping that Bob would connect with the ball. Bob swung into a pitch, and the ball sizzled along the ground to the pitcher. Watching Bob get thrown out at first base, Jim was disappointed.

He turned from the window and went to the bathroom, the first bathroom he had ever had in his own home. He remembered the cottage at Forty-fifth and Wells, with the privy in the yard, and the smelling kerosene lamps, and the dirty five-room clapboarded cottage, and Lizz always slopping around the house in house slippers, with a dirty face, uncombed hair, and an unwashed calico rag around her chin. And Artie, his baby boy, a beautiful child with blond curls, the little face, the laugh and excitement as he was learning to walk, the questions he asked after first having learned to talk, the way he always chased and stumbled after his brothers and sisters, Bob, and Margaret, and Catherine, and Dennis, and Bill. Jim thought of that night in June when he had come home from work with a basket of fruit under his arm, and Artie had had a sore throat. The next morning the child had been worse. And all the kids had had sore throats. Diphtheria! They had telephoned for that damn Doctor Callaghan, and he hadn't come for over twenty-four hours. He remembered his baby boy, with blond curls, dying at its mother's breasts, for Lizz had not weaned it, because she believed that while she was still nursing one child she would not get caught with another. There was the sick child, dying in its mother's arm, at its mother's breasts, in a house full of kids sick with diphtheria.

The kids were all sent to the hospital, and Margaret, the oldest girl, who, like the boy Danny, lived with the aunt and grandmother, also went with them. Himself and Lizz burying the baby in a small white coffin, the beautiful boy turning black in the box from streptococcic poisoning. He had cried that day. Yes, he had cried, and asked was there a God? Remembering it, thinking of those rotted bones of his baby boy out in Calvary Cemetery now, he cried again, alone in his bathroom, the first real bathroom he had ever had in his home in his whole life. He cried.

Jim shaved, his right hand tiring as he ran the straight razor over his face. He went to the kitchen, and fried eggs and bacon, and heated the pot of coffee. He carried his food to the dining-room, shoved the cluttered objects on the table aside, and sat down to eat. He glanced out of the window and saw Bob make a two-base hit. He hoped that Lizz would return shortly. He determined that he would tell her a hell of a lot. He ought to give her a good smack in the teeth. Hell, she was such a goddamn fool, praying all day in the church, until the janitors had to ask her to leave so that they could close up. Why wasn't she cleaning her house, taking care of her children, making things at home pretty and orderly—why wasn't all that as much of a prayer as kneeling down in St. Patrick's church and praying by the hour. That goddamn woman!

She still wasn't back when he finished his meal. He did not remove the dishes from the table, and went out to the kitchen to make some ham and cheese sandwiches for his lunch. He placed them, along with a slice of Ward's cake and an apple, in a newspaper, and wrapped a neat bundle.

He determined that he would tell that goddamn woman what was what.

He waited impatiently in the parlor, looking with pride at the stuffy, ugly installment-plan furniture. Then he looked at his old horned victrola. He went over to it, and ran his hand along the curved horn, almost fondling it. He dug through his records, and put one on, sitting down to listen:

*"Call me back through the years, pal of mine,
Let me gaze in your eyes . . ."*

He re-played the record, thinking of black-haired Elizabeth, his beautiful young bride. His anger with her melted. After all, she and he had stuck it all through, stuck through all that poverty in the days when he was a teamster. And she had borne him eleven kids. She had suffered through all that, seeing nine of her kids die, holding Artie to her breasts while he gasped his last feeble breaths. Yes, she was in church praying, because she was still stricken with grief over little Artie's death. Through these last three years she hadn't forgotten, hadn't forgotten how he and she, tears streaming down their faces, had walked out of Calvary Cemetery in the rain, the freshly dug earth smothered over their dead son. Mothers love their children, and they don't forget. Why should he get so sore? Hell, it still put a catch in his throat.

He slowly wound the victrola, and set the needle back at the start of the record, these practical details diverting his thoughts.

"Let me gaze in your eyes . . ."

He listened to the slow, whining words of the song, and reflected that they had come through it all, goddamn it, they had. He was not the man he had been, and that stroke, too, but he was going to go on pulling through, and his kids would never have to know the same kind of a life that he had known, the drinking, poverty, fighting, strikes, like that teamsters' strike back around 1904, when the company sluggers and thugs had tried to get him. He felt his right hand, the hand that had spoken straight from the shoulder in many a fight. He had pulled through, and goddamn it, he had been honest. He suddenly sat up erectly. He remembered that scrippers' strike during the war, when he had scabbed. Well, a man had his family, and it came first, and it was right after Artie had died. Where would he have been, if he hadn't scabbed.

"Call me back through the years, pal of mine . . ."

Yes, his kids were going to avoid all that.

He wanted Lizz to come back. He wanted to kiss her as he had used

Twenty-five Bucks

FIFTEEN years is a hell of a long time to live in grease. Fifteen years is a hell of a long time to keep getting your jaw socked. Fifteen years is a hell of a long time for a broken-down, never-was of a palooka named Kid Tucker. Fifteen years stretched back through a reeking line of stale fight clubs, of jeers and clammy dressing rooms, and lousy gyms, and cheap can houses, of ratty saloons with sawdust floors—OH, MEET ME TO-NIGHT IN THE MOONLIGHT—of flop houses whose corridors were fouled with musty lavatory odors, of training camps, gyps, speak-easies—IT'S A LONG, LONG TRAIL A-WINDING INTO THE LAND OF MY DREAMS—of mouldy dumps and joints, of crooks, pikers, louses, lice, and war . . . Fifteen years stretched back all the way through these things to a box car, with *Armour's Meats* printed on its sides in white lettering, moving out of Lima, Ohio, and across sweet Ohio landscapes on a morning when the world was young with spring, and grass, and the hopeful if idiotic dreams of a good-natured adolescent yokel.

It was all over with Kid Tucker and there had never been any shouting—only boos. His face had been punched into hash: cauliflower ears, a flattened nose, a scar above his right eye. His greenish eyes were shifty with the fleeting nervous cowardice of the sacked and broken man. He was flabby. The muscles in his legs were shot. There was a scar on one leg, the medal he had received for carrying a badly wounded farm boy from Iowa through a wheat field near Soissons on a day when the sun was mad over a mad world, the earth nauseous from the stink of corpses, and the wheat fields slashed with ripping machine-gun bullets. Kid Tucker was through. Toss him aside. Another boloney drowned in grease and defeat.

Sol Levison matched him with K. O. Dane for a six-round preliminary bout at Sol's West Side Arcade Boxing Club. Sol always wore a derby and a race-track vest. He made money out of a mouldy dump of a boxing club. He made money out of a string of ham scrappers. He made money out of everything he touched. Dane was one of Sol's stable, fresh from Minnesota. Sol was nursing him along on pushovers, building up a reputation so that Dane could get a match with a first-rater for a good purse. It did not matter that the big-time boy would slaughter him in a round. He was being prepared for it just as cattle were fed for the Chicago Stockyards. Tucker was another setup for Dane. And the Kid needed the twenty-five dollars Sol guaranteed him for the bout. He took the match. He earned his living by taking smashes on the jaw. But Sol told him that this time he would have to fight. No taking a dive in this fight.

"Lissen, now, that ring ain't no swimming pool. See! No divin'! It ain't gonna be nothin' like bed or a park bench. It's a prize ring, and you're in there to fight. So don't act like you ain't never seen a bed for a month. Yuh gotta fight this time . . . or no dough. See!"

Kid Tucker had heard that before.

He reported on time at the West Side Arcade Boxing Club, a rambling building in a shambling district. He dressed for the bout, putting on a pair of faded trunks. With his hands taped, and a dirty bathrobe thrown over his shoulders, he sat on a slivery bench, waiting, watching a cockroach scurry up and down the wall. Two seconds sat on tilted chairs, one sleeping with his mug opened like a fly trap, the other reading a juicy rape story from *The Chicago Questioner*. Tucker sat. He didn't have many thoughts any more. He never became nervous before a fight. He had caught every kind of a punch already. He sat and watched the cockroach on the peeling green wall, with its many spots of broken plaster. It crawled up toward a window, turned back, scrambled sidewise, about-faced, turned downwards, and cut across the floor to lose itself in the shadows of a corner.

Kid Tucker wished that the scrap was over. He might manage to catch this kid off balance, and put him away. But then, he mightn't get any more fights from Levison, because this Dane was one of Sol's comers. Sol wanted him to put up a fight, because he was sure he couldn't take Dane. Anyway, he wished that the fight was over, and he was sitting in a speakeasy with a shot before him. He did not think much any more. Fools think. One day he had been a young ox, puking with excitement in a dressing room, awaiting the gong for his first fight. He watched a second cockroach scurry up and down the wall. Up and down it moved. The seconds lit cigarettes, and opened a discussion of the love-nest suit which had put the abnormal relationships of a rich old sugar daddy and a young gold-digger on the front pages of the newspapers. Tucker sat and recalled the lice and cooties in the trenches in France. Up and down the cockroach moved.

When he entered the ring, he received only a small dribble of applause. The crowd knew the bum. Someone yelled at him, asking him if he had gotten his pants pressed for the tea party. Another wanted to know where his patent leather shoes were. Tucker never listened to the comments of the crowd, or its razzberries. He was past the time when he heard or was affected by boos. In France, he had lost all concern and worry when the shells landed. When he had heard one coming, he just casually flopped on the ground. A guy can get used to anything, if he just hangs around long enough. He sat in his corner, waiting, his eyes fastened on the ropes.

The crowd leaped to its feet spontaneously, and roars rose from the murkiness of faces when Dane entered the ring. He was a husky Swede with childish blue eyes, a thick square head, a bull neck, a mountainous pair of shoulders, and legs that resembled tree trunks. Tucker did not look at him.

A slit-mouth of an announcer bellowed out the names of the contending fighters, pointing to their respective corners as he briefly described trumped-up reputations. They shook hands in the center of the ring and returned to their corners. A gong clanged.

The arclights glared down upon them, revealing a contrast between the fighters that was almost vicious. Dane was strong and full of youth; Tucker worn out and with a paunch of a belly. Both fighters were wary; and the crowd was perfunctory. It wanted Dane to make a corpse of the big fat ham. They faced each other, feinted, tapped, and blocked as they continuously circled around and around. Tucker could see that the kid was nervous; but he had learned to be a bit cautious of shaky young fighters when they looked as powerful as Dane. Dane led with a few light lefts. Tucker caught them easily with his gloves. His confidence perked up, and he retaliated with a straight left. It slid off Dane's jaw. They lumbered, feeling for openings. They clinched and their interlocked bodies made one swaying ugliness in the white glare of the arclights. The referee danced in and parted them. They clinched again. They broke. Dane hesitantly attacked, and Tucker clumsily skipped backward.

Roars and boos grew out of the sordidness that surrounded the ring.

"Come on, Kayo. He's only a bum!"

"In the bread basket, you Swede! The bread basket!"

"Lam one in the bread basket, you squarehead, and he's through!"

"Come on, Fight!"

"This ain't no party!"

"Hey, how about doin' your sleepin' at home? Huh?"
"Siddown in front!"
"Siddown, Tucker, and take a load off your feet!"
"No guts!"
"Murder the sonofabitch!"
"Kill the sonofabitch!"
"Fight, you hams. Fight!"
"Come on, you Swede boy, in the bread basket!"

Dane connected with a few inconsequential left jabs. He was clumsy, and when he led, he stumbled about, losing his balance. A good fighter with a willingness to take a chance, and a heart to mix and trade punches could have cut him up and polished him off in short order. But Tucker kept backing away out of range, pausing to jab out with a few untimed, ineffective left-handed stabs. Dane danced about him in confusion, and when his opponent retreated, he stood in the center of the ring, hands lowered ungainly, a stupid expression of indecision on his face.

The crowd roared, and suddenly above the disgruntled roaring and booing there rose a throaty-voiced suggestion that sleeping quarters were upstairs. The bell saved them from further exertion.

The razzing increased during the one-minute intermission. Tucker sat heedless of the mob. He rinsed his mouth out from the water bottle, and puffed slightly. The seconds pointed out that Dane was leaving himself so open that a five-ton truck could be driven through his guard; Tucker said he would watch it, and catch the kid in the next round. He waited. He had five more rounds to go. He wondered if he could slip one through when Dane was off balance and stun him, or put him away. If he wanted to last through, he couldn't take many chances, and the kid looked like he had a punch that could kill a mule. He glanced toward the Dane's corner, where the latter's handlers were instructing him with emphatic gestures. He eyed the ropes.

Round two was duller and more slow than the first round. It was a clinching party. A fan called out that they were like Peaches and Daddy. Another suggested a bed. A third asked was it a track meet or a six-day bike race. The crowd grumbled. And repeatedly someone yelled to kill the sonofabitch.

A pimply-faced punk of a kid arose from his chair, yawned, ignored the commands from behind to sit down, and in a moment of quiet, shouted:

"I tank I go home!"

The crowd laughed, and he sat down.

Near the close of the round, Dane connected with a wild but solid right. The accidental wallop had echoed with a thud, and the mob was brought to its feet, yelling for blood and a knockout. Dane hesitated a moment, and stared perplexedly at his opponent. Then he went for Tucker with a look of murderous, if formal and melodramatic, intent stamped on his face.

The bell ended the round. There was a buzz of excitement. Dane was not such a dud after all. That right had been a beaut. Now he was getting warmed up, and he would do his stuff. He'd crush a lemon like Kid Tucker dry; he'd put him away in a hurry. Watch that Swede boy go now; watch him knock that Tucker bastard out now! One to the bread basket, and one on the button, and the lights would go out for that has-been.

Tucker was a trifle groggy as the seconds started working over him. They whispered that he should fake weariness. That would bring Dane in, wide-open. Then one solid punch might turn the trick. Tucker nodded his head as if to indicate that he knew the whole story. But when he found himself in there punching and taking them, he found himself unable to put anything behind his punches. In France, he had gone through two days of a terrific bombardment. Then he had caved in. He had gone on like an automatic man. He could not give himself. It was the same with fighting. He wanted to go in and take a chance trading punches. He told himself that he would. The haze was now cleared from his mind, and he was determined. But things had all happened like this before. Tucker, willing and determined, and then being unable to carry out his will, incapable of giving himself. He couldn't go in and fight. The war and the prize ring had taken all the fight out of him. His nerves and muscles wouldn't respond to his will. There had been too many punches. He awaited the bell, determining in vain. Tucker's state was called being yellow, having no guts. He sat out his final seconds of rest.

Just before the bell, Levison appeared, and told one of the Kid's seconds to warn him that he had to fight if he wanted his dough. Then, the clang of the gong. Some people in the crowd noticed Levison, but their curiosity was drowned by the roar greeting the new round. They were going to watch Dane take the bum for a sure in this one.

The tired Tucker backed away. Dane pursued him, determined. His handlers had persuaded him into a state of self-confidence. He unscrewed an awkward left which flushed on Tucker's button. Tucker reeled backwards. The crowd leaped to its feet, yelling for blood. Dane *grew far away from Tucker*. Gloves came at the Kid like *locomotives slowly rising from the distance, coming closer and growing larger until they collided with his face. One ran into his stomach.*

"In the bread basket. Come on, you Swede!"

Tucker experienced a heaving nausea, and *far, far away there was a din of shouting*.

Instinctively, mechanically, Tucker fell into a clinch. He made a weak, hopeless effort to sew Dane up. His head swam in a daze, he was glassy-eyed. Dane, *a billowing mass of flesh grew before his dimmed eyes. Something big closed his eyes*. His feet slid from under him. He was blinded for a few seconds. Then he weakly perceived through his sick daze. He arose feebly. *There was a swinging of gloves, a going around of posts, ropes, and gloves*. He floundered forward to clinch. He was off balance, and Dane came up from the floor with a haymaker that mashed into his jaw; the impact of the punch caused an audible thud. The lights went out for Tucker, and about him, dizzy darkness crashed, like a tumbling nightmarish dream. He fell backward, and his head bounced hard on the canvas. He lay there, quivering slightly, while the referee tolled off the necessary ten seconds. He bled from the mouth; blood trickling out to run in tiny rivulets and mix with the dust and resin.

The mob rocketed approval.

"That's the ticket, Swede!"

"That's the babee!"

"You put him out for a week. Oh, you beautiful Swede!"

"You got the stuff, kid. Yay!"

"Christ, what a wallop! Dynamite!"

"Out for a week!"

"Oh, you Swede! Wahooooo!"

The punk kid with the pimply face who had yelled about going home in a Swedish accent evidently recalled Levison's visit to the ringside just before the gong. He jumped on his chair, and shouted:

"Fake!"

As Tucker was lifted back to his corner, and set helplessly on the stool, the cry of fake was suddenly taken up, and it contagiously reverberated through the arena.

Dane left the ring, and the cheers turned to boos as feet stamped and the cry of fake loudened into a booming roar.

The seconds continued working on Kid Tucker. Levison, in the back of the building, nervously spoke with two policemen. Then, after giving hasty instructions to six burly bouncers, he walked to the ringside, climbed through the ropes, and stood turning in the center of the ring, his hand raised for quiet.

"Silence, pleez!" he megaphoned.

He finally received relative silence and shouted through megaphoned hands:

"Ladies and Gents! Ladies and Gents! I wanna say a few words to yuh. I wancha to know I ain't never had nothin' to do with a framed fight, or a faked boxing match of any kind or classification. I wancha to know that any time Sol Levison promotes a bout, then that bout is on the square. A fight that Sol Levison promotes is one hundred per cent on the level. Now to show you all that I'm on the level, I'm gonna offer one hunerd dollars, one hunerd dollars reward to the man that can prove that this last fight was a frame-up. Now some one of you spectators here has been so unkind as to insinu-ate that this here last fight has not been on the level. Now, I'm offering one hunerd dollars to the man that proves that this or that any fight that Sol Levison has ever promoted was not on the level, to the very best, I say to the very best, of his knowledge and intentions."

There was a mingling of cheers and boos.

"When one of my fights is not on the level, Sol Levison wants to know about it. This here last fight was not faked to the knowledge of Sol Levison. Kid Tucker here, he asks me for a chanct to go on so's he could make himself a little stake. I gave him his chanct, just as I always do with a boxer. Now, when I came up here just before the last round of this here last bout, it was to instruct Tucker that he had to fight if he wanted to get his purse. It was a square fight. Kid Tucker was yellah. He was just yellah. He was afraid of Kayo Dane, and refused to put up a resistance. He got just what was coming to him becuz he was too yellah to fight like a man, and like he agreed to when I agreed to pay him. He was yellah."

There were cheers. The handlers lifted Tucker down from the ring, and he was carted away to the dressing room amid many boos.

"Now, Ladies and Gents, to show you how I feel about this here matter, just let me tell you somethin'. When Sol Levison hires fighters, they fight. They fight or Sol Levison knows why. I guarantee that each and every bout I stage will give you your money's worth. If it don't, I guarantee that you kin get your money back at the box office. And when I hire boxers in good faith, they either fight . . . or they get no purse from Sol Levison. Now, to show you how I feel, and to guarantee that you'll get your money's worth after the showing this yellah bum made here, I'm gonna take his purse that was coming to him if he had lived up to his agreement with me and stood up and fought like a man, I'm gonna take his purse because he don't deserve it for breaking the contract he made with me, and I'm gonna give it to the boy who puts up the best fight here this evening, and I'm gonna let you all choose the boy to get it by general acclaim. Now, Ladies and Gents, I ask you, is that fair? He was yellah and he didn't earn his purse. So I asks you, is it not fair to give it to a boy with a real fighting heart. Now is that fair or isn't it?"

The roars of the crowd approving Levison's speech sounded like far echoes down in the mouldy dressing room where the beaten Kid Tucker lay unconscious. His handlers worked on him in vain, dousing him with water, using smelling salts, working in vain. Two bantams, one a swarthy-skinned Italian boy who had won a Golden Gloves championship before turning professional, and the other a bushy-haired Jewish lad, left to fight the next bout.

"He must have got an awful sock," the Jew said.

"He looks pretty bad," the Italian kid said to his manager.

"We'll bring him around," one of the seconds said.

They worked over Kid Tucker for an hour. Cheers echoed down from the other fights while they worked. A doctor was called in, and he could not bring Kid Tucker to consciousness. An ambulance was called, and Kid Tucker was carted out on a stretcher. As he was being put into the ambulance, the crowd was roaring acclaim, shouting out its decision that the swarthy-skinned Italian bantamweight, and former Golden Gloves champion, had merited Tucker's purse.

But Tucker did not need it. He was taken to the hospital and died of a cerebral hemorrhage without ever regaining consciousness.

1930.

Mary O'Reilley

I

ONE morning Mary O'Reilley glanced a second time into her dresser mirror and discovered that she was an old woman. Her hair was completely gray. Her thin, plain, serene face was becoming the frame of a dried, weedy expression. Several wrinkles were making their inevitable announcements about the edges of her faintly drooping lips. Her bluish eyes were sad and tired.

Mary had never considered herself an old woman, not even the last ten years when she had been under a doctor's care because of her heart. Always she had drifted along on the level acceptance of middle age. Senescence, the clinging pathos of change, death, these thoughts had but rarely and briefly interrupted her peaceful days. Always she had lived with a hope. It was a wish nebulous and intangible. It seemed to tell her in a manner almost mystical that some day all the simple problems and irritations of her daily life would be washed out by a calm and absolute comfort and happiness. Deeper than the conscious acceptance of her religion was an intuition that the stains of fifty years would be cleansed, eliminated. But that morning, hope was gone. It had withered without her knowledge. She was an old woman who had been waiting through all of the years of middle age—for death. She had seen in the mirror's realism more than a mere wrinkled face; she had perceived the joy, the richness, the youngness, the pleasure of living, reflected as so many dead things.

Mary was unmarried. She lived with Joe, Martha, and their niece Gertrude. Joe and Martha were also unmarried. They had lived together in stiffly comfortable homes ever since the death of their parents. For two decades they had been at Fiftieth and Grand Boulevard, but the inrush of Negroes had driven them out to the southeast side of the city; and now, they owned a sprawling, red-bricked sample of American suburban architecture at Seventy-fourth and Crandon. Gertrude was the life and joy of their household. Uncle Joe had educated her, given her the refined advantages of a supposedly superior education at

St. Paul's High School for girls, and at Chicago Normal College. Every summer, when she was not teaching, he sent her to the University of Chicago or else Wisconsin. She was charming. Everybody said so. Now she was a grown girl of marriageable age. Her youth was a pathetic announcement for the two old maids. However, life had gone on in the O'Reilley household unruffled, as placid as the conventional lake set in the center of the very conventional landscape oil painting that adorned the stiff and over-furnished parlor. They never quarrelled. That was a privilege of intimacy which they did not share. Each was a personality sealed to the others, inter-acting on a basis of patterned word formulas which generalized commonplaces.

That morning, after vividly perceiving the ruins of her gray hair, Mary could not go down to the breakfast table and explain how she felt. She could not explain to Joe and Martha that she was empty inside, that her soul was a barren field over which were scattered the corpses of her few, emaciated dreams. She must keep the freight of her new sorrow locked within, while she spoke of the accustomed breakfast trivialities, the weather, bridge, friends, Annie and her children, Lizz O'Neill, the news in the *Chicago Tribune,* obvious facts connected with Joe's legal cases.

Joe and Martha were already seated. Gertrude was gone. Joe was a grayed and handsome man, whose mellowed appearance was but slightly time-touched; he exuded a sense of well-being. Martha was dried and sapped like Mary, but her features were pointed, acrid, bitter in contrast with the sweetness and calm which sometimes seemed like a serene glow on Mary's countenance.

Joe read the newspaper. Mary listened while Martha talked of Lizz O'Neill. Martha said she liked Lizz, and that Lizz had a good heart. But she was a little common. And she talked too much of her children. They were good and dutiful children; they supported and respected their mother, like they should. But they lacked class, they lacked the class of Tommy and Annie's children. None of them could touch Gertrude for brains. Johnny's Annie, however, was a little like Lizz, a little common. Joe read on. After Lizz had been definitely described as common, he made a few remarks. Then he said that he was going to bring home a young priest for dinner in a few days. It was Father Malloy, a regular fellow of a priest who rooted for the Chicago White Sox, smoked and had a sense of humor. Joe had a regular-fellow complex. Mary and Martha expressed delight. Joe was a god in the family, a patriarch; his wishes were always devoutly acceded to. If he brought people home for dinner, they were inherently fine.

After breakfast, Joe departed for his office. Mary sat by the parlor window. Martha decided to do some sewing for Gertrude.

It was autumn. A sunless sky was pressing heavily over the gray day. Mary's perceptions were misty. She sensed a soul, a spirit, a thing gloomy, wearied, and unseen, passing up and down the street in company with the monotonous wind, shrouding all objects with its mantling mood of brooding dejection—the red-brick apartment building across the street, pedestrians, occasional automobiles, the wind-split trees, the expired lawns, the cheerless sameness of the pavement, herself, everything.

She would have liked to sit by the window remembering things; but there was very little for her to remember. So much of her time had been spent in trivial gossip, in eventless breakfasts and unemphatic teas, in long hours of doing nothing but waiting. She had sat through countless hours, listening to Martha reaffirm that Lizz O'Neill was good-hearted but untidy, that Father Kildea was a saint and scholar blessed in a special manner by the Lord, that Mamie Moriarity was common. Such things were but slight props for memories.

She listened to the wind rattling the window pane. She reflected how it curiously symbolized her own existence. Sitting at a window, protected from storms and colds, watching people, hoping inarticulately —such was her life. Now it was lost, and she had only a few recollections, which she held like a slim bouquet of desired flowers that had withered. Everything she saw, all her thoughts, were like the unseen soul she seemed to sense traveling with the wind. The wind against the pane, too, was cruel, a cruelty felt to be slashing against her.

Martha asked if anything were wrong.

"Nothing. I just feel a little tired, and thought I'd sit by the window here. It's kind of sad today," she replied.

"Yes, but, darling, you ought to rest a little while. Rest is what you need with your heart."

"I will. I just thought that I'd sit here for a little while first."

"I'd take care of myself if I was you."

Mary did not seem to hear her sister.

"Martha, do you remember John Newton?" she suddenly asked.

"No. Why?" Martha responded.

"Oh, I just wondered. Joe brought him out to dinner once, when he was in law school. He seemed like a nice young man, and I wondered what had happened to him."

"I can't remember him. What did he look like?"

"I don't remember, except that he was a nice-looking young man, and he dressed well, and his grammar was as good as Joe's," Mary said.

Martha spoke of a number of people out of the past whom she did remember, only too vividly. She recalled that the Mahoney twins were fat slobs, and that Catherine Malloy had married a good-for-nothing drunkard, and that Joe Collins, who had always been such a roughneck, was now driving a truck, and becoming an old man.

Mary did not listen. She reflected on the oddness of her sudden recollection of John Newton. And yet it was not odd either. Subconsciously she had carried him along with her through the endless flatness of the years. Yet she retained only a vague if pleasing impression of him. His appearance, his features, seemed to evade her memory completely. All she could recall was that she liked him, and that he had been quiet; a very dignified quiet like Joe's. And she had often wished that Joe would bring him out again, or that she would meet him again somewhere. But John Newton had disappeared.

She had been going with Myles Rierdon at the time that Joe had brought John out. Myles was a successful lawyer and politician now, rich and well-known, with a wife and family. On Sundays, she and Myles used to take walks along Michigan Boulevard. When walking with him, her attention was always attracted to the shiny, transparent window panes of some of the houses, set back from well-tended lawns. They had seemed so much like Myles. She would walk along for blocks thinking that Myles' soul was like a clean, transparent pane of glass. It was a queer comparison, and yet it seemed accurate. After she had met John, she had sensed a difference in quality between him and Myles. Myles had shrunken in her estimation.

She could not recall ever regretting her refusal of Myles' proposal. Now, sitting by the window, she was stung with no lamentations. She would not have altered her life, and re-lived it as Mrs. Rierdon, if such powers were given her. Her memory of him carried with it the same repulsion that he had always caused in her. Confidently and with the insensitivity of a crass male, he had asked her to marry him, vainly unaware that she might decline his offer. There was something about Myles, his brashness, that had often caused her to wince. After Myles would kiss her, she would lie in a hot bed wondering if she were the

Mary O'Reilley who had allowed that man to kiss her, to press his lips heavily upon hers. It had shamed her. Even now she reacted to that sense of shame. She watched a woman pushing a baby buggy past her window, and she experienced a soiled feeling; a lingering nausea from kisses which Myles Rierdon had now probably forgotten. Everybody had thought her a fool for not accepting him. No, she was not sorry, even though she was barren and unfulfilled, going to death without having known a woman's warmest feelings and experiences.

She sat looking out of the window.

"Oh, Mary, Lizz ought to be over today," Martha said, glancing up from her sewing.

"Yes," said Mary.

"She hasn't been to see us lately, and when she was down at Annie's the other night she said that she might be around today."

"That'll be nice. I have a dress I want to give her."

"Well, she needs it," Martha said aggressively.

"Yes, she's poor. The poor thing," said Mary.

"She's dirty and sloppy. She most certainly needs a new dress," Martha said.

"She's had a hard time."

"Yes, but there's no excuse for a woman being so sloppy. She could comb her hair and wash her face. Water is free, and a bar of soap only costs five cents."

Mary did not answer. Martha spoke on. She suddenly changed the subject to a party they had attended when they were young girls. There had been a young man named O'Connell. Martha spoke of him confusedly. Poor Martha! Mary thought. She, too, was oppressed by the past.

Martha's tongue finally lapsed, and she proceeded with her sewing. Mary wondered about John Newton. What had happened to him? Was he married? Was he unhappy, and approaching the end of a stream of wasting trivialities, coming into the hands of death? People went in and out of each other's lives with such strange abruptness. They disappeared—for eternity. There was a certain horror in this realization; and she changed her thoughts to the time she had contemplated entering the convent of the Poor Clares. When she was thirty, she had sensed life shrinking and shrivelling inside of her. Perceptions had commenced to sting her; the laughter of young people who walked summer nights arm in arm, innocent of future misery and the inroads of age; the spring madness of green leaves and trees; Annie and Tommy with their babies; youth; love. The world had seemed to press upon her with insistent fingers. She was stifled, nervous; her thoughts seemed like a succession of boils. She wanted escape, peace, a fortressed calm. At the Poor Clares convent, over at Fifty-third and Laflin, she had learned of the cloistered nuns, who were isolated from all contacts with the outside world. Living in complete solitude, they prayed and meditated, and passed an easeful life. There was neither struggle nor sorrow, but only devotion; so she had felt. When she had attended benediction there on Sunday afternoons, she had heard them sing through a partition. Their voices had seemed sweet and flowing with a spiritual peace. Once a Protestant friend had said that their voices were shrill; but she had never felt them so. She had spent long hours in wishful contemplation of joining them, of escaping from the hurting continuities of everyday existence into a quiet that seemed like an endless summer evening's swoon. But she had never entered the convent. She had lived on into the comfort of middle-age, losing the pain of those final, suppressed, youthful gasps. She had sunken into the final ditches of the human static and the commonplace.

II

In the afternoon Lizz O'Neill, and their sister-in-law, Annie, visited them. Lizz was fat and sloppy, a woman in her middle forties. Annie was thin with angular features. They sat in the parlor and talked and talked. Mary sat by the window, only half attentive, sunken in her own thoughts. Lizz said that her children were fine children. Annie told how Good and Fine her children were. Her Annie, and her Gertrude, and her Tommy, and her Martin, and her William. Lizz became equally as explicit about her brood. Then she switched her subject to the recently beatified eighteenth-century nun, The Sacred Rose of Jesus Christ. The talk spun along. They spoke of Mrs. Nolan's sloppy clothes, Mame's dead husband, the dreadful way in which A. P. A. schools, like the University of Chicago, turned out atheists, and of what Lizz O'Neill heard Mamie Moriarity say to Nellie McBride about Bridget Malloy at the wake of Sadie O'Brien.

Mary glanced out the window.

Lizz was speaking profusely, emphasizing her words with facial and manual gestures. . . . "And the airs of them. Humph! Her Peter is getting a new car, and they are moving out on Jeffery Avenue, and her Nellie is going out with a swell college guy. . . . Now, let me tell you, college guys are slick. Oh, but they're slick! And they don't take girls out for no good reason. You can't tell me that they do. . . . You can't be too careful nowadays about them slick college guys. A mother must watch her girls. Now my Margaret and my Catherine, they never go out with a young fellow, unless they have brought him home and introdooced him to me. And if they're out after twelve o'clock, their brother Dennis is wild and wants to go and get them. Dennis is going to take care of his sisters. But as I was saying, the airs them Dempseys put on. Humph! . . ."

Annie took the floor from Lizz, almost by assault.

"You speak the truth, Lizz. A mother must keep her eyes primed on her girls. Now, I only let my Annie go out with the finest type of young men. Young men with—*class.* Now, there's that Roycroft boy. He's a student at Loyola, and he's studying law, and gettin' educated, and his family has—*class.*"

Mary had heard all this maternal braggery before. At times, it had even interested her. Now it was devoid of meaning. It slid out of her consciousness without the least strain upon her attention. She watched a group of children moving down Crandon Avenue. There was an entangling pathos, an almost tragic beauty about them as they trooped by, their forms wistfully etched against the dull October day. She thought of the intangible beauties of childhood; and she wished that she had had children of her own; children of hers and . . . John Newton's. She dismissed the thought before it became either painful or shocking. She remembered being with Annie when hers were born, the pain and bloodiness of it! And these children she had just seen pass beneath her window, they were born in pain, to live like she had, or else like Lizz and Annie. She again thought, almost enviously, of the Poor Clares. It seemed beautiful to her; lives lived in such quiet noiselessness, lives of escape from . . .

"Mary, would you like to make the novena to The Sacred Rose of Jesus Christ? It starts next Toosday," Lizz said.

"Yes," Mary answered.

Lizz spoke of The Sacred Rose of Jesus Christ, seemingly bragging as if the latter's purity, virginity, and sanctity were her own. Then Mary served tea, and there was more conversation. At five-thirty they both had to rush home to prepare late supper for their families. After they were gone, Martha spoke of how common they both were. Mary was uninterested.

III

Days slipped along, and Mary's strength waned. She tired easily, and her interest in people, parties, and gatherings lagged. She seemed to have given up after that morning when the fact of approaching old age had been imprinted vividly upon her. Joe asked her to accompany him on a vacation to California, but she lacked the resistance for such a journey. She spent most of her time seated by the window, watching autumn coffin the street, her memory slipping through the flimsy satisfactions of her own past. School children always gauzed her spirit in melancholy. She was getting thin. She was suffering from frequent heart-pains. One day, she heard Gertrude remark, "Poor Aunt Mary!" There was no use pretending. She was near to the end.

Yet she was unterrified. Sometimes she even hoped for death. She was in bed most of the winter and did not leave the house until spring had come with its gaudy greenness.

Her first walk was in Jackson Park. The world was foreign, alien with its own happiness. She was but a weakened stranger, allowed merely to observe its parade. And the fresh young and gay impressions of the sticky leaves and trees pained her like a sad melodrama. Sometimes, her depression became like a naked sore. She wished intensely that she were young again, that love and a future were hers. Death was altered into something nightmarish. She even grew to hate youth. She prayed and she cursed, and, alone, she cried because she could no longer identify herself with the freshness that pervaded the park on her walks. She was a sick, old woman.

The summer passed for her, slowly, pantingly, miserably, with its suffocating hotness. Once again the world slid into decay. Mary was happier. Autumn was her season. Its melancholy was hers. She even liked its windy monotony. But after autumn was winter.

In November, she was sent to the hospital, a thin old woman. She had a private room with all possible conveniences and attentions. Joe secured the services of three renowned heart-specialists. The room was often filled with flowers. There she lay, waiting for death. But she enjoyed the quiet of the hospital. It seemed something like the mists of solitude which she imagined as the surrounding mood of the cloistered Poor Clare nuns. Sometimes she would even try to recreate memories where there were none. Sometimes she grew moody with longings for home, wishing for her parlor window, tea, conversation with Martha, Lizz, and Annie, for novenas to The Sacred Rose of Jesus Christ, church socials. Sometimes, she prayed. However, she more often lived in fogs and shapeless, melancholy moods. . . . And she had visitors. They came to see her and tell her that she looked well and would get better. Joe came, and Martha, and Annie and Tommy, and Lizz. She was usually happier alone.

December came; winter came, with ice blasts and holiday moods of simulated joy. Mary remembered other Christmas days. She was gloomy with the realization of an approaching Christmas in the hospital. It was to be her last. She grew more weak, living on borrowed time. She even began to hope that she would die before Christmas. The mists about her mind thickened. She received the last sacraments. The hope of dying before Christmas became almost an obsession. To lie in bed, looking back across a stretch of fifty-one years, remembering the doll her mother had given her on her eighth Christmas, the candy and dress her father gave her for her fourteenth birthday, the whole cluster of memories that had suddenly grown so significant with a lost beauty—she wanted to die.

At five o'clock on a morning of the week preceding Christmas, when a surly wind was crashing against the bleak bricks of the Mercy Hospital, her wish matured in an expiring darkness. As she lay awake, gasping for breath after a fatiguing, sleepless evening, the world was slowly crushed into silence. She sensed her faculties and powers ebbing; and blackness, soothing and restful, spread calmly over her room, engulfing all her perceptions in its tremendous, suffocating hush. It covered her, and her lips grew cold and tight with the imprint of a satisfied smile that she carried with her to the grave.

1928.

Calico Shoes

I

STELLA sat by the window, swathed in a heavy faded blue sweater.

Outside of the store, the crossing of Forty-seventh and Bishop stifled under the relentless sun of a July afternoon. On the northeastern corner and cater-corner from the store, was the fenced-in extremity of the Chicago Stockyards, and the stagnant atmosphere was foul with its nauseous odors. Strewn with bits of papers, the dusty sidewalks burned. Bishop Street, running north, was an unpaved, rutty passageway of baked mud and dirt, and it seethed with loud and untidy children. An automobile, bumping along it toward Forty-seventh Street, scattered dust and children in all directions. It curved into the driveway of the Nation Oil Company filling station, which was directly across from the store. Trucks and trolley cars rumbled along Forty-seventh Street. A drunken Slav, walking eastward, listed in front of the dirty bay window of the store, pointed an index finger ahead of him, and then proceeded zig-zag along the sidewalk. A beefy peasant woman, wearing a soiled gingham apron, turned past the store to go south on Bishop Street. A troop of children paused in front of the fly-thick platform of a meat-packing concern next to the oil station. A girl about nine years old singled herself from their midst, flung a stream of profanity at her companions, and continued to express her scorn by lifting her dresses, revealing filthy underpants. She thumbed her nose at them and tore across the oil station driveway. The gang pursued her. One of the boys paused, clutched a rock, and hurled it at her. She stopped running, drew her hand to her head, and screamed, while blood soaked in her hair. The children turned and ran in the opposite direction, and the girl shouted in pain, staggering along Bishop Street. A fire engine, followed by a long and ungainly hook-and-ladder, screamed westward in the direction of Ashland Avenue. Automobiles, and then hastening pedestrians, appeared in its wake. The echoes from the bells hung momentarily in the air. Another trolley car passed, and an eleven-year-old boy flipped it. Crushed with petrifying odors, torrefied by the torch-like sun, caked with dust and dirt, reflecting all the squalor and the squalid life of a Chicago slum, the crossing of Forty-seventh and Bishop Streets drowsed through the afternoon.

And Stella sat by the window, staring with vacant blue eyes, only feebly understanding what she saw without. She was a plump Bohemian woman of twenty-eight, who looked as if she had passed her thirties. Her yellowish, dish-watery blonde hair straggled from under a cheap and unwashed imitation lace nightcap. Her face was round and full, and she repeatedly pursed her lips and sucked on the upper one. Her back was on the store, a wide and disorderly establishment, plagued with large and buzzing swarms of flies. The floor was unswept, the unassorted cans and packages on the shelves were screened with dust, the candy in the case looked stale, and the long low counter next to the case was littered with newspapers, jars, a bread box, and a slab of bologna sausage upon which the flies repeatedly alighted.

Yashka, an unbathed middle-aged Lithuanian, appeared from the rear of the store. His soiled white collarless shirt was opened down three buttons, leaving a segment of naked, hairy chest. His unshaven face was perspiring and swarthy, and there was a crafty look in his beady eyes. He glanced about the store, yawned, emitted a lazy curse. He scratched his chest, and mumbled to himself that there was no business running a store in a neighborhood full of Polacks. A twelve-year-old boy, blond, dirty, and with a wide, stupid face, entered, followed by a fleet of flies. He asked Yashka if he could have a loaf of bread for his mother on trust. Yashka humped his shoulders, shook his head, exclaimed that he was a poor man, and that he could give no trust, repeating the words no trust three times. The boy laid ten pennies, wet from being tightened in his perspiring hand, on the counter. Yashka handed him a loaf of bread. The boy turned at the doorway, and cursed Yashka. Yashka moved quickly but stiff-leggedly from behind the counter. The boy leaped down the two steps in front of the store, raced across the street, narrowly dodging out of the path of a five-ton motor truck. He halted on the opposite curb. He made sheeny gestures, and muttered:

"Oi! Yoi! Yoi!"

The overalled attendant from the filling station stood in his doorway, laughing. Yashka's face contracted into an expression of hate. He shook his fists at the boy, and cursed back at him, but his words were drowned by a passing street car. He turned back from the curb, and half-aloud he goddamned the whole race of Polacks.

Strabinsky came along and sat on the rickety bench in front of the store. On his left arm, over his khaki shirt, there was a black band; his last child had died after having been bitten by a rat in one of the crumbling wooden neighborhood buildings which Yashka owned. Yashka paced slowly back and forth in front of the store, and Strabinsky, his nose dribbling, followed his movements with the unfathomable eyes of a half-wit. Yashka repeated to Strabinsky that the Polacks were no good, they were dirty, they never had any money, they always had houses full of dirty kids who grew up to be criminals, and they would never pay their bills. All the time, they wanted something for nothing. Yashka suddenly stopped in front of Strabinsky, looked down at him, and told him to wipe the snot from his nose. Strabinsky smiled like a silly subnormal boy, and rubbed the back of a dirty hand across his under-lip. Yashka laughed.

Biting from a plug of tobacco, Yashka re-entered his store. Stella met his approach with childish trusting eyes.

" 'ullo," she muttered, while he stood over her, pinching her cheeks.

"Stella, you looney, cra-azy. Got wheels in de head. Ha! Nobody home upstairs and rooms for rent. . . . Ha. . . . Well, in de fall, you go to de nut house. Yah, dere, dey all got nottin' in de head."

"Yashka, you have Mira go downtown 'n' buy me nize noo dress?" she said, staring up at him, open-eyed.

"Yah, Mira buy you noo dress. Ha!" Yashka said, laughing with a sardonic and deep hoarseness.

He pinched her cheeks, and she smiled happily.

"Stella, you an old s . . t."

"Yashka, when you do dose tings to me, like las' night, you hurt me here," she said, pointing to her matronly bosom.

"Yah, and I hurt you oder places too. Crazy in de head or not, all de women like it," he said, again laughing sardonically.

He pinched her cheek.

"And you have Mira buy me nize dress?"

"Yah. Five noo dress. Noo dress too for de nut house," he said, turning from her to go outside.

He stood in the doorway and yawned, revealing yellow, irregular teeth. He stepped down onto the sidewalk, moved over to Strabinsky, and stood looking down upon his friend, with hands on hips. He spit tobacco juice, which dashed off Strabinsky's shoe, and said that all the women, crazy in the head or not, liked it. Strabinsky's face lit with a recognition that took the form of an ugly leer. Hearing his name mispronounced, Yashka turned around in surprise. Brick-faced, gray-mustached, weazened Karney stood saluting him in a position of drunken unsteadiness. Yashka stepped back a pace, and told Karney that his breath would kill an elephant. Yashka turned to Strabinsky and said that here was that drunken Irish bum whose woman supported him. Karney went into a long, obsequious and flowery preamble, and then asked Yashka for a drink of moonshine, or the price of a can of beer. Yashka laughed sarcastically and told Karney of all his own troubles, taxes on houses where the Polacks would not pay the rent, cheap as it was, expenses, and more expenses. He concluded by asking Karney did he think him crazy in the head. Persuasion failing, Karney cursed Yashka, branding him as one of the foreigners who had stolen the neighborhood away from good Irishmen and Americans like himself. Yashka made a gesture as if to punch Karney. Karney leaped ungracefully backward for about five feet, clumsily raised his guard in a stilted pugilistic pose, and issued the loud proclamation that he was yet to see the day when a spineless miser of a foreigner could whip a good Irishman like himself. Yashka retreated two steps and raised clenched fists. Each challenged the other to strike him. Three passing Mexicans, in wide sombreros, laughed. Two boys crossed the street, watched with eager eyes, and one of them said persuasively:

"Go ahead, Mister, sock him one!"

Yashka unwrinkled his face into a smile. The more Karney fumed out curses, the more Yashka laughed. With a dropping of his shoulders in a gesture of despair, Karney turned and rolled down the street, away from Yashka. Yashka, with a sneer, told Strabinsky that Karney had not been sober for fifteen years.

His hands again found his hips as he observed two girls approaching. They were young and Polish, with tough cynical faces, and cheap gaudy dresses.

"Vel . . . Vel . . . Vel, gels! Gels . . . vat you say? No-o?" he exclaimed, nodding his head and smirking obscenely.

"Go peddle your fish, you old sousepot," the girl on the outside of the sidewalk said as they passed him, their high red slippered heels tattooing on the cement.

"Go hop in the bowl, you dried up old pig," the other girl said, without turning her head toward him.

"Wait . . . here, I got something for you . . . inside," he quickly called.

"Go wash your ears," one of them flung back at him.

"Goddamn Polacks!" Yashka sneered, watching them walk on.

He went inside the store, and Strabinsky ambled off. Stella asked Yashka what he had been saying to the girls outside, and he answered that he had been telling them that his wife, Stella, had nicer dresses than they had. He laughed throatily and ironically. Stella smiled at him with simple pleasure.

Hows-um, the Greek popcorn man who lived on Bishop Street, entered the store. He was short, thin, wiry, and swarthy-complexioned. There were profuse lines and indentations on his scowling face, and a drooping set of mustaches that would have recommended him for the parts of villains in motion picture comedies. He asked for a loaf of bread and laid two nickels on the counter. Yashka hesitated in getting the bread, and inveigled the Greek into a dice game.

He shoved aside a pile of newspapers to provide greater room on the counter and watched while Hows-um shook the dice in the frayed dice cup. Before each roll, Hows-um grimaced. After letting the dice out of the cup, his hand, clutching it, rose in a parabola above his head, and he held it aloft in a statuesque gesture while he screwed his eyes upon the dice, reading and adding their numbers. With the progress of the game, the stakes rose from small change to dollars. Yashka, winning his turn with the dice, furtively substituted loaded ones for those they had been using. In three rolls, he won ten dollars. Hows-um continued losing until he was down to four dollars. With an extravagant gesture, he laid two on the counter, and shook the dice. He rolled two twos, making four his point. He made three passes with no result. Perspiration commenced to drip from his face. He grew intent with greedy concern. He slowly shook the dice in the cup. Yashka, with an assumption of naïve innocence, rubbed a two-dollar bill under Hows-um's nose:

"Come, shoot-um. Two bucks no four. Two bucks no four. Play! Play! Don't be cheap," he shrugged his shoulders with the mention of the last word, "Cheap, don't be cheap. Two bucks no four. I give you chance, win your money back. Don't be cheap skate!"

Hows-um glanced suspiciously at Yashka. He automatically played with his mustache. He sneered, and with elaborate gesturings laid his final two dollars on the board. Yashka glued his eyes on the dice cup, and Hows-um deliberately shook them in the cup.

"Yashka! Yashka!" Stella said, tugging at his sleeve.

"Cris sake! Don't bod-der me!" he snapped angrily, and watched as the dice were propelled out of the cup.

"Yashka, you have Mira buy me nize noo dress?"

He doubled his fists, but read the numbers on the dice Hows-um had rolled, a three and a four.

He relaxed, smiled, pulled in the eight-dollar pot, and turned to tell Stella she could have a dozen new dresses.

Hows-um said he had no more money with him, and asked Yashka to loan him five dollars. Yashka shrugged his shoulders, and asked Hows-um what did he think he was—fool. Loaning his money out so he could lose more. Cris sake, no business that way.

Yashka met Hows-um's envenomed glare with a smile of innocent friendliness. Hows-um shouted, speaking so rapidly that he ran many of his words into each other:

"Croook! Croook! Goddamn Lithwanian Croook! Hows-um you all a time win? You no play fair, on a level. Lithwanian sonofabitch. . . . Me, I play um fair. Hows-um you no shoot-um fair, on a level? I go home, and I come back with my gun, and I shoot-um you in a goddamn pants. Hows-um you never lose, all a time win. Croook! Goddamn Lithwanian Croook, Cris sake, you no play fair. I go home, get-um gun, I come back shoot-um you in a goddamn pants. Hows-um?"

"Go home and get money. I give you chance, all de chance you want. But me, I no fool, give-um you money to play against me, win my money. Cris sake, no business like dat," Yashka said, shaking his head from side to side.

Hows-um exhausted his lung power on the adamant Yashka. Finally, Hows-um picked up his loaf of bread, shook his thin fist at Yashka, promised again to shoot him, and stalked out of the store, slamming the screen door behind him. Yashka watched him cross the street and go down Bishop Street past the filling station; he laughed with satisfaction.

"Yashka, I hungry," Stella said.

"When Mira come."

Shortly afterward, Mira, Stella's seventeen-year-old brother, came. He was a tall, husky, clumsy blond boy, overgrown for his age. He spoke with Yashka in Lithuanian, reporting on the rents he had been collecting, and laid the roll of collected money on the counter. Yashka put it in his safe under the counter. He went upstairs to look at the moonshine whiskey he was making. Mira sat at the counter reading a foreign-language newspaper. He looked up from the paper, yawned, and commenced to pick his teeth with a safety match.

"Mira, you go downtown buy me nize noo dress?"

"Sure, Stella, I'll get you the swellest red catgut dress you ever lamped. Say, Stella kid, when you get into it, you'll look—slick. Get me, kid, you'll look . . . *slick.*"

Stella smiled with childish enthusiasm. At the same moment, Mira's pal, Ruddy, came around. Like Mira, he was big and awkward for his age. They discussed dresses with Stella, and Ruddy told her that he thought she would look best in black catgut. Then he told Mira about the big blonde who had shook that thing like nobody's business at last week's burlesque show at the Empress Theater.

"Mira, she could shake her field artillery like the cat's tonsillitis," Ruddy kept repeating.

They talked lazily, and Stella again sat by the window. In time Yashka stuck his head out from the rear of the store, and said they would eat. Mira and Stella went back, and Ruddy sat behind the counter. He extracted a dollar from the cash drawer and pocketed it.

The kitchen in back of the store was filthy. The table in the center of the room was covered with a greasy, splotched oilcloth and disorderly with unwashed dishes. The room was alive with flies. Pork chops and fried potatoes were heated in a skillet which contained three weeks' accumulations of grease. The meat and potatoes and raw tomatoes were set on plates, and coffee was reboiled in an ancient pot. They ate with their hands, smudging their faces. Stella's chin dripped tomato juice. She asked Yashka about a new dress. Eating cormorantly, he told her to shut up. Their meal was consumed in silence.

II

When Yashka had married Stella, she had been a buxom young immigrant girl. He had brought her to live with him above his saloon at Forty-seventh and Bishop. At the time of his marriage, he had owned many buildings in the section and he continued accumulating them. In those days, she had been a great help to him, cleaning his saloon, waiting on tables in the ladies' room in the rear, keeping accounts for him since he did not read or write English, and ministering to his personal needs and comforts. After the advent of Prohibition, his saloon had become a delicatessen, and he had started bootlegging in a small way. She had tended the store, kept the floor swept, the shelves tidied and dusted, and the articles in their proper places. She had been a good and helpful wife to him.

One day while crossing Forty-seventh Street, she had been struck by an automobile, driven by a drunken driver. She had fallen backward, her head cracking on the cement curb edge. She had been in the hospital for months, and when she had been released, she had returned to Yashka with her memory destroyed and her mind impaired. There was a clear case for damages on the accident, but the suit had been continuously postponed and delayed for several years. One day, a little over a year after the accident Yashka had lost his temper with Stella and thrown her downstairs. She had landed on her head, and her faculties had been further damaged. From that time, she also had less control over her facial muscles, and her mouth would constantly twitch.

The damage suit was finally coming up in the autumn of 1926. As the time approached, Yashka and Mira, who had been sent to live with them by their family in order that he might see that Stella was properly treated, both commenced humoring Stella more than they had ever done before. They regularly listened to her babble about dresses, and one day, Yashka gave Mira the money to buy her a cheap black silkateen dress and inexpensive patent leather shoes at Klein's on Halsted Street. That night, Stella told various store customers about her new black catgut dress and her new calico shoes that Yashka and Mira had gotten for her so that she would look slick. And Yashka often pinched her cheek and spoke kindly to her.

He brought out a doctor and a lawyer to see her, and they listened to her while she told them of the nice new dresses Yashka and Mira were buying her. They pinched her cheek when they departed. The lawyer came a second time, and Stella told him that she would be his wife like she was Yashka's wife. The lawyer smiled, pathetically.

And one morning, Yashka and Mira dressed her up in her new black catgut dress and her new calico shoes and took her away in a large yellow automobile which scared her. Yashka said that it was the suit, and she looked at him, perplexed, and told him that she did not like suits, but only dresses. They brought her to a large room with people in it, and she was more scared, and she saw a man sitting above the others in a black dress that she thought dirty, and only good for dirty Polack women. She clutched Yashka's elbow and told him not to let the man in the dirty black dress take her new dress away from her. They went back to the room for four successive days, and they put Yashka and Mira, and then Stella in a chair up near the man with the dirty black dress, and they asked them questions. When they asked Stella questions, she told them about all the nice new dresses Yashka and Mira would buy her, and she told the man in the dirty black dress that he could not have any of them.

When the suit was ended, Yashka was happy, and pinched her cheek. He was all smiles, but suddenly frowned, telling Mira they better go back to the store, because he knew that Ruddy, who was tending it, was stealing money on him. Stella was happy and she knew that Yashka and Mira were going to buy her nice new dresses.

III

An impoverished dimness pervaded the corner. A sole electric light seemed feeble. A chill sharp wind carried the stockyard odors overhead and scraped and tossed bits of newspapers randomly about the streets and sidewalks. The night traffic was less heavy than the day's, but automobiles and trolley cars continually passed.

Yashka staggered back and forth in front of the store, a new gray fedora set back on his head. In his pocket was the ten-thousand-dollar check for damages that he had just received as a result of the lawsuit. And tomorrow morning he was going to put his X to the final papers selling his store and building at a good price. Then he was going to see about having Stella committed to an institution for the feeble-minded. He was kind of sorry to be leaving this neighborhood, but out in Blue Island he was going to make more money bootlegging. And he still owned plenty of buildings about here. He would sell them one by one whenever he could get a good price for them. Tonight, he was happy and celebrating, and later on, he was going to sleep with a nice sixteen-year-old Polack girl; her father was out of work, and they owed him four months rent, and the girl should just try and charge him too much. He boisterously greeted passersby, and kept looking through the store window.

Inside, Stella sat by the window, wearing her heavy faded blue sweater. Mira and Ruddy talked over the counter. They were talking about Mira's trip to New York, which he was going to make on the money he had forced out of Yashka on the threat of telling, in court, how Yashka had thrown her downstairs that time.

"Well, Stella, I'm going to bring you all kinds of rubber dresses back from New York, and will they be the cat's meow," Mira said; Ruddy guffawed.

"Stella, if you don't know what the cat's meow is, ask Mira, he'll tell you," Ruddy said, while they were still uproariously laughing.

"Mira, you buy me nize noo dress so I look slick . . . cat's meow?"

"Sure, Stella," Mira said; he and Ruddy guffawed.

"Hello, Stella," Yashka said drunkenly, entering the store with Hows-um.

" 'ullo," she responded.

"You get nize noo dress in de nut house. Ha! Ha!"

"Yashka, you let Mira buy me nize noo dress?"

"Sure," he said, laughing throatily.

"Come on shoot-um! Hows-um you say, come on, we shoot-um crap, and then you foolaroun' like crazy man. Jesus Cris, you no 'fraid of me? Hows-um?" the Greek popcorn man said in his serious manner.

"Sure shoot-um for money, not ni-ickels," Yashka said, moving behind the counter.

He procured a roll of ten-dollar bills, held together by a rubber band, from the safe. He bounced them on the counter. Hows-um looked at the money with anxious greed.

Yashka handed Hows-um the dice cup.

"Stella, you an old s . . t, get nize noo dress in de nut house. Ha!"

Hows-um beamed as he won a five-dollar pot. On the next pass, he shook eleven and pulled in a second five-dollar pot. Yashka grew serious, and laid ten dollars down. Hows-um lost. Yashka substituted his loaded dice, and laid another ten-dollar bill on the counter. Stella sidled up to him, and tugged at his sleeve.

"Go way! Don't bod-der me, crazy goddamn fool!" he said to her.

She tugged again, while he was rattling the dice cup. He spit tobacco juice in her face. She turned and walked back to sit by the window.

Yashka shook a seven. He took the money from the counter and turned to Mira.

"Goddamn Mira, dat's de way to play. Come I shoot-um with you, Greek! Money! Money! Money!"

1929.

Sunday

I

A HAPPY man was Peter. He earned one hundred and five dollars a month working as a janitor around the University. His working hours were from noon to ten in the evening, with a two-hour intermission for supper; however, he rarely took his full two hours. He was over fifty, and he worked strenuously, so that he often went home tired; but his job gave him security, and it had its advantages. He had no boss glowering over him all day, and he was able, on occasion, to pause for a breath of air, or for a few words with his friend Charley.

Also, there was variety in the tasks that he performed. He emptied waste-baskets. He swept and mopped floors. He washed windows, a feature of his work that he enjoyed immensely, because he knew that he was the best window-washer about the University. Around supper time he relieved the elevator operator in the main library building, and he was able to pass the time commenting on the weather and the nature of life and the world with students as they rode up and down. And then there was the grandest task of all, that of wearing a braided uniform and guarding entrance ways, collecting tickets, and controlling waiting lines at University functions.

On a Sunday early in June Peter was very tired, and he was grateful for his day of rest. After washing the dinner dishes he decided to go for a walk. Mrs. Cordel, kindly neighbor that she was, had some sewing to do, and promised to sit in with his invalid mother. Peter's mother was over eighty, and he was her gray-haired baby boy. She loved him in a cranky, nagging, jealous old woman's way, and she was always promising him the spanking which she said that he deserved. She was very fond of telling this to Mrs. Cordel, or to whatever other rare visitors they had. She would also tell them that if he was a good and dutiful son she would permit him to get married when he reached the age of sixty-five.

She was extremely difficult, but he cared for her with great devotion. He had vowed to himself that he would provide for her as well as possible so long as there was strength remaining in his body. And he was keeping that vow. Sometimes she told Mrs. Cordel that he beat and starved her, and left her alone while he went out traipsing after evil women; but she was old, and could be forgiven. She was his mother, and a person only had one mother.

Others might have sent her to the poorhouse, but never would he be such an ingrate. She was worth all the sacrifices he made, even that one of the previous summer, when he had postponed his trip to New York City. For three years he had denied himself, saving to visit New York on his vacation. He had gotten the money together. Then, on the eve of his departure, his mother had become seriously ill. He had abandoned the trip, spending his vacation nursing her, and using his vacation money on things for her. He could have sent her to the University clinic, but that would have been filial ingratitude. She was his mother. He was proud of the sacrifice he had made for her, even though it would require at least another three years before he would have sufficient money for that trip to New York.

II

He felt rested, walking along the sunny, dozeful Sabbath streets. The sun was warm, and Sunday was so calm and peaceful. He walked along slowly towards Jackson Park, and life was a chalice of quiet, filled with sunny incantations. He thought of his mother, proud of his dutifulness, happy. But vaguely and inarticulately beneath the surface of his happiness there was a consciousness of the fact that he was declining into old age.

A shiny, newly-washed passing automobile distracted him. Gee, he wished that he owned an automobile so that he could take his mother out driving in the park on a Sunday afternoon. And to the country. Just think, he hadn't been out in the country in years. He wondered what it looked like these days.

His mother, he reflected, would soon be dead. Sometimes he dreamed that she was dead already, and he felt that it was a sign warning him that he would not have her with him much longer. Clenching his fists, he solemnly reiterated his vow to care for her. He was still pretty strong and spry, you bet. But his hair was gray, and he had turned fifty. Once he had had many days ahead of him. But now—well, the days that were ahead were not so many.

The green park seemed healthy with people. He wandered among the crowds, and was warmed and sustained by their presence and number. Unnurtured, hungry little impulses for companionship ached within him. It was so good just to walk along, and see people, and they looked so happy playing, picnicking, strolling, sitting, talking. And the grass spread out so brilliantly under the sun, and was so deeply green and cool in the shade.

Yes, he told himself, it was nice to see people. They were on every bench, on the grass, on the walks, playing tennis, in rowboats on the lagoon. And the young girls, moving in twos and threes, and hanging on the arms of the young lads—yes, the young girls! He looked closely at them, at the hints of breasts and thighs beneath their fresh and summery dresses.

He wished that he had something to do, and he ambled along down a path that was cathedraled with leafy tree spreads. Nice! Glancing lonesomely about him, he observed a contented family of Mexicans, clean, dark, good-looking people, the husband smiling with love upon his slim young wife as she watched their two youngsters chasing squirrels, trying to feed them peanuts, but succeeding only in scaring the animals off. He boiled with resentment, thinking that it was wrong to permit Mexicans in a good white man's park. Down farther he observed a small group of noisy, dirty Irish, two beefy women shrieking at their children who were scrambling in adjacent bushes. There were some people, he thought, who didn't get along together.

He ambled on, and around him was the park, drenched in warming sunlight, alive with sensuous and bubbling life. The world was very, very good. But along the benches were lonely men and women, frustration written clearly on their faces. They were like him. They walked along or sat on the benches, unhappy, and lonesome in the midst of gay, laughing swarms. Frustration was scrawled on their countenances.

His drifting attention centered upon a corpulent aging couple, who were ahead of him. They had a country air about them and they walked with their eyes set rigidly to the front, neither speaking. He followed them for a few hundred yards. Then they occupied a vacant bench and sat speechless, eyes rigidly glued on the bushes directly before them, lips clamped quiet. He passed them, wondering what he would do.

Fat pigeons waddled near him, jerking their heads and necks, and waving their rear ends. He turned his eyes from the pigeons to a girl seated on a bench, a cigarette in her thick mouth. She was a tough-looking one, he felt. Her legs were crossed, exposing naked stretches of thigh. She met his stare with an unwavering sneer, and manipulated her legs to give him a fuller view. She inhaled nonchalantly. He slunk along. Shame lapped within him. But she had been a looker, even if she was brazen.

He reflected that he saw plenty of lookers every day at the University. Some of them were sweet girls and good girls too. But when a fellow has been janitor around a university for quite a while he learns that one can't ever tell what a girl is from how she looks. Yes, sir, a fellow who is a janitor around a university sees plenty of things that are never meant to be seen. Like that little doll of a girl he caught with a fellow on the plushed stairway leading to the chapel tower, and right at the very moment when Mr. Hamilton, the Dean of the chapel, was speaking the word of God.

Them two had thought they wouldn't be caught. Well, they were, and he had called another guard, and he had done his duty, and the officials had only done what was right in expelling them. They should have more sense of right and decency than to do a thing like that in the million-dollar chapel, right when Dean Hamilton was explaining the word of God. He had only done his duty in turning them in. If everybody did his duty like he had, this world would be better off.

Yes, sir, students who had a chance to get an education should put their time in better than doing things like that right on plush stairways of the million-dollar chapel. He certainly wished that he had an education. If he had had the chance to get one, he sure would have taken advantage of it, and he wouldn't be a janitor now. He was satisfied with his job, but, gee, if he had only had an education. Some people just don't have opportunities, and more often than not, them that does get an opportunity don't take the right advantage of it. He shrugged his shoulders. Well, he was better off than many.

A pigeon flew before him, descending in a downward parabola, scooting past his ear, wings flapping rhythmically, and then soaring over the trees, disappearing. Gee, it was nice the way birds could fly.

III

He wondered what he should do, and crossed a driveway, on which automobiles moved ceaselessly. The people in those cars must be going someplace. He wished he had a car, and was taking his mother out in it at this minute. But Charley was saying to him, only yesterday, that most of them that has cars and many such things is up to their ears in debt, borrowing from Peter to pay Paul. He could be proud; he owed not a penny to any man. It was every man's duty to live within his means. But if he only did own an automobile! Gee!

He traveled along the edge of the golf course, watching the knickered golfers, almost like priests performing the rites of a strange religion. He thought that golf must be an interesting game. Everybody, almost, seemed to play it. Millionaires, and university professors, and even the President of the United States put on knickers and played golf.

He yawned, and wished that he could think of something to do.

He sat on a bench near one of the holes, and watched foursomes come and go. Many players were stern and serious about the game, and it caused him to reflect a second time that there must be something to it. In back of him were trees and a clump of bushes. The frail wind sang through the leaves and branches, sad. He grew afraid of the wind, and its monotonous sough seemed like a prophecy of death. The wind was sad all right. He did not like to hear it moan in the trees like that; it made him creepy. He had once been young, and he had never been disturbed or distressed by the wind in the trees. Now he was older, and it made him afraid.

Sitting there, he strove to throw off his sadness watching the people come and go, and especially by watching very closely when girls approached the hole, because their dresses were liable to fluff up. He watched the golfers teeing off for the next hole. It was a great thing the way some of them could drive that little ball. It took a lot of time and thought and practice to do it that good. And it must have taken smart men to think up a game that everybody wanted to play and was so serious about. Everybody couldn't think up a game that even the President of the United States, university professors, and millionaires played.

The wind soughed behind him.

A girl approached, and as she bent over to place her ball for the drive, her dress ruffled, and he saw a narrow slice of bare flesh above her stocking. Girls didn't wear much clothing any more. He watched the ball roll and dribble along after her ineffective drive.

A spindly-legged fat man, in pantaloonish knickers, histrionically stanced himself, and drove. The ball out-curved on a wicked line, and disappeared in the distant grass. The fat man laughed lustily.

The others teed off, and the last of the four, a man with a small thin head, sliced his drive. He cursed volubly.

Peter watched the steady succession of golfers. Then he arose and walked on. He was lonely. But he felt less lonely in the park, where there were so many people, than he would have at home, with only his mother. He stared at the girls. He wished that he would meet someone he knew, someone from the University, perhaps a co-ed. He wanted to talk. Gee, he wished that he would meet Charley. Good old Charley. Golly, he liked good old Charley all right. When the boss had offered him that job at the clinic, with five men under him, he had turned it down because he didn't want to shoulder the responsibility; but he had recommended Charley in his place, and now Charley was doing fine at it. He wasn't at all stuck up, but acted just the same as he always had. There was something between him and Charley that was deeper than what they ever said to each other. They were friends. He liked to meet Charley, and maybe stop to talk and kid with him for a minute or two.

"Quit stalling," Charley would say.

"I don't see you breaking your neck," he would say.

"Never mind me," Charley would say.

"And never you mind me," he would say.

"I bet you ain't done a lick of work all day," Charley would say.

"No!" he would then say, meaning it the other way around, of course.

"No!" Charley would say, all in fun, because Charley was that way.

"You're a great kidder," he would say.

"I ain't neither. I know you ain't done a lick of work all day," Charley would go on and say.

"Listen!" he would go on and say.

"I know you too well to let you bull me along," Charley would say.

"I'm not bulling you. Come on around to my building and I'll show you what I done," he would say.

"I ain't got no time for that," Charley would say.

"Gwan," he would say.

"Gwan, yourself," Charley would say.

Good old Charley. He'd have to ask Charley to come and take a walk with him in the park next Sunday, because there was something very deep between him and Charley.

He passed over grass, delicately colored by the sun. Restful! Good old Charley!

IV

He trooped along westward, toward the baseball diamonds. He stood along the left field foul line, and in back of him was a rectangular stretch of shaded grass, where women sat and mothers watched their children. He didn't understand the game, but it was nice to watch it, although the players on both teams seemed always excited and looked like they were going to fight each other any minute. He hoped there wouldn't be a fight, because once he had stopped to watch a ball game and a fight had started, and darned if he hadn't got punched in the eye.

Peter watched the game, half asleep on his feet. He saw the pitcher wind up. He saw the batter swing, too soon, and drive a vicious curving foul over the heads of the crowd by third base. He heard a frantic feminine shriek, and saw people rushing toward the place where the ball had landed on the stretch of grass. He rushed also, and milled in a crowd around a mother who moaned and yelled hysterically over a two-year-old baby that had been struck in the head by the batted ball.

People shouted to give them air. The mother's wails continued. No one knew what to do. Finally, a park policeman elbowed his way through the crowd and assumed control. Then someone fetched a doctor. Peter heard a man in front of him say that the baby had been killed instantly. The mother wailed, as Peter edged out of the crowd and walked away.

He walked very slowly. He was weak with horror. He did not know what to say or think. He attempted to figure out who was to blame, because if he could figure out somebody to blame for the accident, then he would know what to think about it, and he would feel less horrified. He walked on in a semi-stupor. He tried to eradicate the occurrence from his memory, but it bobbed back, anchored in his mind like an obsession.

He sat down on a bench beside an old codger. He was impelled to tell someone about it, so he described the death and the scene to the old codger, his language confused and unclear. When he had finished, he was relieved. The old codger, losing his temper, declared that the baby's mother should be put in the penitentiary. They talked, and the codger insisted, at great length and with many reiterations, that the cause of such things was the modern age.

Peter nodded. They sat there on the bench, silent, talked out. Peter finally remarked that it was a nice day. The old codger yepped agreement. Peter re-affirmed that it was a nice day. The old codger assured Peter that it was certainly a nice day, and added that he sure hoped it wouldn't rain. Peter also hoped that it wouldn't rain. The old codger reflected aloud that you never could tell about the weather. They sat silent. The old codger arose and hobbled off.

Peter sat. Again the memory of the accident bobbed up. He sat in a daze, watching the people file past him. If he just sat there and watched the people going by, he could forget about the baby.

A pigeon waddled close to his feet. He whistled and the bird drew closer. But he had no food for it, so it flew off. He sat and trembled, again remembering how the baby had been killed, almost before his very eyes. The wind in the trees behind him was again sad and disturbing. The thought of death forced itself upon him. Almost inarticulately, he felt that his life was drying up, that he was slowly dropping away like a leaf drifting from an autumn tree. People strolled on the gravel path before him. Girls, young and disquietingly attractive, lookers, passed by him. He slipped into a state of semi-dozing, and the horror of death lost all its pronged sharpness, becoming an undefined and wordless melancholy. Surprised, he blinked his eyes, and sat erect, and for a moment the park sounds, and the people and the panorama before him were like novelties unexpectedly dropped before the attention. He heard the wind again in the trees behind him. He could not stand to hear it. He arose and walked on, away from the wind.

The wind and that baby! Terrible. He walked more swiftly. An untidy woman, with a bag of peanuts in her hands, was feeding the pigeons. He laughed, hearing her coo at the birds. She was not all there, he felt. He paused to watch a squirrel shying through the bushes. A black bird, slim and sleek as a well-dressed girl, moved close to his feet.

He told himself that nature and trees and birds were all nice, and sort of haunted with something, something mysterious. And the sun was like that, too; it was warmer when he had started out. It had boiled down on his face.

It would be nice if he could forget that baby, but he kept remembering. He walked. The grass was crowded with colors, tenderly refined, softly blending, glad colors. He walked.

Skirting the far corner of the park, down near the end of the golf course, he heard a screech of motor brakes. The sharp, rending echoes sounded like the wail of a mortally injured dog. He became convinced that they were the agonized, ebbing cries of some dog that had been run over. He hurried forward to see the dying dog. He cursed an unknown motorist for having murdered it. He knew that when he saw the dog, bleeding, perhaps already dead, he would feel nauseated. But he ran on. He stopped at the crossing just outside the park. He saw only the ceaseless stream of tangling Sunday traffic. He breathed in relief. It had been only an automobile after all.

He walked along a quiet street, flanked with suburban cottages and large, pastry-like apartment buildings. He paused to look at the geegawed cornices. He wished that he could live in a beautiful building like one of these. He looked at the parked automobiles lining the curb. It would be nice to own one of them, all right. And one of these houses with a lawn, too, so that he could water it at night in his shirt sleeves.

He reached Seventy-first Street. It was lined with stores, and the railroad tracks ran down the center of the street. Across from him, between the parallel tracks, was the long platform of the Bryn Mawr station. The scene looked like one on the main street of a small town. He stood in front of a chain drug store, watching the people eddy around him.

Dinging bells announced the approach of a train. The safety gates were lowered, and automobiles, with sharp soundings and gratings of brakes, halted before the gates. Their horns and klaxons racketed. The warning bells dinged on. The electric train grunted into the station.

This noise and confusion seemed to numb Peter's nerve centers. He stood like one paralyzed, his mouth jarred open, his eyes fixed in an immobile and fearful stare. The suburban train passed, and the gates gradually lifted. Automobile traffic was resumed. Like a man awakening from sleep, he regained his equilibrium. He stood looking at the people on the sidewalk. Gee, he had been scared. Golly! Holy Moses!

He wandered along Seventy-first Street, gaping at the contents of the store windows. He surveyed the sky. He listened before a street radio to a broadcast of a baseball game and heard the announcer describe a home run by Hack Wilson, of the Chicago Cubs, in flowery language. He moved back westward and stood mopishly before the operatic entrance of a neighborhood motion picture theater, where blaring electric bulbs and melodramatic posters announced Dennis King in *The Vagabond King*.

Should he see the show? It would cost forty cents. Could he afford it? He wondered and debated with himself. He walked away from the theater, and on down several blocks, still fighting with the temptation to spend forty cents, fingering the silver in his pocket. He returned to look at the theater posters. On a quick resolve, he purchased a ticket and slunk into the show.

When he entered the sky was clear and blue, and the sun was shining. He sat in the pitch darkness of a poorly ventilated building, seeing romance leap, sing, and bluster across a sheet of cloth. When he came out, it was dark and a trifle cool. He rode home to his mother on the trolley car, thinking of the picture he had seen. He thought of what he'd tell Charley about it. And that song, *Only A Rose*. Across from him sat a girl, her legs crossed. He became interested. He saw so much that he rode several blocks past his corner.

1930.

Well, That's That

I

MIKE sat by the low desk in the center of the large, oval, many-windowed filling station. Outside, on Marquette Road, the automobiles whizzed by, and at the corner trolley cars rattled and rumbled. He opened his lunch package, pulled the cap from a pint bottle of milk, and spread a newspaper out before him. He bit into a jelly sandwich, took a swallow of milk, and read a few lines of the newspaper account of the trial of Gerald M. Upton, chairman of the board of directors of the Upton Oil and Refining Company, who was being prosecuted for the bribery of public officials and contempt of the Senate Investigation Committee which had uncovered this bribery. He shrugged his shoulders, and asked himself what was the difference between himself, an Upton employee who made extra dividends by short-measuring the customers on the gasoline pumps, and Gerald M. Upton who pulled the same kind of stunts, only on a grand scale. That was one they could ask Mr. North, Superintendent of Service Stations, at the next sales meeting for service station salesmen. He laughed ironically, imagining himself asking that one. He remembered the last meeting. Mr. North had exhorted them to work in the interest of the company, and he had threatened that, if the attendants continued sitting down while on duty, he would take all the chairs out of the service stations. Mike could see himself not sitting down to eat his supper. He could see himself turning the station into a palace by polishing the bricks on the outside of the station with a sandwich between his teeth. And then, receiving a note from Mr. North, telling him that he had *ambition*. It was B. S. Life was pretty much of that, and the idea was to get what you could out of everything. That was what fellows like Upton did. Why shouldn't he model himself after the big boss of the outfit?

He munched at his sandwich. Outside, the day was imperceptibly fading, and the twilight shadings from the sun were running and spreading over the sky like dissolving colors. From the street, the succession of traffic noises was almost steady. He liked this hour on the job, because he could sit back like a man of leisure and take his time about eating, and have few worries about any rush at the pumps. There was almost nothing to do now, and there would be little doing until about seven-thirty. That was, unless some motorist came in for a crankcase drain. Well, if he did, send him down the line to the Nation Oil station. He laughed at this idea. Thinking of it had an aspect of bravado to it that pleased him. He finished the remains of his supper, and hastily read items from the newspaper. He did not care much about what went on as long as he got his. Let them have their trials, and conferences and treaties over in Europe. He was only interested in one thing, in getting his, and if anybody asked his private opinion, he would answer that the fellows who ran the show, like Upton, were interested in that very same thing. And something he would like to get would be that telephone operator that he kidded with on the phone all the time. He wished that today was not her day off so that he could talk with her now. He was curious about her looks, and wondered if she was as sweet as she sounded, and if she would be as easy to make as she pretended to be with all that hot suggestive talk of hers over the wire. But she had not kept the date she had made with him last week, and her excuse for breaking it had sounded to him like a lot of bubbling soft soap.

He placed his newspaper back in the desk drawer, crushed his lunch paper into a wad, and carried it and the emptied milk bottle to the small station lavatory. He dropped the paper in the waste-basket, washed out the bottle and laid it under the sink, and looked at his thin, pointed face in the mirror. He took his uniform cap off and looked at himself. He guessed that the telephone operator could not complain about him. He had sufficient looks. He yawned, and wondered how he could pass the time until the rush of business started after the supper hour. Of course, he could find plenty of cleaning and polishing to do, and all the bosses would appreciate that, but work interfered with his digestion, and he told himself that a man was only as good as his digestion. He emerged from the station lavatory.

II

She stood in the doorway, with a weak grin on her pimply face. She was fat, and her figure made her look almost like a human rubber ball. Her shoddy blue dress was splotched with dust, and there was an embarrassing grease spot on it, just below the stomach. She wore a crushed straw hat, which was out of shape, and dish-watery blonde hair escaped from under it. There were runs in the stockings covering her pipe-organ legs, and her garters did not perform their function satisfactorily. She carried a bundle of magazines under her left arm. Recovering from his surprise at seeing her in the doorway, Mike wondered if she would be easy pickings. She looked to him like a bum, not very appetizing. But he realized that he had been celibate for over a month, and that was what they called a long, long time. And could he take a chance in the station? If he was caught, it was the air, and his job was a pretty soft one.

"What do I get if I take a subscription?" he asked, as she timidly advanced toward the desk.

"You get the magazine at a bargain price," she answered in a dull and unsalesmanlike voice.

"Is that all?" he leered.

"Huh?"

"Hell, I don't want those magazines. They're no good," he said, energetically striving to think up a snappy remark.

She humped her shoulders, and her face saddened with a forlorn and defeated expression. She grinned weakly, and turned away from him, toward the door.

"Wait a minute. Why all the rush? There's no fire down the street," he said.

WELL, THAT'S THAT

She turned around to face him, hoping.

"I got to sell some magazines, because I ain't sold many, and well, a person has got to eat and pay her rent."

"All right. That's the problem that we all have to face . . . but I might manage to buy some magazines . . . well, if I was to get something for them, you know . . . a premium."

She seemed puzzled.

"Yes, you might just add something else to make it a bargain," he said, his glance an innuendo.

"Aw, Mister, go ahead and take a subscription. Honest, I ain't sold many today, and I got to eat tonight. Honest!"

"Well, it all depends. I don't want the magazines, and haven't time to read them. I get all the reading I want out of *The Argosy Magazine*, and my old man always buys that like it was his religion. There's no use in paying for something you don't want, or can't use, is there? This world, like my great grand uncle's ninth cousin used to tell me, this world is just not run on a charity basis. Not anyway in this, the year nineteen hundred and twenty-five," Mike said, pleased with his own spontaneous cleverness.

"Go ahead, Mister. You can give them to your mother or sister, or your girl."

"Haven't got them kind of animals. But I was just thinking, before you came around, how nice it would be to have a girl come around, and then you came like the answer to my dreams."

"Go ahead, Mister, be a sport," she pleaded with seeming sincerity.

"Well, let me have a squint at the stuff," he said, after they had faced each other for a silent minute.

She laid a magazine on the desk. It was a copy of a national weekly which contained press summaries of world events. On the cover, there was a reproduction of a painting done by a well-known American artist, who always had fish in his pictures.

"Now this magazine. There's the name of it on the cover. It has all the news of the world in it, everything what everybody's reading, and thinking, and talking about, and we have a special and unusual subscription offer on it, and any one of this list of magazines, that everybody reads, and if you subscribe you'll save yourself two dollars and fifty cents."

Not listening to her, he perused the magazine. He got excited, and he did not know what he was reading. He dropped the copy on the desk, and clumsily ran his hand down her fleshy thigh. She attempted to retreat, but he held her arm and pressed himself against her.

"I don't like the magazines, but there is something that I do like," he said, squeezing her broad buttocks.

"That's not nice or right," she said, dully.

"Sister, it's the only thing in the world that is . . . nice or right," he said huskily.

His compunctions because of the great visibility of the station were completely forgotten. He laid his hand against her sagging left breast.

"Don't!" she said with little determination.

"Why?"

"I don't like that."

"Don't try and spoof me, girlie. There's plenty better than you that couldn't do that!"

He stepped back from her, and tried magnetizing her with a concentrated gaze.

"Really, I ain't that kind. . . . Aw, Mister, honest, I ain't got any place to sleep. My landlady, she kicked me out today, and honest and truly, I got to sell some subscriptions, and get a place to sleep, and eat," she said in a voice of entreaty.

"Well, I *will*, but I got to get something else . . . a little premium."

"That's what all you gas men say."

"I thought you said you didn't do it?" he said roughly.

"I don't," she said in that persistently dull manner of hers.

"Then what did you say about gas men?" he continued bullyingly.

"I said that's what all you gas men want."

"What's your name?" he asked, changing his tack.

"Gloria."

"Just like Gloria Swanson. And just as pretty," he said, causing her to wince.

He took out a package of cigarettes from his overall breast pocket, and lit one. It was against the rules to smoke on the station grounds, and lighting his cigarette he feared lest he be seen by a spotter. But he figured that you had to take some chances on the job.

"Where do you hail from?" he asked, after inhaling.

"Kansas City."

"It's dangerous for girls to be such a long way from home," he said. She lifted her eyebrows in an expression of mild bewilderment.

"How come you're here in Chicago?"

"I thought maybe I would get a job."

"And this is the job you got," he said ironically.

"Well, I had a job in a bag factory down near Thirty-fifth Street, but I was laid off, and with not so much business in the summer time there's lots of girls looking for jobs, and I didn't get another. So I took this, because everybody has to eat," she answered, holding out a magazine, pleading with him with her watery, grayish eyes. He acted as if he were thinking.

"Sell many of them?"

"I ain't sold one all afternoon. But some days I do better than others. One day last week, I made two dollars and twenty cents."

"If you won't give any premium, how can you expect to sell many?"

He pulled a roll of bills, kept for change, from his overall pocket. He held them before her, and she looked at them as if she never in her life had seen as much money. He stuck the money back in his pocket.

"Come on, baby, quit the stalling and let's get down to business," he said, touching her breasts.

"Somebody would catch us here," she said.

"There's a little side room here," he said, pointing back to his right at a green-painted door.

"But somebody might come in here . . . and anyway, I'm not that kind."

"Don't string me. If you want your subscription, you got to come across," he said in a hard, wise-guy manner.

"I don't usually let anyone do that to me . . . but if I did, it would be to please you because you were being a nice gentleman and taking a subscription off of me."

"Now you're talking particulars. Come on, Glorious, and if you give me a nice premium, I might buy a subscription."

He led her by the elbow to the room. She stood hesitantly at the door, and he pulled her in roughly. It was a cramped hole, with an air compressor usurping most of the space, a shelf of cans, form books and supplies, a bulky oil barrel, and hooks on which there hung overalls, a straw hat, and a clean blue broadcloth shirt. He kissed her greedily.

"Don't! Please. . . ."

He quaked, hearing a motor horn on the driveway. He told her to wait there, and rushed out. There was an automobile beside one of the pump islands, and the driver stood by the red-painted Wayne pump. It was a regular customer, and Mike was relieved. He serviced the car with five gallons of gasoline, and was glad that no motor oil was needed. He watched the car drive out of the station, and turned back inside. She was emerging from the room, but was docile when he pushed her back and closed the door.

"Baby!" he said with gusto.

"Please, don't do that. . . ."

III

She stood by the station desk, and told Mike that he was a nicer fellow than most of the gas station men around the city, and she liked him. She held her magazines out before her, and asked which ones he wanted the subscription for. He answered that he would have to decide, and since he would be getting busy any moment, she should go off and come back at about eleven-thirty.

"But you told me you would, and gee, please," she said, disappointed.

"I will. I'm telling you come back. When I close up tonight, we'll have some fun. I'll even buy you a meal."

"You mean it?"

"I shoot square. But listen, it's dangerous for me to have you in from now on until about eleven-thirty. A spotter or my boss might go by and see you in here, and it's against the rules. You come back at eleven-thirty."

"Honest?"

"Yes," he said anxiously.

She laid her magazines on the desk, and with her back to him, bent down on one knee to tie her shoe. He saw the sole of her right shoe, worn through with a hole almost as large as a quarter. A round patch of dirty foot was visible. She arose and took her magazines. She grinned, and tramped slowly out of the station.

Not long after she left the cars started coming into the station, and Mike had to hop, servicing them. Until ten-thirty he had hardly an opportunity to pause from his work. Then the cars became less frequent.

Joe drove in, bought five gallons of gasoline, and parked his car along a side edge of the driveway. He entered the station to chat with Mike. Joe was a salesman, and always bought his gasoline from Mike. He liked to hang around late in the evening and talk with the attendants. He was thin, with a narrow face, bushy black eyebrows, and beady eyes.

"A bum came around peddling magazines tonight, just at supper time, and I slipped the blocks to her. But she wasn't anything to write home about," Mike said.

"What was she, just one of that abnormal kind that flops for anything in pants?"

"If she was normal, I'd hate to see the kind you'd call abnormal. And she must have been the sweetheart of the marine corps. She's like all these gals that come around selling magazines and such things. If she wasn't a bum she would be doing something better. Those broads are just tramps. But boy, the tough luck stories they dish out. It just rolls off their tongue by the yard. And they don't care. It just doesn't mean anything to them. Like a hardened whore, it's nothing more than combing their hair or something like that."

"You say she wasn't much good?"

"Oh, merely so-so. I was hard up," Mike said casually.

"Usually, the bums you pick up are like that. They had so much practice at it that it's second nature and nothing excites them."

"You're wrong there, Joe. Promise them a square meal or rub a dollar under their nose, and see how excited they get."

"They're all alike, the bums. That's why I've been thinking of getting me a decent clean girl and marrying her."

"I want more of my fling before I'm ready to say 'Let the wedding bells ring merrily'," Mike said.

"The bums are pretty maggoty, but a jane is a jane, and for the grand old purpose, they're all the same. That's poetry," Joe said.

"Say, that bum I just spoke about, she might come back. I hope not. Once you get one of them on your neck, they hang like a clinging vine."

"Listen, if she comes back, and you want to get rid of her, let me handle it. I can handle that type. I'll have her wishing she had wings so she could get out of here faster than walking," Joe said.

About eleven-thirty the girl limped into the station. She smiled, and sat in the chair by the desk. Mike watched her, thinking that she had nerve acting like she was at home. He fretted lest a spotter go by, because with her in the chair there, it looked like hell. He studied her dirty face, her unshined shoes, her stockings with runs in them, her dress, and he wondered why such a pig could have ever made him anxious and led him to risk his job.

"Is he going to come along to our party?" she asked.

Mike frowned, sore at the way she was assuming.

"That's the one, Mr. Malloy," he told Joe.

Joe nodded knowingly, and looked up and down at the girl, critical. An automobile rolled into the station and Mike hastened to the pump island. Turning the pump handle, he saw Joe speak to her, saw her turn into an almost motionless statue of fear. He drained the pump hose into the gasoline tank and collected. He watched the car drive off, and looked at the object in his right hand. It was the cap of the gasoline tank. He had forgotten to screw it back on. Damn her, she was causing him to forget about his business. He entered the station, just as she scurried out the side door on the right, like a frightened animal.

"She won't be back," Joe said with assurance.

"Glad it worked. She had me worried. You know, if one of my bosses saw me having a thing like her hang around my station—well, that would be my can. I even forgot to put the cap back on the tank on that car. I'm glad it worked. I was plenty hard up or I sure would never have bothered with her," he said, putting the cap in a desk drawer.

"I told her that I was from headquarters, and that I'd been hearing a lot about girls using the magazine racket to solicit, and that we were cleaning up all hustling. I told her she'd better beat it while she had a chance, and that I was going to watch along the line here to see that she didn't come back. If she did, I told her we'd have to take her into the station and book her. You should have seen her. She turned white," Joe said, both of them smiling with gratification.

"Good . . . and now, if I only don't get burned," Mike said.

"Hell, Mike, don't let that worry you. It's no worse than a bad cold. It's something in every young man's life," Joe said.

They laughed, and lit cigarettes.

"I wonder what kind of lives broads like her live? You know, some of them go around from town to town, selling magazines, and I wonder?"

"They're bums. They come around here with their rackets every day in the week."

"I know, I was only just wondering."

"Well, I'm rid of one more pig," Mike said.

"Yes, and even if I do say so myself, I think I managed her pretty smart," Joe said.

"Well, that's that, and now I got to get ready to close up. I don't want to give old Upton one minute more of my precious time than I have to. I want to get closed up right on the dot," Mike said.

IV

A stout girl, in a dusty dark dress, sat on the park bench. The night was soft and calm, but damp with the misting, falling dew, and there was a low mournfulness in the wind that stirred the trees surrounding her. She shivered slightly, yawned, untied her shoes, and pulled them off to shake the gravel out of them. She took the worn cardboard, used to protect the sole, from the right shoe, and dropped it beside her. She placed her finger through the hole in the shoe. She stuck her feet back into the shoes, and in tying the left one, the lace broke, and she had to knot the broken lace. She placed a bundle of magazines at one end of the bench. She shivered. She scratched herself, and rolled and twisted her back and shoulders because of itching dirtiness. She lay down, using the magazines as a pillow. The evening was soft and calm, but damp with the misting, falling dew. The wind, disturbing the branches in the trees surrounding her, sighed in a low and persistent mournfulness.

1930.

Meet the Girls!

This inhuman world of pleasure.
MARCEL PROUST

I

DOLLY had rented a room in a cheap hotel at Fifty-third and Lake Park Avenue. Now it was messy like disordered intestines, and impregnated with stale gin odors. The carpet was mean and worn. The walls glared a poisonous green. Gin bottles, stale food crumbs, empty and broken glasses, cigarette butts, and odds and ends of feminine apparel were scattered helter-skelter. In one corner was a plate with the crusted leavings of spaghetti and a bed pan.

Spread out on the bed, Dolly looked blown and old. Her hair straggled over her swollen blob of a face. Bulgy sacks hung beneath her closed eyes. Her mouth was opened, exposing toothless gums, and a sick, purplish and yellow-green tongue. Her legs were fan-wise, and her dark green dress, torn and stained, was curled up above her abdomen. Her stomach was swollen out, creating a false effect of pregnancy. She was sleeping off a week's drunk.

Lillian and Marie were slobbering and sobbing on chairs, crossing and uncrossing their legs. Their faces seemed vague, like hastily washed-in effects on a modernistic painting. Beneath their glazed eyes, tear stains had channeled through thick layers of powder.

"Poor Dolly!" Lillian gurgled, shoving back a falling mess of marcelled blonde hair.

"Poor Dolly!" her sister, Marie, said.

"My poor-r fren Dolly!" Lillian sobbed.

"My poor-r dear fren, Dolly!" Marie sobbed.

"Poor Dolly!" Lillian gushed.

"Poor Dolly!" Marie gushed.

Marie arose, and staggered to her sister. She cried, sinking her head in Lillian's lap. With Lillian sitting, and Marie kneeling before her, they were like broken statues. Suddenly, Lillian shrilly repeated a smutty joke, and they tittered into laughter. They began to cry.

Lillian interrupted their tearful orgy to stutter that Dolly had been a fine girl in her younger days. Her sister offered profane agreement. They informed each other that Dolly's uncle, Paul, had been the cause of poor Dolly's downfall. He was a mean man, they simultaneously exclaimed. Lillian shrieked in her sorrow for Dolly. Marie warned her that it was unbecoming for a lady to raise her voice.

Lillian arose, and stood wavering. In a serio-comic voice, she declared that it was unbecoming of a lady to holler, and she added that she was . . . a lady.

"We're all ladies!" Marie exclaimed.

"Yes . . . we're . . . all . . . ladies."

"I'm a lady . . . you're a lady . . . Dolly's **a lady** . . . we're all ladies!" Marie monotoned.

Lillian staggered to the side of her sister's chair, and laid a thick arm around Marie's equally thick neck. In soothing baby-talk, she asked Marie what was the matter, and Marie said that she was crying because they were all ladies. Lillian pondered, and agreed that they were ladies.

Marie said that Bill Van Dye always told her that she was a lady, and Bill ought to know, because Bill was a smart man . . . and rich.

"Marie, Hon! Why, Marie! Marie! Marie, darling, everybody knows that you're a lady."

Marie arose and faced her sister.

"Lil, dear! You know. You're my sister. You know. You're my sister. Blood's thicker than . . . thickerthan . . . thickerthan . . . thickerthan . . . thickertha. . . ."

Marie tumbled. Lillian plunged to assist her. She sprawled ungraciously on top of Marie. They slowly untangled themselves, and tediously won their way to standing postures. Dolly's body twitched. She groaned.

"Poor Dolly!" Lillian sighed.

"Poor Dolly!" Marie sighed.

Grief-stricken for poor Dolly, they drank glasses of gin. Marie talked of how Bill Van Dye had always told her that she was beautiful, and that her body was very, very beautiful. Her body was just B. U. tiful, and she was B. U. tiful. You couldn't hardly find a woman over forty with a body like hers. You could scarcely find a woman over or under forty with a body like hers, because she was simply B. U. tiful.

She screamed that she was ready to prove that she was beautiful, and tore her clothes off. She stood, Eve-like, in the center of the room, posing at *graceful* nakedness. She was flabby and fleshly. Her breasts sagged, her hips were wide, and her thighs were chunky meaty slabs. The effect of her figure was matched by her slow-wrinkling face. She twisted about in various postures, and insistently muttered that she was beautiful. She stood as erect as her condition permitted, and shrilled that artists would commit murder to secure her as a model for their beautiful portraits. She was so beautiful now that it was impossible to imagine how dazzling she had been in her youth. She adopted another forced pose, and said that she would make a beautiful model for a statue of *Eternal Youth and Undying Love*.

Lillian agreed that Marie owned the most beautifullest body in the whole, whole, entire world. She added that her own body was beautiful too. She disrobed. Her breasts hung like well-worn bedroom slippers, her hips approached enormity, and she bore discolorations from childbirth.

They faced each other sobbing, and toasted their beautiful bodies.

Lillian recollected that ladies should not expose themselves. They replaced their clothing in careless haste. Marie spoke of all the men who had loved her, declaring that she could write a heart-rending poem about the men who had adored her and her beautiful body. And they had all been men of . . . means.

They drank again.

"I'm a los' soul. I'm a los' soul. I'm a los' soul!"

Lillian strove to console her by repeating that she was not a lost soul, but a great woman.

"I'm a los' soul . . . A los' soul!"

They drank again.

"Lil, do you believe in God? Hon, Lil, Sister, darling . . . do you . . . believe . . . in God?"

Lillian said that she believed in God, and that God had pity on poor sinners, and that He sent no one to Hell. God was a great comfort to her, and those times when her children had died at birth, she would have gone out of her mind, only for God.

"Well, I don't! I don't! I don't believe in God! I'm a los' soul!" Marie said, interrupting her sister.

In tears, Marie stuttered that she was a loster soul than any lost soul in the whole, whole, entire world. Lillian corrected Marie's grammar, declaring that most lost was proper. Marie insisted on her usage, adding that of all the lost souls in the world, she was the lostest. Lillian insisted that Marie should call herself the most lost soul in the whole, whole, entire world. Lillian stared at her sister, shook her head in a gesture of sorrow, and said that Marie wouldn't be the most lost soul in the whole, whole world, if she had not been proud and turned her back on God. Marie called Lillian unintellectual. Unintellectual people always believed in God because fear and trembling was in their bones.

Lillian denied that she was afraid, and said that she believed in God because she loved Him, and because He was so good and kind to her. God alone understood her poor damned soul. God alone was a comfort and a consolation to her. And because God alone was good and consoling to her, she would some day do the right thing by Him, and join the Church, and be a Catholic like Dolly was.

Marie laughed raucously and drank half a glass of gin. She glared at her sister, and called her a coward. Lillian frowned back. A groan from Dolly distracted them from their sisterliness.

II

Dolly gazed stupid-eyed about the room. She muttered indistinctly. She struggled upward and sat on the edge of the bed. She looked about her, and saw nothing. The girls rushed to her, and slobbered that they were her best friends, and loved her. Marie said she loved her with such intensity that only death could cleave their love. Lillian asked her if she wanted anything. Dolly sat unsteadily, too sodden to speak. She pushed her hand out for something, like a wordless infant. Lillian stuck a cigarette in Dolly's mouth, and Marie lit it. Ashes slithered down on Dolly's dress. Marie brushed them off, leaving a grayish streak on the dress. Hot ashes dropped again, and burned a hole in Dolly's dress. She sat stupidly. She stood up, and listed, too helpless to maneuver about by herself. She tumbled backward and Marie caught her. They sat her on the bed.

"What can we do with her?" asked Marie.

"Poor-r Dolly!" Lillian sighed.

"Poor-r Dolly!" Marie sighed.

Tears came. They drank.

Dolly retched, and Marie suddenly leaped aside to escape from the belch. She carelessly wiped up the mess with an old towel, and hastily wiped off Dolly's dress. Lillian slammed a wet washrag across Dolly's face. They sat Dolly up straight and Lillian supported her so that she would not reel. They debated whether or not they should give her a drink, and Marie poured gin out for herself and Lillian. They continued debating. Marie kissed Dolly, murmuring that she was poor Dolly's best friend. Lillian arose. Dolly lurched forward, toppled sidewise, and swung back, her head narrowly missing the bed post.

"Gimme drink!" she mumbled.

With hesitation, Marie placed in Dolly's shaky hand a glass with a small thimble of gin in it. Dolly gulped it down.

"Now Dolly, you got to come out of it. You're too fine a girl to go on like this. You are. S'finest girl I ever known. S'best fren I ever had," Marie told the unhearing Dolly.

Lillian warmly avowed her high respect and friendship for Dolly, and said that they all three were going to sober up now. Dolly stuttered for another drink. She had to have it, because she was an object of Sorrow. Drink was in her blood, and she couldn't help it. She wanted a drink.

Marie cogitated, studying the gin bottle. There was about one last drink in it. She decided that she might as well have it for herself. She drained the bottle.

Dolly gazed at her friends like a hungry, half-frozen cur dog begging for food. She spoke of her great sorrow, and they all cried. They told her how sad her life was, how sad all their lives were.

While the tears slowly ran dry, Dolly explained how she had known millionaires, more millionaires than she could count on her fingers. She attempted to drink gin from her emptied glass, and said that she was going to write a book some day. It would be *Millionaires That Have Known and Loved Me,* by Dolly O'Leary.

"Les' all write a book," Lillian volunteered.

"About los' souls that haven't any God," Marie added.

They quarrelled over God. Dolly averred her belief in God. All three of them expressed their opinions in concert. Then Dolly announced her disbelief in any God. She cried, stating that God wouldn't punish pitiful sinners like herself. But it all didn't matter. Living was hell. She was going to write a book about her sad life, and about millionaires who had loved her.

"Well, can't we all write a book about los' souls? We're all los' souls, aren't we?" Marie asked.

"Los' souls. I'm a los' soul . . . I'm a los' soul. My life has been the saddest life in all the worl'. A Los' Soul . . . And I was a good girull once," Dolly drooled.

"Dolly, you're still a fine girulll," Lillian said.

"I was, but I didn't have a chance. When I was a little tot of ten years, my father and that ole she bitch of an uncle, Paul, they beat me. And I was only a poor little girull. I never had a chance. A los' soul. Oh, if the worl' only knew. If it only knew," she said lachrymosely.

The three girls sat on the floor in a circle, suspiring over their lost souls.

III

Dolly O'Leary was nearing her forty-third birthday. She had worked for a number of years in the real estate business, where she had established a reputation as an efficient sales woman . . . when she was not on one of her periodic drinking bouts. Whenever she did commence drinking, she was just as likely to be drunk for two or three months as she was for an evening. She had lost or quit job after job, destroying one profitable connection after another, until, shortly after her fortieth birthday, she had ceased working entirely. She descended from lower class Irish Catholic stock, and her family had slowly struggled upward to a safe and comfortable level of existence. Now, her family was all dead, except for her uncle Paul, with whom she had lived since her parents had died in her twenty-fourth year.

Paul was a quiet-living, retiring man, a superintendent in a local chain-store corporation. He had always liked his niece. However, her drinking had melted that fondness into a patient weariness. Now he put up with her only because his sense of duty and his conscience forced him to. He was a scrupulously religious Catholic, who attended mass regularly, defended the Church in all public discussion with business friends, contributed liberally to the support of his pastor and to all collections, said his prayers daily and devotedly, and received the Sacraments on Christmas and Easter Sunday. His Christianity demanded that he suffer Dolly's eccentricities and vices, and it furnished him with the faith and the conviction that eventually, through the mercy of God, she would go straight. He desired from life, principally, an undisturbed comfort. He wanted to dream and doze away his many idle moments, to forget all the stains and emptinesses of living in a sleepy perusal of newspapers, the comic strips being his especial favorites. He yearned to sink into static obliviousness, listening to the songs of yesterday, to Dan and Sylvia on the radio, and to Father Coughlin's broadcasts. At the core of his mental and emotional life was that nostalgia which turns the attention backward, magnifies the hopes and joys of yesterday, and asks only that tomorrow's benefactions be repetitions or shadows of yesterday's. He was a living corpse, mentally and emotionally sealed, quietly snoring through the last of his allotted days. He had always dreamed of a home, but had never happened to marry. And after the death of Dolly's parents, he had hoped that she, until she should marry, would make a home for him. As the years had dragged out, and she had failed to marry, he hoped and yearned for domesticity with increasing intensity. But Dolly had her work, her hysterias of self-pity and her drinking bouts. Between times she served as an excellent housekeeper and cook, and occasionally, she prepared Sunday dinners and arranged programmes of Sunday enjoyment which he could never forget; and which he turned and turned over in reverie, seeking to catch wisps and straws of their vanished and easy contentment. Belching down upon these rare days were those others, when Dolly was drunk and screaming her sorrow to the neighborhood, striding about the apartment in tears, cursing the world in general, and him in particular.

In her earlier years, Dolly had been a distinguished-looking and attractive woman. Her first sex experience had come at the age of thirteen, when she had seduced the boy next door to her in a wagon out in the alley. This had been followed by a long and regular series of boys and men. When she had matured and had achieved a minor success in the real estate business, she had affairs with men of means, and became the mistress of a succession of well-to-do business men. She had had three paramours, in particular, who were extremely rich; one had been a millionaire. She had played them all simultaneously without ever having gotten tripped up. One died; a second disappeared; the third, S. T. Hayden, the millionaire, had abandoned her. There had been others, men who accepted seduction as an inducement to buy worthless suburban lots, stray good-time Charlies, even occasional plumbers and peddlers. But Hayden had been the one man whom she had actually loved. His money had come suddenly and luckily through the ownership of lands on which oil was discovered. She had met him while he was seeking to buy property on which he intended to build a home for his wife and family. They went to dinner and shows together, and she became his mistress. He had recompensed her well for her body, giving her money, expensive clothes, good times; but after she had passed the thirty-three mark, he tired; he searched for younger flesh. She still spoke of him as her sweetheart. Regularly she phoned the downtown hotel where he had formerly registered; but she was never able to talk with him. His home was now in California, and she wrote him letters in a business code. He never replied. He had dropped her. For a few years, following his desertion, she had drunk more heavily, and had slept with almost any man who had asked her. Then, her sexual life had gradually frozen up, and she had remained sober for three years. One day she had casually met an old friend, and they had dined together. He offered her a glass of Scotch, and that had set her off. She resumed her drinking, but her sex life remained meager and sporadic. The lessening of sex and passion drove her into wilder and more extended periods of drunkenness. Her persecution obsession magnified, and she drank to curse the world. She became a public nuisance.

Dolly, Marie, and Lillian had been playmates for years. They had become acquainted at a party at De Jonghe's when it had been a popular place. The sisters came from a large family living in a jerkwater Michigan town. Following the death of their parents, the family had split up. Three of the girls, Marie, Lillian, and Joan, came to Chicago.

They were good-looking girls, and did not care for grinding work. They found that they had something to sell, and each of them was smart enough to get attached to a man of sufficient income. Joan roped in a promising young architect, and drank him under the earth. She had drunk his two successors into the same condition, and she was now in California with a fourth husband, similarly tagging him for the undertaker. Men came easily to Marie, and from each she secured money, clothes, apartments, ocean voyages, stocks and bonds. She was now well off in her own name and liberally provided for by her latest man, a rich sportsman named Bill Van Dye. Lillian had finally married a building contractor with a prosperous business. She had had three still-born children, and the last birth had driven her to vigorous drinking. The sisters had become indispensable to Dolly, both as companions and as an audience. They had quickened her obsessions of self-pity, and they encouraged her when she symbolized her resentment of a cruel world in her hatred of her uncle. They were all idle women with nothing to do; and they were now too old for promiscuous man-hunting. They drank. Paul frowned on this, and on Dolly's girl friends; but he was powerless. Whenever the girls were arrested, he bailed them out. When they were broke, he was tapped for money. To them, he was a chump. They welcomed Dolly's protests against him, and her tearful descriptions of how he had ruined her life. Paul prayed to the good God that this intolerable situation would be altered, but the ways of the good God are not the ways of men, and God's will was done. Their small apartment was a miserable prison, where the aging man and fattening woman each lived in walls of solitude and frustration.

IV

Dolly and the girls faced a critical situation; they had no more gin. They were broke, and they had gotten credit from or defrauded every bootlegger or speakeasy proprietor whom they knew. Dolly was too drunk and dirty to go home and touch her uncle. They sat in Dolly's room, crying, nervously pacing the floor, striving to think. They made three vain sallies to nearby beer flats. They begged the hotel clerk. Finally, they wore themselves out and tumbled exhausted, three into the one soiled bed. Awake and sober with the sunny morning, they faced the gin problem afresh. Dolly slumped into a chair and thought. Marie dumped herself onto the bed, and lay there legs athwart, ready to wait until someone provided. They asked her about her bank account. She lied that she had none. Lillian lugged herself back and forth, double chin cupped in unwashed hands thinking, thinking. Dolly jerked to her feet and paced at Lillian's side. She paused to phone the downtown hotel where she hoped to find Hayden. The cold, official voice of a clerk informed her that he was not registered. She trod the floor and made other unsuccessful phone calls.

"Jee-zus. . . . I want a drink," Marie exclaimed, in exasperation.

"So do I. You know, whenever I'm sober, I think of my boys. You girls never had any, and you don't know what it can mean to carry a baby in your womb. It's different with you girls and your abortions. But when you get to expect the children and want them, and your mother's love comes welling up like a fountain, and it pays you for the labor pains that nearly crack your back, and then they're . . . born dead, it's different," Lillian said.

She paused to sob.

"I'm always seeing my boys. I see them and talk to them. That's why I know there's a God. It's because God will not make them suffer, and He'll keep them in Heaven, and maybe they'll ask God to let their mother in Heaven when she leaves this sad world. That's why I believe in God. And if they hadn't died, I'd never drink like I do."

"Jesus, I want a drink," Marie said, ignoring her sister's monologue.

Lillian wiped her tears away.

"I wonder if Kate Crowley would let me have something?" Dolly pondered aloud.

"Oh!" Lillian lugubriously sighed.

"Who's she?" Marie asked.

"She's a fat-ass cousin of mine," Dolly answered.

"Now I remember her, the fat bitch," Marie said.

Dolly telephoned her cousin, and received no answer. She hovered about the room, making liberal references to her cousin's buttocks.

"Oh!" Lillian sobbed.

Dolly developed an idea. They put on their hats and coats, and tramped down to Sixty-third Street, looking like three Limehouse apparitions. Dolly tackled the manager of a store under Paul's supervision, and borrowed five dollars. Then she visited a storekeeper who was a long-standing friend of her uncle's. While she talked with her uncle's friend, Lillian and Marie stood on a corner, sidling up to passing strangers and trying to beg or borrow money from them. Lillian would halt young girls whom she had never seen before and tell them:

"You're beautiful! You're so beautiful you should go to Hollywood."

But they begged in vain. Dolly was more successful. She told a very convincing story. A very dear friend of hers had just died and she was almost insane with grief. She had been so grief-stricken that she had walked the streets for two days, not knowing what she had said or done. She was nearly crazy and her nerves were so bad they jumped. She needed five dollars to straighten herself out and prepare for the funeral in the morning, and Paul was out of town on business. He hadn't sent her any money and she did not know what she would do. It was too late to go to the bank. She just had to have the money. She got it.

They were able to buy gin, to eat, and to return to the hotel in a taxicab. They were happy on Dolly's money.

V

Dolly was sobbing the blues. Marie was repeating that Bill would return to town soon, and she and Bill would be together. Lillian talked to the ghosts of her children as they played and giggled before her.

Dolly unexpectedly began vigorously lumbering about the hotel room. Then she flung herself on the bed, and gestured with her entire body.

"My life is ruined. . . . Ruined. . . . Ruined!" she wailed.

Marie patted her, soothed to her that it was not so, and that she would brace up and become the Dolly O'Leary of old.

"Ruined! And he did it, that sonofabitching uncle of mine who made me slave my life away as his housekeeper. Ruined."

Marie sympathized and kissed Dolly on the back of the neck. Lillian giggled with the ghosts of her children.

"What good is he? Jesus Christ, the men I knew who wanted to marry me could have bought and sold a piker like him ten times over, and done it, too, just like they were buying a box of cigars. The sonofabitch. . . . The . . . dirty . . . son . . . of . . . a . . . bitch!" Dolly screamed; she concentrated upon crying.

Marie offered Dolly a drink of gin. Dolly held the glass in her hand, and complained that while other girls were happy and lived on the fat of the land, here was she, an old woman, housekeeper for a mollycoddle who wasn't able to get himself a woman. She moaned. Then she drank her gin.

Lillian tucked her ghost children in bed, listened to their prayers, kissed them good night. She sat beside Dolly and motherly tried to assuage the grief which seemed to rip at Dolly's heartstrings. She tried to interrupt Dolly's flow of words to tell her that she should leave her uncle, go back to work, and get a place of her own.

Dolly moaned.

"I would never put up with such a man," Marie said warmly.

"It's a sin against God," Dolly said, emphasizing her words with another long groan.

"Dolly, why not get some nice man and marry him and have a home of your own and a little happiness, and tell that old-woman uncle of yours to lump it to hell," Lillian said.

"I can't now. I'm too old."

They argued the point, and Dolly continued to moan.

"Millionaires would have had me. Millionaires. I was a beautiful girull once. Why, Sheldon Kane, the millionaire, once told me; he tol' me, and he was a millionaire, he tol' me: 'Dolly, you're the beautifullest girull and the smartest girull I know.' And now . . . look at me!"

"Dolly, I always told you you were a fool, living with that mollycoddle," Marie said.

"It's a sin against God," Dolly asserted; she moaned.

"What kind of a bastard is he, to let you ruin your life?" Marie asked.

"You don't know that man. He's the walking image of Satan, he is," Dolly said.

She moaned, and they had a drink. They cried. Dolly talked of her tragic life. Lillian kissed her sleeping ghost children, and drowsed over their cute curly locks. Marie stretched herself out on the floor. She snored. Dolly fell asleep, and snored.

VI

After several more days of drinking the room took on the appearance of a slaughterhouse. They sat in it, talking endlessly. Marie complained that they had cheated her, forcing her to spend too much money on gin. Dolly countered that she had contributed more than her share, adding that she always had to give more than her share to anything. Marie had no right to bellyache. Marie tried to reply, but Dolly banged her words out so rapidly that it was impossible. She recalled everything she had done for the girls, as well as many imagined favors. Lillian sat in a corner, not listening, babbling to her ghost children. A quarrel was imminent when Arch Keene appeared.

Keene was a thirty-five-year-old advertising specialist, a dissipated looking fellow, whose life was strangled with an ennui he sought to escape by constant repetitions of sex and gin. He dressed sportily, smoked expensive cigarettes, and toted canes which were always accounted to be knock-outs.

"Here's something for you girls . . . I mean ladies . . . ah, just look at it! Just cast your blazing orbs on this little bottle of heart-balm! See! Gods swim invisibly in this little bottle of brownish liquid, concocting dreams and forgetfulness," he said, flashing a pint of Scotch.

They argued about the colors of the whiskey. Marie asked him why he had not brought his famous flask along, the one which looked like a bible. Arch said that that particular flask was for the Lord's day only, and they tittered. Dolly called him a blasphemer.

"Yes, girls, I'm a blasphemer, an infidel, a heretic, a rounder, an atheist, an unbeliever, an agnostic, a modern, a cynic, a pessimist, a . . . a . . . sinner, a violator of all the commandments, and others of my own invention, a practitioner of all the seventy-nine capital vices, and I invented a few extra ones of my own. When I die, the Devil will say: 'Keene, you're too goddamn rotten for Hell, go on down further and dig your own spot, and make it deep.'"

"Jesus Christ, give us some air!" Lillian said.

"Archy, we're ladies, and not just girls, if you please," Marie said with all the coyness she could muster from her forty-odd years.

Dolly told Archy that he was awfully smart. Maybe she had never been to school, but she had met scholars, and she worked two crossword puzzles every day.

"I just love Art. You know, I should have been an artist's model. And you know, I ain't so dumb. I ain't. Now, I work a crossword puzzle every day," Marie said.

Arch improvised:

A crossword puzzle a day
Keeps ignorance away.

"I should have been in Art too. I used to go with a girl that went with artists," Dolly said.

"Well, let's drink. . . . For Christ sake!" Lillian exclaimed.

"No, let's drink for Beelzebub's sake," Arch countered.

"Who's Beelzebub?" Dolly asked, mispronouncing the name with slow and serious care.

"Well, I'll tell you. Beelzebub is a gink with a nose like an electric bulb," Arch informed them.

"Ain't Arch witty, though?" Marie said, half-sarcastically.

"I used to be witty and gay before I suffered so many misfortunes," Dolly said in the tragic manner.

They drank. The girls commenced splattering feminine emotions all over Arch. Dolly told how she had been abused and ruined by life. Marie interrupted to tell how beautiful her body was. Lillian leered lasciviously, and stated that she wasn't through yet; then she mourned over her three dead children. Archy snappily assured them that they were three young butterflies flitting about for honey in all the joys and wonders of their feminine . . . *pulchritude*. He pronounced pulchritude with pride. Marie and Dolly seriously told him that they were not so beautiful any more, and they wiped away tears, shed over the lost beauty of their bodies . . . once so lovely. They repeated once so lovely twice. Marie sat up straight with suddenness, and declared that she was not so old, and volunteered to prove it by disrobing. Arch cut them short by telling them a line of new smutty jokes. Arch was the one for jokes, they told him as a compliment.

Arch began to brag about how he had pulled himself up by his own bootstraps, educating himself, rising by his own effort from the position of office boy to his present high estate, where he was earning a hundred dollars a week, and still going on up. And he enjoyed the higher things of life. He loved poetry. Marie cut in to say that she also loved poetry, and she even wrote it. She quoted one of her poems, standing temulently erect, her face a travestied expression of etherealness.

The precious soul,
It stands above the goal
Of life's eternal strife.
The precious soul,
It is bathed in joy and beauty
And to behold, it is lovely.

> *Guard that soul!*
> *Raise it above the mire*
> *And the many dire*
> *Catastrophes of life.*
> *Keep it free and whole.*
> *Do not count the cost*
> *Lest that precious soul be lost!*

They clapped. Arch modestly exclaimed that he also wrote poetry sometimes, but of course he did not feel that it was much good, or as beautiful as Marie's. He said that if they were quiet, he would recite one of his poems. They sat in unnatural silence, and he overemphatically declaimed Swinburne's *The Oblation*. Marie said that it was lovely. Lillian tagged it beautiful. Dolly told him that he was a genius. Marie asked him to write them a poem about lost souls, immediately. Archy, after the proper show of modest reluctance, promised to create one. The girls jabbered, and Arch, seated on the bed, sweatingly wrote in his notebook. His task completed, he arose, and said:

"For Lost Souls, Marie, Dolly, Lillian!"

"Poor Dolly," Dolly corrected.

He asked for silence, repeated the title and dedication, and declaimed:

> *From too much love of living,*
> *From hope and thought set free,*
> *We thank with brief thanksgiving*
> *Whatever gods there be.*
> *That no life lives forever*
> *That dead men rise up never;*
> *That even the weariest river*
> *Winds somewhere safe to sea.*

They gushed appreciation, and demanded that Arch explain what the poem meant.

"Well, well, it's an expression of the desire for the oblivion of death after the fever of a short, gay, and happy life."

They called it marvelous, and told Arch how deep a person he was. He *made up* a few more short poems and epigrams for lost souls, and the girls enjoyed an emotional bath in his extemporaneous masterpieces. Arch was a genius, all right. Beautiful! Marvelous!

The girls wearied of poetry and commenced to ogle overtures at Arch. The overtures became invitations. The invitations approached becoming outright requests. Lillian demanded first preference because she was married, and the unmarried girls, she snickered, must be . . . virgins. At this date, he did not want to be, at this late date, bothering with girls who must be . . . inexperienced.

They laughed. Lillian continued, telling him that he could be the father of her next child. Archy spoke a little piece about lacking any desire for paternity. Marie offered him the opportunity of being the cause of her next abortion. Dolly said she didn't care if she did sleep with him, because nothing mattered any more.

Archy secured a room next door, and took Marie in with him. Lillian and Dolly listened at the thin partition of a wall, and giggled. When there was no more cause for giggling, and they could hear Archy's snoring, they drank with gay courage.

VII

Dolly was alone, and she lay on her bed in a drunken daze, unaware of time. The window curtain flapped. She watched it with curious, eager, and surprised interest, as if she were a child gazing at one of the fresh marvels of life. It was funny, the way the curtain flapped. She called to Marie and Lillian, and assuming that they were within hearing, described for them the comical flapping of the window curtain. Her interest persisted for an indefinite time. Then she arose and moped about the room. She kicked some object. Stooping she picked up the lower plate of her false teeth. She set it in her mouth, and walked about, kicking, finding, and placing the upper plate in position. Her feet were unsteady and she called the girls by name. She searched for gin, and found empty bottles. She phoned the hotel clerk downstairs and attempted to borrow money. He refused, and asked her about the hotel bill. She promised to pay, and telephoned a nearby speakeasy. A Negro porter arrived with a bottle of gin, and Dolly inveigled the bottle from him without cash. She drank, flung herself onto the bed, and cried.

A vague and far past jumbled through her imagination like a disordered freak show. Faces of men who had loved her; faces of men who had slept with her; rooms with passion-moistened beds, their corners sharpened, their walls twisted, and crooked, their ceilings humped out of recognizable contour: Hayden, like a stranger in a nightmare, terrorizing and phallic with misplaced genital organs; a gloomy, long-faced dark man with his ear pasted onto his left elbow; her parents; her father and mother in a darkened bedroom behind a closed door and funny sounds as the small and curious girl, Dolly O'Leary, listened and tried to see through an unrevealing keyhole; huge flies and beetles, buzzing, massing in a threat to attack her; herself with her breasts ripped and dripping blood . . . a drunken, delirium cinema of the imagination.

In the midst of this giddy pathology, God came to her. He came suddenly and soothingly to a miserable and degraded woman, a vision in pure and flowing white robes, His bearded face heavy and melancholy with the world's sorrow and kind with gentle understanding. He hovered over her like a forgiving father, motionless, calm, lucid, a cool figure of consolation. She tumbled to her knees, and tried to pray, begging and supplicating forgiveness and mercy, sighing a deep desire to serve Him. But God vanished, trampled out and erased in a phallic fever. She returned to her pillow and sobbed herself to sleep.

VIII

Dolly fumbled through queer, moving streets. People, buildings and pavement all walked along with her. Street corners jumped at her, like apparitions from nowhere or from some uncharted wonderland. All forms charged about her, robed in dream-strangeness. She paused at a corner, and looked at a policeman. She looked at him. She gazed at him, tilting her head to the right. He seemed like a statue, and the statue wrought an unexplained fascination upon her. It looked at her. It grew toward her. The statue took her arm, and she cried. It asked her what was wrong. The statue became living flesh, and she recognized him as a policeman. Her confusion dissipated, and she told him her sad and heart-torn tale. She had just lost her dear mother. She had been so shaken with grief, that she had become a mass of raw nerves. She had taken one drink to ease her misery. If she hadn't, she would have gone mad. She loved her mother so dearly. She missed her so frightfully. Yes, if she had not taken a drink, with her nerves in the condition they were in, she would have gone stark mad, insane. It was impossible for anyone to understand or appreciate the depths of her grief. Sobs caused her entire body to shake and quiver.

The policeman said, sympathetically but embarrassed, that he did understand. Didn't he lose his poor old father a year ago, himself! He gave her a dollar, put her in a cab, told her to pray to God for help, and try and straighten herself out, because her old mother now in Heaven would want her to pull herself together. She directed the driver to a cheap speakeasy, and secured a fifty-cent pint of gin. She returned to her hotel. The driver demanded his fare, and was adamant to all her wheedlings. She instructed him to drive her to her home.

She and Paul lived in a quiet, respectable, middle-class neighborhood. Drunk and dirty and disheveled, she staggered out of the cab and her bottle of gin fell, breaking on the sidewalk. She emitted an oath. Neighbors gazed out of the window, clucked their simple formulas of good and bad, of decency and indecency, and enjoyed a self-respect that was winged with self-righteousness.

Paul was home, and he paid the cab bill, his expression one of martyred pain. After she had been seated by the dining-room table, he tried to explain to her that she should not do such things. It disgraced them before the neighborhood. She said nothing. He talked, and she did not listen. After about fifteen minutes, she demanded food. He hastened out to a store, and returned with an armful of groceries. He cooked supper for her. She ate crapulently, and as she gutted herself with the food, tomato juice spilled over her chin, butter was smeared on her dress, pork-chop grease and catsup were daubed on her cheeks. She devoured everything before her, and shouted for more. He scurried down to a delicatessen, and brought back ham and milk. He sat watching her consume it, his sense of propriety severely strained.

When she could eat no more, he attempted to persuade her to go to bed. She asked for veronal tablets and a bottle of beer first. He went out and procured both. She drank the beer, but hesitantly fingered the tablets.

They sat vis-à-vis at the table. Her face was puffed, and the bags beneath her eyes seemed to have enlarged. They sat, both of them looking old, victims of the same pressures of time.

She suddenly burst into shrieking curses, and, blaming him for the ruin of her life, she splattered him with all the familiar barroom epithets. He begged her to hush, but the more he supplicated, the louder she became. She screamed that she wanted the neighbors to hear, wanted them to know of her sad life, wanted them to know what kind of a vicious, unfair cur he was. Let them judge; she wanted them to judge, and to see if he was not responsible for her sad, sad fate. If the world knew, the world would judge . . . and forgive. She arose, shouted, tore her clothes off, and placing her hands to her cheeks and ears, she screamed like one gone starkly insane. She was calmed by promises of more beer. He went out and returned with three bottles of needle beer. She quietly drank the beer. She cried softly, expressing a self-lacerating contrition for her conduct, extenuating it with pleas that she hadn't been aware of what she was doing. She resolved that she was through now, and that she would never, never drink again.

With her tears flowing unwiped, she monotonously described how she had once been a very fine person. She spoke of her success in business, of the millionaires who had loved her and asked for her hand. He treated her with Christian kindness, trying to help her brace up and forget all that had happened, and to resolve to start over again. She cried on, shook her head, repeated six times that her life was ruined. She promised to brace up and to make a happy home for him.

The veronal tablets still lay on the table. He offered one to her. She took it, and held it in the palm of her hand, looked at it, put it aside. She spoke of her manifold talents and abilities, and of the promising voice she had once had. Why one millionaire, long ago, had even desired to have her voice cultivated. If she had only allowed him to, today she might be in the grand opera. In a cracked and squeaking voice, she dribbled out the chorus of *My Hero* from *The Chocolate Soldier*. She told the sad story of her life, repeating, adding, embellishing. She was again thirsty, and asked for more beer. He tried to refuse, but her persistence shifted into loud-voiced belligerency. He went for beer. When he returned, she was gone.

She was home again in an hour, glassy-eyed. Paul searched her but she had planted her gin downstairs in the basement. She exclaimed that she had no liquor, and that she had just gone out for a walk, because she had been so nervous. She went to her room and sat in quiet tears. He retired to his room, and knelt before his God. He sobbed with those jerking sobs that wring a man's body. He heaved, and he begged God to help his niece. She sneaked out, secured her gin, returned, sat on the bed drinking herself into a heavy, tossing and snoring sleep.

IX

Days vomited along for Dolly and for Paul also. She did not see the girls, but she continued to drink. Lillian had sobered up, and she was back home with her patient and long-suffering husband. Marie was with Bill. Dolly made Paul's existence miserable. She sneaked out regularly, and returned staggering. She borrowed money, on innumerable and ingenious pretexts, from peddlers, merchants, janitors, filling-station attendants, friends, policemen, hoodlums, cab drivers, and unclassifiable strangers. Her drunk had already lasted over a month.

Lillian and Marie started off again, and secured a room in the same sportive hotel. Dolly fell into the room, surprising them. Drunk, the three girls ate spaghetti, and as they ate, Marie expostulated on the angelic beauty of her features.

"Jesus Christ! You ain't beautiful. You ain't got any looks. You're old and fat, and your can looks like the ass-end of a motor truck. Why, for Christ sake, I could have bought and sold you. Looks! Looks! Jesus Christ!" Dolly snapped, without warning or any overt provocation.

"Yes!" Marie screamed at her.

Lillian tugged at Dolly's sleeve and muttered:

"Dolly? Dolly? She's my sister. She's my sister. You leave my sister 'lone, and don't call her names."

Lillian was ignored, and she slipped into tears.

"Yes, Dolly O'Leary! Yes! Yes! Well, let me tell you you got your lousy stinking nerve, saying that to me. You! why, you're nothing but a faded, lousy nigger whore. Whore!" Marie shouted.

"Well, you bitch, I didn't have an abortion to rid myself of Jack Pierce's bastard brat," Dolly retorted.

"Never you mind! You had your abortions, Dolly O'Leary!"

"Prove it!" Dolly demanded.

"You told me so."

"I did not! I certainly did not! As true as God lives, I most certainly did not!"

"No, and you never had syphilis!" Marie sneered.

Lillian wavered by Dolly, grabbed her sleeve with a feeble hand, and repeated that Marie was her sister. And Dolly was her bes' friend, and she was going to stand up for her bes' friend and her bes' sister. She was unheeded. She floundered into a corner, and fell onto the floor. She sat crying, with her hair streaming down over her face and into her lap, and she babbled with the ghosts of her dead children.

Marie and Dolly raged at each other, exchanging curses, violating confidences, calling each other old women with bitter and rasping voices. They clinched, scratched, shoved, punched at each other clumsily and awkwardly, clawed away like fighting wounded tigresses. Lillian arose, cried to God, and tried to separate them. She was brushed aside, lost her balance, and slipped backward. Dolly drove her nails down Marie's right cheek, gripped two handfuls of hair, and pulled. She shoved Marie onto the bed, and left her there howling. She went for Lillian, who had arisen and was off balance. She ringingly slapped and drove her knee into Lillian's abdomen. Lillian fell, confused and in pain. Marie lurched back at Dolly and they collided. They separated, and Dolly butted Marie in the stomach with her head. Marie held her stomach, and screamed murder. Lillian wailed. Dolly frothed and cursed, and the sisters continued to chorus for help and mercy as Dolly tried to sink her false teeth into Marie's arm. Marie escaped and retreated into an opposite corner, and Dolly followed like a hound on the hunt. She turned and pummelled the defenseless Lillian again, and blood streamed from the scratches on Lillian's bewildered and hurt face. The two sisters retreated from the room, and Dolly flung a bottle at the door just as it closed.

The police arrived, and carted Dolly to the station in a patrol wagon.

X

Dolly sobbed and wailed and keened through the night in a filthy cell at the local police station. When she appeared in court in the morning, Paul was at her side, pained and depressed. Bedraggled, she sat in a court full of miserables and unfortunates. Cases were called and settled in a brisk, quick, and legally impersonal manner. A Negro moron who, in a brawl with himself and his drunken wife, had split her cheek with a flat iron, was dismissed with a lecture. Others moved one by one to the bar of justice, drab and aging prostitutes, alcoholic brawlers, hoodlums, petty thieves, cheap bootleggers, delinquent boys and girls, several homosexuals caught in a raid on a nondescript party. Dolly sat in misery, suffering under a sense of personal degradation, oscillating between baths of self-pity and rages of internal abuse silently hurled at herself, her uncle, the world. There were no charges against her. Paul had paid the hotel, and Lillian and Marie were still asleep under the stupefactions of gin. Dolly listened to the judge's listless, moralizing cut-and-dried sermon, and was dismissed with warnings.

Paul brought her home in a taxicab, a dreary journey for the two of them. Unable to face the shame that welled up in her conscience, she attacked him. She shifted her conversation, and spoke viciously of Lillian and Marie. He winced at her opprobrious language. He sat, trying to think the situation through, wondering what might be done, meditating on God and men, and striving to justify the ways of the Creator to mankind. When she was in tears following an exhausting diatribe, he assured her that she was forgiven and that the incident would be forgotten. He wondered why must it all be? He mumbled sporadic prayers, and she continued to sob.

XI

The next day was Sunday, and Dolly's forty-third birthday. There was no sun, and the murkiness of the day tortured Dolly! It was a sign of disdain sent to her, a poor, racked sinner, by God on her prophetic birthday. In her despair and contrition, she externalized the causes of her condition, and blamed others. She was growing old, and she was unloved because of human viciousness, which was personified and concentrated in her uncle. She was a woman of sorrow. Her wild thoughts dissipated the poignancy of her situation, made it vague, and sadly comforting. She paced the floors, relieved by her tears. She twitched in unceasing nervousness, smoking cigarette after cigarette. She bellowed. She ripped her soul out, and hurled it obscenely at Paul. Then she sat gazing down upon the uninspiring street. People walked below her, suffused in their characteristic Sunday apathy. They went, slow-moving, comfortable, contented, stupefied, their gaits and their demeanors bespeaking a self-righteous pride in their sleepy-souled satiation and satisfaction. She watched them with comminglings of hate and envy. They were living, she felt, on the fat of the land; they were happy; she was a WOMAN OF SORROW. If they only knew the misery corroding in the soul of the old woman watching them, if only . . . then their hearts would be wrung and choked with pity and sympathy. It was unfair; and a just God would punish the world for its unfairness to Dolly O'Leary, for its callousness; for the ruin which it heaped on a woman, an old woman of forty-three.

But she was not so old. Only forty-three. Some day she would break away from it all, start all over and make something of her life.

The minutes passed like the smoke-belching, choking, slow irritating gasps of an engine; she nervously walked up and down and about the house. She felt stifled, and went out for a walk. She strolled aimlessly, obliviously, like one insane, up and down the street. Sometimes she noticed passers-by, and imagined what they might be thinking of her. She cried, and constantly wiped her tears away.

She sat by the lake, and watched the sullen swirling of the gray-green, white-capped waters. The waves pushed in, slow, and quiet and inevitable, undemonstrative of their power until they smashed, like pile-drivers, against the cold, gray-white stones of the breakwater. She imagined herself committing suicide, and enjoyed a melodrama of borrowed emotions. She saw herself sinking down into the unfriendly, insensate waters, sinking to forgetfulness. She saw herself a discolored corpse, dragged to shore, carted to a dingy, dirty morgue, her purpled body set out for strangers to gape at curiously. She imagined herself being taken from the morgue to a pauper's grave in Potter's Field. She thought of a different funeral, a gorgeously sad occasion with all the world paying tribute to the heroism of her ruined and mangled life.

Children scampered along the breakwater, happy, excited by the sheer joy of throwing stones into the water; children giggling, laughing, effusing an innocent, unreflective, muscular and neural joy of life, while they were watched by pleased and contented parents. Children who cut her with the realization that no life had sprung from her womb. Vaguely, and with an inadequacy of expression, she realized that all her life was but a scramble to make up for her childlessness, for the pain, burden, and joy of giving life. She sneered, and quietly cursed the passing mothers, the mothers of the world. She told herself that the majority of them were whores unfit to raise children. She broke into tears.

While she was crying, an aged, kindly-expressioned gentleman sat beside her. She blurted out her sorrow and her life history to him. He was moved by her tale and promised to help her. She said that she was unable to go home for a few days until she could get herself straightened out. He offered to have her cared for. They went to a restaurant and had supper; she ate greedily. Over the table there was more conversation, and then he took her to the Westgate Hotel, and paid her room rent for three days. He pressed a five-dollar bill into her hand, and promised to return and talk to her the next evening. She cried. He returned a short time after his departure, saying that he felt that she would be blue. They sat and talked, and he told her the story of his own dead daughter, a girl who had been seduced by a rake, and who had died of septic poisoning, following an abortion. He almost cried, but finally, he went away.

The hotel was lonely. Dolly attempted to pray, promising God that she would mend her ways. She grew sad and nervous, and the thirst for liquor scourged her like a whiplash. She felt that she needed just one drink to straighten up. She telephoned Marie, and patched up their quarrel. Marie and Lillian arrived with a bottle of gin and they held a noisy birthday celebration.

XII

On the following morning, the three of them were ejected from the hotel. Dolly returned home and went to bed. She awoke with a headache, and sorrowed through the remainder of the day. When Paul arrived home, she cooked his supper. A blue dreary week followed. Their home took on its normal colorlessness. Dolly promised that she would abandon drinking for life, and that, as soon as her nerves were rested, she would look for work. That would give her something to do, and would make something out of her life. One afternoon, two weeks later, Marie and Lillian were invited over for tea. They came, and the three girls sat sipping tea in the stuffy parlor. A sunless day stared through the tasteless parlor curtains. They talked, each one elaborating on her intentions to remain on the water wagon. They spoke of the past, but the past had no significance, no depth, no store of memories; it was like wasted semen. Yesterday was a drunk, and today a hangover. They sat, all of them with wrinkling faces. Dolly complained of heart pains. They sat in empty talk. Their lives were empty and futile. They sat, Lillian with her ruined womb, Marie and Dolly with their empty wombs. They talked and gushed. They sat and sipped their tea, and the sunless day stared through the tasteless parlor curtains. Before six o'clock, they had a bottle of gin.

1930.

Guillotine Party
AND OTHER
STORIES

Lost, wholly lost without an inward fire
GEORGE SANTAYANA

Soap

"WHAT are we going to do?" she asked disconsolately.

He shrugged his shoulders. It was a rhetorical question.

"Anything left to eat?" he asked, drawing a crumpled package of *Elégantes Bleues* cigarettes from his pocket. He lit his last cigarette and tossed the crumpled package in a large ash tray.

"Nothing but coffee, only we haven't any sugar or milk," she apologized.

He puffed at his cigarette.

"But, honey, I'm not hungry. I'm not really hungry. I've been wanting to go on a diet and lose a few pounds anyway," she said.

He tightened his lips as if in thought. He glanced at the worn brownish carpet. Theirs was a small apartment on the sixth floor of an ancient building situated on the *rue Berthollet*. It was a raw February day, dark and dreary outside. The chilled room was scrupulously clean, but everything in it looked old and shabby, and it also seemed disorderly because he had so many canvases lined up along the walls. And in one corner there was a broken easel.

"Did you go to the steamship companies today?" she asked.

"There was nothing doing there. They all complained of the *crise*. I went to some of the galleries, but they said the same thing. The *crise*."

"And there wasn't any mail?" she asked.

"Nope. There were four mail boats in Tuesday, but nothing for us."

"Gee, I wish we had an income," she said wistfully.

"Yes," he said abstractedly, listening to an autobus as it rumbled by on the street outside, "and there isn't anyone left from whom we can borrow money."

"I'm ashamed. I'm ashamed whenever I see all those people to whom we owe money. I don't want us to be always having to borrow money," she said.

"Neither do I," he said.

"I wonder if anyone will be dropping in to see us tonight?"

"Probably not. They all know we're broke, and they're probably afraid that they'll have to loan us more," he said, squashing his cigarette butt in an ash tray.

"And you had to walk around all day in those shoes, too, didn't you? My dear, I was so worried about you," she exclaimed, wiping away a tear.

"I did some walking. But I found some old *carnet* in my pocket, and I rode down and back from *L'Opéra*."

"I'm glad," she said, kissing him, "but I want you to have some good shoes. I worry because you haven't. And it's so cold out."

"These will do. And since I put that brown polish on them, they don't look so bad. If you get far enough away from them, they look like oxfords instead of tennis shoes. That's what you call art," he said, forcing a smile.

"But it's cold out," she said.

"It could be colder," he said, taking their last one-franc piece from his pocket, looking at it, feeling his whiskers.

"You go and buy something to eat for yourself with that," she said, observing his action, "I'm not hungry, so you can get bread or something, and I'll make you some black coffee."

"I'm not hungry," he said.

He walked to the wash basin in a corner and looked around the sink.

"No soap?" he asked.

"It's all gone," she apologized.

He fingered his beard. He turned and studied his reflection in the long wardrobe mirror opposite the sink. His shirt was dirty, and his unpressed suit looked old, splotched, greasy. He bent his right elbow forward and saw that the coat was beginning to fray at that spot. And the ball of his right foot was sore from having walked so much on cobble-stone streets in tennis shoes. He felt humiliated and insignificant. Ordinarily he was unaware of his clothing. Now, he was only too conscious of it. He had felt almost naked as he had walked into the offices of shipping companies to ask if they had any commercial art work which he might do. Moving about Paris streets, with all the people speaking an alien tongue, he had felt rootless, completely out of place. And his shabbiness had emphasized this feeling, attenuated it. He didn't belong. He was poor, shabby, just out of place, worse than a beggar.

And he was losing faith in himself. He and his wife had come to

Paris from Chicago, full of high hope and confidence. They had been poor but determined. He had believed in himself. And others had spoken highly of his talents and his promise. But now, with his poverty, he had lost all confidence. He was beginning to hate and detest his art. He felt that even were he permitted to work at it uninterruptedly, he would be able to do no decent work. His poverty had sapped his spirit, choked him of character and moral courage. That was how he felt. He was thoroughly ashamed of himself. He was unable to work. No paints. And his easel was smashed. And every day he had to go out and beg for odd commercial jobs or else haunt the galleries in a vain effort to be taken on. And after this failed, he had to go to Montparnasse, a district which he loathed, and hang around there until he could meet somebody and try to make a loan of a few measly francs. He was swiftly losing his awareness to life, to color and forms and shapes, to all the beauties of Paris. He had no more sensitivity. He went around, more and more, like one in a daze. He no longer desired to hear, to feel, to see, or to sense anything. All the time his main desire was to be almost completely unconscious. Yes, he had been considered a promising young artist when he had first come to Paris.

"I suppose I'll have to start raising a beard," he said.

"I don't want you to look so bad. Tonight I had wanted to wash your shirt. I was down to the *blanchisserie* today, but they wouldn't let me have our laundry without money. It makes me worry and feel bad to see you having to go around so dirty," she said.

"It's all right. It might make me look like Modigliani's successor," he said, unable to keep the bitterness out of his voice.

He scratched himself. Needed a bath, too. But that cost five francs. And they already owed six weeks' rent. If they asked for baths, the *patron* would tell them to pay up, and he might even get sore and kick them out.

"I'll buy a bar of soap with the money," he said.

"No, you won't. You are hungry. You go and buy some bread. You're hungry, and it makes me sad. I don't care about myself because I want to go on a diet anyway," she said.

"I'm not hungry," he said.

He washed himself without soap, and they sat facing each other.

"It will be better to get soap. We can take sponge baths, and get ourselves cleaned up. I'm sick of feeling so damn dirty."

"Me, too, only I want you to eat," she said.

"I ate. I met Art and he took me into that *Bar Automatique* on the *Boulevard Haussmann*," he lied.

"I don't believe you," she said.

"Sure he did. I'll get soap."

He sat there listless, and she wiped away another tear.

"I might be able to borrow something tomorrow," he said.

"From whom?"

"Oh, Art or somebody."

She arose, walked over to him, sat beside him on the couch-like bed.

"I'll get soap," he said.

"You most certainly will not. You will go out this minute and buy some bread. If you don't, I shall not speak with you," she said, forcing herself to prevent crying.

"It won't hurt us to miss a meal," he said.

"I won't have it. I worry about you. You're losing weight, and oh, dear, I worry so," she said, crying, and he strove to kiss away her tears.

"Maybe there'll be some money for us in the next batch of American mail," he said.

"From whom?"

"Oh, somebody might send us a dollar or two."

"I don't like that. I don't want people pitying us," she said.

They sat in silence. Suddenly she burst into sobs.

"I want my baby."

He blinked, and blew his nose. He couldn't cry. It wasn't manly. He remembered their baby. It had been born in December. He recalled her moaning in the labor room, her screams filling and piercing the corridor outside as he had paced it, wrung with the fear that she might not live. He had gone into the labor room, and seen her twisting and agonizing on the bed with a contorted face. She had curtly ordered him out of the room, and he had left it, hang-dog. That had been at eleven o'clock in the evening. She had gone on suffering like that until the next afternoon when the baby had been delivered. The nurse had come out with the swaddled, wrinkled-faced baby under her arm. His son. It had cried, a thin, sharp sort of a cry. She had hurried with it down the corridor to the nursery. And he had seen it in the nursery the day before it had died. The little thing had looked so cute, its face had been clear, the head well-shaped, the eyes a deep rich blue. It had lain sniffling and gasping, unable to breathe, suffering as it had taken in oxygen. Her body had been torn and bruised by the baby, and she, too, had nearly died. She had only been permitted to hold the baby in her arms for a few seconds on the third day. She had been brave, too, when he had told her that their son was dead, but he had seen all her crushed maternal impulses on her drawn, struggling, wearied girl's face.

"I want my baby," she cried.

He kissed her. He wanted it also. When she had been caught, neither of them had wanted it. They had thought of going to a *sage femme,* but didn't trust such practitioners. So they had decided to have it, and do the best they could. And by the time she had gone to the hospital, they had wanted it. Their friends had said that it was good for the baby to have died. But friends did not understand.

He kissed her.

"And my baby looked like you," she said.

Thousands of fathers had had their babies resemble them, and had felt proud over the fact. He was no exception. He recalled the pitiful little thing gasping for air at the oxygen tube in the hospital nursery, while all around there had been healthy squalling infants.

"Our baby was nice," she said.

"Yes."

He thought that if it had lived, they would not have had to decide whether to buy soap or bread.

He was hungry. He knew that she was hungry. He touched his whiskers.

She dried her tears.

He glanced at his canvases along the wall. Would he ever paint again? And would he be able to pick up where he had left off?

"I want you to eat," she said.

He had known all along that he would buy bread. Only he felt so damn dirty. And more keenly and acutely he felt his will and his self-respect dissipating as he walked around unshaven, with a dirty shirt and a greasy suit.

He kissed her, and she tried to smile.

He went out and ran two blocks to a *boulangerie*. There were closer ones, but he owed them money. He ran, not only because it was raw and cold, but also because if he ran, there was less chance of the shopkeepers stopping him and asking for money he owed. He bought a franc's worth of bread. When he returned, she was heating coffee.

They ate in silence, eating ravenously, like animals, and he had to force her to take half of the bread. Finishing, they were still hungry.

She took his coat, and commenced to sew up the frayed elbow. He lay on the bed.

"In America, we could get a bar of soap free," he said.

"You catch the French giving away anything," she said, bent over the coat.

"Well, maybe I can steal a bar of soap somewhere tomorrow."

She sewed patiently. He figured that it was between eight-thirty and a quarter to nine. They had to get through the night somehow. In the morning they would feel better, because it was easier to hope that they might have a bit of luck. In the morning, well, it was just easier to hope.

The room seemed extremely dreary, and their silence made it seem even more dreary. Now and then a tram car or an autobus rattled down the street. They listened for the noises.

"Our baby looked just like you. He was cute, and I loved him when I held him in my arms. I don't care, he was cute, and there was nothing the matter with him, only it took so long for him to be born," she said, tightening her face to prevent crying again.

"Yes," he said, thinking of the infant pitifully fighting for its frail life, gasping at the oxygen tube.

She sewed on patiently.

"Something might happen tomorrow, and anyway, I'll steal a bar of soap some place," he said.

1932.

The Open Road

I

AHEAD of him and behind him the open road stretched in a long, straight line of parched, unrelieved, and dusty concrete. It was flanked on the left by a monotony of weeds and railroad track. To its right was a continuity of rolling, half-baked prairie land, wavering with corn and oats.

He trudged along, fatigued, a bundle wrapped in a yellow slicker under his arm. He was dirty, filthy. On the previous night he had slept in a railroad depot in Indianapolis, and his white shirt, which had already been gray with dirt, bore the checkered imprint of the floor. He was thirsty. He was hungry. His unprotected head throbbed. His eyes ached. To escape the boiling sun, he glanced down at the concrete. He saw flame-like, quivering black lines. He removed his glasses and wiped his watering eyes with a soiled handkerchief. He gently touched his eyelids. He trudged along.

There was a humming noise ahead of him. He saw the noise grow into a moving speck, then into a roaring Cadillac that cannonaded forward. The driver waved to him as he flashed by, and he waved in response. He cursed that it was not going his direction.

He trudged along. He paused to watch the arrow-like flight of crows across the sky and away into the vanishing, slippery distances of space. He crossed the road and stood looking on as sparrows exultantly chittered and fought along the sides of the mounded railroad track. He recrossed to the right-hand side of the road. He listened to the monotonous sigh of the summer wind through bending stalks of corn, and to him it became a theme of death. Suddenly the wind seemed like a far, faint cry of human pain. He listened, struggling to find words expressing his mood and the sad, nebulous music of the wind. He trudged on, and the countryside sounds stirred his tired perceptions disconsolately.

Behind him, he heard the roar of a motor. He turned. An automobile came forward, its headlights aglare. He jerked his thumb, motioning for a lift. A Studebaker passed him. The wearing friction of its balloon tires and the turning of its motor hung in the air, a momentary echo. The world dropped into silence. Lonely, he trudged along.

He cursed himself. The day was almost over, he believed. He had left Indianapolis at nine. Now it must be nearly three, and he had made only about eighty miles. Chicago was a hundred miles ahead. If he didn't make it! Well, he could sleep by the roadside. He could wake breakfastless, dirty and stiff, and he could stand and watch a silly dawn floating over the world, insensate and alien. He could quote Walt Whitman for sustenance. But he was hungry! Tired! He wanted to make Chicago.

He trudged along.

The scene about him seemed to grow increasingly frugal. He saw the weeds by the track as poisoned. The prairie on his right seemed scorched, graceless. He looked beyond them at a wistful blue mist of trees which sank into the distant horizon. He watched them. He caressed them with his eyes, and their sight made him more thirsty. He wished somehow to possess them, touch them, at least to describe them and his own emotions in apt words. He trudged along.

An automobile whizzed by him.

He trudged along, too nervous to sit and wait for a lift.

In the morning, he had felt gay, hopeful, free upon leaving Indianapolis. Two weeks there of nickel hamburgers and starvation. Two weeks of torrid summer weather. Sitting in the library reading books on an empty stomach. Panhandling around the Circle Monument with its atrocious statues dedicated to a martial patriotism. Two weeks as a hungry stranger in a burg he hated. And that night he had gone into a Thompson restaurant and asked if he could wash dishes, do anything for a meal. The oleaginous manager telling him that he could drink all the water he wanted to. The funny traffic system in the town. The girls, strange girls, pretty girls, apple-cheeked, buttery girls in bright printed dresses. Dirty, a bum, looking at them, wanting to speak with them, and touch them, and kiss them, and stroke and pet them. Goodbye, Indianapolis.

And just outside the town he had walked along the country road, breathing deeply, exulting in a feeling of release, on the go again, hopeful. Now his morning's mood was gone. He had an almost aching nostalgia for it. And he trudged along. He recalled riding in an open Ford, watching the lovely graceful flow of the land as he passed, inhaling the sweetness of country air, seeing haystacks, richly golden and silently bowed in morning sunlight. And trees with silver-stippled caps and jackets of leaves melting into the horizon. Hollyhocks, fresh before doorways. Gabled houses looking cheerful with new coats of white paint. A mellow, red-stoned Protestant church in Lebanon with bright, stained-glass windows and a gold steeple. It had been a world full of happy surfaces, and his mood had matched it. He trudged along.

He grew melancholy, sad, with the reflection that every spring and summer the world thrilled with such surfaces. Then there would come one spring and summer and . . . He trudged along. He emitted a foul curse, the one adequate expression he could find for the feelings welling up in him, drawing tears of anger from his tired eyes.

Another car passed.

He slopped along, striving to keep his eyes closed, not looking at the sun-burnt ugliness around him.

Another car.

II

He paused by a pasture fence and watched several cows dully and contentedly chewing their cud. No hunger there. No thoughts of death.
MMMMMMMMMMMMMMMM! he throated.
An aging, blackish cow looked at him with dumbly quizzical eyes.
MMMMMMMMMMMMMMMMMMMMMMM!
The blackish cow commenced to jog slowly and suspiciously forward.
MMMMMMMMMMMMMMMMMMMMMMMMMMMMMM MMMMM!
The other cows became restless. They gazed at him with eyes shot full of question marks. They jogged closer to the barbed-wire fence.
MMMMMMMMMMMMMMMMMMMMMMMMMMMM MMMMMMMMMMMMMMMMM!
The cows whined and started to stampede around the fence.

"See here! You let them ka-ows be, and mind your own affairs! Go and be about your way before I call my man. Go on and be about your way, you dirty bum," a slatternly housewife called, standing, almost like a caricature in a comic strip, against the background of a sunken farm house.

He looked at the excited cows while she cursed him. He bowed elaborately, and remarked that it was merely sex appeal.

MMMMMMMMMMMMMMMMMMMM, he throated, trudging on.

III

Chicago. All day he had been anticipating a warm reception there from his old friends. He had repeatedly visioned himself bursting in upon them while they were having a party. They would be having a party because they threw one every night. He would cause an adjournment to a restaurant, where someone would stake him to a juicy roast beef with mashed potatoes, coffee, pie. He laughed at himself for these anticipations. He was an anti-climax there. He might just as well have gone on to New York, as he had intended. He was hungry, though. He trudged along. Cars zoomed past him. His head throbbed. More cars.

Fagged out, he sat down by the roadside. A Buick appeared. He jumped to his feet and jerked his thumb for a lift. He sat down again.

A bug crawled over his leg, and he squashed it. He listened to the murmur of grasshoppers. From far away, he could hear birds singing. Creatures born to sing their little day and die. And himself. Born to live in this restlessness, and die. And he wondered how a decent meal tasted. He mumbled Edna St. Vincent Millay's poem to himself.

> *The railroad track is miles away,*
>   *And the day is loud with voices speaking,*
> *Yet there isn't a train that goes by all day*
>   *But I hear its whistles shrieking.*
>
> *All night there isn't a train goes by,*
>   *Though the night be still for sleep and dreaming,*
> *But I see its cinders red on the sky*
>   *And hear its engine steaming.*
>
> *My heart is warm with the friends I make*
>   *And better friends I'll not be knowing,*
> *Yet there isn't a train I wouldn't take,*
>   *No matter where it's going.*

It didn't matter where he was going, and whether or not he lilted about it in neat little affectations. If he went or he didn't, what? When he went, he wanted to be somewhere else. When he didn't go, he wanted to be going. And then he had gone again, and he had gone, and now he was eighty miles south of where he had gone. And the smoking room at the depot where he had slept; and how it had been rancid with body odors and the sweat of men who might go or not go, and it didn't matter. And they were hungry men, too. Restless, he arose, trudged on.

He became acutely conscious of his appearance, the dirt which covered him, and his clothing. He walked. He didn't want to think, or even to reverie. He didn't want to feel. He wanted his mind and his consciousness to become like the wood in a tree. He wanted to move on in a vacuous state of oblivion until he got a lift. He paused, aimlessly, by a field of oats, reached through the fence, and picked a handful of seeds. He squeezed them, and the white juice chalked his hands. Moody, he pondered the irreducible mystery of life. He had come from a white juice, and maybe they would throw him in a field, and he would rot, and part of him would become like these seeds, and on and on endlessly, with others after him feeling, sensing, suffering, loving, sensing, always sensing, always their consciousness drawing in from life, sensing, on and on endlessly until that final day of thermodynamic reckoning. He quoted to himself a memorized passage from Job.

Have pity on me, have pity on me, at least you my friends, because the hand of the Lord hath touched me. My flesh is consumed, my bone hath cleaved to my skin, and nothing but lips are left about my teeth. Have pity on me, have pity on me, at least you, my friends.

All those beautiful wailings of mankind for itself. And blah! Here he was, an animal organism containing elements worth about ninety-two cents, also wailing for himself. And he was afraid. He was a young man and he was afraid because some day he was going to die, and until he was going to die he was going to go on, sensing, seeing other people, seeing them flounder and blunder and suffer like himself, seeing them hungry and poor, too, realizing that they were going to go on sensing, always sensing, and they were going to die and they were afraid, too, and have pity on me, have pity on me, you indivisible three-in-one, self-creating, perpetual-motion machine wagging your gray beard up there beyond the hot clouds and the hot sun, have pity on me, blah! He walked on, counting his steps, one, two, three, four, one, two, three, four.

A farmer rattled along at the wheel of a dilapidated Ford.

"Down away?"

The man scowled beneath a wide-brimmed straw hat. He moved after the Ford, cursing the man.

Four more automobiles hummed by him.

He wondered if he would ever get a lift. He drew a comb from his stuffed pocket and ran it through his tangled, gritty hair. He crossed to the left side of the road and changed his bundle from his right to his left arm. Such little movements and actions now were events to him, almost swollen with meaning. He stopped, bent down, and re-rolled his bundle. A truck groaned southward. The driver waved, and he waved in response.

Dullness tagged him with insistent fingers. He thought of girls. Those girls in Indianapolis, buttery, their young bodies, and bright dresses, and how he had looked at them and had wanted to fondle them. And there were several in Chicago. The letter in his pocket from Texas. She was everybody's sweetheart. If he arrived in Chicago, she was sure-fire. She had wide hips, and thick ankles, and she was always willing to help out anybody who was hard up, and it meant nothing, and even that wouldn't trouble him now if she only washed her feet. And Jill. He hadn't made the grade there. Beautiful with thick, dark hair and dark eyes, and dumb with some synapse somewhere tangled up behind that beautiful dark hair. . . . And the novels he wanted to write, and how he got drunk and bragged that he would write them, and where were they, and would they ever be? And would he write them, and go to New York, and he wished he were back there. He remembered a party he had gone to on Eighth Street, and he had met that girl with the olive skin, and he had sat beside her, and wanted to stroke her silky hair, and he hadn't gotten to first base. And what was her name? He walked on.

A Studebaker with a new coat of shiny blue drew up in front of him. He had not heard it approach, and he looked up in surprise to see it stop. He clumsily ran to it, and entered the door thrust open to him, to squeeze in beside two stout and middle-aged Jewish women.

"How far you going?"

"Chicago. Going that far?"

He noticed the child beside the driver. She wore a blue-striped calico dress and a red beret.

"We're not going that far but we can take you a little way," the driver said.

"We're not going very far, but you're welcome to go as far as we are going," one of the stout women said, her voice friendly and non-patronizing.

They spun along. There was casual conversation about where he was going and where he had come from, the distance between Indianapolis and Chicago, the weather, and the admiration of the man at the wheel for President Coolidge. After every statement he made, he seemed to cast a furtive glance back at his wife, as if for approval. The conversation lapsed, and all in the car seemed to become absorbed in their own thoughts, their faces moody. They kept hitting it along at about thirty miles an hour, and he watched the countryside bounding past him. He tried counting the telegraph poles. They seemed to him, glimpsed so briefly from the car, to be crooked and staggering. He edged sidewise into a painful position to look out of the rear window and watch the road as it seemed to jump up from under the car. He edged back and counted telegraph poles.

They swept by a tumbling farm house. Before it was a pathetic old woman, bent, a walking ruins of flesh, wearily entering a gate with a ragged young boy tugging and pulling at her right hand. The contrast, the woman worn and drooping, the child young and eager and spontaneous, was striking, impressing itself in his mind as a flashing picture of human life, painted in streaks of an unwitting and eternal pathos.

"Daddy, aren't we going too far?" asked the child, her voice sweet, young.

The father answered no, and automatically glanced back at the stout women. The child insisted, and, pert and pouting, she seemed a lovely little thing. She smiled, and looked out the window to wave at a passing worker who stood by the road permitting the car to pass. He looked at the girl, at the mother beside her. Would she, too, grow up to be a reeking, overstuffed bag of kindly and good-natured human flesh, tyrannizing over her husband, warning her own children to keep their hands in out of the window lest they get hurt.

He counted the telegraph poles.

He was dropped off at Atkinson, Indiana. Atkinson seemed to consist of a small and apparently disused railroad station platform to the left of the road, a combination garage, filling station and hot-dog stand across from it, an all-weather road shooting by the filling station and across the Indiana prairie, and the sign. He stopped in the shed or garage and asked for a drink of water. Two stolid-faced fellows labored over the fan belt of a junky Dodge. He stood there. They worked, ignoring him, sweat oozing from their dirt-seamed faces.

"Can I have a drink of water, please?" he repeated.

The older and more inept-looking of the two paused to gape at him. He replied that he didn't know about it, because he didn't know if there was any water drawed yet.

"Never mind. Thanks," he said sarcastically, starting to walk back toward the concrete road.

"Jist a minute there . . . I was jist a-gonna draw some water this minute," the fellow called in a friendly voice.

He waited, and after about five minutes the younger of the two went off with a bucket. He drank, and between gulps asked the distance to Chicago.

"One hundred and five miles," said the fellow who had drawn the water.

"Know the time?"

" 'Bout three o'clock daylight saving time."

He walked off, followed by suspicious eyes. He trudged on along the side of the road, a bit refreshed by the drink. But it seemed to make him more jerky. He again hoped to get a long jump, perhaps a ride all the way in. Cars passed him, sometimes in whizzing bunches. He lost his temper and flung unheard curses at the occupants of the passing cars. He cursed humanity at large, and he was steaming himself up to the point of cursing the cosmos when he was distracted by a blabbering horn. It was a large car coming toward him, a Cadillac, which slowed down in front of him and curved to a stop by the side of the road. He ran toward it, noticing the Illinois license in the rear. He stopped by the driver.

"Down away?"

The horn blared. The car shot forward, and he caught a smirk on the driver's face before he disappeared. He stood in the center of the road, shaking his fist after the speeding car.

He trudged on and a Ford halted beside him.

"Goin' as far as Otterbein?"

He got in. The man driving was past fifty, wearing overalls and a wide straw hat. The car seemed to creep forward, and many automobiles cut past it.

"You always go around like this?"

He did not answer, and out of the corner of his eye he perceived that the man's face was thick, dull.

"You always travel around like this, I said?"

"Sure. Been around the world six times."

"You must have had some experiences. Gee."

"I should say I have. Once I was just about to be cooked by cannibals in Africa, but a Y.M.C.A. secretary came along and saved me. He used to live in Brooklyn, and we went through the jungle for four days. All the monkeys tossed cocoanuts at us."

The fellow turned, his mouth dropping agape. He didn't know whether to believe or not. They rode on, and the subject of conversation changed to farming, and then to Purdue University which, the driver said, had a summer enrollment of about five hundred students. Then they talked about automobiles.

He got out at the edge of Otterbein and hastened through the town, noticing that it was, like so many American small towns by main highways, dreary and depressing. It lay there naked and asleep in the harsh and blinding August sunlight. Its main street possessed the same store fronts, the same line of cars parked along the curb at an angle, the same three or four witless, soporific faces in front of the hotel, the same air of waiting for eternity to justify its existence, that so many other small towns he had seen possessed. He passed the two blocks of dusty-windowed stores, walked by a sprawl of bungalows. At the edge of the town where the frame houses dribbled off like outposts, he met a chunky young fellow with tortoise-shelled glasses.

"How's it goin'?"

"Rotten."

"Goin' to Chicago?"

"Yes," he said, his manner bored.

"College fellow?"

"No."

"You look like one. . . . Me, I'm goin' to Georgetown this fall."

"Where's that?"

"Washington."

"Oh, yes, that's out on the Pacific coast."

"No. Washington, D. C."

"Oh!"

"I guess I better move on so's you can catch a lift."

"So long."

"So long."

A few yards down he came to a gray-painted Nation Oil Company tank station, and in front of it he read a sign in red letters against a tan background.

THE CITY OF OTTERBEIN
WELCOMES
YOU
POPULATION 982
SPEED LIMIT 15 MILES PER HOUR
WATCH OUR KIDDIES

He laughed and trudged on.

It was commencing to cool, and shadows dropped across the road. Veils of pink were hung over the sky. He walked on slowly for about a mile, and it seemed to him like five. Cars paraded past him. He turned and looked behind him. Two black dots were moving in his direction. This was tough luck. Two more fellows bumming lifts, and they could catch one, most likely, before he did. He determined that he would wait and let them pass him. Suppose they wouldn't. Well, he'd wait, too! He chewed grass to pass the time, arising as automobiles passed and sitting down again after they had whizzed by him. The black dots turned out to be two tramps even dirtier than he was. They came up to him. A Buick, packed with people, loaded with baggage, and strung with pennants, went by, honking. He talked with the two tramps and gave them one of his last two cigarettes. He watched them move on along the road.

He figured that it must be late, and guessed that at least three hours must have passed since he had reached Atkinson. Dots seemed to careen before his eyes. He was gnawed with hunger. Fatigue was wearing him out. Suddenly, he realized that the countryside was banded in an intense silence, as if the world hung wombed and suspended in a vast quietude. He was alone in it, alone in this tremendous hush that extended aimlessly and endlessly beyond and beyond and beyond the sky. He paused, as if to listen to the silence. He was alone in this tremendous and suddenly noiseless world, and he would always be alone in it. He was hanging by his heels on a second-rate planet in this tremendous world, while the planet spun around and around, and in his way he just seemed to spin around and around, and he was alone, alone, and small, and unimportant, and dirty, and yes, hungry, and he felt himself to be as ridiculous as a caricature, and all around him was this world large and insensate. He gazed at the countryside, the scene seeming sickly. A bird traced its silent flight across the sky. He smoked his last cigarette. He knew that he loved this world, and this silence, and he was afraid of it, and he was afraid of the death that would sever him from feeling and sensing it, sending him back to become part of this feelingless vastness. He trudged along.

A dusty Hudson drew to a halt in front of him. He hastily got in.

There were two fellows in the front seat. The driver was slovenly and in his thirties, and the lad beside him was about twenty-five.

The driver talked. He was going to Chicago. Him and his buddy, Lem, needed some money to pay fifteen men that was working for them, that is, for he and Lem. He had been driving all day, and him and Lem had a business. In 1927 him and Lem had built forty-seven houses, no, it was forty-eight houses, in Quincy, Illinois, nine in Blue Island, three at Round Lake, and fifteen at Chicago. This year they would build even more houses, him and Lem. They were hustlers, him and Lem were, and they did good work and had good times, him and Lem did. They hadn't had a vacation for a long time, but this year they, him and Lem, they were going to get one. The lad beside the driver mentioned women. The driver was off again. He didn't need to never go lookin' for them, because he had his lady friend back in Cincinnati, and every time he felt like it, why he just sent her the money and she came up on to Chicago and they had a time together. That was the way to manage it because then there was no trouble, and you didn't go gettin' burned. The fellow up front was playing Lem's partner for a job, and assented. Lem's partner turned around and asked him if he was broke. He nodded, thinking that the fellow might buy him supper. Lem's partner said that young fellows shouldn't go hoboing around, being wards of charity and of society. A young fellow should settle down on a job, and get himself a stake. The young lad in front agreed. Lem's partner said sure, that was the thing.

"That's what me and Lem did. Now look at us!"

He sat back, too tired to listen, and dropped into sleep. He awoke to find the car stopping. Lem's partner and the young fellow beside him got out to eat, not inviting him. He was disappointed, and cursed, but sleep eased him of bitterness and hunger. He awoke again to find the car bumping along. He tried to feel glad that he was really getting into Chicago for the night. But what of it? Another city. First there was one city, and then there was another. Between them were parched and dusty roads. He thought of a line from one of Masefield's poems.

But only the city of God at the other end of the road.

Nice lines for poets to write, and what did they mean? Soon, anyway, he would be in Chicago again. First one city, then another. He fell asleep seeking words to discover what he really felt.

He awoke at Sixty-third and Western and got out of the car without thanking Lem's partner. He hung around the corner for an hour trying to bum a ride. Finally, he stomached his pride and panhandled carfare. He got on the street car and fell asleep. He opened his eyes at Cottage Grove and glanced out the window at the lighted shows and windows. Familiar, and meaningless. He changed at Stony Island, and rode on a north-bound car, alighting at Fifty-seventh Street.

He found some of his friends in a studio of the deliquescent art colony at Fifty-seventh. They were all talking. They always talked. When they had parties, they talked. When they didn't have parties, they talked. They always talked, and generally the conversation was about somebody else's sexual life. He walked in, and one of them said that he had no money. Another said that they all had their problems and didn't want to hear of his. Another said they were broke. They continued talking about somebody else's sexual difficulties. He went outside.

He sat on a bench in Jackson Park. The evening was cool and moonless, a black August night. He sat. He had come all the way from Indianapolis to do something like sit alone in Jackson Park, while the black August night was crushed around him, and the wind grew rough in the deep green trees. Anyway he was hungry, and the world was full of cities. He fell asleep.

1928.

Guillotine Party

I

"JESUS, I pity the poor bastard. Just think, tomorrow while I'm comfortably taking my afternoon siesta, well, this poor guy, he'll be in such a condition that his head won't know where his neck is," Jack Soules languidly said.

"Jack, you're ghastly," Mrs. Soules said.

They were a part of a group which had been gathered together nondescriptly and as one of the accidents of travel in the semi-modern apartment of Art Reynolds, an American novelist, on the *Rue de la Glacière*. They were talking, eating sandwiches, drinking wine and coffee, yawning, waiting for dawn when they would go around the corner to witness a guillotining at the *Boulevard Arago* and the *Rue de la Santé*.

"Now, if I were still on the *Times Picayune* instead of leading my quiet and leisurely life, why, I'd like to cover a story like this. Such a story is worth yards of furniture-sale and department-store advertising. Love crime. With true Gallic sense a *titi* from *Montmartre* saves his girl friend's soul. And how does he manage this noble achievement? He ups and slays the dame, and then says rosaries over her dead body until it stinks so that the neighbors call in the *flics*. And now he expiates the crime," said Jack Soules, his voice flowing in a drawl that was occasionally punctuated with a midwestern accent.

"It's an utterly fascinating crime. I'm going to write a story about it and call it *The Perfect Passion*," frail Alvin Dilling lisped, rolling amorous eyes at Chuck Smith.

"Alvin, do it, please! I know you can make an exquisite thing of it. I have faith in you, if you can only get back to your writing," Chuck said lovingly.

"At all events, this poor unfortunate will have lived longer than the President of France. That's fate," Morton Brooks, a University of Chicago graduate studying history at the Sorbonne, said.

"Small loss," said Jacques Sorel, poet and translator, in an accent. "Small loss. The assassination of the President of France only lends distinction to a name which would otherwise have gained no historic embellishments. We, in France, we have plenty of political old men to spare. So, as you Americans say, what the hell!"

"Yes, but now isn't this question of oblivion and fame in history one of great relativity, with the elements of circumstance and fortuity playing a dramatically impressive role? How do we know who will be famous and given the most attention in the works of future historians? It's a profound subject. Now, take any one of a number of cases, oh, say, well, the Duke of Wellington . . ."

Mrs. Soules interrupted Brooks to deplore a public execution.

"Soon we might all lose our heads. So what the devil!" Sorel said, ignoring the previous remarks of both Brooks and Mrs. Soules. "These politicians! These fools! Assassins! Crooks! Lice! They have nothing else to do, so they are making a nice shambles of a war for all of us. And it's all foolishness. But when these assassins make this war, then," Sorel shrugged his shoulders in a gesture of utter weariness, "but then, since I'm an officer in the reserve, I'll have to go to my post. I'll have none of the war, but I'll do my duty. Maybe everybody will be killed, or else forced to live in the shambles they are making. So what the devil! This poor fool has his head severed by *Monsieur de Paris*. Another poor fool who was elected President of France, because the politicians didn't know what else to do with him, he is assassinated by a crazy Russian. And I shall be killed in a war that I will have none of." Sorel again wearily shrugged his shoulders.

"But honestly, do you think there will be another war?" Mrs. Soules asked dubiously.

"The frontier of civilization on the Vistula must be defended," Art Reynolds said, looking pointedly at Sorel.

"Reynolds, you are a fine chap with much talent. You write like a Frenchman. But you think like an American, a child. You have your sympathy for the common people. It is sentimental. It is weak. The common people!" Scorn grew in Sorel's voice. "Fools! Cattle! And you and your Russians. They are all crazy. They want to make a paradise for pigs, so that they can destroy civilization. So sooner or later we French will have to save civilization."

"You're right, Jacques. A social system that will enable all of the masses of people to share in their own productions, that will enable them to benefit by the results of human science and effort, a social system like that is a threat to culture and decency and civilization," Art Reynolds said.

"You know, I was reading *Ulysses* the other day," Brooks said before Sorel replied. "Stephen Daedalus says at one place, 'All history is a nightmare to me.' When you study history, you slowly grasp the profound truth of that statement. Almost every conceivable instrument of torture which one human being can devise to use in torturing another human being has already been used. History is a nightmare of suffering and torture."

"That's something, Mort, to put in a letter and send back to the history department of the University of Chicago. It might help them in their support of the next war," Reynolds said.

"Men are fools, except for a few noble human beings, artists and noblemen. They are pigs. Your common people! Pigs. Beasts! What do they always do? Destroy men of superior ability and talent," Sorel said acidulously.

"Sure, the poor bastards!" Reynolds said, sipping wine. "All they do is destroy virtue and talent by producing the goods of life that we can all enjoy. Yes, I know the kind of pigs they are, working in coal mines."

"I tell you, you are a sentimentalist," Sorel said, lighting a French cigarette. "Why do you waste your time with this sympathy for those who deserve a whip, not sympathy?"

"They are my people," Reynolds said.

"Say, do you people know who came into the library the other day while I was working?" Alvin asked, bored.

"Who? Marcel Proust?" asked Phillip Hirschman, an American artist who had hitherto been very silent.

Alvin's face broke into a childish pout.

"But I don't believe that there'll be another war," said Mrs. Soules.

"There is one already between the Japs and China, only the Japs have polite manners and consideration for the feelings of others. So they won't call it a war. They are just blowing the Chinks into hell-and-gone and refusing to call it a war," Reynolds said, his mouth twisting in sarcasm.

"There has to be a war. Mussolini has bought new suits for his army. The Italians have not won a battle in five centuries, but Mussolini has new suits for his soldiers. What can they do with their new suits if they don't march off to war in them?" Sorel said, causing laughter.

"That gives me an idea. Why not let them fight the Poles? The Poles won their last battle before John Sobieski died. And they all love Poland. They can't run their country. I don't know how they can stand to live in it. And they'd all love to die for dear old Poland. And then make it a three-cornered fight for eighth place and toss in the Irish. They haven't won a fight since Saint Patrick booted the snakes out of Ireland, and Saint Patrick wasn't even an Irishman," Jack Soules said, and they laughed again.

"But I'm serious. Do you really think there can be another war?" said Mrs. Soules as she munched on a sandwich.

"It won't be a war. It's going to be a defense of civilization," said Reynolds with a sneer.

"There cannot be a war. Civilization cannot stand a war. So all intelligent men must support the cause of pacifism," Morton Brooks said.

"Say, that reminds me of a good story, even if it's an old saw. The story of the elephants," said Jack Soules.

"Do tell it. It's screaming," said Chuck Smith as he arose and poured himself coffee.

"Well, a prize of five thousand dollars was offered by a philanthropist for the best treatise on the subject of the elephant. It was open to all nationalities. So an Englishman submitted his contribution, titled *Hunting the Elephant in Darkest Africa*. And a Frenchman sent in a small, neat manuscript called *Les Amours Des Elephants*. A German submitted two volumes, weighing a ton, called *Preparation for the Introduction to a Systematization and Study of the Sources of a History of the Elephant*. An American college professor sent in *The Elephant and Sales Resistance.* A Russian decided to submit a contribution called *The Elephant: Has He a Soul?* But he procrastinated and procrastinated. And he drank tea and vodka, and as the contest drew near, he talked and talked night after night, asking and pondering the question of the soul of the elephant. So he finally sent in his title page. And then a Pole turned in a treatise called *The Elephant and the Polish Question.*"

They laughed.

"I'm beginning to get jittery. Just think. At sunrise we will see a man get his head cut off," Alvin said, growing pale, and Hirschman arose, dropped his sandwich on the table, turned livid, walked to the French windows, and stood there, still pale.

"Well, let's have some more wine," said Soules to break the spell of silence that had been cast over the room, and Reynolds poured wine and distributed filled glasses.

"I need this," said Mrs. Soules.

"Don't worry, my lady. You won't see much. It's just like a circus, as if you would be going to the *Cirque Medrano*. The crowd will be too large to see anything, and I give you my word there is nothing much to see but people standing around like dogs looking at their own shadows, and *poules,* and pickpockets and peddlers. Ah, humanity! These fools!" Sorel said.

"But the idea is so grisly. You know tomorrow morning I was planning to read some more of Proust in the *Cathedral of Saint Germain des Prés,*" Alvin said, and they looked at him curiously, Hirschman sneering at him from the window.

"Ah, this world is crazy. It is only we French who save the human race from being ridiculous," Sorel said, and they laughed.

"What do you think of Hitler?" Mrs. Soules asked, and Sorel looked contemptuously at her.

"He's a German. I tell you, the German, he is crazy. Crazier than the Russians. Some day we French will have to erect a huge wall around Germany and Russia and keep civilized nations out of it. That fellow Hitler is crazy enough to get into power in Germany and when he does, War!" Again Jacques shrugged his shoulders. "Well, the fools want to make a shambles. And I will have to do my duty and be killed."

"Why not a Revolution?" said Reynolds, ashes from his cigarette dropping onto the wine-red carpet as he spoke.

GUILLOTINE PARTY

"I tell you, Reynolds, my dear chap, you are too talented to concern yourself with such foolishness."

"You guys can talk, but I want to say that since I went to that Russian wedding, I now got an ambition in life, and a hope to rescue myself from either newspaper work or writing detective stories," Jack Soules said. "When I go back to Louisiana, I'm going to start a church with Russian weddings for the niggers, and charge them five bucks a throw. I'll make my pile in a year and then go to the South Sea Islands, and let Jacques save civilization, and Art here fight the revolution."

"Capitalism and war will pursue you there. There's no corner in the world where it won't," said Hirschman bitterly.

"All I can say is that I think it barbaric, guillotining in public," Mrs. Soules said.

"Why? You cannot be so soft. Look at your own American newspapers. When this Lindbergh baby is kidnapped, I read that your Al Capone wants to get out of jail and help find the kidnappers. In France, do you think that could happen? Why, you think we let our criminals read newspapers and turn our jails into hotels," said Jacques, arising, circling about the room.

"Since I have been reading Proust, I have been thinking of how each human being is such a complicated human organism, and to think of how much there is involved in any single human life. Just think. Each human mind is a complicated and dramatic world of its own, rich with feelings and passions and hopes. And in a war when millions are killed, millions of worlds are just destroyed, blotted out," Morton Brooks said.

"You are young, Brooks, and a sentimentalist. It is no tragedy when pigs chew each other to death," sneered Sorel.

"Jacques, I see we'll meet on opposite sides of the barricades," said Reynolds laconically.

"I cannot understand you, Reynolds, giving your sympathies, wasting it on fools," said Jacques, picking up another sandwich.

"You know politics just bores me," lisped Alvin.

"Anything that disturbs my afternoon siesta is too much for me. After all, I'm a southerner from Illinois," said Jack Soules.

"Politicians are all alike," Jacques began, ignoring these last remarks. "They get the people's money and they have jobs. So they got to do something. They go to their desks each morning, and they have

an ass he had . . . Jeff wanted to be like the other kids . . . wanted to be one of them . . . he was too big and fat . . . Jeff tried to play marbles . . . he knelt down to shoot . . . got a dozen boots in the tuchas . . . Jeff stole money from home . . . bought the little girls candy . . . Jeff loved little Clara Schmaltz . . . Jeff stuck his hands in the old man's pocket . . . the old man caught him . . . gave Jeff a hell of a beating . . . Jeff loved little Clara Schmaltz . . . Jeff walked down the hall at school . . . Jeff heard little Clara talking . . . Denny Dennis says Jeff is a big fatass hehehe . . . Jeff heard Clara . . . Jeff waddled away . . . Jeff lugged his heavy fanny by Bathcellar's poolroom . . . the big guys gave him the horse laugh . . . Jeff had too much fanny . . . too much of a load to carry . . . Jeff was slow . . . lazy . . . dopey . . . crazy . . . Jeff helped clean house . . . ran the oil mop over the floor in two hours . . . his old lady cursed his big tuchas . . . Jeff tried to play ball in the playground . . . Jeff was always kicked out of the game . . . too much lead in his fanny when he ran bases . . . You got too much lead in your ass Jeff . . . Jeff tried to play baby-in-the-hole . . . the kids always let him . . . Jeff ran out of the circle like a steamroller . . . Jeff was always hit . . . got ten babies first . . . Jeff was placed against a wall . . . what a target . . . each kid threw at him six times . . . smack-whack . . . you couldn't miss that Jewish tuchas . . . Jeff played blue-my-blackberry in Washington Park . . . he was tagged . . . he was down . . . Denny Dennis didn't try to guard him . . . the kids put stones in their caps . . . blued his blackberry . . . Jesus it was funny . . . and Jeff's can stayed blue for three weeks . . . Jeff walked through Washington Park . . . Jeff's pudgy face lit with a smile . . . Jeff smiled a lot . . . Jeff waddled through the park . . . Big Schmaltz the wolf saw him . . . Big Schmaltz got hot . . . Big Schmaltz took him in the bushes . . . Coady the flatfooted cop saw them . . . Big Schmaltz ran . . . Jeff tried to run . . . got caught . . . there was hell to pay . . . it cost the old man something . . . and Big Jeff got saved from reform school . . . anyway Jeff's can was good for something . . . Jeff never passed in school . . . he got bigger and bigger . . . and his classmates got smaller and smaller . . . the teachers wanted to sock him . . . they said he would end up in jail . . . maybe on the gallows . . . but Jeff smiled . . . nobody knew what made Jeff smile so much . . . the punk kids picked fights with him . . . he fought like an ox . . . the kids socked him and re-

BIG JEFF

treated . . . socked him and retreated again . . . Jeff was always waddling along Fifty-eighth Street with a pair of shiners . . . and Jeff's fanny kept swelling and swelling.

Big Jeff got wise . . . Big Jeff started using his Jewish noodle . . . Big Jeff started gyping everybody . . . he stole marbles . . . candy . . . money . . . anything he could . . . he devised schemes . . . talked the kids out of their money . . . somebody was always laying for Jeff . . . to punch hell out of him . . . Jeff was always working his Jewish noodle to gyp hell out of somebody . . . Jeff stole everything and his ass kept swelling . . . and he kept smiling through life.

Jeff was easy to laugh at all right . . . Jeff, you'll make a fat man in a circus . . . Jeff you'd make a mint in a peg house . . . Jeff, you're a dirty louse . . . but you're funny . . . Jeff, how old are you . . . sa-ay you couldn't get that fat in fourteen years . . . and Jeff kept right on bloating and bloating . . . until he had more ass than a dozen Negro mammies.

Big Jeff got kicked out of school . . . put on long pants . . . yards of long pants . . . he didn't get a job . . . who the hell would hire him anyway . . . Big Jeff sold things . . . he sold baseball pool tickets . . . where there was no pool . . . he took bets on horses . . . when the nags never ran . . . he sold French postcards . . . he sold postwar gin . . . he sold bonded stuff . . . and never delivered . . . he sold everything . . . and he made good jack.

He walked down Fifty-eighth Street . . . turned down a side street . . . walked smiling along . . . he fell down a manhole . . . Jesus it was as funny as a Keystone Comedy . . . Jeff groaned from a manhole . . . they needed a derrick to pull him out . . . and they damn near needed a horse doctor for his broken leg . . . holy Jesus it was funny . . . Big Jeff came out of the hospital and started pimping . . . Big Jeff stood on street corners in the Black Belt . . . hailing the boys . . . married men . . . farm boys . . . blushing high school kids . . . hailing business . . . he waddled up to them . . . want a little nooky lad . . . want a girl to make you glad . . . want a three-way broad . . . want a frail that'll love you like a French frog . . . come on, lad, I got the nigger whore that's going to change your luck . . . Big Jeff led many a lad to heaven . . . and many a lad to syphilis, clap and the Chicago Public Health Institute . . . and Big Jeff took in the shekels . . . and Big Jeff spent his money on the whores . . . sweet cookie . . . he liked his nooky . . . he liked his gals . . . and he paid them hard iron men . . . Jeff came around the poolroom at Fifty-eighth Street . . . described the frails he had . . . Jeff that's bad . . . Jeff how can you get in the saddle . . . listen brother if you slept with the peach I had last night . . . listen brother she was a blonde and she wasn't tight . . . B.S. Jeff . . . all right brother but that means nothin' . . . that don't take away the lovin' ah gets . . . Big Jeff . . . gyping . . . pimping . . . rimming . . . jazzing . . . doping himself up . . . waving his fanny along . . . Big Jeff made his dough pimping . . . took a course in reducing . . . got fatter and fatter . . . don't worry Jeff the first ton is the hardest . . . but Big Jeff kept using his noodle . . . he always caught the boys from the poolroom on a new racket . . . he had to . . . the whores soaked him twenty-five and fifty bucks . . . Big Jeff paid a hundred grafted dollars for a new suit . . . hey Jeff who's your tailor . . . Omar the tentmaker . . . listen brother this is a suit . . . hundred berries good goods . . . Jeff you're a wagon-load of manure . . . all right brother but you can't shell out a hundred bucks for a suit of cloth like this . . . B.S. . . . listen brother I got a scheme now and I can get you some prewar stuff . . . Big Jeff on another racket.

Big Jeff went swimming to Fifty-fourth Street beach . . . where there was no bath house . . . and he wore his suit under his clothes . . . Big Jeff took his pants off in a half hour . . . mother look at the fat man . . . hey see the big ham . . . boy is he fat . . . if he goes in the water there'll be a flood and we'll all row home . . . the lake must be that boy's bathtub . . . Big Jeff lumbering into the water . . . everybody watching him . . . Jesus he couldn't sink if he wanted to . . . Big Jeff on the beach . . . pinching girls' legs . . . Big Jeff putting on his pants . . . for a half hour . . . Big Jeff just waddling his fanny through life . . . listen brother do you want me to fix you up with a real broad . . . a three-way doll . . . and what she don't know about lovin' . . . well I don't either.

Big Jeff kept on pimping . . . good dough in it . . . he pimped for black babies in the Black Belt . . . made and spent his shekels . . . led many a boy to heaven and many a boy to syphilis, clap and the Chicago Public Health Institute . . . Big Jeff paid big for his women . . . and got the syph . . . he gyped too many people . . . had to blow town or get his old tomato pumped full of bullets . . . shoved off with a thousand bucks in his kick . . . Big Jeff spent his money in New Orleans . . . then Big Jeff didn't go so well there . . . Big

Jeff was sick with the syph . . . Big Jeff walked the streets broke . . . Big Jeff kept smiling along . . . and the rackets got goddamn tough . . . Big Jeff panhandled . . . pimped for two-bit whores . . . but Big Jeff didn't hit it off so well in New Orleans . . . the load was too heavy . . . too much lead in his pants . . . too much syphilis . . . too much of Big Jeff for one world . . . Big Jeff slept with his last whore . . . diseased her . . . and smilingly pretended to sleep . . . stole her money . . . bought a gun . . . and the gravediggers cursed all holy hell when they lowered his crated body . . . they said they needed a derrick.

And then the maggots got busy . . . they rubbed their paws together . . . smiled sleekly, said . . . well I'm eating with my feet under the table tonight . . . the maggots said well this is a feed you don't get every day . . . the maggots said this is real meat . . . the maggots said I ain't never had grub like this . . . the maggots said we'll put some flesh on our bones now . . . the maggots thanked Jesus for having put so much ass on one corpse.

And the guys from Fifty-eighth Street stood in front of the poolroom . . . he was no good anyway . . . the cheap grafter he should have been killed long ago . . . good riddance to bad rubbage . . . he was one big load of garbage . . . they must have had a crate or a steamship for a coffin . . . the stiffs will sue him for taking up so much room in the morgue . . . he should have been sent to a booby hatch . . . well anyway Jeff had the world's biggest ass . . . he was a sonofabitch . . . cheated his own mother . . . he'll make enough fertilizer for the fields of all Russia . . . when he shot himself he should have blown the lead out of his pants.

1931.

In Accents of Death!

I

WITH the approach of April, Alvin Norton tended to grow moody and introspective. He was president of the class of '24 at Saint Stanislaus High School on the south side of Chicago, and soon he would be graduated, and all the fun and good times of high school life would be gone. Since his father could not afford to send him to college, he would have to work, although, later on, he hoped that he would be able to earn his way through college, only it would have to be a Catholic university. At the end of each day he would moodily reflect that he had one day less of all that glory of going to Saint Stanislaus, one day less before he had to go out into the world and struggle and earn his way.

Often, also, he would remember his days as a freshman in short pants. Kids with whom he had gone to grammar school had told him about their high schools, making him ashamed of Saint Stanislaus because it had no gymnasium and it did not win as many championships in the Catholic high school league as some schools did. And he would reflect on what Saint Stanislaus had given him—school spirit. He knew that there was not a school in the country better than his Saint Stanislaus. He was proud of his school, proud that he was to graduate as president of the senior class, proud that he would be an alumnus of good old S. S. And all year he had been constantly reminded that he was leaving it, leaving it when he hated to, when he wanted to stay on and continue all his fun and education. For there was a new spirit at school. The long-dreamed-of new building was rising rapidly across the street from the oblong gray box of a four-story building that now served all the needs of the school. Next year the students would move across the street into one of the most modern high schools in the country, a six-hundred-thousand-dollar building, with a capacity for one thousand students, a large gymnasium and auditorium, a swimming pool, and adequate facilities for large classes and for chemistry and physics experiments. Next year, too, there would be student self-government, and a cafeteria, and various things that had not yet been inaugurated. He sensed how he would miss all that, and the additional pride in his school was constantly intertwined with a nostalgia for what he would not have. All year, things had hummed. There had been more successful athletic teams, more activity in the Literary and Debating Society of which he was a member. And there had been a steady pressure placed upon all students to do their share, to work to the utmost to bring in every added penny which they could to enlarge the building fund for the new school. And Alvin had. He had been the collector in his class, and he had dunned, and persuaded, and insisted that every student contribute more and more to the building fund, and his class had gone way over the top, almost doubling its quota. There had been plenty of activities and excitement besides the regular course of studies, and the school had been given considerable publicity in the local papers. It even had a press agent, a member of the class of 1919, and all its dances, the breaking of ground for the new high school, the building of a new grammar school, all these had been in the papers. More and more Alvin grew proud of his school, and hated to be leaving it.

He felt, though, that his senior year showed a real measure of accomplishment. He had thrown himself into all activities the way a real S. S. student should. He had not missed an athletic contest and had not refrained from cheering his teams on to victory and the honor and glory of S. S. And when a local Catholic weekly newspaper had turned over a page of one issue to be edited and written by the students of Saint Stanislaus, Father Geraghty had included one of Alvin's compositions, an essay on *Law and Order* which Father Geraghty had marked one hundred. He had written in it of the Bolshevists and sob-sisters who decried the use of poison gas in war, and he had told how the Chemical Warfare Service of the Army had proven that the use of gases was not as deleterious as the weak-minded sob-sisters declared in their un-American propaganda. He had read an article in a popular magazine, based on information released by the Chemical Warfare Service, and he had quoted it and shown that the Bolshevists and sob-sisters were wrong. He had shown, too, that the use of these gases to prevent mob violence only caused sneezing and tears, and that those propagandists who were opposed to chemical warfare were really encouraging mobs to disturb law, order, and the peaceful progress of industry. When his father and mother had seen his composition printed in a Catholic newspaper they had been very proud.

His feeling that the year had been such a success made it all the harder to face the fact that he had only two more months of high school. He would think, too, of how then all that would be left of his career at Saint Stanislaus would be memories and the principles that he had been taught by the priests. He would resolve never to forsake these principles, never to dishonor the name of his alma mater, always to work and struggle in the world so that he would be a pride to his school. He would think how lucky he was to have been sent there, to have been favored with the best education that a Catholic boy could receive in any high school in the city, because he knew that his S. S. was the best. This realization always heartened him, because he would at least be going out to earn his right and his way and his bread in the world, prepared, prepared with knowledge, with the principles of Americanism, and with a Love of God and knowledge of the doctrines of Holy Mother Church.

II

On a morning in March, Alvin sat in the classroom gazing out the window at the blue sky and the warm and sunny day. A lassitude flowed through his body, and as Father Henry asked questions based on the chemistry text book, Alvin allowed his thoughts to wander, and he thought of past and future, of his school, of himself, of what he might do, of how great a success he would become, a lawyer, a senator, or a rich business man and prominent Catholic layman. And he thought of the boys around him who would, like himself, go out from here to face life. He wondered what they would become, how many of them would be successes, who among them would be the richest, who the most famous. He felt warm and friendly toward every one of his classmates. He wished them all well, although there were many he envied, boys whose fathers were richer than his, who would go to college, some even to Notre Dame University, boys who were football and basketball stars and had already been given offers for free tuition at various colleges and universities. He would not have what they had, but he would go out prepared to fight for it.

There was a knock on the door. Father Henry opened it, and many of the students shuddered. They saw Father Robert N. Geraghty, Prefect of Discipline, and they trembled lest he would call one out to punish him. Seeing him so unexpectedly at the door, clothed in the brown habit of his order, his freckled, broad, bull-dog face set in its characteristically stern expression, each of them feared, almost trembled. Alvin was called. A lump seemed to come into his throat. He tried to think of what he might have done to cause his being disciplined. He walked slowly out and faced Father Robert in the long, shadowed corridor. Father Robert smiled, and Alvin felt relieved. He observed a folded slip of paper in the priest's hand.

"Alvin, you've seen the newspaper accounts lately of the wave of pacifistic sentiment sweeping through the student bodies of some American non-sectarian universities, and of the meeting which occurred the other day on the campus at Evanston, where the American flag was insulted?"

Remembering headlines and unread accounts, Alvin nodded, because he didn't want Father Robert to think that he did not keep completely abreast of current events.

"Well, Alvin, we've decided that the Catholic schools should speak out against this un-American sentiment, and this afternoon we're going to have a pep meeting to denounce such un-American tactics. Since you are president of the senior class"—there was a catch in Alvin's throat, and he was uncomfortable lest he would have to address the demonstration—"I think that the duty of presenting resolutions devolves upon you. Hence, at this demonstration, you are to read these resolutions. Read them slowly, and enunciate every word clearly. There are going to be newspaper reporters and camera men present, and you wouldn't want them to hear you slurring your pronunciations."

"No, Father," said Alvin, smiling.

"I believe that Saint Stanislaus will be one of the first schools in the country to denounce un-American pacifistic sentiments, and we'll be able to refute the lie so often made that Catholic schools are un-American."

"Yes, Father," Alvin said.

Father Robert suddenly broke into one of those rare good-natured smiles of his.

"I suppose you are wondering if you'll get a half-holiday?"

"Well, Father . . ."

"That's to be wondered about. You'll find out in due time," Father Robert said.

When Alvin returned, Father Henry cut short the question period, relieving those who had not prepared their lessons. He gave them a brief talk on the glorious contributions Catholics had made to America, of the manner in which Catholics had always willingly borne arms and laid down their lives for their country, its principles, and its Constitution.

III

The four-hundred-odd students of Saint Stanislaus were gathered in the yard, happy and boisterous with the prospect of a half-holiday, of release from their classrooms, and of the opportunity which they would have to shout at the top of their lusty voices. Boys from twelve and thirteen to seventeen, eighteen and nineteen, they were massed in the rectangular brick-paved yard behind the school. Those in the front row center held a large American flag before them, and removed from the students was a small group of brown-frocked priests and newspaper men. Alvin stood in the front rank of the students, near the flag, waiting until he would read the resolutions. He was nervous and jerky, hoping that he would make no blunders. He repeatedly determined to remain calm, and to read the resolutions clearly, slowly, loudly, firmly.

Father Robert stepped forward and raised his right arm for quiet. Instantly, there was quiet among the students. They knew what would happen if they attempted any monkey stuff now in the presence of the newspaper men, and on such a serious occasion.

Father Robert spoke briefly, in a slow, clear-voiced, poised delivery. He explained that the purpose of the meeting was that of demonstrating to the public at large that the Catholic schools, of which Saint Stanislaus was a good representative, were not harboring or teaching un-American principles. On the contrary, they would strike out in an unequivocal denunciation of all disloyalties to American institutions. He explained to them that the principles of Americanism, written into the Constitution, were precious—principles of liberty, justice, freedom, freedom of conscience. All who deserved the name of American should hold these principles dear, should hold them next in their hearts to the principles of their religion. And it was an honor to everyone connected with Saint Stanislaus, faculty and students alike, to be the first Catholic school in America to affirm these principles at a time when they were threatened by a wave of pacifistic sentiment. He concluded with the words:

"It is a fundamental tenet of Americanism that love of your country should stand enshrined in your minds and your hearts next to the love of your God. In our Catholic schools, this is a teaching that has always been honored and haloed in tradition, even though there have been those who, through ignorance or bigotry, have called Catholic institutions and Catholic education un-American. The willingness to serve your country in a time of stress and need, and to bear arms in its defense, is a duty which no American citizen, or future American citizen, can ignore; it is, further, a duty which no true American would think of ignoring. Americans must be prepared to serve their country, just as Catholics must be prepared to serve their God and His Church."

Prolonged cheering greeted his words, and he stood smiling upon the students during their five-minute excess of shouting. Then Father

Dennis, a husky, bucolic priest, who spoke with a nasal twang, addressed the students. His talk was longer and less organized than that of Father Robert, and he ranted about Bolshevists, sob-sisters, and other weak-kneed pacifists, who, having not full-fledged ideas, but just notions, strove to weaken American institutions and overthrow the government. He said that their ideas had been spread, like a contagious disease, through non-sectarian colleges and universities, and that, undisguised, they were Bolshevistic ideas, and that, unless they were checked, America would be reduced to the chaos, anarchy, and terror of Russia. Pacifism was threatening the principles of Democracy, those principles which were affirmed in the true religion of God and for which Catholic Americans, yes and even alumni of Saint Stanislaus, had fought and bled and suffered on the fields of France. Before he finished, there was shuffling of feet, but at his final words there were more lusty cheers.

Then Alvin stepped forward, and, with shaking hands, slowly read the resolutions:

"We, the student body of Saint Stanislaus, unanimously condemn the unpatriotic movement now sweeping through institutions of learning throughout the nation, and we condemn all those particular students who have subscribed to pledges of disloyalty in times of war.

"We further condemn and denounce all those who insulted the flag at a recent unpatriotic demonstration in Evanston.

"And, in addition, we hereby affirm, upon our solemn honor, to meet the call to defend the flag and our country, wherever and whenever we are needed."

The resolutions were cheered. Pictures of the group were taken, *The Star-Spangled Banner* was sung, and the demonstration closed with a short prayer asking that the grace of God shine down on America and the democratic institutions upon which this great nation of liberty and justice was founded.

Father Robert announced that there would be no more school that day, and there was still another outburst.

Alvin left the grounds with a group of his classmates, and they were giving three cheers for the pacifists because, if there were no pacifists, they would not have had a holiday. Alvin was moody. He remembered the words of the priests, and he thought romantically of fighting for his country, defending it against a foreign invader, the Japanese or the Bolshevists or the English. He thought of dying for his country, and it caused a quiver and sudden terror, and he did not like to think of himself shot to death on the battlefield, even though it was a glorious death in defense of the stars and stripes. But all soldiers did not die, and, in case of war, he might not, and Patrick Henry had said:

Give me liberty or give me death!

The next day both of the morning papers carried pictures and first-page accounts of the demonstration. The account in the *Chicago Questioner* mentioned Alvin's name and the resolutions. Alvin cut the pictures and reports out of the papers and pasted them in his scrap book. He had one more memory, one more enforcement of principles, one more teaching, one more lesson from his high school to carry out with him into the world where he would earn his bread.

1934.

The Little Blond Fellow

I

"HE looks queer to me," Marty said as he stood in the lavatory of the Everglades Roadhouse, washing his hands.

"If you ask me, I'd say that he's hiding something," Pete Studebaker said.

"There's something about him that I can't make out. And it's something queer or flukey in some way," Marty Mulligan said.

"Think he's a faggot?" asked Al Bleecker.

"It wouldn't surprise me none if he was, only he doesn't act or talk like one," Pete Studebaker said.

"Where did you pick him up?" Al Bleecker asked.

"In the saloon across from my station. I was swilling beer there one night after I locked up, and I just met him after that. I'd see him there now and then, and he seemed all right to talk to and a nice guy, only he did seem kind of shifty and nervous, and he'd never seem to look a lad straight in the eye. Anyway, sometimes he'd treat me, and sometimes I'd treat him. And so once in a while then he started dropping in to see me in my station, driving an Oakland, and buying five gallons of gas off me. So tonight I stopped over in the saloon for a glass of beer, and he was there. We got to talking again, and I said I was going out on a beer party with some pals of mine. So he said he'd like to come along if it wasn't private, and I couldn't very well refuse. And so that's the story."

"Well, there's something about him. It might be that he's been a jail bird or that he's even an escaped con," Al Bleecker said.

"There's something in him that makes me wonder. But then he's nothing in my young life, so what the hell," Pete Studebaker said as they left the lavatory.

They walked past the crowded noisy tables, and when they reached their own place the little blond fellow said hello to them. He was short, nervous, with a thin, sensitive, ascetic face, blue eyes, and a narrowed, almost tortured, mouth. He ordered another round of beers, and sat with them fumbling with his hands, glancing continually around the place, avoiding their glances when they strove to look him straight in the eyes.

"Well, here's luck to all around," he said with uncertainty in his voice, touching glasses with them after the waiter had brought their order.

"Say, this is goddamn better than most of this Prohibition needle beer, and it's got kick to it, too," Al said, laying his half drunk beer mug down on the table.

Again the little blond fellow glanced nervously around the place, as if he were looking for someone.

"Say, fellows, I met a real bum in Jackson Park the other night. It was a nice night, and I didn't have much to do so I took a walk before going home, and I picked her up. She looked so goddamn maggoty I wouldn't take a chance . . ."

"If you wouldn't take a chance, Marty, she must have been the essence of maggotyness," Pete Studebaker interrupted with friendly sarcasm.

"All right, boy, all right, don't you try and kid me. I've seen plenty, plenty of the bums you've taken on. But anyway, I let her exercise her knees, and gave her a half a buck. Jesus, you should have seen her eyes and seen the way she clutched that dough. You'd have thought that it was a twenty-dollar gold piece. I tell you, I never met as crummy a bum in all my life."

"Maybe she didn't have any home or job, and had to do something," the little blond fellow said, flushing as he spoke, seemingly embarrassed by the story.

"A bum is a bum," Pete said.

Catching the flush on the little blond fellow's cheeks, Al winked to Pete, who responded with a knowing smile. The little blond fellow, catching this by-play, became more ill-at-ease and finished his beer with a hasty gulp, which made him sneeze, and the beer ran out of his nose. The others smiled. They had another round.

"Well, Marty, how's the Nation Oil shark these days?" Al Bleecker said, and the little blond fellow smiled as if he were in perfect rapport with them.

"Oh, don't worry about me," Marty laughed, his ruddy face expanding with good nature.

"Sure you're getting yours?" asked Pete Studebaker.

"I'd be a fool not to. What do you say, Murphy?" Marty responded, looking to the little blond fellow, who grinned weakly in return.

"You're not an oil magnate, too, are you, Murphy?" asked Pete Studebaker.

"No, I'm a salesman," Murphy said.

"What line? Notions?" Pete asked sarcastically.

"Paint."

"Good racket?"

"Pretty good."

"Oh, say, fellows, did you hear about Dick Osborne?" Marty asked.

"No, what?"

"His wife tied the can to him."

"How come?" asked Al.

"Ran off with some guy, a tap dancer in a vaudeville show."

"Well, the guy must have had what Dick didn't have," Al Bleecker said philosophically.

"And that's a five-letter word," Pete Studebaker said, causing the little blond fellow to wince.

"Say, do you fellows know any girls we can get tonight?" he asked, showing his embarrassment.

"Well, now, that's a good philosophical question," Al Bleecker said.

"Hell, too bad it wasn't last night. The folks were away again, and I had the whole house to myself," Pete Studebaker said.

"Why didn't you tell us?" Al complained.

"I didn't see you."

"You haven't got a telephone, and I suppose you'd break your leg going down to a drug store to use one," Al said.

"Well, I'll fix it up next time, and we'll have another one of our famous bare-ass parties," Pete said, and Marty flung a questioning look at Murphy.

"Every time this guy's family goes away, we throw a party. We get a couple of Pete's bum broads, because that's all he knows anyway, and everybody parks his underwear at the door," Marty said.

"Sure there, Murph, how'd you like to come in on one of our B. A. parties?" asked Al.

"You'll have to let me know about one of them," Murphy nervously replied.

"Sure, Murphy, I'd like to see you at one of them," Pete said cuttingly.

"Can it, Pete," Al whispered, leaning toward Studebaker.

"How about seeing some girls tonight?" Murphy asked.

"Let's. I wouldn't object to seeing some floosies," Al said.

"Me, neither," Marty said, taking out a notebook. "I got it. There's two Polacks I got lined up in South Chicago. I'll call them up."

Marty went to the telephone.

"Pardon me there, old top," Murphy said arising.

They watched him walk to the lavatory.

"Pete, I got the guy doped out now," Al said, a light of discovery coming into his eyes.

"What?"

"I think he's still got to lose his cherry. Do you notice the way he blushes when we talk about jazzing, and the way he keeps on asking about seeing some girls?"

"Might be. But, hell, he looks older than any of us. He must be over thirty," Pete said.

"Well, there are guys like that. There's everything you want to find if you'll look for it on Christ's green earth," Al said philosophically.

"What the hell do such guys do? Seems to me they'd have worn holes in the palms of their hands a long time ago. And if that's the thing that's eating him up, he sure is one freak. They ought to put him in a circus and charge people money to look at him," Pete said.

"That's it, all right. Because otherwise he doesn't seem to be a bad sort of a guy."

"I guess you've hit the nail on the head that time. Well, as an act of simple charity we ought to help the guy out. Just think of it, Al, he's gone all these years without getting it, knowing what it's like, how sweet it can be. And think of guys like us who can get so much of it, we got to keep turning it down," Pete said, pity for the little blond fellow creeping into his voice.

"Well, we'll fix him up," Al said.

"No soap. Those two damn Polacks aren't home," Marty said, falling back into his chair.

"Say, Irish, I got that guy doped out," Al proudly said.

"What's the dope, Houdini?" asked Marty.

"I think the lad is o.k., only he's cherry."

"Boy, he must be a real dope then," Marty said, laughing in surprise.

"And we're going to get him fixed up tonight."

"What are we, a charity bazaar?" asked Marty.

"No, we're going to a can house. I need to get my luck changed anyway," Al said.

The little blond fellow returned, still nervous and flushed.

"Say, Murph, we're going to a can house," Pete said.

"All right . . . only say, now, isn't there, I mean, well, now, wouldn't it be better if we could find some girls rather than going to . . . well, to a place?"

"Yeah, if we were sure of finding them, and if we were doubly sure, after finding them, that they weren't just goddamn teasers."

"Let's have a shot," Marty said, and they all nodded.

They ordered four gins, and sat over their glasses.

"Well, boys, we're getting nowhere moping here this way," Marty said with sudden impatience.

"And those drawers of mine are starting to heat up," Pete said.

"Let's have another drink first," Murphy quickly said.

They had another round.

"But mightn't such a place be raided?" Murphy asked after taking a sip of his gin.

"Not the joint we're going to on Twenty-second Street. Big shots own it, and if the cops raided it, what would they do for their jobs and where would they be getting dough to buy baby an extra pair of shoes?" asked Al.

After a third round of gin, they left. Riding in the cab, the little blond fellow kept getting more and more jittery, and finally he suggested stopping for one more drink. They stopped, and went dutch treat on the cab bill.

"This bastard's yellow," Marty whispered to Pete as they were entering a dimmed speakeasy.

"We're going to get that cherry of his copped if we drag him by his ears. Hell, we're only doing him a favor," Pete said.

Murphy stalled time at the speakeasy, but they taunted and hurried him, and he got more and more drunk, and finally said all right, he was game to go. They staggered out and took another taxi cab.

II

"Oh, Lamb of God, Who takest away the sins of the world! Oh, Lamb of God! Oh, Lamb of God!"

Reciting these words aloud to himself, and walking along on aimless and unsteady feet, the little blond fellow commenced to cry, and a sadness seemed to suffuse his body. He stared overhead at the clear sky and was astounded by the sparkling wealth and profusion of stars. He stared at the starry sky, feeling as if it were a door opening a crack beyond to the mystery of life, and a voice seemed to drone within his mind like some strange, wailing voice in a dream.

Father, forgive them, for they know not what they do!

He staggered on, telling himself that he was drunk. He entered a Greek restaurant and slouched over a stool at the deserted counter. He hastily drank a cup of black coffee, and again found the street, to wander on.

Yes, he was drunk, and sin, ugly, black, vile, contaminating sin was upon his soul like a cancer, and it was stinking his soul until it wallowed in filthy, ordurous sin.

Lamb of God!

No, there was no sin. Sin was a myth. Because there was no God, and without God there couldn't be sin.

Look at the moon on a clear and beautiful night, feast your eyes upon the glory of the stars, and then, do you in all your feeble mortal ignorance, do you say there is no God? Then do you doubt the existence of Him Who created all out of nothing, made every living thing that breatheth and walketh and liveth on this green earth? Do you?

I do!

And the fool, he crieth out in his heart, there is no God!

And he, he was a fool. God or no God, he was a fool. A fool there was, and it was he.

You say there is no God?

I do.

No, no, I say no, no!

Father, forgive them, for they know not what they do!

But he had no excuse. He knew what he was doing. Sinning. Tonight, he had left the parish house fully determined to expose himself to the temptation to sin, fully determined to sin. He had drunk to gather courage so that he would not fear and back down at the last moment. And he remembered the girls in their flimsy slips, their bare flesh, their ogling eyes, and the dark-haired girl he had taken and paid and sinned with alone in a bare and dirty bedroom. She, touching him. He flinched at the memory.

But suppose now, suppose that God was only a dream, a monstrous lie, and there was no sin. And he was free to live as other men did, and live with a woman openly and freely in love, not go slinking into dens of vice, into brothels? Suppose? And there was no God. He knew it! He knew it!

He paused and shook his fist at the sky.

"I defy you, God, Father, Son, and Holy Ghost! I defy You. Wreak your vengeance on me! Strike me dead like a petulant old nun punishing boys in a classroom for throwing spitballs!"

He had said it. He had uttered the blasphemy that had grown in him from cankers of doubt these last few years. It was out. He felt purged now. He was clean. And he was unhappy. He was alive, and he had said it, and now his soul belonged to no God, to no bishop, to no pastor. His soul belonged to himself. He would walk on, out of it, into a new, free life. He would be free now to be a human being instead of a fake saint and a hypocrite living by what he did not believe. After all these years, the best years of his life, he was going to be free.

And the voice of his conscience suddenly struck in his brain like the God of the Hebrews roaring down in thunder from the mountain tops.

I AM THE LORD THY GOD AND THOU SHALT NOT HAVE STRANGE GODS BEFORE ME!

He laughed in drunken hysteria.

I have blasphemed when there is no blasphemy. I have sinned when there is no sin. I have cursed God when there is no God!

Again he laughed in drunken hysteria, and he walked on unevenly along a darkened street, his gait becoming gradually slower.

A wave of self-hate and contempt gushed up in him. He was a coward. If he wasn't a coward, he would take his freedom, he would become a man, and live like other men, and not continue the life of a hypocrite, with his collar turned around backward, preaching like a medicine man in a dark African jungle. He was a coward, an object of something too contemptuous for words—*pity*.

He had permitted himself to be pushed and shoved into it, and these last years he had gone on in his rut. He was a pawn. A pawn to the ignorant vanity of his mother, who had wanted a priest in the family in order to show off and win herself a high place in the Irish mothers' sewing circle among the golden angels who played their golden harps. A pawn to an institution which he hated as he served it, an institution that crushed the life out of him, made him into a walking mummy in a cassock. It was a machine, his church. It was a machine that took boys and girls, as it had taken him, and ground them into unhappy and unbelieving priests and spiteful gossipy neurotic nuns. And its engine was a lie called God. And he was too cowardly to break away from it. What if his mother did cry? What if his family did feel disgraced? What if people looked at him as a pariah? He could go away, be a free man. Thirty-four years of his life lay in ruined torture behind him. Was not the rest something to him? Take it! He should take it, walk over their feelings, wade through their tears, step on their disgrace, laugh at their scorn, and go forth and live like other men. Instead of doing this, what did he do? Lead others into the same net that had trapped him. He was a vocation salesman. Every spring, he told boys and girls of the graduating class to become priests and nuns. He put vocations into their minds. And when some of them had come to him in the confessional? What? Told them to pray that God might call them to be priests and nuns. Pray! Prayers. Daily, he prayed. For what? Pumped people full of that same conscience that tormented him. He was a coward.

And so here he was, miserably drunk, and he told others to be sober. He was returning from a brothel, and he told others that thou shalt not commit adultery. They had made a fool out of him, and he was making a fool out of others, and it was going on like an endless process, spinning around and around in an eternal vicious circle. And next Saturday he would be back again, sweating in the confessional, listening while others confessed their sins. Bless me, Father, for I have sinned. I violated the sixth commandment. Alone or with another? Both. I stole. I lied. I cheated. I defrauded. I sinned with my sister. I sinned with my friend's husband. I forgot to say my prayers on three nights before going to sleep. Bless me, Father, for I have sinned. And your penance will be five Our Fathers and five Hail Marys, and say a good Act of Contrition, and go and sin no more.

He wanted to cry, and again in drunken hysteria he laughed.

He wished that God would reveal Himself to him. He wished that God, if He existed, would strike him dead. He wished, and he opened his arms, and his mind, and his eyes to the sky that was silent and serene. He wanted to feel clean and free. And the memory of his experience in the brothel returned to him hot and searing so that his brain roared and burned like a miniature Hell.

Oh, Lamb of God, oh, Lamb of God, Who takest away the sins of the world . . .

The details of his sin crowded into his mind, the whore in her pink slip, black-haired, cynical, laughing, calling him dearie, laughing silently at him, he had felt, when she had stretched out her hand for money, her movements, his own sensations. He wanted to go back to her, and he wanted to rip his sin out of his soul. Why had he done it? But he had had to. He had had to go, to know what a woman was like, to escape from that torturing curiosity, that onanism that had filled him for years with a sense of personal and spiritual vileness.

Life was evil to him. He remembered the conversations of those boys who had been his casual companions. The gusto with which they had spoken of women. Why couldn't he be like that? Why? He knew. His teachers and his church had poisoned his mind. He wanted to live and be human, and how could he? Sin. They had pushed sin down his throat, original sin, sin until the life of humanity seemed to him like a gutter of sin and sex. And now here he was, almost thirty-five years old, and they, it, had poisoned him. He could not live. He could not be natural. He could not face life. And what did he do? He told the same things to boys and girls. And they went out and snickered and leered as these boys had tonight, so that they never could be completely natural.

Oh, Lamb of God . . .

Pray. Yes, pray. Prayers just came naturally to him. They were like a river running through him. He was stuffed with them, stuffed with prayers, and God, and the Ten Commandments, stuffed, stuffed. And so he would go on sneaking out like this, and drinking, and going back to women, until he was discovered, driven out of the Church in disgrace. And then what? Why couldn't he just walk away and be free? He couldn't. They had him. They had him with invisible chains. He laughed hysterically at himself. He walked on, harassed, flustered, miserable.

III

The nervous little blond fellow, his face flushed, slunk into the Illinois Central Railroad station at Sixty-third and Dorchester, his chin sunk against his chest. He quickly unlocked one of the doors in the row of public lockers, drew out a bundle, moved into the lavatory.

Wearing his collar turned around backward, Father Pat Doneggan walked out of the lavatory of the Illinois Central station. Ahead of him, some young fellows were cursing. One of the lads nudged another, and they glanced furtively back at him, talked in lowered voices, walked on. Outside, a girl smiled at him, bidding him good evening, and a passing man tipped his hat. Father Doneggan smiled pleasantly in response. He boarded a west-bound street car and returned to the parish house, hastened to his room, undressed, and knelt by his bed praying to the God Whose existence he doubted, for succor and strength. He lay tossing in bed, thinking of himself as a coward, hating himself, mumbling over and over again to himself as if he were reciting a mechanical formula.

"Oh, Lamb of God, Who takest away the sins of the world . . ."

1933.

The Merry Clouters

I

*Oh, my name is Tinker Tommy.
I'm the bum from Omaha.
I was born in a grist mill,
With corn meal in my jaw.
The first job I ever had
Was ridin' on a hack,
Till one fine day the horse . . .*

MILT ROSENSPLATZ had a number of lads on the grass outside the boathouse practising harmony. All of the Merry Clouters who were not outside with Milt giving their ears a treat sat on the right side of the crowded Washington Park boathouse. Down the center of the boathouse, extending from the ticket stall on the landing and running back against the wall, was a queue of people waiting for rowboats.

Glenn Reaves, a dark, wiry fellow with Semitic features and only eighteen-inch bell-bottom trousers, arose from his wicker chair and friscoed in the center of the group, twisting his feet rapidly and rolling his abdomen, singing as he danced.

*I'm runnin' wild! I'm runnin' wild!
I lost control . . .*

"*Comon* now, Jew! *Comon* now, Jew! *Comon* now!" Coady, the flat-footed, beefy, ruddy-faced park policeman said.

Glenn clamped his trap shut and made a gesture to sit down, but Coady grabbed him roughly by the sleeve and pushed him toward the exit. The gang smiled defensively, and Glenn walked out nonchalantly, Coady muttering and flat-footing after him.

"Get a move on! Get a move on, Jew!"

Glenn joined the harmony boys outside.

> *I'm the sheik of Araby,*
> *Without a shirt.*
> *Your love belongs to me*
> *Without a shirt.*
> *At night when you're asleep,*
> *Without a shirt,*
> *Into your tent I'll creep,*
> *Without a shirt.*

Three Star Hennessey, who was all sheiked out in the widest and flappiest pair of bell bottoms in the neighborhood, a striped tie that looked like the flag of Montenegro, and a straw katy with a red and blue band, mimicked the cop's brogue, and the gang laughed raucously.

Man Bleu interrupted Hennessey's mimicry to denounce Johnny Law, the old sb.

Manuel was a tall, well-built lad of eighteen or nineteen, with dark, fine and intelligent features. He wore a tight-fitting dago brown suit with a hick cut to the trousers which were tight at the bottom; his coat sleeves were too short, and the pockets were long, wide, and sensationally cut. He had on purple socks, a yellowish tan pongee shirt with a low, white stiff collar, and a stringy brown tie. He wore a seven-dollar-and-fifty-cent straw hat, the straw darkish, flexible and mashed in a number of places.

"Let's the bunch of us get him some time," Connell, the sixteen-year-old punk who didn't have to shave his cherry cheeks, said toughly.

It's three o'clock in the morning,
We've danced the whole night through;
And daylight soon will be dawning;
Just one more dance with you.
Ding-dong, ding-dong, there go the three o'clock chimes,
Chiming, rhyming, I could just keep right on dancing, forever . . .

"Well, I know something sweeter than getting put in the jug for trying to slough cops," Three Star Hennessey said.

"Hennessey, you never think of nothing but gash," Young Rocky Kansas said. He was caked out in a black suit with wide trousers but not bell bottoms, and he wore a soft-collared broadcloth shirt and a black knit tie. Like most of his companions, his hair was well-pomaded with vaseline and meticulously parted in the middle.

"If you ask me, I turn down nothing," Hennessey said.

"Not even dark meat?" said glassy-eyed Swede Larson whose infectious laughter set them all to haw-hawing.

"Swede, you're a card," Connell said.

"Hell, didn't you guys know that Hennessey loves dark shanks?" Young Rocky said.

"Big boy, don't you all speak against mah pok chops," Hennessey said, extravagantly imitating Negro dialect.

Andy Le Gare suddenly broke into one of his idiotic fits of laughter, and he nearly fell off his chair. Hennessey said that Andy better get himself attended to. Andy jumped to his feet and let fly a mule-driving right at Three Star. Hennessey ducked out of range. Man told Andy to can it, and Andy said that Hennessey was just pig-pen Irish. Hennessey said Andy was just of froggy French descent. Man said that there were two lads of froggy French descent present who didn't bar anyone. Andy looked gratefully at Man.

"But, fellows, we're all Merry Clouters," Man said.

"And, Man, we Merry Clouters stick, and I mean stick," Connell said.

> *If her eyes are blue as skies, that's Peggy O'Neill.*
> *If you miss your watch and chain, that's Peggy O'Neill.*
> *She went out with a young millionaire,*
> *She took his millions and gave him the air.*
> *If she walks like a sly little rogue,*
> *If she talks with a cute little brogue . . .*

"I smell dark clouds around here," Andy Le Gare suddenly said, sniffing.

Connell took up the theme of Negroes, and complained bitterly that Washington Park was no longer a place for white men.

"Why, a decent girl can't come over here at night," Andy said.

"No, not with the jiggs and the purse-snatchers like Three Star Hennessey around," Young Rocky said.

"But no kidding, the Merry Clouters ought to become a sort of vigilance committee and run all the eight-balls out of the park. This is a white man's park," Darby Dan Drennan said.

"It's going to stay a white man's park as long as the Merry Clouters have anything to do with it," said young Ted Houlihan, the dirty-faced mascot of the bunch, who still wore short trousers.

"And you know, most jiggs are morons. They're subnormal," Young Rocky said.

Sweet Adeline . . . Sweet Adeline . . .
Sweet Adeline . . . Sweet Adeline . . .
For your dear heart . . . for your dear heart . . . alone I pine . . .
    alone I pine.
In all my dreams . . . in all my dreams . . . your fair face beams . . .

Hennessey entertained them with an anatomical description of the last beetle he had picked up.

"The nearer the bone, the sweeter the meat," he concluded, smacking his lips.

Connell spoke of the time he had pulled a gat on some tough eggs from Sixty-third and Halsted, and Man Bleu told of the time he was thrown from a freight car by the dirty-fighting micks from around Fifty-fifth and Wentworth. Young Rocky interrupted to refer to the time he had broken up a Sunday afternoon dance at Louisa Nolan's up at Sixty-third and Stony Island, by starting a fight.

> *With someone like you,*
> *A pal good and true,*
> *I'd like to leave it all behind*
> *And go and find*
> *Some place that's known to God alone.*
> *Just a spot to call our own.*
> *We'll find perfect peace . . .*

Nettie and Martha, two broads from around Fifty-fifth Street who were always putting out for charity, came around, sitting demurely by themselves. Half of the lads thronged around them.

"How about a little put-and-take, girls?" Hennessey suddenly said, breaking in on the boasting of his pals.

"The flag's out," Nettie said.

"You wouldn't kid me, would you?" said Hennessey knowingly.

> *You got to see your mama every night*
> *Or you can't see mama at all.*
> *You got to kiss your mama, treat her right,*
> *Or she won't be home when you call.*
> *Now, if you want my company,*
> *You can't fifty-fifty me . . .*

The other boys flagged some strange beetles, and sat around them trying to make an opening and take them over to the wooded island across from the boathouse.

Cakey Phil Rolfe, the blond Jewboy, happened in, wearing an oxford gray suit with twenty-two-inch bell bottoms, a gray broadcloth shirt with collar attached, a tie with slanting black and blue stripes, a handkerchief in his lapel, a soft gray fedora, and patent leather pumps.

"How goes it with the Patent-Leather Kid?" asked Young Rocky.

"Where you stepping to tonight?" Ellsworth Lyman, who was with some strange broads, hollered over to him.

"Boy, I'm stepping high," Phil said mysteriously.

He told them that he had a date with a keen number, and would divulge nothing else about her except that she was hot stuff and lived over on the other side of the park. They razzed him. He friscoed for the lads, snapping his fingers and singing.

I'll be there to get you in a pushcart, honey.
Better be ready about half-past eight.
Now, dearie, don't be late;
I want to be there when the band starts playin'.
Tickle toe, and shimmy too,
I want to dance right out of my shoes,
When they play those jellyroll blues,
Tomorrow night at the Darktown Strutters' Ball . . . and that ain't all . . .

"You must be struttin' some tonight, Phil," Young Rocky said.

He strutted out of the boathouse. They looked after him enviously, most of them thinking that the damn Jewboy sure did rate gash.

They sat around, talked, smoked, gassed with the broads, and outside the harmony boys persisted.

One grasshopper jumped upon another grasshopper's back
And they were only only fooling . . .

II

Ted Houlihan had gone outside with the harmony boys. He suddenly dashed in and spread the good word that there were a couple of jiggs outside who ought to be smacked down. The gang was roused to importance.

"Merry Clouters, ahoy!" Man called loudly.

They scrambled outside and collected the singers, Milt protesting that they were breaking up his concert.

"Listen, Rosey, the Merry Clouters got serious business ahead. It's up to us to keep the coons out of this park, and if we don't, one day they'll flood it, and then maybe we might all even get our throats slit with razor blades," Young Rocky said.

"The niggers killed poor Clackey Merton from Sixty-first Street in the race riots of 1919, and I fought against them then, even if I was only a kid. I know 'em," Andy Le Gare shouted.

"Well, they're going to pay. The Merry Clouters ain't foolin'," Ellsworth said.

"Come on, gang, or they'll get away," Man said.

They asked which way the jiggs had gone, and Ted said south. The Negroes turned out to be one lone black lad who was ambling around the south bend of the lagoon and singing in a deep and resonant voice. Man told them to go quietly, but they raised a war cry and bellowed that the Merry Clouters were coming. Frightened, the Negro ran across the grass in the direction of South Park Avenue. He was caught in the small circle where the path leading from the boathouse to the Fifty-eighth Street entrance converged with a gravel walk. In the center of the circle was a small pond and fountain. The Negro begged to be let off, pleading that he had done nothing. He let out a shrill yell for help, but was told that if he tried that stunt again he would catch it twice as bad. He stood in the center of the gang, docile, almost quaking, his eyeballs a seeming ghastly white, his expression a plea for mercy. The guys shouted at him, and debated what form of punishment he deserved, and while they shouted at one another Ted Houlihan spit tobacco juice in the Negro's face.

"Don't you do that, white boy!"

"Why?" Ted rejoindered snottily.

"Listen, nigger, what the hell business have you got in a white man's park?" Young Rocky asked.

"I wasn't harmin' nobody. I was just walking," the Negro said.

"Well, after this, try walking in your own neighborhood, you eight-ball bastard, or else maybe you can find out how it feels to be the guest at your own funeral," Ted Houlihan said.

"Yes there, black boy, did you ever go home in a coffin?" asked Andy.

The victim's teeth began to chatter. They frisked him, and found a rusty knife with a cracked pearl handle, and they knew that he had carried it to slash a white man. They cursed him for his supposed murderous intent. They bellowed in further debate on the proper punishment to give so that they would teach him to stay in the Black Belt where he belonged.

The Negro suddenly slipped away, darting across the grass in a northwestern direction. The mob tore after him, and Andy Le Gare brought him down with a flying tackle. He was dazed, and as he started slowly to get to his feet, Young Rocky clipped him on the jaw. He shook his head in confusion, and as he begged for mercy, Glenn Reaves slapped his face. Hennessey spat in his eye. Connell moved forward to swing on him, and the Negro impulsively put up his hands to guard. Connell jumped back warning them to look out for a razor. Ellsworth Lyman snuck behind the Negro and got down on his hands and knees. Wils Gillen gave him a shove, and the Negro tumbled over Lyman while everyone laughed. Lyman arose.

"Hey, what's the idea of falling all over me?" he said, kicking the Negro.

Everybody laughed, and Connell timidly kicked him. The Negro arose on command, receiving simultaneous belts in the face from Lyman, Andy, and Young Rocky. He went down backward, his lip bleeding. Man told them to stop it. Ted Houlihan suggested dumping him in the fountain. They carried him back to the fountain where they had first caught him. He was ceremoniously baptized, and the mock ritual was concluded when he was shoved head first into the pond. They ranged around it. The inside was slippery and sloped downward, and the Negro slid on his face again and again, and it was all so funny that they roared. He reached his way to the edge, and Ted Houlihan shoved him back.

"Black boy, this hyeah is the fust bath you all's had in years," Ted said as they laughed.

"Don't catch cold there, shine," Swede Larson said, and they laughed again.

Park amblers paused to enjoy the spectacle. One fellow protested, but was told that the niggers were getting too gay and this was the only way a white man's park and decent white girls could be protected. He stood by to laugh.

They wisecracked and imitated conventionalized Negro dialect. Hennessey broke off a long thin switch from the nearby bushes, and made the Negro dance in the fountain until he slipped and splashed again. It was so funny they laughed until tears rolled from their eyes. After about fifteen minutes of it, they wearied of the sport and let the victim out. He was told to be on his way, and not to come back to Washington Park if he placed any value on that black hide of his.

They returned to the boathouse, laughing, bragging, congratulating themselves. All but Man. He walked alone, ashamed of himself. He said that after this, the Merry Clouters would give everybody a chance to fight one of their gang, fairly and squarely.

"But niggers are treacherous. Didn't that jigg have a knife?" Connell said.

"No one gets away with anything on the Merry Clouters," Ted Houlihan said.

Before re-entering the boathouse, they gave nine rousing cheers for the Merry Clouters.

III

Phil's keen date turned out to be a flop, and he was two-timed. He walked along Fifty-fifth Street toward Cottage Grove and the park, thinking up an excuse he would give the guys. There was a large gang on the corner of Fifty-fifth and Ellis, the tough Kenwoods, led by the battling Ascher brothers who were feared all over the south side.

"Hello, cake!"

"I say, cake, don't trip over them skirts of yours."

"I hear you calling yoo-hoo!"

"Hey, boy, you sing in a church?"

> *Oh, here he comes, oh, there he goes,*
> *All dressed up in his Sunday clothes,*
> *But oh, how sweet to smell the stink of his dirty feet.*

The gang made other cracks, and several of the lads waved handkerchiefs at Phil. He walked more swiftly. He broke into a run. They made a pretense of chasing him and stood in the street laughing and watching him leg it. He hailed a passing cab and ordered the driver to speed to the Washington Park boathouse.

"Yeah, Andy did a brave stunt. But I didn't see Man around when there was any fighting. You know, I think he's yellow, and we ought to elect a new president of the Merry Clouters," Young Rocky said.

"Listen, we ought to get somebody who didn't run away tonight when it looked like a hard fight," Lyman said.

"Well, I know one thing. One of the guys I smacked will remember it until kingdom come. Look at that hand," Connell said, showing his bruised right fist.

"We could elect Andy but he's too goofy," Young Rocky said.

"Listen, I'll propose you," Lyman said.

Young Rocky said that he really didn't deserve the honor, but that if Lyman and the guys thought they wanted him, well, he couldn't refuse, because the Merry Clouters meant more than did the wishes of one guy.

"I'm with you, Rocky boy. You stuck, like Lyman and Milt and myself."

Milt said no, he hadn't stuck because he didn't want his head beaten off, and he was perfectly willing to be called yellow because anyway he thought gang fighting was just too dumb for words. They agreed that at least Milt had stood by his convictions.

"And next time I'm going to have my gat," Connell said.

They stood there discussing whom they could get to vote with them for ousting Man and electing Young Rocky as the new president of the Merry Clouters. Milt listened, and kept suggesting that they go over to the park again and try a little harmony. They walked with him and sat at a bench near the drinking fountain by the Fifty-eighth Street entrance. They sang.

> *When you come to the end of a perfect day,*
> *And you sit alone with your thoughts,*
> *While the chimes ring out with a carol gay,*
> *For the joy that the day has brought;*
> *Do you think what the end of a perfect day*
> *Can mean to a tired heart?*
> *When the sun goes down with a flaming ray*
> *And the dear friends have to part.*

They saw Phil Rolfe and Three Star Hennessey strolling out of the park with Nettie and Martha.

1931.

Reverend Father Gilhooley

I

ALBERT SCHAEFFER, from the sixth grade, sounded the sanctuary bell, its echoes knelling through the hush of Saint Patrick's barn-like church. Heads lowered in pews, and closed fists beat against suddenly contrite breasts. Low, sweet organ tones flowed, and Miss Molly O'Callaghan sang.

Agnus Dei, qui tollit pecatta mundi,
Agnus Dei . . .

Communicants slowly and solemnly marched to the altar rail, heads bent, lips forming prayers, hands palmed together in stiff prayerfulness. Father Gilhooley, the corpulent, ruddy-faced, bald, gray-fringed pastor, choked his Latin, mumbled. Miss O'Callaghan's voice lifted, evoking and spreading through the church a spirit of murmuring contrition, a deep and feelingful Catholic humility.

Oh, Lord, I am not worthy
That Thou shouldst come to me,
But speak the words of comfort
And my spirit healed shall be.

Father Gilhooley descended from the altar carrying the golden chalice. His Irish blood plunged with pride, pride in his ascent to the priesthood from his lowly Irish peasant origins, pride in his power to change flour and water into the Real Presence and to carry it comfortingly to penitents and sorely troubled sinners.

Oh, Lord, I am not worthy . . .

The cassocked acolyte shoved the silver communion plate under the fat chin of the first communicant. The priest extracted a wafer of unleavened bread with his consecrated fingers, crossed it in the air, and placed it on the out-thrust tongue, muttering simultaneously:

Corpus Domini nostri Jesu Christi custodiat animam tuam in vitam aeternam.

"Sir, that is a matter for your own conscience. My action is impersonal, and I am thinking not simply of your temporal happiness, but of the soul of this girl which has been placed in my care, since I happen to be her pastor, and thus her spiritual guardian. And also, I am thinking of the souls of many more young people like her in my parish. I am older than you two people, and I am drawing on long experience, and the wisdom of my church through long years and centuries of history when I speak. You two are young, and you are letting yourselves be blinded by what you call love. I am older than you, and I see more. I see the danger to this girl's immortal soul, and to the souls of any offspring you might have."

"But, Father, Graham, Mr. McIntosh, is perfectly willing to let our children be raised Catholic, and he will not interfere with my fulfilling my religious obligations," Peggy said, blushing.

"My dear girl, a house divided against itself will fall. A home cannot be built unless there is sympathy and understanding erected on the religion of God. There cannot be sympathy unless both parties see eye to eye on religion, because religion is the foundation stone of the Catholic home."

"But Father, we love each other!" Peggy exclaimed impulsively, almost despairingly, and Graham glanced at her with raised eyebrows, pained.

"You young people take my advice. Forget this marriage, and stay away from each other for six months. Then come back to see me and see if I am not right. Mixed marriages are the principal cause of the pagan evil of divorce which spreads through the world these days like a cancer, and in so many cases it paves a sure road to Hell. I have given my decision, my dear girl, because I am your pastor, responsible to Almighty God for your soul."

"But Father . . ." Peggy exclaimed, startled, ready to cry.

"Father, you can't stop us!" Graham said, his face white, set.

"There is nothing further for me to say. Good evening!" Father Gilhooley said, arising and leaving the room with a swish of his cassock.

IX

From a window he saw them pass slowly, arm in arm, under a lamplight, and move on, their figures growing vague in the spring dusk. His blood rose. He frowned, reassuring himself that he was right, and acting wisely for the best interests of both of them and in accordance with the dictates and spirit of God and of God's True Church. And in his whole time as a pastor at Saint Patrick's no one had ever crossed him as this chit of a girl had.

I'll have none of it, he told himself in rising fury.

His anger cooled. You could take a horse to water, but you couldn't make him drink. He had done his best to explain and guide the girl, and under the circumstances he was forced to recognize that marriage was the lesser evil. But he felt, sure as the summer followed the spring, certain as the night succeeded the day, that the girl was paving the road to her own perdition. He called Father Doneggan and instructed him to telephone the girl in the morning and arrange all the details. But he would not perform the marriage as the girl had requested when she had first come to him.

He returned to the window. They were gone somewhere with their love and their hugging and kissing. The spring night now quilted and shadowed the yard, and he could hear voices and street sounds through the opened window. He thought again of how gray towers would rise above this quiet and darkened grass, piercing the blue heavens of God on nights like this one. The gray towers of his magnificent church, with vaulted nave, marble pillars, a grand organ, a marble altar imported from Italy, stained glass windows, hand-carved woodwork, a marble pulpit from which he would deliver the first sermon to be preached in the new church, packed with faithful parishioners for the first mass. He could see how the edifice, in stone and steel and wood and marble, would stand in beauty and inspiration to goodness and the doing of God's holy Will amongst his flock . . . and it would make him Monsignor Gilhooley.

But that chit of a girl! Suddenly he enjoyed the realization that she was making for herself a fiery bed in the eternal flames of Hell. A slip of a girl crossing him who might some day even be . . . Bishop Gilhooley.

He turned from the window, the excitement of his dream ebbing in his mind. And for the first time in his long pastorhood he knew that he had been . . . defeated.

1932.

Jo-Jo

I

Jo-Jo was on one of his drunks. His red and overripe nose was dirt-smeared. His thick, square face framed a primal obtuseness. His stenched ragged clothing was torn.

Jo-Jo blundered, stumbled, staggered, tripped, fell, crawled, sprawled his way through the weedy vacant lot which extended away from and in back of the Nation Oil Company filling station near Thirty-fifth and Morgan, a street crossing in Chicago's Central Manufacturing district.

People passing in this lazy dusty Sunday afternoon world paused and watched him. Strangers shook their heads, registering self-disgust. Sweeney, the policeman on the beat, walked along, twirling his club. A few of the loafers on the corner in front of the gas station laughed and said that Jo-Jo was drunk again.

For Jo-Jo, the world was all black. It was a dizzy, crazy blackness of seeming atomic energy, swooping, streaking, cometing against and within his alcohol-sodden body. He lurched through this world of smashing darkness. He tripped and fell face forward in dust and weeds. He lay there, alternating between dead fits of motionlessness, and brief sloppy spasms, punctuated with muffled groans. Eventually, he bent himself into a semi-erect position and twisted forward. He stumbled and scratched his cheek-bone. He tripped and bruised his knee. He fell and cut his finger on a tin can. He went forward slowly, slowly, through the tricky darkness.

An alley, layered with black dust, ran parallel to the prairie and opened onto Morgan Street. Jo-Jo crawled across its coaly surface and climbed onto the pile of old logs set beside the brick wall of Liebenstein's junk shop. The sun disappeared, and Jo-Jo lay senseless on the boards.

II

The morning sun came like a crash. Its brilliant light beat white streaks of pain against his eyes, and he opened them, bleary and bloodshot, upon a world of noise, and crush, and activity. He muttered because of the nausea that gripped him. He blinked stupidly and gazed where the sun smashed into the street-car rails along Morgan. He watched the factory crowds pour down to the tall, dull-colored industrial prisons. Trucks grumbled. Street cars rocketed. Foreigners went stolid-faced to their piece-work jobs. Girls, young and alive with sex; girls, young, with bodies still immature, giggled by to earn their fifteen dollars a week. And Jo-Jo sat, slowly regaining his equilibrium, mumbling to himself that only fools worked.

The early flocks of workers had all passed when Jo-Jo arose and walked unsteadily to the gas station.

"Hello, Jo-Jo, drunk last night?" the attendant asked, sipping coffee from a milk bottle as he sat on an oil barrel.

"And bo-oy! Am I sick!" Jo-Jo replied.

"You look like you been on a tear."

"I was. I was drunk. And the way my head aches. Bo-oy."

"Yes, you look gone."

"I am. I'm gone, all right. Gone."

"It must have been pretty lousy stuff."

"No. Jake and I got it at Moloney's."

"You feel as bad as you look?"

"Worse! Jesus Christ! I feel like a sick case of the monthlies."

Jo-Jo disappeared in the service station lavatory. He came out ten minutes later, leaving a stench behind him. His face was half-washed, and there was a water mark on his neck. He exclaimed that he felt better. The attendant handed him a quarter for breakfast. He left, muttering a cursory thanks, and walked away, his gait more steady.

A few minutes later, Sweeney stopped into the station.

"Say, Jo-Jo's on a bender. I saw him blind yesterday, and he just passed me, looking a little wild-eyed."

"He just left here. Last night he must have slept on the logs beside Liebenstein's junk shop," the attendant said.

"It's too bad," the cop said, sadly shaking his head and flicking ashes from his cigar.

"Yeh, he drinks like a tank. I guess the reason is that he can't work steady because he gets those epileptic fits."

"His family's got dough. They'd give him anything if he'd brace up and live a decent life. If he would put on a clean shirt and a good suit of clothes and not hang around with these here corner bums, or drink with that old scrouge, Jake McCoy, they'd do anything for him," Sweeney said.

"I guess he can't. But it's too bad," the attendant reflected.

"But you know, Jo's honest. He ain't like most bums," Sweeney said.

"I know it. I often leave money laying around here, and when he comes in he never touches it."

"He does a little work for Liebenstein now and then," the cop said.

"Yeh, but it isn't much. Liebenstein lets him do it because he likes Jo," the attendant said.

"It's too bad. And you know, when he was a young fellow he was one of the classiest dressers in the neighborhood. He was a dude. But he just went to hell, and nobody can figure out why, except that it's because of them epileptic fits he gets," the cop said.

"Yeh, drink and the fits must have got him."

"Well, them, or it might of been a skirt. Skirts can do a lot of queer things to a man," the cop pondered.

"Yeh," the attendant muttered philosophically.

"Yeh," Sweeney said, slowly shaking his head.

"Some day he'll get drunk and just go off," the attendant said.

"Or else have a fit and cash in his checks without knowing it," the cop said.

"Yeh," muttered the attendant.

"It's too bad."

"Yes, sir, it's too bad. Too bad, all right."

"He's not such a bad sort. He's honest. Too bad! Too bad!"

III

Jo-Jo had breakfast in a greasy restaurant and went home. He lived with his two old maid sisters in the frame house they owned on Laflin, near Thirty-fifth Street. They were eating when he came in, and they said nothing. Mary, the older and the more dried-up in appearance, blessed herself and her lips moved in the muttering of a Hail Mary. He drank five glasses of water, silently left the kitchen, went up to his attic, and tumbled into bed without removing his clothes.

In the kitchen, Mary cried. Lily sighed that it was too bad. Mary said that Jo would be better off dead. Lily warned her that such a remark might be tampering with the will of God. Mary uttered a frightened Jesus, Mary and Joseph. Lily said it might still all be for the best.

The two old maids sat the morning through in their musty, faded parlor. The room was thick with the clinging pathos of dead yesterdays, and the women recurrently prayed, beseeching the Mother of God to redeem their brother, just as they had beseeched Her on numberless other mornings. Now and then tears splattered down their sunken cheeks. Lily looked out at the dirty street. They had spent their chaste lives on it. It was a Polack street now, but it throbbed with Irish memories. Jo-Jo had played and flirted on it. Jesus, Mary, and Joseph! How times change, and people change, and things die and grow old! The two old maids sat and prayed, and Polack kids shouted beneath their window, just as they and other Irish children had once shouted and romped. Oh, God! Oh, Mary, Mother of the Savior! Oh, Bleeding Sacred Heart of Jesus! Oh, good Saint Joseph, please, please, drive the devils out of Jo-Jo. Please! The two old maids prayed, and Polish kids shouted beneath their window.

IV

Jo-Jo awoke at six o'clock. His sleep-deadened face was sweaty and stupid. He perfunctorily washed. His eyes were bloodshot and his beard had sprouted black bristles. On his dresser was the fifty cents Lily sometimes left for him. He pocketed it, and walked silently past his sisters, who sat eating their supper in loneliness. After he had gone, Mary cried. When they finished supper they said the rosary.

Jo-Jo returned to Thirty-fifth and Morgan. Red and Jake were in the gas station, barbering with the attendant. Jake was a long, limp character with a rectangle of splotched flesh for a face. He was like a rubber ball which bounced in any random direction. Red was a truck driver, who liked to come around at nights and chew the fat with the boys.

"Hello, Jo," Red said.

"Hello," Jo-Jo said dully.

"Where did you go yesterday?" Jake asked.

"Where in the hell did you go?" Jo asked.

"Somebody took me home. . . . And did I catch hell from the old lady!"

They razzed Jake about his old lady, but he replied that she wasn't so bad. . . . Didn't she feed him!

"Well, I passed out, and this morning I felt like a sick case of the monthlies," Jo-Jo said.

"I saw you. You was pretty drunk," Red said.

"And was I sick!"

"Yes, you must have been. Jo, you're gettin' old," Jake said.

"You ain't no chicken yourself," Jo answered.

"I am down here," Jake said, making the appropriate gesture.

"Go way! Don't pull that stuff around here. We know you. Go way!" Jo said, gesturing with his hands.

"Bah!" Jake muttered.

"Well, Red, how's your quail?" asked Jake.

"She's all right," Red answered.

"Out with her last night?" Jake asked.

"Yeh."

"Any luck?"

"No . . . I couldn't get my hand above the garter," Red answered, and they haw-hawed.

"Did you hear that? Red was out with his broad last night and he couldn't get his hand above the garter," Jo said, and they all gave Red the haw-haw.

"Well, it's true love," Jake said, causing Red to blush.

"Red's been chasing that floosie for years and he ain't never yet got his hand above her garter," Jo said.

"Red, I'd advise you to marry her," Jake said.

"What for? You're married, ain't you?" Red answered.

"Well, never mind my old lady. She feeds me . . . and she lets me get my hand above the garter," Jake replied.

They haw-hawed, and Nort happened in.

"Say, Nort. You know the Redhead here, he's been going with his broad for a couple of years, and he ain't never got his hand above the garter. Now what do you think of a guy like that?" Jo said.

"Maybe she hasn't any garters," volunteered the attendant.

Coloring, Red told him to shut up. But Red laughed in good-natured acceptance when Jo-Jo kept on razzing him, suggesting that Red buy her elastic garters that could be shoved down to the ankle.

Nort asked Jo-Jo how he felt, and Jo-Jo said rotten. Nort also felt rotten. The night before, he had gotten drunk on dago red and gone to a can house at Madison and Halsted. The joint had been raided, and he'd spent the night in the jug. The judge had fined him ten bucks, and his old lady had had to come down and pay the fine. He felt rotten. He and Jo-Jo ragged each other about who felt the rottenest.

A fat Polish girl passed, and the fellows stared at her, enumerating how many in the neighborhood were known to have made her.

"Well, Jo-Jo, think you'll ever go to work?" Red asked, changing the subject.

"Only horses work, and they turn their backs on it," Jo-Jo laughed.

"Well, I'd like to get a job for a few weeks. The old lady is sure gettin' on my tail pretty hard. She threatens to kick me out. You know, I wish I had a trade. When a man has a trade, he can always find work," Jake said.

"You said it, bo! Don't I wish I had me a trade of my own," Nort said.

"Well, Jake, what I say is this. You just better keep your eyes peeled on that Greek popcorn man," Jo-Jo said.

"No, it ain't nothin' like that. When I push my old lady, she stays pushed," Jake boasted.

"But just answer me this. Just answer me. She's human, ain't she?" Jo-Jo said.

"Yeh," said Jake.

"Well, then, she's got to have a man, and you're all worn out," Jo-Jo said, and they all guffawed.

Jake tried to refute Jo-Jo but the more he strove, the more they laughed at him.

"Well, you know, I can't see nothing to this here hanging around and loafing. All you do is hang around. When you got a job, you got something to do, and you can buy yourself decent clothes and have dough to spend when you want to do something," Red said.

"Sure, you can spend it playing with garters," Jo said.

"Well, I wish I had a trade," Jake said wistfully.

"Yeh," said Nort.

"Yeh," said Red.

"Think you'll ever go to work, Jo?" asked Nort.

"A judge once asked me that. I was hauled in for vag and brought up before the bar of justice. He asked me will I ever go to work, and I said, I said: 'Judge, your honor, only horses work, and they turn their backs on it, your honor.' The judge, he laughs, and I was released. Yes, sir . . . only horses work and they turn their backs on it."

They continued barbering. Suddenly Jo-Jo walked away without saying a word.

V

Sadie was an Irish hag with forty-five slovenly years in back of her. She was toothless and earned her living sleeping with any man who would pay her from a quarter to a dollar. She lived in a shack near Thirty-second Street in back of a tumbling frame house where a Hungarian worker lived with his voluminous family. Almost every year his old lady had a baby, and while she was in confinement the husband visited Sadie and paid her fifty cents a throw.

When Jo-Jo came to see her, Sadie greeted him with fat kisses. Suddenly she recoiled from him.

"You been drinking again. How many times have I asked you not to drink? Huh? You've been drinking. I saw Jake and he told me. You been drinking? You know that stuff ain't no goddamn good for you. Well, all right. If you're going to drink, get your money from someone else. I work too hard for my money to be buying that goddamn poison for you. Me, here, selling my soul to Polacks, to Polacks, for you to buy it . . . Goddamn you!" Sadie shrieked.

"Come on, let's go to bed!" Jo-Jo snapped.

"But it ain't right. You know it ain't no change . . ."

"Let's go to bed!" Jo-Jo interrupted.

She obeyed.

VI

Jo-Jo happened back around the corner at nine o'clock. The filling station was closed. A few beams of yellow light slunk over the quiet dusty corner. The factories, strung along the south side of Thirty-fifth Street, slung ominous shadows over the dreary stone paving. The scene seemed like an ugly mystery. Jake stood alone, propped against a lamppost. Surrounded by the night, he appeared small and weak. He had fifty cents and suggested a bottle. Sadie had given Jo a half dollar, so they had a dollar and fifty cents.

"We can get two pints," Jake said.

They hastened to Moloney's speakeasy at Thirty-fifth and Racine, Jake limping, Jo-Jo dragging and scraping his army boots against the sidewalk. They killed a pint of their liquor at Moloney's, and started on the second. They wandered around, and for an indefinite period they leaned over the bridge railing and stared down on the quiet, scum-topped Chicago River. The dirty water flowed under them and moonlight spilled shaky silver upon it.

"I had lots of stuff in my day," Jake said.

"Go on! You can't even make your old lady," Jo-Jo said.

"Never mind. I had lots of stuff."

"Don't pull that gag on me."

"If you had all the floosies I had! I said, if you had all the floosies I had, you wouldn't have a backbone left. That's how much I had in my day. If you had all the floosies I had, you wouldn't even have any backbone left."

"Can it! You're gettin' old. The old lady's got to take on the Greek popcorn man to get satisfaction now," Jo-Jo said.

"There was one baby. She was Irish. She had never let anyone get above the garter. Well, I got above the garter," said Jake.

Jake suddenly shrilled the chorus of *My Wild Irish Rose* and then he changed to *Sweet Rosie O'Grady*. Jo-Jo laughed sarcastically. They killed their second pint, leaning over the bridge railing. The river slipped under them. They reeled back to Moloney's, and got some liquor on Jo-Jo's credit. They staggered back to Thirty-fifth and Morgan, and sprawled on the logs beside Liebenstein's junk shop. They sat. Jo-Jo retched.

"There's garters and floosies in the river," Jake mumbled.

"No. Boats."

"No. Boats in the ocean. Garters and floosies in the river."

"You're drunk. You're gettin' old," Jo-Jo muttered.

"I got a cast-iron belly," Jake said, his chest threatening to fall away from his hips.

"You're old."

"Belly's cast iron," said Jake.

Jo-Jo swayed, his head wobbling.

"Old cast iron . . . old . . . old lady . . . old . . ." muttered Jake.

They sat side by side, too drunk to talk. Suddenly, Jake was gone. Jo-Jo was bent over the logs. He retched a second time. The world went black, mad, swirling blackness. He moved on, his chin stuck forward. He staggered into a telephone post. He bounced back. He eddied in all directions. He fell, bumping his head, and blood trickled from his nose into the dirt. Eventually he arose and moved forward like a somnambulist. He zigzagged across Morgan and bruised his shins against the curb. He pitched forward on the sidewalk. He sat, his head reeling like a slow-motion top. He flopped sidewise and lay curved on the cold stone.

He circled upward, and his body hurled ahead. He draped himself around a lamp-post. He gargled inarticulate sounds. He parabolaed away from the post, and spun into the street.

A Cadillac, cut-out open, roared westward. It hit Jo-Jo and roared on. The echo of motor and cut-out crashed a terror through the silent streets. Jo-Jo was thrown back and his head struck the curb.

His form lay quivering and convulsed. At dawn, a policeman found the forlorn heap. The skull was smashed, and blood had coagulated over the face, the neck, the clothes, the stone, dirt. Jo-Jo was carted away in a police ambulance, dead.

VII

"It's too bad about old Jo," Red said that night while they were gathered in the gas station.

"Poor Jo," Jake sighed.

"He was a great kidder," Red said.

"It was tough, the way he got killed," Nort said.

"The lousy bastard that hit him," Jake said.

"And you know, Jo used to be such a classy guy when he was young," Red said.

"I remember him then. He had dude clothes, and every jane on the street was giving him a tumble," Jake said.

"It's tough," said Nort.

"We'll miss him," the attendant said.

"He was always saying funny things," Red said.

"He had a good heart," Nort said.

"Jo and I got drunk many's the time together," Jake said.

"It was drink that killed him," Red said.

"Yeh, poor Jo didn't know how to take it. Last night, I kept telling him. But you know how Jo-Jo always was when he got a holt of a bottle. He always wanted to down the hull thing in one swallow," Jake said.

"It's tough, all right," Nort said.

"It's too bad," the attendant said.

"He was always a great kidder," Red said.

"He always used to say that only horses work and they turn their backs on it," Jake said.

"Well, if a guy does work, he hasn't got the time to do all the drinking Jo did," Red said.

"It's what I say. If a fellow only had a trade," Jake said.

"Yeh, a guy's got to learn a trade these days," Nort said.

"Yeh," Red said.

"Let's get a bottle," said Jake.

"O.K.," said Nort.

"Not me. I know better," Red said.

"We'll drink a toast to poor Jo-Jo," said Jake.

"Yeh," said Nort.

1930.

All Things Are Nothing to Me

I

"Who was the jigg I seen you talking with?" Jim Doyle asked Cousin Joe.

"That must have been Lincoln. He was on the track team with me in high school. He's a crack sprinter, and we have a class together this quarter. He lives near here."

"He does, huh? The goddam nigger! He's living around here, huh?"

"Why shouldn't he?" Joe asked.

"Why should he!" Jim stormed, becoming so angry that he paused, inarticulate, his face bloating with his wrath. "What are you, a nigger lover? Did that A.P.A. University do that to you too?" Jim turned to his younger brother, Tommy, who joined them in the musty and dim parlor. "He's starting to love niggers now."

"I suppose that next he'll be taking out a black dame," Tommy said with heated sarcasm.

"I wouldn't put it past him," Jim said.

"I don't see why we should think that we're any better than they are because our skin is a different color," Joe said calmly.

"You wouldn't. That's what comes of reading all those books the atheistic college professors tell you to read," Jim said.

"And I suppose you like a nigger's stink. Well, I don't. I worked with them, and I know how they smell. If you like their smell, you're welcome to it. They're animals, just like dogs. They ain't human," Tommy said with confidence.

"A white man can have perspirational odors."

"Never mind using them big words. Can that highbrow stuff!" Jim shouted.

"For Christ sake, talk American!" Tommy sneered.

"Well, what's the matter with them?" Joe asked.

"I'll tell you. Look at your aunt out there in the kitchen now, cooking your supper. She's getting old, and this building is all she has in the world. What are the niggers doing to its value? They're trying to come into a good white man's neighborhood, spoiling and degrading property values. They're robbing your aunt of the value of her building, and it's her bread and butter. Just to love niggers I suppose you'd even see her in the poorhouse," Jim bawled.

"He's got no appreciation or gratitude after all she's done for him. She took him as an infant when his mother died, and raised him, and that's all the gratitude he shows," Tommy said.

"I always said he never should have gone to that damn school," Jim said proudly.

II

"Hello, Unc," Joe said, smiling as they sat down to supper, and Unc's creased, unshaven face tensed into a scowl, his glasses set down toward the center of his nose.

"Stop plaguin' him," said Aunt Maggie, a stout, bovine, sad-faced woman with gray hair.

"Just because you think you're smart and educated, you don't have to be acting superior to him. There's plenty of people in the world smarter than you are, and they didn't go to an atheistic university to get their education, either," Jim said.

"I was only saying hello to Unc, that's all," Joe said, and Unc ate, heedless of their talk.

"Unc and me saw a movie last night, *Broken Hearts,* and I tell you it's a shame what these modern girls and women are doing with their smoking and drinking and cutting up something shameful," Aunt Maggie said as she cut a slice of meat.

"And those bobbed-haired dolls over on the campus, they're not slow," Tommy said.

"Don't be picking up with any of that trash," Aunt Maggie said with a mouthful, looking at her nephew.

"Yeah, you! Nix on the running around with the dames. You're going over there to get an education," Tommy said.

"You know, you can't get an education and make the most of your time if you go chasing after those shameless she-devils, with their bobbed hair and their cigarettes, and hardly a stitch of clothing to hide themselves. You got to mind your studies," Aunt Maggie said.

"What do you think, Unc? Think that bald head of yours would make the flappers fall for you?"

"Shut up!" Unc whined, scowling.

"Now, Joe, I told you to stop plaguin' him!" Aunt Maggie said.

"Well, I just thought the girls might like Unc's whiskers."

"You think you're wise, don't you!" Tommy said.

"If I was wise, I wouldn't have to go to school," Joe said.

"All that University does is make him half-baked like the professors he's got," Tommy said.

"I hear that Mrs. Swanson down the street is sick, and that her daughter has bobbed hair, and is cutting up something fierce. Poor woman, I seen her on the street two weeks ago, and I told myself that now there was a woman who should be home and in bed. And today I met Mrs. O'Neill and she told me."

Unc spilled gravy on the white tablecloth.

"It'll soon be spring, and all the trees will be green. I guess I'll have to fix a nice garden in the back yard," Unc said.

"And mother will be able to take some nice drives on Sundays soon," Jim said.

"I hope not next Sunday. I was planning on usin' the car," Tommy said.

"You're always planning on using the car," Jim said angrily.

"Why shouldn't I when it's idle in the garage?" Tommy quickly and hotly retorted.

"That car is mother's. And any time she wants to go riding you can forget about using it as a taxi service for them hoodlum friends of yours," Jim said.

"Boys, please, now, don't be quarreling!" said Mrs. Doyle.

"Hey, for Christ sake!" Jim yelled as Joe collected the plates. "Hey, don't be pulling such stunts. Take a few at a time and never mind a load like that. We don't want you breaking those dishes. They're a wedding present of your aunt's."

"All right, Coz," Joe said from the kitchen as he set the soiled plates on the board by the sink.

He brought in coffee and cake.

"I suppose he'd like it better now if he was eating with a nigger," Tommy sneered.

"Sure and glory be! He isn't going with the black ones, is he? What will be the end of it with him going to that school! And wasn't his father, Mike, telling me only the other day that Joe O'Reilley, the lawyer, wouldn't let his nephew go there because they hate the Catholics. And didn't I know from the start that no good could come out of that school where they have abandoned the word of God," complained Aunt Maggie.

"He could have gone to Saint Vincent's night school like Tommy O'Reilley, and he would get just as good an education," Jim said.

"He wanted the frills," Aunt Maggie said.

"What's wrong with the Jesuit university?" Tommy belligerently asked Joe.

"It's too far out on the north side," Joe said.

"It would have been better than that A.P.A. dump across the park," Tommy said.

"That house of the devil," Aunt Maggie added.

"Aunt Margaret, sure 'tis a terrible place, I tell you. Why, they take every Catholic student who goes there and lock him up in one of the towers of the main library building and keep him there until he promises he'll become an atheist," Joe said.

"Nix, wise guy! Never mind making fun of your aunt," Jim said.

"Somebody ought to kick his pants," Tommy said.

"I'd like to see one of your half-baked professors stand up to a priest like Father Shannon, the missionary, and give the arguments they use, weaning inexperienced half-baked students like yourself away from the faith. Those professors wouldn't know whether they were coming or going when Father Shannon got through with them," Jim said boastfully, as if he could take credit for the priest's abilities.

"If Father Shannon went over there he'd be locked up in a tower,

ALL THINGS ARE NOTHING TO ME

too, and held until he swore to become an atheist," Joe said, drawing looks of disgust from the whole table.

"Some people talks too much," Unc said laconically.

"Why don't you go and try to give some of your arguments to Father Gilhooley?" Tommy challenged.

"He'd ask me for a contribution to the next Coal Collection," Joe said.

"He's even disrespectful of priests. See! I told you what would happen to him when he went over to that dump on the Midway," Jim gloated.

"Indeed, 'tis a bad business!" Aunt Maggie sighed.

"Well, he'll learn some day when he gets older and has to face life," Tommy said, arising and dropping his unfolded napkin beside his plate.

Jim frowned as Mrs. Doyle arose and followed her son out of the room. He shouted a warning for her not to be giving him any money, and nervously wrung and fingered his napkin. He arose, dropped it, left the room. Looking at Unc's stolid and unilluminated face, Joe heard shouting and cursing. He shook his head and thought of Edgar Guest's poem on the home which he had once read somewhere.

"Hop in the bowl!" he heard Tommy yell before slamming the door as he went out.

"But he's my son," he heard his aunt saying in answer to long and loud recriminations from Jim.

"Well, he'll be drunk again," Jim said, raising his voice.

"God forbid! He said he only wanted to see a show, and that he'd be in early and up in the morning to look for a job."

Joe cleared the table and washed the dishes. Unc, complacently smoking his corn-cob pipe, dried them.

"The grass and the trees will be green again soon."

"Yes, Unc. The grass will be green, and there will be leaves on the trees. That's indisputable," Joe idly said as he hung the dishpan on a hook above the sink.

III

The house was quiet now, with Aunt Maggie and Unc gone to see another movie at the Prairie Theatre and Jim out to see his girl. And always when he was alone in the house, Joe felt queer, with a vague unhappiness trickling through him. He had the feeling of being in a tomb that had been turned into a museum. The lights were dim. The parlor was stuffy and musty, and hardly ever used since his uncle, Aunt Maggie's husband, had died. He had the feeling that nothing could be touched, nothing disturbed, that most of the chairs were not to be sat in, that the victrola could not be played. Music, life, these were held without the door. He sat striving conscientiously to study his Pol Sci notebook, carefully proceeding through the notes he had so diligently scribbled down from his readings and from the classroom discussions and lectures, struggling as he read to retain as much as possible in his memory. The winter quarter exams were only a week off, and he was anxious and uncertain, because he always worried before his examinations, no matter how hard he studied. He lacked confidence in himself. And he felt that he knew why. His home, his background. It was only after having started at the University that he had become aware of the poverty in his home life, his background, his people, a poverty not only of mind, but of spirit, even a poverty of the senses, so that they could scarcely even look at many things and enjoy them. And he, too, he had been afflicted with this poverty. He wanted to live more, he wanted to know more, he wanted to see and enjoy more of life, and this limitation of his background was like a hook pulling the confidence out of him. And now, when he was preparing for his examinations, he worried more than he should. For the University had unleashed in him a kind of hunger. Doors to unimagined possibilities in life had been opened to him on every side, and here he stood, surrounded by all these opened doors and lacking confidence to enter them, trying to substitute intense determination for this deficiency. He bent over his notebook, gritting himself to grind on in his study. And stray thoughts intruded. He became restive. He discovered again and again that he was losing track of what he read and letting his mind float through vagrant thoughts and fancies. And he would pull himself back to the book, not even aware of what had been the content of his thoughts and fancies. And then again his mind resisted concentration, and he dreamily tried to imagine himself after the exams, free, feeling that so much more accomplished in his university career had been put behind him. But to do that he had to study. And tonight, study was hard.

Suddenly he gave up the struggle, left his study table, and donning a cap and old sweater went out for a walk. The night was clear in

Washington Park, and the early March winds were stiff and invigorating. In the distance the lagoon glittered as he walked toward it over the hard, choppy ground. Once outside the house, he lost that sense of gloomy constriction. He was no longer restless. He could walk slowly, think. And these days, what he needed to do more than anything else was to think. And he scarcely had the time for it. He had three classes, and had to study two hours a day for each of them. Then there was the work on term papers, field work in sociology, daily work-out with the squad out for the track teams, and the housework he had to do at home. He was turning into a machine, and just at the time when he had to think, and think hard.

Here he was, twenty-one now, and he was just discovering how he had been brought up and educated on lies. All these years, at home, in church, in grammar school and high school, they had built up his brain on a foundation of prejudices, of things that were not true. Now he was seeing, learning how they had turned him into a walking pack of lies. And how was he going to go on? Was he going to pretend that he still believed in all these lies, or wasn't he? Because if he wasn't, it meant a break, it meant that scenes like the one tonight were only the merest dress rehearsal. He had one foot still in the world of lies. He carried it with him wherever he went, in memories and nostalgias, in ties that bound him by invisible threads. He was sunken in it, in the world of Fifty-eighth Street, and no matter what he did he felt that he would always carry it with him, as a sense of pain, as a wound in his memory. And it was stupid and prejudiced, and he no longer felt as if he fitted into it. He did not want to be insincere, a liar. And how could he retain his sincerity and live in it? He wanted to be honest, and honesty was impossible in a life built upon lies. And they all believed in lies, would live for them, even perhaps sacrifice their lives for them. His aunt, and his father, and his cousins, and his brothers, and friends, they all lived benignly in these lies and stupidities. And he had to, or else he would wound and hurt them, fight with them. They would not let him attain his freedom. He had to pay a price for it, and the price was they. And now that his eyes were opened, what would he do?

He had never expected that such problems would face him when he had started in at the University. He had gone there thinking that he would acquire the knowledge that would make him a success in life, the same way that Joe O'Reilley, the lawyer, and Barney McCormick, the politician, were successes. And now, after five quarters in college, he was all at sea. Every truth in life seemed to have been ripped out of him, as teeth are pulled. The world was all wrong, and he felt that he should help to make it right, and not continue agreeing that it was all right, plucking profit out of wrongs and lies.

He felt, too, as if reading more books and studying was not going to help him unless he made up his mind. No book could really help him very much now. Will power alone could. For what he must do was to make up his mind. He must cast these lies out of him, cut them out as if with a knife. And he realized now that that meant that he would be forever estranged from the world of Fifty-eighth Street, and that never again could he be in rapport with its people, and its people were his people. He was saddened, and he stood still, thinking, idly listening to the wind as it shaved nearby bushes like a razor. His bonds were broken, or would be, once he announced his changed convictions without any equivocation. They would all look at him as a traitor, a stool pigeon. They would think that he had lost his mind. And because he liked them, yes, loved them, it would hurt him. And he would be alone, without moorings. Everything that he believed, held as truth, all that he had been brought up in . . . was gone. And again he heard the wind as if it were a melancholy song.

It was not just that they, his people, could not accept him. He could no longer really accept them. Worlds had been placed between them both. At best, he would go on, and his love would turn to pity for them. The very fact that he was going to college made them suspect him, as his cousins had shown at the supper table. And he had thought, too, that when a young man had tried seriously to work his way through school and win an education for himself, the world would applaud and praise and help him, and that, at least, his closest relatives would give him all the encouragement and assistance they could. In the abstract, they all favored the idea. They assumed that it was the way to become a success. In the concrete, in his case, he was met with distrust, envy, suspicion. They nagged him. They seemed to try and hinder him at every turn. Every day, almost, it seemed that they strove to discourage him by telling him that he was wasting his time, and that he would be a failure.

It was jealousy, envy, spite. And it was fear. And hatred, the hatred begotten from narrowness, bigotry, ignorance. They hated knowledge. It was something mysterious and dangerous. Knowledge in politics would disturb the politicians with their hands in the grab bag. And the politicians were leaders, models, heroes, in the Irish milieu that had been his. Even his cousins, Jim and Tommy, fancied themselves to be politicians. Like two weeks ago, when Tommy had seen people looking at the vacant apartment over them and talking with these people he had said that he was in the political game. He was a politician because he wore a badge on election days and handed out cards asking people to vote Democratic. And Jim acted as a kind of assistant precinct captain and had a minor political job. So they, too, were politicians, and they had their fingers in the political grab bag. And they knew all that was to be known about politics. Knowledge in politics disturbed their petty little grabs, and their egos. It destroyed faith in the Church, and the Church was the heart of their world, and so many of the hopes that they saw frustrated in this life—these would be fulfilled in the Heaven of which the priests preached. Now he could see clearly why the Church had carried on such a relentless warfare against science, why priests attacked the University. And also, next summer, he would have to read through that book of White's.

He had talked with Schwartz about these problems, Schwartz who had read so much more than he, who had attained his freedom so much earlier. And Schwartz had told him about a book, *The Ego and His Own,* by Max Stirner. Schwartz had quoted one of the statements made in the book, and Joe had been so impressed by it that he had copied it down and memorized it. Now, thinking of the Church, of politics, he quoted it to himself:

If an age is imbued with an error, some always derive advantage from that error, while the rest have to suffer from it.

And these last quarters at the University he was learning how his own age was so imbued with errors, and how some profited from them, and how so many who did not profit from them wanted to. They were even suffering from the very errors out of which they wanted to snatch a profit. Like Jim and Tommy, and their being in the political game. And that was what he had planned to do, enter politics after he passed his bar examinations. Now if he did, he knew that it meant failure, or profiting out of errors, injustices, dishonesties. It would make him a crook and a liar. It would make Jim a crook. Jim was naturally good and honest and hard working, and he worked hardest to become part of a whole system of graft. And he was stupid, and in his own stupidity he wanted to keep others that way. Joe again asked himself, was that his ideal?

And still, he wondered why did they hate knowing things so? It brought to his mind an incident that had recently happened at home. Tommy had asked him a question about the Civil War. He had been reading about it in a history book, and he had handed the volume to Tommy, showing him the answer to the question, contained in two pages. Tommy had flung the book on the floor, sneered, and hadn't even spoken to Joe for several days. Such reactions made him want to give up and let them go their own way. At first he had tried to explain to them, to help them, to tell them the things he was learning so that they could learn, too. He had wanted to correct their errors, cut down the margins of their ignorance, break down their prejudices, such as the ones they held against Negroes and Jews. He had tried to tell them that the poor were not always poor because of laziness, that men out of work often could not find jobs, and even with the example of Tommy before them who would not work, they had condemned the shiftlessness of others and contended that there was some kind of a job for anybody who wanted to work. The same way, he had, after his field trips in sociology to Italian districts, tried to tell them that the foreigners were the same as any other people and wanted just to live as others did, and be happy. And it had only precipitated another of those stupid and hot-tempered quarrels. Knowing so little, they acted as if they knew everything. Nothing, it seemed, could be done to dent such self-conscious ignorance.

He stopped by the wrinkling lagoon where an aisle of moonlight reflected over the surface to the wooded island. He thought of how the last time his father had been up, he had looked so very old. His father was the same, though. He had worked for forty years in a railroad office. And during the Wilson administration, he had gotten a raise. So Wilson was the touchstone to all knowledge with him. But at the table his father's hand had shaken noticeably, and now the memory of it saddened Joe. It meant that perhaps soon his father would be dead. And what had the poor man gotten out of life? In a clear-cut focus Joe sensed and visioned his father's life for these last many years. His wife dying at Joe's birth. The family split up. The father living in a succession of rooming houses, ruining his stomach in cheap restaurants, lonely with his family separated. And soon now the father would be pensioned off to die. His hopes were centered in

ALL THINGS ARE NOTHING TO ME

Joe. In him, he saw the triumph, the success, the happiness, that he had never sucked out of living. A beaten, frustrated old man now, waiting for his son to make amends for him. All he had ever seemed to have gotten out of life were those occasional drunks he went on. And even when drunk, the old man seemed sad and usually ended up in a crying jag. Joe shook his head. Because he saw clearly what it would mean for him to hurt his father. And hurt him he must, or capitulate. And could he surrender himself as a sacrifice for such things, the contentment of a few people, the broken dreams of an old man? Even if they were his people, his father? It was so damned unfair, too. And needless, if they could only be intelligent. If! His Aunt Maggie, too, she looked for him to do big things. And she, poor woman, had had her troubles. Her husband, a good man, had been a heavy drinker. And now Tommy, drinking, not ever working. And they would be so hurt. It would leave them bewildered, with a wound cutting them to the core of their consciousness. They would feel betrayed as he now felt betrayed. And the whole situation made him see so clearly how life was not something soft, something harmonious, something that was without contradictions. It was hard, stern, and demanded sternness.

He walked on. He knew that he could no longer aspire as they wanted him to, believe as they expected that he would. He could no longer retain his faith in their God, their church, their ideals of success and goodness. He had tried to, these last days. And now he was at the end of his resistance. To continue as he had meant compromising himself, and going on meant turning his whole life into lies and hypocrisy. And at home, their suspicions were not unjustified. They sensed it, all right, just as they had shown tonight at the supper table. And soon, if he told them of his loss of faith, he could imagine the scenes, the scorn they would pour on him. And at times it seemed also that they wanted to drive him to it, so that they could indulge themselves in self-righteousness and self-justification at his expense, so that they could stand superior to him. He shrugged his shoulders. It was all coming. He would have to tell them. He would have to show he had changed, and build his life on truer foundations. Because he was choking with hypocrisy. How could he go on like this much longer, pretending, going to church on Sundays, kneeling to a God in Whom he did not believe, pretending, faking, saying yes as if he agreed with so much of their self-assertive ignorance.

He had an impulse to pity himself. Here he was with no belief, no

God, a world inside of himself twisted into a chaos. He often, these days, had the feeling that nothing mattered. Just like the statement he had heard Schwartz quoting from that Stirner book.

All things are nothing to me.

Again he stood by the dark waters of the lagoon with the wind sweeping them. A sense of mystery seemed to settle over them, pervade them. He was without words. He felt that beyond these waters there must be something. Beyond life, there must be something. This living as men did, all this suffering, all this defeat, and unhappiness, and self-inflicted pains and poverty, it could not be all that there was. If so, everything was useless. And if there was no God? And there was none. He could not believe in Him. He suddenly hurled a stone into the waters, and listened to the splash and watched the widening ripples in the moonlight. He hurled another stone, and turned his back to walk home.

He thought of how he would some day die, and there was no God. He was living in a world of death, and if he did not free himself from it he would die twice, many times. He would never have any honesty in his own life. And a pervasive pity seeped through him. He could not hate them, his people. He could only feel sorry for them. How could he hate his father, sitting at the dining-room table, his hands palsied, thin and sunken-cheeked, that ghostly dried-up look to his face? How could he hate his own past, even though it was part of a world that would kill anything that was honest within himself?

And he remembered how, as a boy, he had played in this park where he now walked. He had raced, wrestled, played football, chase-one-chase-all, run-sheep-run, looked at girls who reduced him to flustering shyness and speechlessness. Long and sunny days of boyhood idleness, and they now fell through the dark reaches of his brooding mind like sunlight filtering a feeble warmth on the cold stones of a cellar. Now he wished for them back, wished for their obliviousness to doubts, their acceptance of the stupidities he must now vomit out of himself, their faith. And it was just in those days that he had been betrayed. It was all through those years that false faiths had been implanted in him, that the threads knitting him to what he must now destroy, had been sewn. And yet, he wished, if only things were just simple again.

He heard footsteps behind him, and turned to see a stout familiar figure approaching.

"Hello, Mr. Coady."

The park policeman was older, slower now on his flat feet, than when Joe had been a boy.

"Out looking for them tonight?" Joe asked.

"Oh, hello! Hello, boy! How are ye, Joe?"

"Fine, Mr. Coady. How are you feeling these fine days?"

"Well, Joe, me feet, they ain't what they used to be."

"It's nice out tonight, Mr. Coady."

"Grand, Joe, grand, but still a little chilly for a man when he gets to be my age."

"I was taking a walk."

"Well, it's grand if ye don't catch a chill."

"Pretty soon it will be nice, all green. My uncle is getting ready to start his garden."

"Sure, and it will be spring in another month or so."

There was a moment of silence.

"And what are ye doing now, Joe?"

"Studying at the University."

"Fine. And study and apply yourself well, me boy, and make something of yourself, instead of becoming the same as the likes of them that's always about the boathouse in the summer looking for trouble. And I suppose it's the law you'll be going into."

"Yes."

"Well, work hard, boy, and apply yourself."

Joe turned toward home. No use thinking or brooding. And anyway, he had better be getting back to his studying. He suddenly crouched into a sprinting position and shot off, tearing fleetly away. He pulled up, crouched again, sprinted, exulting in unthinking muscular release, feeling his body as a well-developed instrument that would do his bidding, expending himself in a way that was release, was like a clean wind blowing through him. It made him feel better. He stopped, a trifle breathless, the joy of running and motion ebbing in him. He hastened out of the park. Back to his studies. And he had to keep his mind on them this time. Only . . . no, he had to keep his mind on them.

IV

As Joe walked up the steps of the building, he heard drunken shouting down at the corner, and saw some of the neighborhood hoodlums yelling with a female bum in their midst. And he heard Tommy's drunken voice rising. He went inside to study.

1932.

A Practical Joke

I

"HELLO, Lillian! Hydrox! How you, Ben Turpin, on this scrumptious evening?" Noel Merton said over the telephone with blithe self-assurance.

Lillian forced a meaningless laugh, and asked who was speaking.

"Gee, Lil, you're certainly looking grandiloquence tonight. Why, you look so beautiful as a whole pile of clouds, I mean you look just as swell as a twenty-dollar gold piece in a bank full of Russian kopecks."

"Thank you. . . . But who is this, *please?*" Lillian asked in a flat and unpleasant voice.

"Well! Well! Well! How many wells make an ocean? Who'd a thunked it? You don't know who this is? So you don't know who this is? So you don't know who I, the great I Am, am?"

"No!" she said sharply.

"Gosh, but this is humoresque. Just like finding a cough dropsy in a car load. Well, Lil, I'm the mysteriousness that even Shylock Holmes-For-Rent couldn't solve. But you ought to know me. Heck, I'm only the guy who just signed a contract with Flo Ziegfield, leasing all my old sweethearts to him, and I'm going to have my handsome pitcher plastered all over the Sunday papers, next Monday morning on Tuesday afternoon if the sun is shining on Wednesday when it rains next Thursday," Noel said, laughing at his own humor.

"That's certainly grand but . . . who is this?" Lillian querulously asked when his laugh had died.

"Honestly, Lil, can't you even guess who would be leasing his ex-sweethearts to Flo Ziegfield?"

"No."

"Not even if I give you a clue?"

"Please do," she asked cuttingly.

"Well, as Abe Lincoln said to King George over a bottle of Valley

Forge! But, by the way, Lil, and all kidding aside, did you hear what happened at the beach last week?"

"What?" she asked in suddenly escaping curiosity.

"Why, six girls fainted, five more were drowned—and about 'steen fellows committed hari-kari out of jealousy and despair when I strolled my manly self along the surf."

"It must have been very exciting," she said coolly.

"It used to be exciting when I was young and innocent, but now I get tired and bored with it all. You know, a bit monocle-less, as I once complained to Theda Bernhardt in Abyssinia back in 1913. You know, I can't fight them all off when there are such numbers of girls chasing me, and it's a hard life, because the first trillion of them is the hardest."

"I wish that I knew who I was speaking with."

"Well, Lillian, seeing that it's you, and not your Siamese twin, I'll break down and confess. To cut a short story long, as I once said to my old buddy, Rex Sabbitinit when he told me I was too Scaramouche, this is none other than the one, only, original, and unlimited copy and model of Mrs. Merton's son, Noel, and no thank you, I'm not Merton of the movies yet. They wouldn't meet my terms."

"Well, this is certainly a surprise," Lillian mocked.

"Well, Lil, how are you?" Noel said after an awkward silence.

"Oh, I'm just fine, and how are you, Noel?" she replied icily.

"Always glad to hear that, Lil. And as for me, I'd be one hundred per cent better, which means that I'd be just about two hundred per cent with no friction only Jack Dempsey, Glorious Swenson, Cal Hooeylidge, Dot Dalton, Polly Negri and Eddie Windsor, you know Eddie, the Clown Prince of Whales, well, they all pester me to go out with them, and it's simply jolly well frightful the way they won't even give me a minute's rest and sololiquitude."

"That is *really* too bad!"

"Yes, a frightful nuisance, a frightful nuisance, don't you know. But then it's all wrung out in the wash, and anyway, it will soon be finesse because I decided to drop them. I just turned thumbs down on an invitation to the White House I got from Cal Hooeylidge."

"Perhaps it would save you a lot of trouble."

"But all kidding aside, do you think you could guess why I telephoned you, other than the fact that I worked the phone box with a wet penny."

"No, I can't . . . unless it is a message from Marty."

"I'll have to tell you then. I have been wondering if Marty had tossed any cream puffs or Charlotte Russians at you lately?"

"Of all the foolishness!" Lillian exclaimed in exasperation.

"But has he?"

"Noel, don't be so silly!"

"And anyway, Lil, don't forget my application for best man was the first one in, and when the day dawns I'll be there with rubber boots and fish hooks to fling at you two happy brides."

"You're simply preposterous!"

"*Pre* . . . who? . . . Say, listen, don't let Marty hear you using a word like that or he'll think you're mad at him."

Lillian coughed artificially.

"Anyway, Lil, to continue as aforesaid and yours cordially until the ninety-eighth inst. of Januembers forthcoming, what's the dirt? Much of it shovelled at your last sorority meeting?"

"Ours is not that kind of a sorority," Lillian said curtly.

"Yeah, I know that story. It's just what Belle says, and then she goes right ahead and spills me all the mud slung out at her sorority meetings. I know just how you sorority girls are when you get together at a meeting."

"How is Belle?" Lillian asked uninterestedly.

"Oh, she hasn't died, caught pneumonia, or learned bridge since I last spoke with her, which was at the bewitching hour of one-thirty-six and nine halves of a split second last night, or to be more exact, this morning. Tonight I confined her to the bosom of her mother on generous principles."

"On account of that *stag,* I suppose?"

"Nope, wrong again. It was just on generous principles."

"Aren't you going to . . . *it?*"

"Don't feel like it. Didn't care to make a date."

"You didn't care to make a date? Why, I thought that it was a *stag?*" Lillian quickly said.

"What's that? I didn't get you," Noel said, suddenly puzzled.

"What about the . . . *stag?* Is it a stag where you go with . . . *girls?*" Lillian said, slurring the last word.

"Wait a minute, Lil, I got my dates all crossed. I confused last night with tonight. Last night, Alpha Nu Sigma of Park High gave a hop at the Coop. You must have heard of it. Most of the fellows went, and they were asking me to get a date with Belle and go along, but I didn't feel like it. I got that confused with tonight. Tonight I just don't feel like going to the stag to drink and chew the fat," Noel said, straining to be convincing.

"Drinking?" she asked knowingly.

"Yes, soda pop."

"Oh!" she exclaimed knowingly.

"But listen, Lil, what do you say we take in a movie tonight?"

"Why, thank you, Noel, but really I couldn't."

"Why?"

"You know, Noel, that I'm going steady with Marty," she replied accusingly.

"I know, but this is nothing serious. I'm Marty's fraternity brother, and you don't think that I'd go and steal his girl. I just thought that I'd like some company at a movie tonight, because I never care to go alone."

"I'm very sorry, but I couldn't, Noel. But thank you very much for the invitation."

"But, Lillian, what the heck, I'm not going to steal you from Marty," Noel said insistently.

"I know that!" she snapped.

"But why? Gee, I just thought that it would be a sort of a joke we'd play on Marty."

"I couldn't appreciate such a joke, and since I am going steady with Marty, I really can't go out with you."

"But gee, Lil, I don't see anything wrong with it. We're just going to a show, and then maybe we'll drive out to Naylor's at Seventy-fifth Street and have a barbecue sandwich, or waffles or something."

"I'm very sorry!"

"Aw, come on, Lil."

"No, Noel."

"Gee. I don't see why Marty should have to get sore. He's going out tonight to the stag, isn't he? Well, why can't you go to a show with me then? I don't think he'd get sore, but if he is liable to, we wouldn't have to tell him because anyway, it wouldn't be anything serious. I'm his fraternity brother, and I'm not out to two-time him or pull any dirty tricks. I just thought it would be nice if we went to a show and drove around a bit. I just got my buggy overhauled and it runs smooth as ice."

"I'm very sorry, but I can't. And I don't think that you even should ask me to go out with you, because you know that I'm going steady with Marty, and you are supposed to be his friend and fraternity brother."

"I am."

"Well, if you are, it is not right for you to ask me to go out with you. . . . But thank you, Noel, for having telephoned me."

"Aw, gee, Lil. . . ."

"Good bye, Noel."

"Well, Olive Oil, Lil, only . . ."

He heard the click as she hung up the receiver.

II

Most of the members of Alpha Chapter had already arrived. They sat waiting in the parlor at Ike Dugan's for the arrival of Marty Mulligan, to begin the regular Tuesday evening meeting. The fraternity had been organized at Saint Stanislaus high school, had grown to an enrollment of thirty-five active members in three chapters, and had been continued after the original charter members had graduated from high school.

They discussed the stag of the previous Saturday evening. They had decided that it was just about time for another fraternity party, and they had rented a suite of three rooms, two of them bedrooms, in a hotel near Sixty-third and Cottage Grove. Marty Mulligan, because of Lillian, had contributed the idea of calling it a *stag*. He had a standing Saturday night date with her that could be broken only by an iron-clad excuse. And the party had been the best of its kind, a hot shindy, as Ike Dugan said. They sat now recapitulating their experiences at it.

"That's funny, though. Marty no sooner gets in with his pig than Hugh McNeil grabs her and drags her into a closet. Marty didn't know what happened to her. But he didn't get sore. He said she was a hot number, but lousy, the kind of a broad who only favors her friends, and has no enemies. She was a neat-looking bum, though, and she knows her onions. I know that because two weeks ago Marty fixed me up with her," Al Herbert said.

"She was keen," Shorty Leach said emphatically.

"I don't think you guys is moral," Ike kidded.

"Yeah, and was Ike here a card! He's an angel though. He ought to be a priest, he's so holy and pious. He picks up a bum at the Bourbon Palace that had her heels all runned down, and feeds her gin. I suppose he got her stiff to save her soul," Al Herbert said with good-natured irony.

"I was educatin' her," Ike said, enjoying the affable razzberry they were giving him, and playing havoc with the pronunciation of his words.

"McNeil's girl won the booby prize. Hully Moses, did you hear how she screamed because Hugh made her come across even if she was sick?"

"Say, why didn't Merton show up?" Al Herbert's kid brother, John, asked.

"He was too cheap. He didn't want to put out two bucks for his share of the expenses. He's the only guy in the frat who's cheaper than Ike Dugan," Dopey Carberry said.

"Say, that reminds me, I called up Marty at his gas station this afternoon, and he's sore again," Al Herbert said.

"What's wrong this time?" Dopey asked sarcastically.

"Did Lillian find out about the *stag* and tie a can to him?" asked Wils Gillen.

"Noel tried to date her on Saturday night, and she spilled the beans to Marty," Al Herbert said.

"Marty ought to pin a medal on Noel for that," Dopey said.

"He made some break that it wasn't a *stag*. From the way Marty told it to me, it was evidently just a slip of the tongue that Marty could have covered up if he wasn't so goddamn dumb and didn't fly off the handle in that bull-headed way of his," Al said.

"What the hell is he sore about?" asked Joe Cross.

"He's blistering and swears that he's going to get Merton."

"Merton's pretty big. He might be able to take Marty on in a scrap," Mike Doyle said.

"Not a chance," Dopey said.

The others agreed, and Al Herbert said that it would be lousy for Marty to take a poke at Noel. Noel was really not healthy, and he was weak in the poop.

"That damn bitch. She's caused trouble between Marty and his friends before. She hates all our guts. She thinks we're always leading her Marty astray," Dopey said.

"Sure, if you'd believe her, we poke a gat into Marty's guts and say here get pie-eyed or we'll pump the heat into you," Al Herbert said.

"Remember how Marty and Robert used to be such good friends. Well, Robert's girl came down from New Orleans and Robert and Marty agreed to go out on a double date one Saturday night. When Marty told Lillian, she got sore as a boil and wouldn't go because Robert is so dark, and has curly hair, and she was afraid that some people might think he was a shine. She said that she and Marty couldn't be seen in any place with a fellow who looked like a nigger. Now Marty and Robert hardly even speak to each other," Dopey said.

"Robert is a swell guy, too," Mike Doyle said.

"We ought to tell Marty what's wrong with him, and how he is so stubborn and bull-headed. After all, we're his fraternity brothers," Wils Gillen said.

"And she makes him twice as pig-headed. Jesus, the two of them are a pair. When they get married, well, I'd just hate to be one of their kids," Al Herbert said.

"I don't like her," Shorty Leach sulkily said.

"She's his ball-and-chain, all right," Wils Gillen said.

"Anyway, fellows, Marty insists that we'll have to kick Noel out of the frat or he's going to resign," Al Herbert said.

"Jesus Christ, we can't do that. You guys all know how Noel is. He has his queer spots, but he's all right. If we do that, it will not be fair, and it will hit Noel like a ton of bricks," Mike Doyle protested.

"Marty is a fine fellow. He's loyal, and holds everybody to his idea of being loyal. The only trouble with him is that he's so damn bull-headed. He can't see anybody else's way. He's the only one who's ever right to hear him tell of it," Al Herbert said.

"Noel might be cheap, but he's regular," Ike Dugan said, and they again kidded Ike for calling Noel cheap.

"We can't let Marty do that. We got to reason with him," Cross said.

"Well, try it," Al Herbert said ironically.

"He ought to be getting here soon now," Wils Gillen said.

"Yes, he closes up his station at nine, and it's nine-twenty now," John Herbert said.

"Say, Merton ought to be along, too," Mike Doyle said.

"He's not coming. He had to drive his mother somewhere tonight," Shorty Leach said.

"Jesus, Shorty, you win the fur-lined dog kennel. Here we've been talking all night about Noel, and you suddenly wake up and tell us he won't be here," Al Herbert said.

"Nobody asked me," Shorty Leach protested.

III

Marty Mulligan sat at the head of the oval, mahogany dining-room table, and the brothers were ranged around it. Marty was a fattish young man in his early twenties, weighing about one hundred and eighty pounds. He had reddish cheeks, coarse sensual lips, blond hair, and a smiling, boyish face. He wore a brown sweater with the letters S. S. woven in white onto the chest, emblem of his having been a high school guard, and now he pumped gas in a filling station for the Nation Oil Company.

He called the meeting to order, and all arose. Mike Doyle, sergeant-at-arms, moved from brother to brother, shaking hands in the involved, thumb-linking fraternity grip and receiving the password. Wils Gillen and Shorty Leach forgot the password, and their lapse of memory occasioned heavy humor. Marty called for order. They sat down, and Marty looked down at his hands which lay on the table, then glanced at his brothers, then back at his hands.

"Fellows, as president of the chapter and a charter member of our frat, I got something serious to tell you," he said, speaking slowly and weighing each word he uttered.

"Mr. President!" Wils Gillen said, raising his hand.

"What?"

"I don't want to interrupt, but you remember we all decided at our last meeting that we should say fraternity instead of frat, because fraternity sounds more dignified," he said.

"The point is well taken, but now to get on to a serious matter . . ."

"I think we ought to go ahead with the regular way of doing things, Marty," Wils interrupted fatuously, and several of the brothers smiled at him.

"Just a minute," Marty said, slightly nettled, his face reddening. "You got to ask for the floor. This is a meeting now. And it isn't that I care, but you fellows elected me as chapter president, and when I am conducting a meeting I think you should ask for the floor in the parliamentary way, and instead of calling me by name you should call me Mr. President!"

Gillen smiled superciliously, chastened.

"Mr. President, I have the treasury report with me tonight, and I'd like to read it," Shorty Leach said.

"And I have the minutes of the last three meetings," Dopey Carberry said.

They congratulated Dopey and Shorty on these achievements, and the president had to call angrily for order.

"I'd like to set aside formalities for special business," Marty said with quiet restored.

They wrangled for many minutes, and then decided to postpone the regular business until the president's special business was considered.

"All right, fellows," Marty began, his face tight with determination. "Al has probably told you about it. It's this. Saturday night, while we were having our *stag*, that skunk, Merton, called Lillian up. He tried to date her. You fellows all know that I'm going steady with Lillian, and none of you would try to cut in on me. It's not the way real fraternity brothers should act toward one another. Noel's acted like a rat, a skunk, not like a true fraternity brother. He's a louse."

"But Mr. President, I can't see that he did anything so rotten or serious," Dopey said.

"Just a minute," Marty said, his face flushing, "Just a minute! Please let me finish! I saw Lillian last night, and she said, 'So you had a stag, huh?' And me, being so innocent, I said sure, and started shooting her a lot of crap about it. She said, with a suspicious look in her eye, 'And there were no girls there? And you didn't drink?' I figured something was wrong, but I went on with my story. She starts then, telling me about my fraternity brothers, getting excited and sarcastic, saying that they meant no good for me, only got me drinking and spending my money, making me neglect her, and all that. I starts defending you fellows, and I said that all my fraternity brothers were honest and true friends of mine who would stick with me through thick and thin, just as I would stick by them. 'They are your friends, huh?' she said in that sarcastic way of hers. I knew there was something up, all right, but I never expected to hear what she had to tell me. She asked me about Noel Merton, and I praised him. And then out of a clear sky I learned what that bastard had done to me. He tried to string her along with that dumb kiddish goofy line of his and he called her Lil. You know how she hates to be called Lil, and he did that, he was being disrespectful to me, his fraternity brother. She's my steady, and when you call a girl a name like Lil, the way he did, it's almost as much as saying . . . well, as saying . . . well, fellows, you know what as well as I do. Lil is just not the kind of a name to call a decent girl. And he tells her that she ought to go out with him. There was no reason why she shouldn't, if I went out on a Saturday night. And that wasn't all. He spills the beans and tells her that it wasn't a stag, and makes one of those goddamn wise cracks of his, saying that we're only going to drink lemonade. It was a dead giveaway that we were drinking. I felt like a fool when she pulled it on me. I tell you, he proved himself to be nothing but a goddamn rat!"

Finishing, Marty's face was red, his lips drawn, his fists clenched on the table. They tried to convince him that it had all been one of Noel's kiddish jokes, but Marty met their arguments like an immovable rock.

"He not only insulted me. He insulted every member of our fraternity. He didn't at all act like a loyal fraternity brother should act," Marty said hotly in answer to an argument of Al Herbert's.

"But, Marty, you know Noel. I don't think we ought to take it so seriously."

"I told you the facts, and I think they are serious. He knifed me, and this fraternity cannot afford to have members who knife their frat, I mean, their fraternity brothers."

"Marty, you need a sense of humor," Dopey said.

"Yeah, well, I'd like to see you fellows take such knifing," Marty quickly retorted, his face again brightening with a flush of anger. "Sense of humor, huh!" Marty sneered. "I'm sick of that bastard anyway. He's nothing but a cheap skate and a skunk. I've been fed up with him and his goofy talk for a long time. I'll introduce him to a friend of mine, as my fraternity brother, and then he goes on talking like an idiot and people begin to think what the hell kind of a goddamn frat, pardon me, I mean fraternity, is that, when it has to get members into it like Merton, fellows who act like they belong in a booby hatch. And then him and his goddamn junky car. He gets the old pile of tin out, and asks us to go riding with him. We pay for the gas, and then he starts fooling around with it, and won't go any place or do anything, and he sulks like a cry-baby. If we kick, he tells us that we don't have to ride in it if we don't want to. I'm sick of that bastard, and I'm going to kick his teeth in when I see him. I suppose he didn't show up tonight because he's just too damn yellow to face me."

"He had to take his mother some place."

"Well, that's his luck."

"But, Marty, what do you want us to do?" asked Mike Doyle.

"Fellows, either he goes, or I quit. I like all of you, and consider the rest of you as true fraternity brothers of mine. But not him. I can't be in the same fraternity with him. He either goes out, or I resign. I'm a charter member, and I have always tried to act for the best interests of the fraternity, and I wouldn't want to meet a finer bunch of fellows. But I can't stay in if he does, after the way he knifed me."

"We can't lose Marty," Wils said.

"But, Marty, can't you postpone any action and think it over, and wait until he can come to a meeting and let him explain his side?" said Al Herbert.

"I don't want to hear it. If I see him I'll poke his face in."

"Marty, that's no attitude to take," Cross said.

"Fellows, I think Merton has done the same thing on other fellows. When I was going with Catherine Lyman, before I joined the frat, he used to call her up on me," Wils said, and the others looked at Wils, some of them with contempt.

"There! You see! This isn't the first time. I can't see any reason why he should be one of us any longer. I gave you the facts, and it's up to you fellows to decide."

"But, Marty, can't you postpone action until we give Noel a chance to defend himself?" said Cross.

"I told you my side, and I laid all my cards on the table. I told you the facts just as Lillian told them to me, and I don't see anything more in the case. It's either he goes, or I'll have to quit."

Marty remained dogged and stubborn, resisting their attempts to change his mind. Deciding that the argument was getting nowhere, he arose and said that he would leave the meeting, and they could discuss it among themselves and then vote whether or not they wanted Noel to stay in the fraternity. But if they did, he was handing in his resignation.

IV

It was a windy autumn night. Noel's car was being repaired, and with nothing to do he was walking around the neighborhood where he lived at Fifty-seventh and Calumet. He was over six feet, thin and gawky, with an elongated neck, a goitre, and large, floppy ears. His clothes were modishly loose fitting, his jacket coat dropping to his knees, his top coat almost sweeping the sidewalk.

He strolled around, and he was lonesome. It had been three months now since he had been ejected from the fraternity. And in that time he hadn't seen much of the fellows, and he missed them. They were a fine bunch, and he liked every one of them. He even liked Marty Mulligan, and didn't hold anything against him. Marty was just a little bit too quick-tempered and bull-headed. When he saw Marty, he would explain things to him, and then everything would be jake again, and he would be taken back into the frat.

He reflected on how he had never had the same kind of good times with other bunches that he had had with his fraternity brothers. And now he certainly did miss their meetings, their parties, their benders, and card games. But he was confident, all right, that he would straighten it all out and go back with them. It would be all just like it had been before that Saturday night when he had thought it would be such a joke to call up Lillian. And he remembered the time that he and Wils had been initiated and they had tried to pass out toilet paper at Sixty-third and Cottage as part of the initiation. And the party they had had at Tommy Collins' when young Johnny Herbert had gotten drunk for the first time in his life and he'd passed out like a light. He recalled many other good times he had had with the fellows, and he was lonesome. He liked them all. He wanted to get back. And he liked Lillian, too. Lil was just a suspicious kind of a person, but she was a good kid. Heck, he would apologize to her if Marty wanted him to. He had only meant it all as a practical joke, and he had planned to tell Marty how he had taken his girl out, and just kid him a little. He laughed, thinking of what a good joke it would have been, and he told himself, in a sudden defensive mood, that he wouldn't think of two-timing a frat brother and a friend. And besides, he really liked Belle, and she was his own steady. Only he wouldn't have cared at all if any of the fellows took her out. But if he was only with some of the fellows! He thought of how it would be straightened out, and then he would be back with them.

He heard someone calling him. He turned. It was Marty. What luck! Now he could explain and patch it all up. They would go to a restaurant and have coffee an', and he would even treat. They would talk it over now. Good old Marty Mulligan! Good old Marty! He rushed to him, his hand extended, his face beaming with a smile.

"Hello, Marty! Hydrox. How you Ben Turpentine?"

Marty, wearing a sheepskin coat and looking as if he were on his way from work at his station, sneered.

"Gee, Marty," Noel said, surprised, pained.

"Don't try to shake hands with me! You bastard, I've been gunning for you for three months."

"But gee, Marty."

"Never mind that crap. I want you!"

"Honest, Marty, I've been wanting to see you and talk things over and explain to you."

"You don't need to explain nothing!"

"But honest, Marty, gee, let me tell you."

"Put up your fists. That's the only way to talk with me!"

"Heck, Marty, that was all a joke. And I don't want to fight with you. I consider you my friend, and my frat brother."

"Nix on that crap! You lousy bastard, you're no friend of mine, and no fraternity brother, either! Listen, you bastard, if you ain't yellow, come on, let's go!"

"But honest . . ."

"You sonofabitch!"

Noel fell from the force of Marty's punch. He sat on the sidewalk spitting blood, and looked up at Marty, who stood tensed, with poised fists.

"Please, Marty."

"Get up and fight, you dirty rat!"

"Listen . . ."

"Get up, you dog!"

Noel edged backward and tried to arise, exclaiming, as he did, that he did not want to fight. Before he was balanced on his feet, Marty was pitching into him, working both fists like pistons, and Noel toppled backward, fell, surprised and hurt.

"I ought to give you more. But Merton, you're yellow! You're yellow!"

"But honest, Marty, won't you please let me explain to you?" Noel begged, putting a handkerchief to his bleeding lip.

Marty sneered.

"Honest, Marty . . . Ouch . . . OOOOOO!"

He went down again from Marty's punches.

"That's what I think of you. Merton . . . you're a p . . . k!"

Leaving Merton stunned on the sidewalk, Marty walked off, satisfied that his own honor and the honor of his fraternity had been avenged.

1932.

Wedding Bells Will Ring So Merrily

I

"Honey, will you see what's the matter with Snooky?" she asked when they were awakened by Johnny Young, Junior.

"Yeah," he said in a surly voice, sitting up in bed and yawning.

He got up, turned on the electric light, dug his feet into his slippers, and flung his bathrobe about his shoulders. He saw the baby crying, its small fingers tightened against the bars of the crib in the corner. His expression became one of divided pride and weariness as he picked up the infant.

"Ugh!" he exclaimed, immediately setting it down.

"Honey, you better change Snooky's diaper. The clean ones are in the bottom dresser drawer."

"Yeah," he said, going to the drawer and pulling out a clean diaper.

He walked back to the bawling baby. He laid the diaper over the crib, and turned again to the dresser for a piece of cotton. Unpinning the diaper, and letting it drop to the floor, he handled it as if it were poison ivy. He wiped the baby with the cotton.

"You better put some olive oil on a new piece of cotton and wipe Snooks so that he doesn't chafe."

"All right," he grumbled.

He looked down at the whimpering baby.

"Now, you keep quiet!"

He followed instructions and pinned on the clean diaper.

"Now, what's the matter?" he asked as he returned to bed to find his wife crying.

"You don't need to be so mean."

"I wasn't mean. It just woke me up, and you know I have a hard day's work tomorrow."

She turned away from him, and sobbed quietly.

"Don't cry, dear! I didn't mean anything. I was just grouchy at being woke up."

"You know I'd do it myself if I felt better. I got things to bear as well as you."

He tried to think of some word to use in telling her that he was sorry. He couldn't. He kissed the back of her neck, and drew her, still sobbing, toward him.

"Please, dear!" he said hesitantly.

"Well, you got surly. Snooks is yours as well as mine, and oh . . . sometimes I get so tired."

He wished it were daylight as he lay with her head on his shoulder, feeling her nearness. If he were only out working now, he would be forgetting. He put his hand under the cover and caressed her girl's body that was commencing to swell with another child.

"I'm sorry, honey," he said, feeling her tears soak through his pyjamas.

"What'll we do, dear?"

"We'll get by, honey."

"But I'm so worried about Snooks."

"It's just his new teeth. Jack down at the office has three kids and he told me that every one of them had diarrhea when they were teething."

"But Snooks must have nourishment, and everything I give him runs right through."

"I'll call Doc Morris tomorrow."

"But we can't afford it, owing money to him still, and now we'll have to save up for this new one."

"I pay Doc Morris something regularly. He knows he won't be cheated."

"I feel ashamed, owing him so much money."

"We'll get by!" he said with determination.

"I know. But I worry."

"Now, dear," he said, kissing her.

She fell asleep, and he lay stroking her shoulder. He loved this girl at his side. He tried to regain a sense of the way his love for her had seemed different in those first days that he had known her. He wanted to remember what his feelings had then been, when everything he had done and seen and thought had somehow been tied up with her, and everything in life had just seemed like the right kind of a song. He stared out at the frosty autumn evening, and he still tried to remember and get back those feelings he used to have always after her good night at the doorway, on just such an evening as this one.

He remembered, too, how he would sometimes stop in Gus' over on Fifty-eighth Street for coffee an'. He'd usually meet some of the old bunch there, and he'd sit with them while they barbered away. He'd never been much at jawing, so he'd always just listened. Even if he didn't have a gift of gab like some of the boys, still he got along all right at selling. Yes, sir, he was a good salesman, even if he had to say so himself. He could remember now how, sitting with the boys, he'd feel proud and equal to them, because he, too, had a girl of his own and no one could take her away from him. And when they'd ask him what he was doing, he'd say that he'd had a date with his girl. He had been able to sit with them unashamed, knowing that he had something.

He tried, also, to remember how he used to feel when they would sit, hands clasped, in the Tivoli Theatre, listening to the moonlight songs that Milton Charles played on the organ, and of how he used to feel afterward when they would be eating waffles in Kling's Restaurant, their knees touching, himself looking at her, thinking how lovely she was, how she was made just for him to kiss, and to pet, and to love. He wanted to remember all these things, and he couldn't regain the feelings that had welled up in him, and now they were only a fading set of memories. He glanced out at the frosty night again, so like those other frosty nights. He looked down at his girlwife, and kissed her. He lay back, drowsy.

It seemed as if he had only fallen asleep when Little Johnny Junior again awakened him with loud and pitiful cries.

"I'll get up this time, honey."

"No, babe, you need rest," he said, throwing the covers aside.

II

In the morning, Young came out of the bathroom, his face still bleeding from a small razor cut, and he saw Beatrice setting the table. Suddenly, her face contorted from pain. He rushed to her side, held her firmly, feeling himself helpless and unnecessary. She went to the bathroom to vomit, and came out smiling, but her young face seemed as if it had accumulated five extra years.

"You go back to bed, dear, and I'll make my own breakfast," he said kindly.

"I'm all right now, honey."

"Go on. You've already been up at six to feed the little fellow, and you'll have a hard day. You go back to bed."

"I'm all right," she said as he gently led her to the bedroom.

He tried to sing as he went toward the stove, but there weren't any songs in him. He was tired, and life was a pretty heavy thing that thinned one's face and fell like a lump on one's shoulders.

He disregarded her instructions, and made the coffee by putting it and water into the pot together. He broke eggs on the frying pan before the oil was hot, and he stirred them around hastily. They dried on him. He decided that he didn't feel like frying any bacon, and then he guessed that he'd just eat bread instead of toast. He cut four slices, leaving the board filled with crumbs.

"Now, John, don't bolt your food," she called in to him.

He finished his breakfast in about four minutes. He kissed her goodbye, and then looked at his boy. It resembled him sleeping there, it was getting teeth, and soon it would be saying Daddy. He smiled. He kissed Beatrice goodbye a second time, and left carrying his small sample case.

"Hello, Young," Joe said as they met at the corner of Fifty-eighth and South Park.

"Going to school, Joe?"

"Yeh, John, I got an eight o'clock class."

"You ought to be finishing up at the U pretty soon."

"I got a couple of more years to go."

"It takes a long time, doesn't it?"

"Six years for a law course, and it's hard work. All I'm hoping is that I don't have to flunk and stay longer."

"It'll be worth it when you're a lawyer."

"I hope so. And how are you these days, John?"

"Pretty good, Joe. I'm working every day."

"Good. Getting along?"

"Yeh. My baby is sick now, though."

"I'm sorry to hear that, John. Gee, I hope it isn't anything serious."

"No, just getting in its teeth."

"Well, I'm glad it's nothing serious."

"How is your aunt, Joe?"

"Fine, John, fine."

"Say I asked for her."

"And, John, did you hear that Dan is in New York?"

"No."

"I got a letter from him. He's got a pretty good job there, selling advertising, and he likes it."

"That's good," Young said without interest.

"Well, John, I got to dash to make my class."

"Say, Joe, come up and see us some night, and we'll talk about old times."

"I will, John, as soon as I can. Only for a while I'll be busy studying every night. It's hard work. But as soon as I can get a free night, I will."

"Do, Joe. We stay in most nights on account of the baby and we'd like to see you."

"So long, John."

Young tried to figure out the sales talk he would use selling the new Silver brand of toothpaste. This week there was a good premium on it, and he wanted to sell as many as he could. Boy, wouldn't it be great if he could sell five or six gross of them, maybe more.

Joe was going to school, and Dan was free in New York having a good time. He didn't like Dan, and suddenly he envied him. He remembered when they had been kids. Dan had been considered a good scrapper. Well, he'd never been afraid of the goof. And when he'd fought Andy Le Gare, and everybody thought that he'd been licked, he hadn't at all. And he remembered the day they had had that big snow fight in Dan's backyard. He'd packed a snowball tightly, held it under rainpipe drippings to get it icy, and then let go. It had plopped Dan square behind the ear, and that had ended the snow fight. Funny. Young smiled at the remembrance. And he sort of wished . . . but then, well, he had his baby, and none of the fellows could say *my baby* the way he could. The baby and his wife, they both meant more and were worth more than going to school like Joe, or being free in New York like Dan, or chasing around with the old bunch that hung out over at Fifty-eighth Street.

"Hello, John."

"Hello, Runt."

"Say, am I shot! I was blind last night."

"Yeah."

"Some broad over around Sixty-fifth and Ingleside threw a party. And let me tell you, she was swell muggings, too. But I don't know how the hell I got home. It must have been five o'clock. Say, with the head I got, I sure don't savvy the idea of going down to the office. I won't be worth a nickel all day."

Young smiled. His old difficulty of not being able to talk much seemed to be checking his tongue.

"Well, how's the happy married man?"

"Oh, all right, Runt."

"That's good. And how's Beatrice?"

"Fine . . . But say, Runt, you promised to come up and see us some night."

"Gee, that's right. Well, I will soon. Tell Beatrice I'm coming, and that I want to get a good squint at Johnny Young, Junior."

Young smiled.

"Business all right?"

"Pretty good," Young said.

"Glad to hear it," Runt said, offering Young a cigarette.

"You got to be hustling now to bring home the bacon to the family, I guess," Runt said after Young had refused the proffered cigarette.

Young nodded affirmatively.

"But maybe it's better at that, being married. You don't get headaches and hangovers like I got now."

Young smiled thinly.

"But I guess I better be hitting it. Still, I don't know how in hell I'm going to get through the day."

"Don't forget to come and see us, Runt."

"I won't. So long, John."

Young walked on. He and Runt had used to be good friends. Well, they still were, only they didn't seem to be much interested in talking to each other any more.

He tried to think about the line of approach he would use in selling that Silver toothpaste.

III

"Hell, I thought that I got rid of you the other day," Syzmanski said as Young walked into his drug store.

"I got something special."

"You birds!"

"How does that Silver toothpaste go here?"

"Lousy. I got five left out of the half dozen you rimmed me into taking. Don't talk that junk to me. If I don't sell the rest of it soon, I'm going to spread it around the back of the store for rat poison."

Young opened his sample case and waited toward the back of the store while Syzmanski took care of a customer.

"What, you starting in this high-pressure stuff? Hell, I was just beginning to like you because you seemed to be the only salesman coming around here who wasn't one of the high-pressure boys."

Young smiled, a bit vacuously.

He offered some pieces of advertising copy to Syzmanski, pointing particularly to one which showed a flapper with ivory white teeth against a silvery background. Beneath her pert chin there was a silver tube of toothpaste and the words . . . *My teeth just get the bow-wow-wows when I don't give them Silver's.*

"How you like it? It's only one of many that will be used in a national advertising campaign which is being launched next week."

"Now, do you believe all that?"

"Well, that's why I came to see you. It looks like it's going to click! You know, business men don't spend money in national advertising campaigns for nothing."

"I guess not. But I tell you, that stuff hasn't gone around here."

"Wait until this campaign makes people Silver-conscious. Here, we're furnishing window displays like this one," Young said, handing Syzmanski a cardboard on which were suggested window displays. "And we're giving a coupon with every package. Three of these coupons entitles a customer to receive free either a tube of shaving soap or else cold cream. And look at this announcement. We're holding a contest, and paying three thousand dollars in cash prizes for slogans. I tell you, it looks like it'll go over."

"Christ, a poor struggling druggist hasn't got much protection from you guys."

"Well, you know, I always give you the straight stuff," Young said.

"Sure, I know. Only those fellows that pay you can think up more schemes than Yellow Kid Weil. They're birds!"

"It's the same for all of us, I guess. We got to make a living," Young said.

"Yeh, we all got to make a living. I suppose none of us would be

IV

"You poor dear, you look tired," Beatrice said as he sat down to the supper table.

"I tried hard today to keep up my record, but I don't know, it didn't go so well. I don't know! Particularly that Silver's. I sold thirty-three dozen on Monday, and fifty-one on Tuesday, and then I thought that I'd have a record week. And these last three days I only got rid of twenty-eight. I used good arguments, explained the advertising campaign carefully, did my best. I don't know. I just couldn't sell much. Maybe I'm just no damn good."

"Now don't you worry. You've still got tomorrow morning, and there's always another week."

"Yes, but I'll get put on the carpet for it when I go into the office tomorrow, and then next week there won't be that premium."

"Honey, you just eat your supper and forget about it."

"How's Snooks?"

"Much better. The formula is very good for him."

"I'm glad," Young said, eating.

After drying the dishes he sat down to read. His newspaper was at least thirty minutes of forgetfulness. He read slowly, with greedy eyes. The longer he read, the longer he had something to do, and the shorter the night seemed. Finally he was finished, and had to lay the paper aside. He yawned. He looked at Beatrice as she knitted for the new baby. He was envious of her, and guessed that all women were like that. They could be satisfied and happy and sing while they did things for their babies and their husbands, and they didn't feel, well, like he did now. They didn't feel that same need of finding something to do that men did. The right kind of wives didn't anyway.

He went and looked at his sleeping baby. Yeah, soon it would be saying . . . Daddy.

He came back, kissed his wife, slumped into a chair, yawned.

"Think we might take a chance of leaving Snooks alone and go see a show at the Prairie?"

"I'm afraid, dear. But you go ahead."

"I don't want to without you."

"Now you go ahead."

He did want to, all right, but he wanted to be fair and not leave her home alone. He wanted to see pictures of pretty women in swell clothes. Because they made him think of those times, back before they had had the baby. Some pictures almost made him feel like then. She had been prettier in those days, too, and pretty women in the pictures helped him remember her. And somehow he felt that it was very important and very necessary to remember those feelings he used to have.

Again he looked at his sleeping baby. He came back and kissed his wife as she sat absorbed, knitting, singing as she worked. He got out his bank book and studied it. Only an account of fifty-two dollars. He needed much more than that. He tried to think of having a record Saturday morning's sales. He yawned.

V

About nine o'clock, Young went out to buy a copy of the morning's edition of *The Chicago Questioner*. It would get him through the rest of the evening, and anyway, in the morning he didn't have time to read a paper. And tomorrow afternoon he would go out marketing with Beatrice, and in the evening they had a woman in to watch the baby while they went to a movie. On Sunday they would spend the day with his father and mother, and it would be easy to get through.

"Hello, Nate," he said to toothless Nate at the paper stand under the elevated station.

He paid for a paper, and Nate, expressionless, with tobacco juice slobbering down his chin, told him about a chicken he had made lay eggs, and she had been a real hot one, too. Young recalled how all the kids in the neighborhood had played tricks on Nate. Studs Lonigan, his cousin, Taite, Kenny Kilarney and the guys in that bunch had once kidnapped him and hung him by the shoulders to a telephone post in an alley. When he thought of things like that, it was suddenly hard for him to realize that he was a man now, with responsibilities and a family to support, and not still a kid.

"Hello, John, where you been keeping yourself?" Ellsworth Lyman, who stood with some other fellows near the station, said.

"Hello, mister," Denny Dennis added.

"Where you been hiding?" Marty Hockstein asked.

"Hello, boys," Young said, smiling thinly.

"How does it feel to be a father?" Denny asked, and Young grinned.

"Seems to me the lad is a fast worker," Phil Rolfe said.

"No tricks. It just happens," Young said.
"And how's Young Junior?" Denny Dennis asked.
"Fine."
"Does he call you daddy?" asked Marty.
"He will soon."
"I suppose you're workin' hard these days," Lyman asked.
"Yes, I'm selling wholesale drugs."
"Must be pretty good pay."
"Fair."
"Anyway, break down and tell us the secret of how it feels to be a daddy," said Phil.
"My kid is a good little brat."
"Yes, and I'll bet that all you do at night is walk the floor in carpet slippers and plead with it to please go sleep," Marty said, causing them to laugh.
"Not any more. He cried at first, but we got him trained."
"But anyway, boys, what I want to know is what are we going to do tonight?" asked Lyman.
"Gloria Swanson is at the Michigan," Marty said.
"How about taking in a jigg somewhere, boys?" Phil asked.
"Don't your feet ever get tried?" asked Lyman.
"Phil doesn't dance with his feet," said Denny.
"Come on, let's go before we miss the last show," said Lyman.
"Want to come along, John?" asked Marty.
"Not tonight, thanks," Young said.
They said so long, and Young drifted on home.
"Young doesn't look so good," Lyman said as the group walked down to the Michigan Theatre at Garfield Boulevard.
"He was bigger than any of us when we were punks. But it was funny, he just stopped growing," Dennis said.
"His face is thin, and no color in it. He looks bad," said Marty.
"Maybe his wife takes it all out of him," Phil smirked.
"Something has taken the life out of the poor bastard," said Lyman.
"He was always quiet when he was a kid. But now, when he's quiet, he somehow seems different. When he smiles, you get the feeling that he's apologizing to you for something," Denny said.
"And once he almost beat up goofy Andy Le Gare in a fight," Marty said.

"He couldn't lick his baby now from the worn-out look he has," Lyman said.

"But if you guys asked me, I'd say this. If we went to a hop, we might not dance with Gloria Swanson, but we could find plenty of nice beetles to rub ourselves against, and maybe afterward, who knows. If we go to the Michigan, all we can do is see Gloria Swanson on a screen," Phil Rolfe said.

"Don't you ever think of anything except gash?" asked Marty.

"Tell me something, kid, that's nicer to think of, and I'll try it out right off," Phil countered.

VI

Young walked home slowly. He had never had the life the bunch had, or done the things they did, or run around the way they did. He'd just never felt like doing those things. He wondered now, were they better off than he was? He didn't know. But he'd like to see Gloria Swanson, and just sit in the show remembering. Sometimes he thought that maybe it was better, being free and without responsibilities, like the lads were.

At home, he read his newspaper. He glanced up from an account of a raid on a minister's love nest to notice his wife singing as she knitted. She was beautiful in a way, this girl, his wife, with her expanding maternity. Having a baby was supposed to make a woman ugly, but there had been times like this, when Johnny Junior had been coming, and she had knitted and hummed, with a beam in her face, and she had seemed very beautiful. Only men couldn't feel that way and be satisfied. There was something different about them. Sometimes, like now, he even thought that he wasn't happy. It was dull and hard, dragging through the evenings. Anyway, the weekend wasn't so bad. And Sunday he would be showing off the baby to his mother and father. He turned back to the account of the raid on the minister's love nest.

He yawned, and let the paper drop to the floor. He went and looked at the baby, bent down and brushed a kiss on its forehead. He hoped that it wouldn't be squalling and waking them up tonight. Soon it would be saying . . . Daddy.

"I'm going to bed," he said, covering another yawn.

1933.

The Benefits of American Life

Ye orphan sons of Greece,
Scattered hither and beyond,
Persecuted and forlorn,
And by all nations beshun.
From a Greek poem translated by Paul Javaras

TAKISS FILLIOS was a strong shepherd boy whose homeland was located just at the hollow valley of two mountains in Arcadia, Greece, in the central section of the Peloponnesus. He grew up on goats' milk and on pitch black bread whose cinders were not separated so as to produce more bread per pound. His hard-working mother sold a piece of land, which produced enough wheat to pull the family through the whole year, in order to pay his steerage fare to America. For in America the streets were paved with gold; the buildings were taller than mountains; the women all dressed like princesses and the men had their pockets lined with money; every boy had a bicycle; and every man and woman owned an automobile. At the age of thirteen, Takiss, large for his age, arrived in a paradise known as Chicago.

He was met at the railroad station, a scared and bewildered boy, by a relative who took him to a home on South Halsted Street. With voluble beneficence, the relative immediately employed Takiss, offering him a salary of fifteen dollars a month and the privilege of sleeping on marble slabs in his candy kitchen. He told Takiss that all successful Greek men started that way, and he showed the boy Greek newspapers with pictures of stern, mustachioed Greek restaurant owners and candy-store proprietors who recounted the story of their rise to fame and offered themselves as favorable candidates for marriage. And as a final word of advice, the relative told Takiss that his mother was getting old now, and that he should send her some of his wages to help her out.

Takiss quickly discovered what it meant to live in paradise. It meant working from six in the morning until six in the evening, and until even later on week-ends. It meant sweeping out the store, washing dishes and windows, polishing, arranging, mopping, running errands. It meant attending night school to learn English when he could scarcely keep his eyes open and where he was frequently laughed at for his blundering efforts. It meant walking along, living in the midst of dirty streets where coal dust, soot, smoke, and the poisonous fumes of automobiles choked his nostrils and made him cough. It meant lonesome memories. For a long period, Takiss was a lonely boy remembering his homeland and his Grecian mountain, remembering the long, slow days with the sheep, remembering the games he had played with other boys, remembering the smile and kiss of his old mother, remembering always.

And he was afraid of America, and of that tremendous paradise known as Chicago. He worked doggedly day after day, earning his fifteen dollars a month, catching a cough from sleeping on marble slabs. He worked doggedly, and from his wages he saved a pittance which he deposited in an immigrants' savings bank. But he looked ahead to the day when he would be famous, with his picture in the Greek newspapers, a pride and an honor to his native Greece and to the great tradition of the great Socrates about whom his relative so frequently boasted. He dreamed of the time when he would become like Americans, talk like them, wear their clothes, ride in automobiles just as they did, walk along the streets with pretty American girls.

In time, Takiss learned things. He learned American words, but never how to speak them like an American. He learned that he was considered a dirty Greek greenhorn, and that many Americans would have been just as pleased if he and many of his countrymen had never come to their land. And he learned that American girls laughed sardonically at a young Greek greenhorn. Also, he learned of a place owned by a cousin of his, where for a little money he could go and find American girls who did not laugh at a Greek greenhorn, at least for five or ten minutes. He learned how to buy American clothes on installments, to wear a purple silk shirt, purple socks, and an orange tie. And he learned, also, that in the store he could put some of the money received for sales into his pocket instead of into the cash register.

Eventually, the cousin employing him discharged him in anger, branding him a crook, a robber, a traitor. In the heated quarrel, Takiss asked him why, if he wanted honesty, he paid only six dollars a week wages, when he made so much money himself selling bad products and got his picture in the Greek newspapers as a successful pioneer in America.

Takiss was employed by other of his countrymen, in fruit stores, soda parlors, at hot-dog stands, and in restaurants. He acquired additional American knowledge, and more American words. And sometimes when he was dressed up, wearing his purple silk shirt with socks to match, and the orange tie, he would walk in the parks or along Halsted Street, seeing American girls, wishing that he had one of his own, a blonde girl with a beautiful pink-white complexion.

Time slid from under Takiss, and he was a young man in his early twenties, with his first citizenship papers. He had worked like a dog, and he was still slaving at the same jobs, performing the same tasks and chores as he had always done since he had come to America. He earned eight dollars a week and was busy twelve hours a day in a candy store. He cleaned and he mopped; he scrubbed; he polished; he washed; he waited on trade. And often when he was alone in the store he pocketed money from the cash register. Every week he deposited money in the bank, and almost nightly he looked in his bank book, proud of his savings, thinking of how he was going to achieve fame in America. But he was never able to save money, because he was always quitting or losing jobs and having to use savings to support himself between jobs, as well as to send money to his mother.

And he learned another thing . . . he learned how to dance like Americans. A Greek-American friend told him of a dancing school called a taxi-dance hall on West Madison Street, and showed him an advertisement from the Greek-American owner, Professor Christopolos, who stated in the ad that anyone could be as graceful as he if they learned dancing from his beautiful girls at only ten cents a dance. He paid a dollar and was given ten tickets and entered the dimly lighted dancing school of Professor Christopolos on the fourth floor of a dingy and decrepit building. Each ticket was good for one dance which lasted from a minute to a minute and a half. Any girl in the place would dance with him, because she received five cents for each dance. Takiss' tickets were quickly used up, and he bought more. It did not matter if he danced woodenly and clumsily, and the girls acted delighted to teach him. He went to this taxi-dance hall regularly, spending three, four, and five dollars every visit, and once in a while a girl would ask him if he wanted to take her home, and for a few more dollars he could get other favors, too. After he started going to the taxi-dance hall regularly he was able to save less money, and he sent little to his mother.

Takiss then spent some of his savings for a suit with bell-bottom trousers. He cultivated a mustache and long side-burns, greased his hair and parted it in the middle with meticulous attention. He began to look like a sheik, and listened to pick up all the words which the American-born sheiks used. He went to public dance halls where there was only an admission fee and longer dances. At these places, there were always swarms of girls, pretty American girls, some of them tall and beautiful blondes with milky skins and red lips like cherries. He would ask them to dance. Often they would dance with him, once. He would talk, and they would catch his accent, and when he asked them for a second dance they would thank him with great regret and exclaim that all their other dances were taken. So he would quickly be driven to dancing with the homely and ugly girls who were called wallflowers. And then he would go back to Professor Christopolos' dancing school, where all the girls would dance with him for ten cents a dance.

One day, Takiss was twenty-five. His native Grecian mountains seemed to have receded in time and he saw them only in painful mists of memory, recalling their details and contours with lessening concreteness. Greece to him was a memory. He had been in America for twelve years, and he was working ten hours a day in a hot-dog stand for ten dollars a week, and able to graft from three to five dollars a week extra. He wanted to make money and to become famous like some of his Americanized countrymen. And when he was a rich man with a hot-dog stand or a restaurant of his own, he would return to Greece with an American wife and act like a millionaire. And he had thirty-five dollars in the bank as a start toward these riches. He wanted to get more money, but not by running a brothel as his fourth cousin George did, and not bootlegging as did George's friend, Mike. He remembered the things his mother, now dead, had told him, and he wanted to make his money and his fame in a way that his mother would have approved of. And then he would have his picture in a Greek-American newspaper.

And hard times came to America. Takiss was out of work in the winter, and again his savings melted. He was employed for ten dollars a week in a candy store, still working twelve hours a day, and in four months that job was gone. He worked for seven dollars a week washing dishes in a large restaurant, and then his pay was cut to five dollars, and he went home every night tired, with chafed hands and an aching back. He had less money, also, for taxi dances. And he lost that job.

He walked the streets looking for other work, and always he learned the same story . . . hard times. He ate very frugally, lived in a chilly, rat-infested room, and wished that he was back home again in his native Grecian mountains, or else that he was a rich and famous American Greek. Every day he went out looking for a job, and sometimes he found work for a few days or a few weeks and was able to skim along while he tried again to find work.

One day he saw an advertisement with large letters at the top . . . DANCE MARATHON. The word Marathon struck him. Greek. He would win it and win another victory for his country as it had been done in ancient times. He would become a famous Greek athlete. He investigated, and learned that it was a contest in which everybody tried to dance longer than the others, and the winner received a five-hundred-dollar prize. And maybe if he won it, he would get a job in the moving pictures and become the idol of American girls, or go on the vaudeville stage, or be hired to dance in a cabaret. And while he was in the contest, he would be cared for, fed, and there would be no room rent to pay. He was strong and husky, even if he had been getting coughs in his chest for years ever since he had slept on those marble slabs. And he could dance. He was used to standing on his feet all day at work. And this was his chance to become rich. He would no longer have to tramp all over town to be told that there were no jobs because it was hard times. This was much better than saving up to own a candy store and grow fat like the American Greeks for whom he had worked. And after he won this contest, and became famous, he would go back to Greece with a trunk full of clothes and money, and maybe a rich American girl whose skin was like milk.

Takiss entered the dance marathon, and when the rules were explained to him, he only understood that he was to stay out on the floor and dance, and if he was able to do that longer than anyone else, he would get five hundred dollars. A number was pinned on his back, and he was assigned a partner named Marie Glenn, a beautiful blonde American girl of the type he had always dreamed of as a possible wife. At first, when she met him, she shuddered, and her face broke into an expression of disgust. But then she saw that he was strong and husky with broad shoulders, and she smiled, offering him a limp hand and sweetly telling him that she knew they were sure going to be the winners.

The dance marathon was conducted in a public dance hall on the south side of Chicago. A ring was placed in the center with an orchestra dais at one end. Around the ring there were box seats, and behind them, rising rows of bleacher benches. The opening was described, in advertisements, as gala. An announcer talked through a microphone, and the promoters and judges wearing tuxedoes also addressed a full house. The contestants were introduced and some of them, but not Takiss, spoke to the crowd and the large radio audience all over America. It was all a new and promising, if confusing, world to Takiss, and he walked around the floor, feeling as lost and as out of place as he had on those first days in America. But it was leading at last to paradise.

The contest swung into action. They danced for three minutes out of every ten, and walked around and around the floor for the remaining time; and they were given fifteen minutes rest out of every hour. There was glamor in being watched by so many people, in eating sandwiches and drinking coffee before them, in receiving attention from doctors and nurses, and meeting all the others who, like himself, saw at the end of this contest five hundred dollars and fame. As the contestants got to talking to each other, Takiss heard them using one word over and over again . . . celebrity. A celebrity was somebody who was important, like Jack Dempsey and movie stars and Mr. Delphos, the famous American-Greek who was wealthy and owned a large dance hall known as the Bourbon Palace. They all wanted to be celebrities. And Takiss, too, he determined that he was going to be a celebrity.

Takiss had not imagined that anyone could dance for more than a week like this, and that maybe after a sleepless and tiring week he would be the winner. In less than twenty-four hours he learned that it was a grind more gruelling than he had calculated, and while he doggedly gritted his teeth, he determined that he would not let himself drop out. Still, he wished that he had not entered it. He wished he were back working in fruit stores and ice cream parlors the way he had been before hard times had come. He wished that he were a shepherd back in the Grecian mountains.

When his partner was tired, she put her arms around his neck or hips, laid her head against him, and fell asleep while he dragged her heavily around the floor, and when he fell asleep she did the same with him. Again and again their bodies were jolted, shoved, pushed against each other, and he began wanting her so that her very nearness became excruciating. And he noticed that she, particularly in the early dog hours of the mornings when there were scarcely any spectators in the hall, began brushing herself against him at every opportunity, looking feverishly into his eyes and telling him smutty jokes. And the other dancers became the same way, and the fellows used to tell him how much they wanted one of these girls, any girl.

Day after day the marathon grind went on. His eyes grew heavy. His back ached. His feet became sore and raw, so that each step was pain and he felt often as if he were walking on fire. The hall was almost continuously stale with cigarette smoke and foul with body odors. He felt constantly dirty, sweaty, itchy. Dust got into his nostrils and his eyes. He began to cough again. His muscles knotted. He became like a person who was always only half awake, and everything took on the semblance of being a semi-dream. Marie, also, changed. She began to swell around the buttocks. Deep circles grew under her eyes. She became haggard and blowsy and looked like a worn-out prostitute. She used more and more cosmetics, and her face became like a ghastly caricature of the pretty girl who had entered the contest.

In the beginning, particularly because of his accent and Greek heritage, Takiss became the butt of many jokes. Constantly, he would be asked why he wasn't running a restaurant, and he would be given orders for a piece zapple pie kid. He was nicknamed Restaurant, Fruit Store, Socrates, and Zapple Pie Kid. In time, this wore down and failed to anger or disturb him. The grind settled into habitual misery and torture. He, like the other contestants, would long for fresh air, and during rest periods, when they were not so tired that they would be dragged like walking somnambulists to the rest cots, they would enter the vile and filthy dressing rooms or the equally unsavory lavatory and jam their heads out of the windows to breathe fresh air and to look yearningly down at the street where people walked free to do what they wished, not tired, able to breathe fresh air, even the fresh air of a city street that was saturated with carbon monoxide fumes and sootiness.

Day after day dragged on. Sometimes Takiss, Marie, or the other contestants would live in stupors of six, twelve hours a day, even longer. As the time passed, the contestants would switch from affected and over-stimulated good spirits to nasty, fighting nervousness, and then into that glaze-eyed stupor. Particularly in those dog hours of the early morning, they would be raw, if awake, and fight and curse. Sex, too, became a growing obsession, and in time was almost madness.

THE BENEFITS OF AMERICAN LIFE

Living so near to one another, their bodies touching so frequently, they told smuttier and smuttier jokes. Perversities and desires or propositions for perversities sprang up among them. It became a relentless process of both physical and mental torture. Constipation, diarrhea, sudden inabilities to control their kidneys so that now and then a contestant would be walking around the floor, drugged in sleep, with wet lines down his trousers, or if a girl, down her beach pyjamas which most of them wore regularly. Broken blood vessels and swollen veins in the legs. Headaches, eye troubles, sore throats, fevers, colds. Periods of sweatiness, followed by shivers and chills. And always that returning stupor, caused by sleeplessness and fatigue, and by the dreams and fantasies which they entertained as relief from that endless procession around and around the floor. And at the end of it all, money, the chance to become a celebrity, sex, and clean white bed sheets and a soft, fresh bed.

Ways of making money from day to day quickly developed and were used to the utmost so that all of the contestants started bank accounts. Every one of them developed some trick or act, a song, a dance, a stunt of some kind, and after putting it on, they would be showered with money from the crowd. One of the contestants, a raw country youth of Lithuanian origin with a nasal twang to his voice, chewed razor blades as his stunt. Takiss learned a dance. Stores, theatres, and politicians also paid them fees to wear signs or sweaters and jerseys with advertising printed on the front or back. Money was sent to them, mash notes, written in as ignorant and as bad English as that which Takiss used and wrote in. The various spectators picked favorites, cheered for them, shouted encouragement.

And still the days stretched out, past the first month, with contestant after contestant dropping out, and the field narrowing down. One day there would be a birthday party. Another day there was a floor wedding between two of the contestants who had met on the floor, and the wedding provided endless hours of raw jokes and humor about when they would have their wedding night, until, sex-crazed, both of the newlyweds went temporarily out of their heads and the girl screamed until she was dragged off the floor. Disqualified, they were out of the marathon, and a new note was introduced in the humor. Another day, a girl had an abscessed tooth extracted on the floor, and immediately afterward she rejoined the endless walking procession that tramped around and around in this ever dullening stupor. Another day, an Italian boy, who with his wife had entered the marathon because they were both unemployed and had been evicted, required crutches and ran a high fever. With his eyes intense from the fever, with suffering imprinted on his haggard face, he hobbled around and around. After twelve such hours he was forced out by the judges on the advice of a doctor.

Again and again Takiss wanted to quit and satisfy himself with the incidental money he had taken in, and as repeatedly he would go patiently on. Like the others, he would fall into that lumbrous sleep, and external means would be necessary to awaken him so that he might continue. The male nurses would slap him in the face with wet towels, put his shoes on the wrong feet, strap him into an electric vibrator machine, poke their fingers down his throat, tickle his calloused soles. During one period, his cough developed into a severe cold in the chest. For another period, he was not out of his stupor for three days. And Marie, his partner, experienced the same tortures. They went on. Days and nights, and days and nights, with the field narrowing to thirteen, ten, eight, five, finally two couples. Then Marie collapsed and was carried off the floor and shipped to a hospital, and Takiss was disqualified. They each collected the two hundred and fifty dollars second place money.

After recuperation, Takiss entered other dance marathons, and became a professional. He secured a copy of *Yes, We Have No Bananas* with a Greek translation, and this, with his dance stunt, became very popular. He was able, with both attractions and with a growing audience of fans, to earn from ten to fifteen dollars a day in extra money. Even when he was forced to retire from marathons or was disqualified, he departed with added money. Again the desire to return to his homeland like a rich American grew upon him, and now his bank account, with foreign exchange rates, would make him very rich in Greece. He was something of a celebrity in this new world of his. His biography and picture appeared in Greek newspapers. A Greek merchant who sold a raisin beverage paid him and Marie each a hundred dollars to be photographed for a newspaper advertisement in which there was their signed testimony that they drank this beverage. He had a run of a week at a small theatre on South Halsted Street where there were many Greeks. Takiss became a famous American Greek.

In all, Takiss participated in sixteen dance marathons. In eight of them, he collected money and was the winner of a thousand-dollar super-marathon in which only finalists from other marathons were permitted to enter and in which there were no rest periods. He had money now, five thousand dollars. He returned to Greece. But the strain of the marathons had ruined his lungs and he had tuberculosis. Resorts for tuberculosis had been developed in his native mountains, and when he returned it was necessary for him to become a patient in one of them, and the money he had earned was paid out while he lived there with his lungs rotting away on him. Well could he recite his favorite Greek proverb:

> *I ate practically the whole cow,*
> *Why must I forget the tail?*

1934.

Nostalgia

AL sensed something familiar in that unhealthy fat face. He noticed the eyes. They were a boy's blue eyes, and they presented a contrast to the thick lips and the lines about the nostrils. He looked closely and saw the developing double chin and the sagging pink flesh about the jowl. He looked and the face opened into a smile.

"Hello, Mort," Al said.

Mort held out a limp, perspiring paw, and they shook hands.

"Hello! Gee, I'm glad to see you. How are you? What you doin' now? Gee, I'm glad to see you. Say, let's get a cup of coffee, so we can talk."

"O.K.," Al said, and they stepped into a one-arm Greek restaurant on Randolph Street, near Michigan.

"Gee, I ain't seen you in a couple of years. Say, but I'm glad to see you. Why don't you ever come around? You know, we got the class organized into a frat now, and we meet every other Thursday evenin'. And say, come to think of it, you're the only one that ain't been around. Say, why don't you ever come around?" he asked, his tone almost unchanging.

Al said that he would. He asked Mort what he was doing for a living. Mort said he was a salesman.

"Yeh, I'm gettin' along. Peddlin' paints. I make good dough. Two hundred a month, and I don't have much work to do, and they give me a car of my own to roust about in."

"Like it?" Al asked.

"Well, a guy's got to work, an' I'm makin' more than most of the guys we graduated with. But say, remember the time we went down to Peoria to play that football game, and coming home we turned a trolley around on that geezer of a hick that was the motorman. And he was so sore, only he was afraid to do anything, and he didn't say nothin' because we had a gang. You know, we had fun, didn't we?" Mort said.

"Yeh," Al said, disinterestedly.

There was a lull in their talk, and then Al asked him how Nellie was, and had he married her yet.

"Nope. But say, remember when we were in third year, and we played football in Springfield, and after the game Artie was smoking a cigar bigger than himself, and he walks into the railroad station and who should he meet but our coach. Them was the days! You know, it's too bad Artie never was bigger and that he got thrown out of college for drinking. He might have been a football star in college."

"Yeh," Al said.

"You know, them was the days. Say, I saw Georgie. He's doing well. He got himself lined up in some religious spiritual racket and he's knocking down about a hundred bucks a week. He was smart though, and a good writer. Funny he never got to be a writer, and you who were drunk all the time with me, you did. Funny things happen, don't they? But anyway, Georgie's got a better racket than writing. Say, you know Georgie's the only guy that gets more dough than me out of the whole class. That's doin' pretty good, ain't it? That is, unless you make more than two hundred a month."

Al shook his head negatively. Then he asked Mort how his mother was.

"Oh, she died," Mort said.

"That's too bad," Al said.

"Yeh, she died. She was good to me. No thanks, I can't smoke. You see, I got something wrong with my heart, and the doctor said I shouldn't do no smokin' or drinkin'. I gotta be careful. I was goin' to the Y for exercise to reduce a little, but I had to cut it out. But say, I ain't so fat, am I?" Mort asked.

"No," Al said.

"Say, remember the time you got us all to stay out of school and paid our way to a burlesque show on dough you cleaned up in a crap game, and the teacher found out, and you talked him out of suspectin' you, and he didn't say nothin' to you. But the rest of us almost got kicked out of school?"

"Yes," Al said.

"You know, you should have got yourself some racket like selling or law or something. You had a line," Mort said.

"Yeh," Al said.

"If you want to be a big shot nowadays, you got to get yourself a racket and have a line. Yes, sir, that's the only way you can be a big shot. That's why I'm sellin'. On the side, too, I'm musclin' myself into the political racket."

"Yeh."

"And say, remember Larry? Well, he's dead."

"Yes. Too bad. He was a nice kid."

"Yes, Larry's dead. And little Spike. Well, he's married. But he still puts brilliantine on his hair."

"But how come you're not married yet?" asked Al.

"Oh, I don't know. But I saw Domek. He was asking for you."

"Yeh."

"He's a clerk somewhere. He ain't never organized that revolution to free Poland."

"That so?" Al said politely.

"Yeh, and say, I saw Cokey. Remember the time he socked Kogan. Well, Cokey's in a brokerage house now, and his kid brother's married. Anyway, Cokey was givin' me the razz yesterday. He said I was fat. You think so?"

"No," Al said.

"Say, remember Paul Schaeffer. He's workin' for his old man."

"How is Goop?" asked Al.

"Goop, oh, he's lazy as ever. I used to see him a lot, but I never do any more. You know, them guys just never want to do anything. Well, me, I'm different. I want to do things while I'm young. Now, take the last four Saturday nights. Each time Nellie and I, we went to some place different, and we had swell times. Well, them guys just ain't got no ambition nor interest in life. They give me a pain," Mort said.

There was another lull in the conversation.
"Remember Anderson?" he asked.
"Yes," Al said.
"I wonder what happened to him."
"I don't know."
"You know Jean's married."
"Yeh."
"Boy, there's one guy that's tight. I used to go out with him. He's so cheap he squeaks. And his wife is dizzy. Whenever I went out with 'em, they'd always fight and she'd give him his ring back, and they'd spoil the party and he never broke his arm reaching for checks, neither."

There was another pause.
"How's your dad?" Al finally asked.
"Gettin' old. He had to retire. He misses my mother. But say, remember the time we went out walkin' on the ice and almost fell in. And remember Hussy? She's married. She was nice."
"Yes."
"Phil and Ed got the same jobs," he said.
"Yeh."
"Remember Holy Ike, our algebra teacher? He never liked me," Mort said.
"He wasn't a bad guy," Al said.
"No," Mort said.

Mort talked on. He suggested a get-together party some weekend. He said his girl was going away. He said times would never be like the good old days. Al said no they wouldn't. Mort suddenly was silent. They didn't have much more to say. Finally they just looked at each other nervously for about five minutes. Mort said one cigarette wouldn't kill him. So he smoked.

"Things ain't like they was," he said after a while.
"No," Al said.
"A guy's got to work. But what does he get? Not much. He don't never have much fun like he had when he was a kid. Remember when we used to play handball and basketball every day after school? We didn't have nothin' to worry about then, did we?"
"No," Al said.
Another pause.
"Nellie working?" Al asked.

"Yeh. Say, remember Bernice? I think she liked me. And she used to think you were nice, too."

"Yeh," Al said.

"Well, say, we got to see each other and talk things over sometime," Mort said.

"Yeh," Al said.

"I better be hikin' now. I'm glad I saw you. You know, I'm glad I saw you. Say, remember our senior prom, too?"

"Yeh."

"Well, so long. Give me a ring some time, won't you? We got lots to talk over."

"Yeh," Al said.

"Well . . . so long."

"So long."

They left the restaurant, and Mort offered Al a limp hand. Then he moved off. Al watched him waddle away, walking as if he were very tired.

He turned once and waved. Al never saw him again.

1930.

For White Men Only

I

"Boy, I tell you, don' you go there," Booker Jones, a small and yellowish Negro, said.

"Booker, there is no white man alive who's gonna tell me where I is to go swimming, and where I isn't. If I wants to go swimming this lake here at Jackson Park, that's where I'm going swimming," Alfred, a tall and handsome broad-shouldered and coppery Negro, replied.

They were shirtless, wearing blue swimming suits and old trousers, and they walked eastward along Fifty-seventh Street.

"Oh, come on, Alfred, let's go to Thirty-ninth Street," Booker said with intended persuasiveness as they passed across Dorchester after they had ambled on for a block in silence.

"You go! Me, I'm going swimming over in Jackson Park, whether there's white men there or not," Alfred said, his face hardening, his voice determined.

"Alfred, you is always courtin' trouble, and just because you want to show off before that no-account mulatto gal . . ."

"What you say, nigger?"

"Well, no, I'm sorry, Alfred," Booker cringed. "But some day, you'll go courtin' trouble, and trouble is just gonna catch right on up with you, and it's gonna say, 'Well, Alfred, you been courtin' me, so here I is with my mind made up to give you plenty of me'."

"Shut up, black boy!" Alfred said curtly.

Booker shook his head with disconsolate wonder. As they passed under the Illinois Central viaduct, Booker again suggested that they go down to the Thirty-ninth Street beach, and Alfred testily told him that Thirty-ninth Street wasn't a beach at all, just a measly, overcrowded pile of stones. The black man had no beach. But he was aiming to go swimming where he had some space without so many people all around him. He added that if the Negro was to go on being afraid of the white man, he was never going to get anywhere, and if the Negro wanted more space to swim in, he just had to go and take it. And he had told that to Melinda, and she had laughed at him, but she was not going to laugh at him again. Booker just shook his head sadly from side to side.

They entered Jackson Park where the grass and shrubbery and tree leaves shimmered and gleamed with sunlight. The walks were crowded with people, and along the drive, a succession of automobiles hummed by. Alfred walked along with unconcerned and even challenging pride. Booker glanced nervously about him, feeling that the white men were thrusting contemptuous looks at him. He looked up at Alfred, admiring his friend's courage, and he wished that he were unafraid like Alfred.

Turning by the lake, they passed along the sidewalk which paralleled the waters. Sandy beach ran down from the sidewalk to the shore line, and many were scattered along it in bathing suits. Down several blocks from them, they could see that the regular beach was crowded. More white people frowned at them, and both of them could sense hate and fear in these furtive, hasty glances. Alfred's lips curled into a surly expression.

Halfway along toward the regular beach Alfred jumped down into the sand, tagged by Booker. He gazed around him, nonchalant, and then removed his trousers. He stood in his bathing suit, tall and impressively strong, graceful. Booker jittered beside him, hesitating until Alfred, without turning his head, taunted him into haste. Booker removed his trousers, and stood skinny beside Alfred whose arms were folded and whose gaze was sphinx-like on the waters. They heard a gentle and steady rippling against the shore line.

Nearby, white bathers stared with apprehension. A group of three fellows and two young girls who had been splashing and ducking close to the shore saw them, and immediately left the water and walked down a hundred yards to re-enter it. Alfred seemed to wince, and then his face again became hard and intent. Booker saw various white bathers picking up their bundles and moving away from them, and still afraid of these white men, he hated them.

Alfred trotted gracefully to the shore line, again plunged into the water, followed by Booker. They cut outward, and Alfred suddenly paddled around and playfully ducked Booker. They again hit outward. Catching his breath and plunging beside his companion, Booker told Alfred that they had made a mistake coming out here where they were two against a mob. Alfred retorted that he was not going to whine and beg the white man for anything. Some black men had to be the first to come, if they wanted to have the right of a place to swim. And he wasn't scared anyway. Booker shook a pained head, caught a mouthful of water, and splashed to keep himself up. Alfred dove under water and reappeared a number of yards away, laughing, snorting, glorying in the use of his body. After they had swum around, Booker again chattered that he was afraid.

"Here is one black boy that's not going to be mobbed," Alfred said.

II

Buddy Coen and his friends emerged from the water laughing, shaking their wet bodies and heads. They found a space of sand within the enclosure of the regular beach and dropped down, hunting for the cigarettes they had hidden.

"Well, boys, I was just going to say, if you lads want to provide the bottle, I'm all set for a bender tonight," Buddy said after lighting a cigarette.

"If you'd go back driving a hack, you'd have dough enough for your own liquor," fat Marty Mulligan said.

"If they want Jackson Park, they got to fight for it!" Buddy sneered.

"Just think! Look at all these white girls bathing around here. With niggers on the beach, it ain't safe for them," Morris said.

"And do you fellows know, my sister nearly came out here swimming today?" Morris said.

They saw the two Negroes coming in and heard the smaller one trying to convince the big one about something, but they could not catch enough of what he said. The two Negroes walked slowly toward their small bundles of clothing, their wet bodies glistening in the sunlight. After they had sat down, Buddy arose and led the group toward them. Seeing the white fellows approaching, Booker grabbed his clothes and ran. Four of the white lads pursued him, yelling to stop that nigger.

With a sulky expression on his face, Alfred arose at the approach of Buddy and Morris.

"The water nice?" Buddy asked, his voice constrained and threatening.

"Passable," Alfred answered, his fists clenched.

"Been out here before?" Buddy continued.

"No. . . . Why?" Alfred said with unmistakable fearlessness.

A crowd gathered around, and excitement cut through the beach like an electric current because of the shouts and chase after Booker. A white bather tripped him as he ran and joined the four other pursuers in cursing and punching him, mercilessly disregarding his pleas to be let alone. They dragged him to his feet, knocked him down, kicked him, dragged him up, knocked him over again while he continued to emit shrill and helpless cries.

"Anybody ever tell you that this is a white man's beach?" Morris asked Alfred.

"You know we don't want niggers here!" Buddy said.

Buddy went down from a quick and surprising punch on the jaw, and Alfred countered Morris' left swing with a thudding right that snapped the white lad's head back. Buddy sat down, rubbed his jaw, shook his dazed head, leaped to his feet, and went into Alfred swinging both hands. While the Negro fought off the two of them, others dragged back the howling Booker to the fight scene. The big Swede broke through the crowd of spectators and clipped Alfred viciously on the side of the head. Two other white bathers smashed into the attack. Defending himself, Alfred crashed Morris to the sand and was then battered off his feet. A heel was brought against his jaw, and as he struggled to arise, five white bodies piled onto him, punching, scratching, kneeing him. Spectators shouted, females screamed and encouraged the white lads, and Alfred was quickly and severely punished. Booker opened his mouth to beg for mercy, and a smashing fist brought blood from his lips, and another wallop between the eyes toppled him over backward.

A bald-headed Jewish man with a paunchy stomach protested, and a small, pretty blonde girl screamed that he must be a nigger lover. A middle-aged woman with a reddish bovine face called in an Irish brogue for them to hit the black skunks, while a child strained at her waist and shouted.

A park policeman hurriedly shoved through the spectators, and the slugging ceased. The two Negroes sat in the sand, their faces cut and bleeding.

"You fellows better go home!" the policeman said roughly, sneering as he spoke.

They slowly got up, and Booker tried to explain that they had done nothing.

"Don't be giving me any lip," the policeman said. "I said you better go home or do your swimming down at Thirty-ninth if you don't want to be starting riots. Now move along!"

He shoved Booker.

"And you, too," he said to Alfred who had not moved.

Booker hurriedly put his trousers on and Alfred did likewise slowly, as if with endless patience. They wiped their bleeding faces with dirty handkerchiefs, and Booker sniffled.

"Go ahead now!" the policeman roughly repeated.

"We will, but we'll come back!" Alfred said challengingly.

The crowd slowly dispersed, and the six fellows stood there near the policeman.

"Shall we follow them?" asked Marty.

"They ain't worth hitting, the skunks, and the dirty fighting they do, kicking me that way," said Collins, limping.

They turned and walked heroically back toward the enclosed beach.

"That black bastard had the nerve to hit me," Buddy said, pointing to his puffed eye.

"Like all niggers, they were yellow," said Morris.

"Well, we did a neat job with them," Norton bragged.

"Boy, I caught that big one between his teeth. Look at my hand," Marty said, showing his swollen knuckles.

"Look at that, fellows! There's somethin'. I say there, sisters!" the Swede said to three girls who were coquetting on the sand.

Looking covertly at legs and breasts, they leered.

1934.

Footnote

JACK took a northbound subway at Sheridan Square. He looked collegiate, without a hat, wearing a bright gray suit and a tie with red, white and gray stripes. As soon as Jack was seated and opened the book he was reading, the fellow noticed him and slid along the seat. He looked over Jack's shoulder at the book, which was a study of Germany by Gooch. He asked Jack if he was a German. Jack said no. He asked Jack if he was a college student at Columbia. Jack nodded negatively. They looked at each other and Jack said nothing.

The fellow was fifty, and looked quite ordinary. He might have been a plumber, a carpenter, a janitor, a bartender, the father of five kids, a watchman who spent his days arguing with a stout wife and tending a garden. His face was long, the eyes greenish and small, and he had a lightish brown moustache.

Jack looked across the car aisle at a couple. The man could easily have passed as a vaudeville type of sugar daddy. He was gray, jowled, dignified. A cane depended from his left arm. She was loudly dressed, garish, her lips almost purple, the creases in her face coated with powder. Their relationship seemed obvious.

"Look at that bitch," the fellow said.

Jack said nothing.

"The nerve of the goddamn bitch," the fellow said.

"Yeh," Jack muttered, reading on in his book about the social patriotic role that Gerhardt Hauptmann had played in the world war.

"Women are bitches, I tell you. They're bitches. Look at that guy! Too old to be any good. Look at him! And the bitch has got him hooked," the fellow said, and his insinuating tone of voice made Jack uneasy.

"What's that to me?" Jack muttered.

"Oh, you don't care for women?" the fellow said.

"I don't know many," Jack said.

He looked at Jack tenderly. He said that women could give a clean young boy a dose. Jack read on in his book.

"I'd like to cut that hag's tits off," the fellow said venomously after a moment when he had sat in gloomy silence. "The bitch! Women are bitches, Kid, and don't ever pay attention to them. They're bitches, I tell you!"

Jack yawned.

"You look queer," the fellow said.

"Yeh?" Jack said.

"What do you do with yourself?" he asked.

Jack did not answer, and he slowly reread a translation of one of Hauptmann's war-hate poems.

"Look at her! She ought to be put to work scrubbing floors. She's a whore. A whore with an old fool like that. The bitch!"

Jack yawned again.

"Listen, Kid!" he said. "Don't never fool around with a woman. I tell you. You're a nice clean kid, and it would be a shame to see you going home to your mother with a dose or with syphilis. There's more damn syphilitics in this town. And why? Women. That's the answer."

"Well, what of it?"

"Look at her! Ain't it a disgrace?" the fellow said.

"No."

He asked Jack why. Jack said that it was a nice day out, and that he hoped the Pirates would win a game from the Yankees in the world series.

"Say, you're queer," the fellow said.

"Why?"

"Who the hell gives a goddamn about the Pirates and the Yankees. Now, why ain't it a disgrace to have whores publicly defrauding old men like that?"

"Oh!" Jack exclaimed.

"You know it is. She's a bitch."

Jack said nothing. The fellow's eyes suddenly got watery. His expression softened and it was apparent that he was being carried up on a wave of emotion. His lips twitched. He swallowed nervously.

"You know what I am?" he asked, as if in self-torture.

"Yes," Jack said casually.

"I'm a c . . . ."

Jack said all right.

"Now you know what I am!"

"Yes."

"Well?"

"What of it?" Jack asked.

"You know what it means to be like that?"

"What?"

"Say, isn't she a bitch?"

"No."

The train pulled into Pennsylvania Station and they sat watching people enter the uncrowded car.

"Say, I got a room at Ninety-eighth Street," he said as the train started up again.

"That's nice," Jack said.

"Listen, a young lad like you has got to watch out for a dose," he said.

Jack yawned.

"Come on, Kid?" he said.

"It's going to be a nice evening," Jack said.

"It's tough to be what I am. You think it's not even human, don't you?" the fellow said.

"No."

"What do you think?"

"That Gerhardt Hauptmann was a louse in the years 1914 to 1918."

"Answer me. You think that I'm not human but that that bitch is, don't you?"

"Wrong, there."

"You're like all the rest. You like the bitches. Well, I hope you get yours!"

"That's all right. Forget it."

"Well, Kid, what do you say?"

"I'm getting off here," Jack said as the train stopped at Times Square.

The fellow followed Jack. Broadway was lit up, and above the glare of lights was the calm of an autumn night, hazy with a vaporous moon. Jack walked slowly along Broadway looking at the crowds, and the fellow tagged at his side, telling him what he was, and condemning

Broadway as a street full of whores. At Fifty-second Street, Jack turned onto Seventh Avenue and started back toward Times Square, the fellow still tagging him, bumping against him in the crowds.

"What do you think of me?" the fellow again asked.

"I think you're a pest."

"You think I'm not human. Well, I am. I'm every goddamn bit as human as you are, or as that bitch on the subway."

"What of it?"

"Listen, Kid, where do you live?"

"Let's get some coffee," Jack said.

They had coffee in a cafeteria below Forty-second Street. As they were leaving, a bum approached Jack. Jack handed him a quarter. They watched the bum shuffle away. The fellow took several steps after the bum. He paused, turned, looked watery-eyed back at Jack. The bum had gained some distance. The fellow turned, hastened after him, and they both disappeared down a side street.

1930.

Comedy Cop

I

RED KELLY, with a growing pot belly, and a sleek, shiny, puffed face, shoved his pudgy arms into his camel's hair coat, drew it around himself, stretched his arms and hunched his shoulders in order to work himself into the coat so that it would look like the good fit it was. Holding his newly purchased gray fedora in his hand, he kissed his wife, a thin, slender, pretty-faced girl.

"Darling, now promise me you won't drink?" she asked in a coaxing voice, draping her arms behind his coat collar, smiling meekly up into his face.

"You know I won't on a Christmas Eve like this. I'll only take one or two shots and that's not enough to get me snozzled. I just want to say hello to some of the boys and wish them a Merry Christmas."

"Only one."

"All right, only one," he promised, looking frankly and with affection into her brown, adoring eyes.

He thumbed her chin playfully, kissed her, made a gesture as if to punch her which he had learned from James Cagney in the talkies. He kissed her flush on the lips.

"Who you love?" he asked.

"You," she muttered as if answering a question in a child's game.

"There isn't a man alive who's got a better wife than I got," he said gently but with pride.

"Mean that?"

His answer was another kiss.

"Now don't you forget what you promised, darling."

"How could I?" he said, revealing an even set of white teeth with his smile.

She pinched his jowl.

"Sweet cakes," he said.

"I'll wash the dishes and put baby to bed. Then you'll be back so we can go to confession early because you know there'll be a big line there. And then, honey, you mustn't forget that you got to decorate baby's first Christmas tree."

"I won't. I'll be back by the time you're ready."

II

A mild breeze from the nearby lake tickled Red's shaven neck as he sauntered eastward along Fifty-fifth Street, his shoulders thrown back and as erect as those of a soldier on the march, his hands sunk deeply into his overcoat pockets, a cigar sticking from the corner of his thick lips, his face expressing a benign contentment. He walked along, a snapshot of health, prosperity and well-being.

He flicked ashes from his cigar with a professional gesture. Under the Illinois Central viaduct he paused, opened his coat, and looked with pride at his bailiff's badge pinned on the inside of his jacket coat. He dug his left hand into his inside overcoat pocket and caressed his revolver. No need to carry them, except that they both always came in handy in case of trouble. But he liked to feel them, look at them because they were the signs of his success in the world.

He heard a train rumble overhead, and buttoned up his overcoat. His cigar had gone out, and he slowly relit it and stood watching people pour through the high, rattling, turnstile gates of the I.C., many of them carrying brightly wrapped and ribboned Christmas packages.

He strolled on, and out of sheer well-fed good spirits he began singing to himself.

Jingle bells, jingle bells, jingle all the while . . .

He smiled in satisfaction, dreamily thinking that at the age of thirty-three he had done pretty well by himself. Compare where he was with some of the boys he used to hang out with in the old days around Fifty-eighth and Prairie. Most of them were dead, like poor Studs Lonigan, Lord have mercy on their souls. But of those who were alive, not that he wished them any bad luck, but had any of them gotten as far along the road as he had? Yes, he could certainly say that this was a Christmas when he could afford to be happy.

Fifty-fifth Street, west of Lake Park Avenue, was lit with store windows, and its atmosphere was slightly garish with saloons, delicatessens, hardware stores, cheap hotels, grocery stores, stationery and cigar stores, shoe-shining parlors, restaurants, Chinese laundries. He noticed the N.R.A. blue eagle in most of the windows, which were stocked with goods in Christmas decorations, and he saw that inside there were many people making last-minute purchases. He smiled passing a short Jew who stood beside Christmas trees which he had stacked inside of and in front of an unrented store. Just what Kelly liked to see. Christmas and ribbons and brightly colored papers and boxes, Christmas, with everybody seeming to be happy, full of spirits.

Jingle bells, jingle bells, jingle all the while . . .

He dropped a nickel in a Salvation Army lassie's plate, figuring he would do it even if the Salvation Army was not Catholic.

III

Red strolled into O'Connell's saloon near the corner of Fifty-fifth and Blackstone, posing, his manner cocky, his looks suggesting the politician.

"Merry Christmas, Bill," he said cheerfully to the sunken-cheeked, bony bartender as he stepped up to the half-filled bar. He casually glanced around to see if there were anyone around whom he knew. Not yet. Well, the boys would all happen along soon. He hoped that they would shake their tails though, because he had to get back to the wife. He was married to the best kid in the world, and a father. Funny.

And swell. He liked it, too. And he was able to provide for his family decently.

"Whiskey straight. Ginger ale chaser, Bill," he ordered, leaning his left elbow on the bar.

Yes, there would be plenty of lads he knew around, and many of them, too, would like to be in his boots. But he cautioned himself. Because he was getting along now in the political game, that didn't mean that he should let himself go getting a swelled head. But he wouldn't. Everybody who knew him knew him better than that. He imagined friends talking about him, saying how he was a precinct captain and a bailiff now with a little drag, but adding that he was still the same kind of a regular guy that he had always been.

"Well, Red, how's tricks?" Bill asked, placing Red's order before him.

"Can't complain, Bill, can't complain," Red answered, paying for his order and lavishing a twenty-five cent tip upon the bartender.

"Thanks, Red. And I was going to say, Red, the way I look at it, things will be getting better right along now. But by the way, Red, how you like the liquor?"

"Fair. It will have to take time before we get real good stuff."

"Yes, Red, it takes time. But some day the liquor will be just as good as it used to be before the goddamn bluenoses shoved Prohibition over on us. But now that's a closed chapter and we're going to have good liquor and good times."

Red nodded, pleased with the warming sensation in his stomach.

"Yes, Bill, it looks like this is ticketed to be the best Christmas we've had since the depression set in."

"So they say. And I've been reading it in the papers. And business has been, well, fair, but it hasn't been nearly as good as the boss calculated it would be," the bartender said, while from outside there came the noise of a passing street car.

"Yes, Bill, Roosevelt has pulled the country back on its feet, and things will hum now. Nineteen thirty-four ought to be just like old times before we got the depression."

"I hope so. God, I hope so."

"Another, Bill," Red said.

"Merry Christmas, Kelly."

Red turned and greeted the newcomer, a tall lanky fellow in his thirties, with a narrow unpleasant face.

"How's tricks down at the Hall?"

"Oh, all right. Can't complain, Red, can't complain. I'm getting my check every week again now, and I been paid up for all that time when they weren't able to pay us, and that's just the little ducat that counts the most in this man's world."

"Same here, Jack," Red smiled.

Red thought of his promise to return home as others kept coming in and the saloon buzzed with conversation. But he could stand one more drink and spare an extra five minutes. It was so pleasant in the saloon, with talk, happy drinking with regular fellows, everybody having a good time. Five more minutes of it and another drink wouldn't hurt him. The kid at home was a little slow in getting dressed and fixed up anyway.

After the fifth drink, Red's face flushed and he began looking around him with eyes slightly bleary. He began to forget about going home.

"Say, Jack, we're Democrats, ain't we, pal?" he suddenly said to the narrow-faced fellow.

"You wrote it that time, Kelly, my boy, you wrote it," Jack said, shaking hands with Red.

"And our party is going to stay in the saddle until hell freezes over. We're going to run this city, ain't we, goddamn it. You know we ain't ever had a man in Washington, except Woodrow Wilson, who's a great man like Roosevelt," said Loomis, a squat husky lad in the group clustered around Red.

"Boys, a drink to F.D.R.," Red said, and they drank.

Red glowed. His fat face beamed, his cheeks seeming feverish. Around him were all regular fellows, all feeling fine and happy. No disagreements. He suddenly looked down the boisterous, crowded bar and sneered at several fellows whose faces he didn't like. He touched the revolver in his overcoat pocket, wagged his chin knowingly.

"Hi, boy!" Red suddenly said as a burly tough lad joined them.

"Hello, Bob. Merry Christmas," another of the group said to the new arrival.

"Merry Christmas, Kelly," Bob said, shaking hands with Red.

"How's the boys?" Red asked.

"Oh, Red, they're O.K."

"I haven't seen them around the club much lately," Red said.

"Well, I got them all in the bag, Red. You can count on that. But

"And he leads a great party," Red said.

"And there's his picture," Jack said, pointing to a picture of the President, draped in an American flag and hanging over the center of the glass mirror opposite the bar.

"That's him," said Red.

The talk went on, punctuated with recurrent holiday greetings, loosened with regular drinks.

IV

"My old pal," Red said warmly, seeing red-faced Les.

"Merry Christmas, Red, and how are you, goddamn you," Les smiled.

"Same as you, Les, goddamn you, and Merry Christmas to you again."

"My old pal, Kelly, goddamn his filthy soul," Les said, both of them laughing good-naturedly.

The air in the saloon was stale. The talk rose, and increasing numbers of customers thickened around the bar and the tables. Red and Les drank, and other newcomers clustered around them. Suddenly the talk in their group shifted back to politics.

"Now listen," Red said, interrupting another fellow who was speaking, "when you guys start talking politics I got something to say." He paused, spread his unsteady feet widely apart, stood with his head falling forward and his torso swinging to and fro. He revealed his bailiff's badge. "The name's Kelly. I'm in the political game, I am. Judge Gorman's court. Bailiff. Precinct captain in this ward over by the lake. Now what do you guys want to know?" Red challengingly stared at the stranger who had previously excited his suspicion.

"Sure, I agree with you," the stranger smiled flatly, in conciliation.

"On what do you agree with me?" Red asked, his voice growing more snotty as he perceived cowardice in the stranger's expression.

"Come on, Red, have a drink," a friend said, putting his hand on Red's shoulder.

"Fellow, on just what do you agree?"

"Why, I agree with you."

"Well, what in the name of all hell does that mean? Why, I just agree with you. Now you said that. You said you agree with me. But what, what do you agree with me?" Red said, the group about them becoming tense, expectant.

The stranger grinned.

"Well, I'm waiting," Red sneered.

"Oh, let's can it, friend," the stranger said.

"No, we won't can anything. I want to know what you agree with me in."

"Politics."

"Well, fellow, that's a big order. And what aspect of politics do you agree with me in?"

"Let's have another drink," the stranger said.

"Sure, we'll have another drink. But first I want to get an answer from you. Now what do you mean you agree with me?"

"Well, I thought I did from what you said."

"You thought you did? Well, what did I say?"

"You said that in politics . . . oh, hell, come on, friend, it's Christmas Eve and we're all jolly, let's have a drink and forget it."

"Sure we will. We'll drop it. But before we drop it, I want to tell you what a goddamn crap artist you are, because I didn't say anything that you could agree with me on."

"Red," Les said, with attempted persuasiveness.

"Come on, Kelly, it's Christmas Eve and we're all friends," Jack said.

"Sure, it's Christmas Eve. Sure, we're all friends. But I don't like crap, and I'm not used to having anybody try and crap me. Get that, lad, I don't let myself get crapped! Kelly's the name."

The stranger flushed, turned pale, looked at Red with a weak and conciliating grin.

"Got any more to say?" Red asked, his voice still snotty.

"No."

"Then we got your number. You're a goddamn crap artist!"

"But listen. . . . You're drunk. I don't want any trouble with you, but I don't like the way you talk."

"You don't like the way I talk! You don't like the way I talk! You don't like the way I talk!" Red said with heavy sarcasm, his right hand going to his inside overcoat pocket, clasping his revolver. "Go ahead, now, say something else! Say it again!"

A larger crowd was now gathered about them. Two bartenders rushed from behind the bar and Red's friends pleaded with him.

"You didn't understand me, friend."

"Don't call me friend, either!"

"Well, I didn't mean anything. I was just agreeing with you on a convivial occasion, drinking, you know, and I wasn't looking for trouble or anything like that."

"But you like to crap people, don't you?"

"Come on, Red. He's a pal of mine, and regular. And we don't want regular fellows scrapping on Christmas Eve."

"If you say so, Bill, all right. You know me, and you know the one thing I don't like is to be crapped."

"Sure, Red, I know you. Now shake hands with my pal."

Red and the stranger shook hands.

V

"Now where to?" Red asked, leading a staggering, noisy group out of the saloon.

"Say, I got an idea. Let's go down to these Communists at Fifty-seventh Street and give them the works."

"They don't believe in love, God, the family, or the human race, do they? They think they're too good for the human race," Red said.

"You said it."

"What's the schedule there?" Les asked, looking perplexed at Red, and they told him about the Reds at Fifty-seventh and Harper Avenue as they staggered forward.

"Say, do they get their hair cut?" asked Les.

"They're not human. Come on, boys!" Red said, his hand on his gun as he marched forward to the head of the drunken procession.

They turned into Cable Court, off Harper, a dark and narrow one-block street. Car tracks cut through it from Harper to Lake Park Avenue and it was lined with old brick buildings that housed stores on the first floor and contained apartments where working people lived above the stores.

"This is the joint."

"None of them here," one of the lads said in disappointment as they stared into a darkened store window and could see within white signs plastered along the walls.

"A break for them, the bastards," Red said.

With the butt of his revolver he cracked the window, and one of the others followed by hurling a brick through it, causing a crash of breaking glass. They ran to Lake Park Avenue, and they cut down to

Fifty-seventh Street, gleefully shouting as they dashed under the Illinois Central viaduct, and drew to a halt breathless, excited and happy at the corner of Fifty-seventh and Stony Island Avenue.

"Jesus, we might have got pinched for it," Les said walking beside Red and still breathing heavily.

"See this!" Red said, flashing his bailiff's badge.

"Well, boys, let's do something else now."

"O.K., pal!"

"Me, I'd like to go to a can house. I feel the imminent need of getting 'em off."

"I'm laying off that. I'm a married man, and I love my wife," Red said.

They straggled around, and got another drink at a saloon, roamed the streets again, talking in raised voices. Soon Red, Les, and a swarthy lad named Tom were alone together and walking south along Blackstone Avenue from Fifty-fifth Street. At Fifty-sixth Street, Red saw a drunk across the street wobbling out of an automobile. He crossed to the fellow, followed by his companions.

"Where you going there, fellow?" he asked.

"Why?" the drunk, a middle-aged and large-boned man, asked in surprise.

"Never mind why! Where are you going?"

"Say, is this a free country, or isn't it?"

Red flashed his bailiff's badge.

"Officer, I'm not violating any laws."

"I just asked you where you were going?"

"I'm here to see my girl."

"All right. When a police officer asks you questions the next time, don't try to evade answering them. What's your name?"

The fellow drew a card from his wallet and handed it to Red.

"What do you do?" Red asked after reading the name on the card.

"I sell vacuum cleaners."

"Well, it's all right. Only the next time don't try to get out of answering questions like you seemed to be trying this time."

"I didn't. It was just a misunderstanding, officer, because I didn't know who you were. Come on, have a drink," he said, handing a bottle of bourbon to Kelly.

They drank, and then Red and his pals proceeded along Blackstone Avenue toward Fifty-seventh Street.

"Well, boys, would or wouldn't Kelly make a good dick?" he asked.

"You were perfect, Red," Les said.

"Say, Kelly, I like this. They think we're dicks, all right. I get a kick out of it."

"Yes, Red, you were swell. I always knew you had the stuff in you. Me, now, I'm no good for nothing. I'll spend all my life rotting away and only working extra, at that, for the Continental Express Company," Les said.

"Come on, Les, old pal. This is Christmas Eve. And you've been singing that same blues song ever since I've known you."

"Now here's something that looks interesting," Tom said, stopping, gazing up into a lighted first floor window where they could see a party in progress with dancing couples and girls seated near the window.

"Come on," Red said, entering the building, his right hand gripping his revolver.

He rang the first-floor bell. The buzzer sounded and a tall, handsome, slender girl in an abbreviated dress opened the door. They could see that she was slightly drunk.

"I beg your pardon," she exclaimed, striving vainly to mask her sudden fright.

"We got a call from headquarters that you were making a lot of noise and disturbing the peace," Red said curtly.

"Who are you, may I ask?" the girl said, regaining her composure.

Red flashed his badge and Les and Tom stood behind him, hands in overcoat pockets, frowning in the effort to seem official.

"Will you officers step in a moment, please?" she said with an inviting smile.

Entering, they heard laughter, talk, music, the clink of touching glasses, and suddenly, above this, a full-throated and spontaneous male roar.

"But, officer, please explain this to me," the girl said.

"We got a call."

"Yeh, we was told you was disturbing the peace and raising a racket," Les said out of the side of his mouth.

"But that must have been a mistake. This is a perfectly proper and respectable party."

"Well, let's take a look," Red said.

Red's hat slanted over his right eye and his face and jaws were set in an unrelenting frown. Followed by Tom and Les, who continued posing like moving-picture detectives, he stepped into the parlor and coldly eyed the surprised party guests. A girl, who had been sitting on a fellow's lap, blushed, retreated coyly and meekly into a corner. A couple that had been shimmying, ceased. Red looked fishy-eyed from face to face.

"The house is pinched," a party wit said, causing only strained laughs and giggles.

A sexy girl smiled at Red.

"I got a call there was trouble here," Kelly said, still frowning.

"That must have been a false alarm, officer," a thin fellow said.

"Do I look like I'd be where there was trouble," the sexy girl said, giving Red another come-on, hinting smile.

"Girlie, if you ask me, you look like you could cause plenty of trouble," Tom said, his remark easing the strain.

Red turned and walked through the house, accompanied by Tom, Les, and the tall slender girl who was very cordial and polite to them.

"I guess everything is o.k. here. But see that you don't make too much noise. We don't like to be sent around on these kind of false alarms. Not on Christmas Eve, anyway," Red said.

They accepted drinks and left. Outside, Red laughed and asked them how they liked it that time.

"I'd like to have stuck there and tried to make something," Tom said.

"I wouldn't have complained at that, either. A nice piece is what I need to set me off for my Christmas drinking, and the turkey marathon we'll have tomorrow at my Aunt Maggie Doyle's house," Les said.

"Well, where to now?" Tom asked.

"Let's just cruise around, and we'll see what happens," Red said.

VI

"Come on," Red said, leading them into a cheap hotel at Fifty-third and Lake Park Avenue. He walked impressively by the seedy desk-clerk, marched his companions up the dark stairs covered with a frayed carpet, and abruptly knocked at a door on the third floor.

"Who's there?" a deep female voice called.

"Open up!"

A woman in a red kimono, with mussed black hair, opened the door, and behind her on the bed they saw a younger and prettier girl with curly blond bobbed hair, who sat cross-legged in pink teddies. Red brushed into the room, Tom and Les following him a trifle hesitantly.

"What's this?" the girl in teddies asked indignantly.

"Now, sister, don't give me any mouth!" Red snapped.

"Well, this is nerve! What's the big idea of coming into our room like this. We didn't ask you, did we?"

"Not much of an idea. Just checking up on you hustlers," Red said, sending a flush of fear into their faces as he quickly flashed his badge.

"What do you mean by insulting us? We're decent."

"Now, sister, no lip! Don't try any gags and rough stuff, and just let's can all comedy acts," Red said, pointing a threatening finger at the woman in the red kimono.

"Well, what do you want?" the black-haired one said, her voice more relaxed.

"I think we better pull you in," Red said reflectively.

"Why? You ain't got a thing on us. Not a thing!" the girl in teddies protested, her voice shrill.

"Haven't I? Soliciting men? Where's your alibi? Think your word will go with the judge against ours? Say, what the hell do you think they put us on the vice squad for?"

"So you can terrorize girls trying their damnedest to make a living," the dark-haired one said, flashing a look of hatred on them and then dropping wearily down on the bed.

"All right, let's come to the point," the blonde said.

"Well, this is Christmas Eve, and on Christmas Eve, business ought to be pretty good, yes?"

VII

"Say, Red, I got to compliment you on the way you handled them. That was neat. Neat."

"Clever, Red, old pal, the way you told them that Christmas Eve was good business. You know, told her the way you did," Les said.

Staggering a trifle, Red proudly smiled.

"And Kelly, I sure want to thank you for chiseling that hunk for us the way you did. The young one I got, I could see she hated my guts, but still there was something that made her go through with it. Maybe she was afraid. I tell you she just had me hanging on there.

And maybe it was just her sense of efficiency. Anyway, she was damn good," Tom said.

"It must have been Red standing there with his gun in his hand while we climbed into the saddle, and then maybe they were jealous of each other's talents, and the girls wanted to show each other up," Les said.

"But, Red, why the hell did you lay off? I never imagined you was the kind of a lad to refuse free tail," Tom said quizzically.

"I love my wife. I don't object to you fellows having 'em off, but me, I love my wife. When you got a wife as good as mine, and love her like I love mine, well, such broads are just scum."

"I see how you feel, Kelly, but don't forget this little lesson from your bible. Tail is tail, the world over," Tom said.

"Well, I just got what I needed to set me off right for my Christmas drinking," Les said.

Red beamed, staggered. He pulled out a five-dollar bill and said they should take the shake-down money. He didn't want it for himself, and he had just taken it in fun and to carry the act through the right way. They entered a saloon on Lake Park Avenue, and Red was greeted by many cordial voices.

"Merry Christmas, my lad," the fat bartender said.

"Same to you," Red said patronizingly.

"What's the ticket, boys?"

"Three whiskey straights," Red said, laying the five on the bar.

"How's tricks, Kelly?"

"Why, Jack Collins! How are you? Things are great, Jack. Merry Christmas!"

"Same here, Red."

They looked at a picture of President Roosevelt hanging on the wall beside that of a fat burlesque dancer.

"Let's drink to F.D.R.," Collins said.

They drank to the President.

"Yeh, things are looking up for us boys now. We're getting paid regularly, we're staying in power, too, ain't we, Kelly boy?" Collins said loudly.

Red introduced Collins, another precinct captain, to Tom and Les, and they beamed. Collins set them up for a round of drinks and suggested they sit down.

"How's Squeaks Gorman?" Collins asked when they were seated.

"He isn't a bad fellow, and he's becoming a big shot," Red said.

"Well, he's horse to me. Of course, that's my private opinion. He's not regular. He's horse to me."

"But he's going to be a damn big shot," Red said.

They drank.

"Well, boys, this has been a good year for me, and I'm drinking in the hope and knowledge that next year is going to be a better one," Collins said.

"You wrote the ticket then, my lad," Kelly said, and Les grew wistful.

"I wish I could say that. But me, I'm just rotting away as an extra for Long Johnny Continental," Les sighed.

"Come on, no blues. I heard that sob story years ago."

"Times will be good now," Collins said.

They drank to good times, and they continued drinking. About one o'clock, Red staggered out of the saloon with one arm slung helplessly around Collins' shoulder and the other draped over the shoulders of a stranger.

"Boys, I love my wife, dead or alive, and I should never let myself get so cockeyed," he muttered as they half carried him home.

He vomited in the street, and continued to dribble out that he loved his wife.

1934–1935.

Two Sisters

SLOVENLY dressed, her beefy face dirty and unpowdered, Bridget waddled through the crowd which flowed out of Saint Clement's church after the ten o'clock mass. At the foot of the steps, she met her younger sister Susie who, while corpulent, was lighter than Bridget and also more neat in appearance. Wreathing smiles on one another, their greeting was tender, and they decided that since it was such a fine spring morning, they would take a walk over to Jackson Park.

"I'm not going home and cook for the mob," Bridget said as they walked toward the park on heavy feet. "I'm not their housemaid. I'm their mother, and they have to take care of me. I'm a lady, a lady, and I'm going to stay a lady, and not soil my hands over a kitchen stove."

The commandment says, *Honor thy father and thy mother.* If they don't, the Lord will curse them with evil days all their lives."

Susie tried to explain to Bridget how she thought that the children needed a good home-cooked meal on Sundays. They were dutiful children, supporting their mother without any complaint, and it was their due. Bridget said that she had suffered enough bearing them, and done enough for them, washing their dirty diapers, and that was all that any woman should do for her family. She could just see herself slaving for them now when she was beginning to age. Susie said nothing in reply, and Bridget told her that she had been to Sadie McCarthy's wake a week ago.

"Glory be to God, I mean, Lord have mercy on the poor thing's soul!" Susie said.

"Yes, poor Sadie is gone. She died a hard death of a cancer of the stomach. And oh, wasn't she laid out like an angel, though! Her poor mother was heartbroken. She's going to miss poor Sadie, may the Lord have mercy on her soul, so much, because Sadie was the last of her children. And Sue, guess who was there, and guess what she said?" Bridget remarked, waxing loud with enthusiasm.

Susie made a wrong, and half-interested, guess.

"Nora Moran. Nora Moran who used to live at Twelfth and Blue Island. Remember how her father, Tim Moran, used to get drunk and beat her poor mother with a horse whip every Saturday night? Nora was such a pretty girl, too. Oh, but she was just a perfect doll! And remember, Nora married Frank Drake? Frank Drake was a good man. He was a good man, but he died on the other side of the fence. I always did say that mixed marriages was against the law of God, and that Catholic should marry Catholic, Protestant, Protestant, and the Jews should stick to each other. It was the sorrow of poor Nora's life that Frank was never converted. But he was a good man, and a good husband, a good provider, even if he was a Protestant. Nora, she told me at Sadie's wake, poor Sadie, that Frank Drake never as much as once opened his own pay envelope. And he died, leaving her enough insurance to take care of herself and the children, and her own house. And Nora asked for you. She said to me, 'How is your dear sister, Susie?' Why, she nearly cried when I spoke your name. Sue, you're the cake of the walk with all the old people from Blue Island Avenue. Every place I go, people are asking me, 'And how is your dear, beautiful sister Susie?' At the wake, Nellie Brannagan, she cried when she

Christopher for protection from automobile accidents. But for all special difficulties, the Little Rose of Jesus Christ was the best.

Bridget suddenly interrupted her discourse on the powers of the saints to tell Susie that at the last novena to the Little Rose which she had made, she had seen fat Mrs. Mahoney. Susie should just see that one, the airs she was putting on these days, she with her fat ass. She was just so killing, bragging about her Lily who was keeping company with the son of a Congressman, and her Patrick, that dude son, who couldn't hold a candle up to Bridget's own Charlie, and her clubs, and her pet canary, and her husband who got his start selling meat not fit for pigs to eat. The airs of her, she with a rump on her that looked like a tub of butter!

A sixteen- or seventeen-year-old couple strolled arm-in-arm past their bench, hungrily interested in each other.

Bridget elevated her nose and sneered after them, snarling that the boy should be home studying his lessons and the girl helping her mother with housework.

They again lapsed into silence. A slight wind ruffled Susie's brown hair. A leaf dropped at Bridget's feet. Sparrows chirped about them. A baby ran bow-legged on the lawn extending away from the gravel path and opposite their bench. A young man sang from somewhere nearby. And Susie seemed to grow melancholy, and moodily she told her sister that it was peaceful in the park. Bridget did not answer. Then suddenly she again spoke of what Mrs. Mahoney had told her about the Cardinal Archbishop. He was German and the Irish priests did not like it having a German as their superior. And she didn't blame them because she knew from her own life that the Germans were tricky. Yes, they were tricky, even trickier than the Jews, and almost as tricky as the black niggers. Susie said that she thought the Cardinal was a great and a good man. Bridget said that he was a great and a holy man because all Cardinals and Archbishops were great, but that if you asked her, he was like all Germans. He was all for himself. He did not give the Irish priests good parishes. And Mamie McDonald, who was housekeeper for the saintly Father McDermott over west, Mamie had told her about what the Cardinal had done when he had first come to the diocese. Why, he had gone around to the parish houses in an old Ford disguised as a priest. Imagine the commonness of it. An Archbishop who would drive his own automobile, and a tin lizzie, at that. And he would knock on the doors of parish houses like a common beggar, and when the housekeeper would answer and ask who was it, he would ask her, with oh, such a sweetness in his voice, he would ask her to tell Father that the Archbishop wanted to see him. Yes, Bridget repeated, none of the Irish priests liked him. He was a German, and favored the Germans and Dagoes and other foreigners instead of the Irish. And why? She knew, and she wasn't afraid to say why. Because he wanted to be Pope, that was why. And the Lord spare them all from the day when they would have a German in Rome as Christ's Vicar on earth. The Lord spare them!

Susie attempted to disagree with her sister, but Bridget loudly repeated herself, and Susie again became broodingly quiet. Bridget again reverted to the wake, and soon the two sisters were nostalgically talking of the days of their childhood and young girlhood, their eyes softening into dreaminess, their voices becoming tender. Young people flowed by them on the path like pinching remembrances of what they had once been. Susie, her sadness increasing, suddenly remarked that anyway Bridget did have the consolation of her children, who were so young and fine, and a parent could live again the days of youth through her children. Bridget sharply said that little comfort they were, bickering all the time, and expecting their mother to stand over a hot stove ruining her complexion cooking their Sunday dinner so that they could stuff themselves like hogs. Susie said that it reminded her that she would have to be going home to cook Pete's dinner. Bridget flushed, glanced angrily at her sister, told her suddenly to mind her own goddamn business, and never mind hinting for her to go home and cook. Susie said she hadn't. Bridget told Susie to run her own house and not go trying to burn her nose by sticking it into other homes. Susie looked at Bridget nonplussed, too shocked to speak. Bridget said she hated jealous people, and of all jealousy that of blood sisters was the worst. And she said that Susie was jealous of her because there had been no fruit from her womb. She said that Pete had good grounds, even for separation, because Susie had an empty womb. And Susie's empty womb was the punishment which God had visited upon her for having had that abortion before she married Pete. It was a sin against God and nature, having an abortion, letting a tinker like Joe O'Malley do that outside of lawful, holy wedlock. It was a sin against God.

Susie flared, and called Bridget a goddamn slob, told her she could mind her own goddamn business, and said that Bridget was just jealous and envious because she had always wanted to be jazzed by Joe

O'Malley, and he never would do it to her. There was nothing in a fat ass like Bridget to entice a man or make another woman jealous of her. And if she were a child of Bridget, she would leave, and let Bridget stay home and sit in dirt on her big fat can.

"Humph! Humph! Well, let me tell you! Let me tell you! My children love their mother. They know that she was always a good woman, that she has never been a whore and she will never break their hearts."

"Why, you, you always were a devil. Even Dad when he lived, he used to call you that she-devil. You always were a dirty selfish devil, and I don't see how you ever got a man. And you certainly made life miserable for poor Pat, God have mercy on his soul!" Susie said, her voice rising until she was shrieking and people were stopping to enjoy the quarrel.

"May God have mercy on you and forgive you for talking like that of me. . . . A Catholic, a Christian, a sacred mother."

"Well, I'm a Catholic, too."

"But you're no good. You were a whore with Joe O'Malley, and you went to a midwife."

"That's none of your goddamn business, and let me tell you, you big fat slob, you wanted Joe and you wanted him goddamn bad. Why, you ran after everything in pants around Twelfth and Blue Island."

"Oh, no! Oh, no! Oh, no! I'm a lady. If I didn't go to school, still, I'm a lady! I'm a lady! Oh, no! I was always a lady! And see this blessed wedding ring! Look at it! A man had to give me that! My bed was blessed by God! But the garbage can in an alley that Joe O'Malley stood you up against, it was cursed by the devil."

"And yes, you just let me tell you something, and don't you forget it. You're nothing but a dirty old hypocrite. You go to church and pray, and then you come out and fight and backbite everybody. You won't even cook a decent meal for your children who support you, you're so busy being a gadder and a backbiter. You're ignorant Irish. What kind of a Catholic is that? You're a fine kind of a Catholic, a fine kind! A fine kind of a Catholic!"

"Oh! Oh! I'll have you know that I'm a decent Catholic woman. A decent Catholic woman! This ring. See it! It was never made filthy by an abortion. I never killed a poor unborn babe and bashed its innocent soul into the eternal fires of Hell. I never murdered a poor unbaptized little innocent. No, I never did that. I'm not that kind of a Catholic. I'm not that kind of a murderer!"

"Why, Jesus Christ, you goddamn lousy hypocrite!" Susie said while the crowd about them increased, many laughing.

Bridget arose, and sneering, she stood before her sister performing a clumsy jig.

"Oh, how refined we are! How swell we are! Da . . . da . . . da . . . dee," she sang, continuing her jig.

Suddenly Bridget flung her dresses up around her neck, and shoved her abdomen toward her sister.

"Kiss my ass," she said.

She walked away, her nose elevated.

Susie sat on the bench, crying, and she told her sad story to a sympathetic young girl. Then she went home to dinner with her husband, and cried as they ate. Bridget returned home to find her children clumsily trying to assemble a meal for themselves. Afterwards, Susie's husband hastened off to a ball game, and Bridget's children left. About three o'clock, Bridget telephoned Susie. They met and went out to the shrine of Saint Jude, in a South Chicago church, to pray. They prayed until the janitor asked them to leave, and closed them out of the church. Coming home, they waddled side by side, talking of old times as if they had never quarrelled. Bridget told Susie how powerful Saint Jude was, and how she stood, next to the Little Rose, in God's sight. As they were climbing up the steps at an Illinois Central suburban station, they saw a young Polish girl smoking a cigarette.

"Humph! If she was my daughter, I'd beat her ass with a strap until the flesh cracked!" Bridget said.

They parted in good spirits, agreeing to meet and make the novena to the Little Rose which was commencing on the following Tuesday.

1930.

Studs

AUTHOR'S NOTE

This, one of my first stories, is the nucleus out of which the Studs Lonigan trilogy was conceived, imagined, and written. It should suggest the experience and background of these books, and my own relationship to their background. But for the accident of this story, and of the impressions recorded in it, I shrould probably never have written the Studs Lonigan series.

After writing this story in the spring of 1929, before I had ever published any fiction, the impressions here recorded remained with me so vividly that I could not let them rest. It was then that both *Young Lonigan* and *The Young Manhood of Studs Lonigan* were begun. Originally they were planned as one volume, to end with a scene similar to the one presented in this story. As I worked over them, they were changed, split into two volumes, and finally they grew into the trilogy as it has been published. However, to repeat, this story is the nucleus of the entire work, and so I include it here.

JTF

It is raining outside; rain pouring like bullets from countless machine guns; rain spat-spattering on the wet earth and paving in endless silver crystals. Studs' grave out at Mount Olivet will be soaked and soppy, and fresh with the wet, clean odors of watered earth and flowers. And the members of Studs' family will be looking out of the windows of their apartment on the South Side, thinking of the cold, damp grave and the gloomy, muddy cemetery, and of their Studs lying at rest in peaceful acceptance of that wormy conclusion which is the common fate.

At Studs' wake last Monday evening everybody was mournful, sad that such a fine young fellow of twenty-six should go off so suddenly with double pneumonia; blown out of this world like a ripped leaf in a hurricane. They sighed and the women and girls cried, and everybody said that it was too bad. But they were consoled because he'd had the priest and had received Extreme Unction before he died, instead of going off like Sport Murphy who was killed in a saloon brawl. Poor Sport! He was a good fellow, and tough as hell. Poor Studs!

The undertaker (it was probably old man O'Reedy who used to be usher in the old parish church) laid Studs out handsomely. He was outfitted in a sombre black suit and a white silk tie. His hands were folded over his stomach, clasping a pair of black rosary beads. At his head, pressed against the satin bedding, was a spiritual bouquet, set in line with Studs' large nose. He looked handsome, and there were no lines of suffering on his planed face. But the spiritual bouquet (further assurance that his soul would arrive safely in Heaven) was a dirty trick. So was the administration of the last sacraments. For Studs will be miserable in Heaven, more miserable than he was on those Sunday nights when he would hang around the old poolroom at Fifty-eighth and the elevated station, waiting for something to happen. He will find the land of perpetual happiness and goodness dull and boresome, and he'll be resentful. There will be nothing to do in Heaven but to wait in timeless eternity. There will be no can houses, speakeasies, whores (unless they are reformed) and gambling joints; and neither will there be a shortage of plasterers. He will loaf up and down gold-paved streets where there is not even the suggestion of a poolroom, thinking of Paulie Haggerty, Sport Murphy, Arnold Sheehan and Hink Weber, who are possibly in Hell together because there was no priest around to play a dirty trick on them.

I thought of these things when I stood by the coffin, waiting for Tommy Doyle, Red Kelly, Les, and Joe to finish offering a few perfunctory prayers in memory of Studs. When they had showered some Hail Marys and Our Fathers on his already prayer-drenched soul, we went out into the dining room.

Years ago when I was a kid in the fifth grade in the old parish school, Studs was in the graduating class. He was one of the school leaders, a light-faced, blond kid who was able to fight like sixty and who never took any sass from Tommy Doyle, Red Kelly, or any of those fellows from the Fifty-eighth Street gang. He was quarterback on the school's football team, and liked by the girls.

My first concrete memory of him is of a rainy fall afternoon. Dick Buckford and I were fooling around in front of Helen Shires' house bumping against each other with our arms folded. We never thought of fighting but kept pushing and shoving and bumping each other. Studs, Red O'Connell, Tubby Connell, the Donoghues, and Jim Clayburn came along. Studs urged us into fighting, and I gave Dick a bloody nose. Studs congratulated me, and said that I could come along with them and play tag in Red O'Connell's basement, where there were several trick passageways.

After that day, I used to go around with Studs and his bunch. They regarded me as a sort of mascot, and they kept training me to fight other kids. But any older fellows who tried to pick on me would have a fight on their hands. Every now and then he would start boxing with me.

"Gee, you never get hurt, do you?" he would say. I would grin in answer, bearing the punishment because of the pride and the glory.

"You must be goofy. You can't be hurt."

"Well, I don't get hurt like other kids."

"You're too good for Morris and those kids. You could trim them with your eyes closed. You're good," he would say, and then he would go on training me.

I arranged for a party on one of my birthdays, and invited Studs and the fellows from his bunch. Red O'Connell, a tall, lanky, cowardly kid, went with my brother, and the two of them convinced my folks that Studs was not a fit person for me to invite. I told Studs what had happened, and he took such an insult decently. But none of the fellows he went with would accept my invitation, and most of the girls also refused. On the day of the party, with my family's permission, I again invited Studs but he never came.

I have no other concrete recollections of Studs while he was in grammar school. He went to Loyola for one year, loafed about for a similar period; and then he became a plasterer for his father. He commenced going round the poolroom. The usual commonplace story resulted. What there was of the boy disappeared in slobbish dissipation. His pleasures became compressed within a hexagonal of whores, movies, pool, alky, poker, and craps. By the time I commenced going into the poolroom (my third year in high school) this process had been completed.

Studs' attitude toward me had also changed to one of contempt. I was a goofy young punk. Often he made cracks about me. Once, when I retaliated by sarcasm, he threatened to bust me, and awed by his former reputation I shut up. We said little to each other, although Studs occasionally condescended to borrow fifty or seventy-five cents from me, or to discuss Curley, the corner imbecile.

Studs' companions were more or less small-time amateur hoodlums. He had drifted away from the Donoghues and George Gogarty, who remained bourgeois young men with such interests as formal dances and shows. Perhaps Slug Mason was his closest friend; a tall, heavy-handed, good-natured, child-minded slugger, who knew the address and telephone number of almost every prostitute on the South Side. Hink Weber, who should have been in the ring and who later committed suicide in an insane asylum, Red Kelly, who was a typical wisecracking corner habitué, Tommy Doyle, a fattening, bull-dozing, half-good-natured moron, Stan Simonsky and Joe Thomas were his other companions.

I feel sure that Studs' family, particularly his sisters, were appalled by his actions. The two sisters, one of whom I loved in an adolescently romantic and completely unsuccessful manner, were the type of middle-class girls who go in for sororities and sensibilities. One Saturday evening, when Studs got drunk earlier than usual, his older sister (who the boys always said was keen) saw him staggering around under the Fifty-eighth Street elevated station. She was with a young man in an automobile, and they stopped. Studs talked loudly to her, and finally they left. Studs reeled after the car, cursing and shaking his fists. Fellows like Johnny O'Brien (who went to the U. of C. to become a fraternity man) talked sadly of how Studs could have been more discriminating in his choice of buddies and liquor; and this, too, must have reached the ears of his two sisters.

Physical decay slowly developed. Studs, always a square-planed, broad person, began getting soft and slightly fat. He played one or two years with the corner football team. He was still an efficient quarterback, but slow. When the team finally disbanded, he gave up athletics. He fought and brawled about until one New Year's Eve he talked out of turn to Jim McGeoghan, who was a boxing champ down at Notre Dame. Jim flattened Studs' nose, and gave him a wicked black eye. Studs gave up fighting.

My associations with the corner gradually dwindled. I went to college, and became an atheist. This further convinced Studs that I wasn't right, and he occasionally remarked about my insanity. I grew up contemptuous of him and the others; and some of this feeling crept into my overt actions. I drifted into other groups and forgot the corner. Then I went to New York, and stories of legendary activities became fact on the corner. I had started a new religion, written poetry, and done countless similar monstrous things. When I returned, I did not see Studs for over a year. One evening, just before the Smith-Hoover election day, I met him as he came out of the I. C. station at Randolph Street with Pat Carrigan and Ike Dugan. I talked to Pat and Ike, but not to Studs.

"Aren't you gonna say hello to me?" he asked in friendly fashion, and he offered me his hand.

I was curious but friendly for several minutes. We talked of Al Smith's chances in an uninformed, unintelligent fashion and I injected one joke about free love. Studs laughed at it; and then they went on. The next I heard of him, he was dead.

When I went out into the dining room, I found all the old gang there, jabbering in the smoke-thick, crowded room. But I did not have any desire or intention of giving the world for having seen them. They were almost all fat and respectable. Cloddishly, they talked of the tragedy of his death, and then went about remembering the good old days. I sat in the corner and listened.

The scene seemed tragi-comical to me. All these fellows had been the bad boys of my boyhood, and many of them I had admired as proper models. Now they were all of the same kidney. Jackie Cooney (who once stole fifteen bottles of grape juice in one haul from under the eyes of a Greek proprietor over at Sixty-fifth and Stony Island), Monk McCarthy (who lived in a basement on his pool winnings and peanuts for over a year), Al Mumford (the good-natured, dumbly well-intentioned corner scapegoat), Pat Carrigan, the roly-poly fat boy from Saint Stanislaus high school—all as alike as so many cans of tomato soup.

Jim Nolan, now bald-headed, a public accountant, engaged to be married, and student in philosophy at Saint Vincent's evening school, was in one corner with Monk.

"Gee, Monk, remember the time we went to Plantation and I got drunk and went down the alley over-turning garbage cans?" he recalled.

"Yeh, that was some party," Monk said.

"Those were the days," Jim said.

Tubby Connell, whom I recalled as a moody, introspective kid, singled out the social Johnny O'Brien and listened to the latter talk with George Gogarty about Illinois U.

Al Mumford walked about making cracks, finally observing to me, "Jim, get a fiddle and you'll look like Paderwooski."

Red Kelly sat enthroned with Les, Doyle, Simonsky, Bryan, Young Floss Campbell (waiting to be like these older fellows), talking oracularly.

"Yes, sir, it's too bad. A young fellow in the prime of life going like that. It's too bad," he said.

"Poor Studs!" Les said.

"I was out with him a week ago," Bryan said.

"He was all right then," Kelly said.

"Life is a funny thing," Doyle said.

"It's a good thing he had the priest," Kelly said.

"Yeh," Les said.

"Sa-ay, last Saturday I pushed the swellest little baby at Rosy's," Doyle said.

"Was she a blonde?" Kelly said.

"Yeh," Doyle said.

"She's cute. I jazzed her, too," Kelly said.

"Yeh, that night at Plantation was a wow," Jim Nolan said.

"We ought to pull off a drunk some night," Monk said.

"Let's," Nolan said.

"Say, Curley, are you in love?" Mumford asked Curley across the room.

"Now, Duffy," Curley said with imbecilic superiority.

"Remember the time Curley went to Burnham?" Carrigan asked.

Curley blushed.

"What happened, Curley?" Duffy asked.

"Nothing, Al," Curley said, confused.

"Go on, tell him, Curley! Tell him! Don't be bashful now! Don't be bashful! Tell him about the little broad!" Carrigan said.

"Now, Pat, you know me better than that," Curley said.

"Come on, Curley, tell me," Al said.

"Some little girl sat on Curley's knee, and he shoved her off and called her a lousy whore and left the place," Carrigan said.

"Why, Curley, I'm ashamed of you," Al said.

Curley blushed.

"I got to get up at six every morning. But I don't mind it. This not workin' is the bunk. You ain't got any clothes or anything when you ain't got the sheets. I know. No, sir, this loafin' is all crap. You wait around all day for something to happen," Jackie Cooney said to Tommy Rourke.

"Gee, it was tough on Studs," Johnny O'Brien said to George Gogarty.

Gogarty said it was tough, too. Then they talked of some student from Illinois U. Phil Rolfe came in. Phil was professional major-domo of the wake; he was going with Studs' kid sister. Phil used to be a smart Jewboy, misplaced when he did not get into the furrier business. Now he was sorry with everybody, and thanking them for being sorry. He and Kelly talked importantly of pall-bearers. Then he went out.

Some fellow I didn't know started telling one of Red Kelly's brothers what time he got up to go to work. Mickey Flannagan, the corner drunk, came in and he, too, said he was working.

They kept on talking, and I thought more and more that they were a bunch of slobs. All the adventurous boy that was in them years ago had been killed. Slobs, getting fat and middle-aged, bragging of their stupid brawls, reciting the commonplaces of their days.

As I left, I saw Studs' kid sister. She was crying so pitifully that she was unable to recognize me. I didn't see how she could ever have been affectionate toward Studs. He was so outside of her understanding. I knew she never mentioned him to me the few times I took her out. But she cried pitifully.

As I left, I thought that Studs had looked handsome. He would have gotten a good break, too, if only they hadn't given him Extreme Unction. For life would have grown into fatter and fatter decay for him, just as it was starting to do with Kelly, Doyle, Cooney and McCarthy. He, too, was a slob; but he died without having to live countless slobbish years. If only they had not sent him to Heaven where there are no whores and poolrooms.

I walked home with Joe, who isn't like the others. We couldn't feel sorry over Studs. It didn't make any difference.

"Joe, he was a slob," I said.

Joe did not care to use the same language, but he did not disagree.

And now the rain keeps falling on Studs' new grave, and his family mournfully watches the leaden sky, and his old buddies are at work wishing that it was Saturday night, and that they were just getting into bed with a naked voluptuous blonde.

1929.

Can All This Grandeur Perish?

That many things, having full reference
To one consent, may work contrariously:
As many arrows, loosed several ways,
Fly to one mark;
As many several ways meet in one town;
As many fresh streams run into one self sea;
As many lines close in the dial's centre;
So many a thousand actions, once afoot,
End in one purpose, and be all well borne
Without defeat.
     SHAKESPEARE: HENRY V

The doors were cedar
and the panel strips of gold
and the girls were golden girls
and the panels read and the girls chanted:
 We are the greatest city,
 the greatest nation:
 nothing like us ever was.

The doors are twisted on broken hinges,
Sheets of rain swish through on the wind
 Where the golden girls ran and the panels read
 We are the greatest city,
 the greatest nation,
 nothing like us ever was.
  FROM "FOUR PRELUDES ON PLAYINGS OF THE WIND"
     BY CARL SANDBURG

Can All This Grandeur Perish?

I

TOM GREGORY and his wife, June, held open house for the family on New Year's Day. Starting into business as the partner in a butter and egg store in an Irish district on the Southwest Side, Tom had become the president of the Peoples' Stores, Incorporated, one of the largest chain-store corporations in the Middle West. The corporation had remained in the family for years, with Tom owning a major portion of the stock. Just before the stock-market break in 1929, Tom had sold the Peoples' Stores, Incorporated, to a larger chain-store group, netting a handsome profit of millions for himself and sizable profits for all members of the family who owned small blocks of stock. Although remaining on the board of directors of Peoples' Stores, Incorporated, and also becoming a director in the buying corporation, Tom was practically in retirement from active business. He was an energetic, roly-poly man in his late sixties. He had a ruddy, round, bull-dog face, wispy gray hair, and a Santa-Claus smile. Sometimes when he smiled he almost seemed like a schoolboy. His wife, June, was well into her fifties, but she did not look her age. She alone among five sisters of an old-line Dutch family had preserved any semblance of her looks and her figure. Her hair was a fading strawberry, and her oval, unintelligent, pouting face sagged only slightly, its wrinkles small and not numerous. The principal signs of age were observable in her neck, the skin of which was beginning to sag. She was not fat, only a trifle stout, and her legs were relatively slender.

The Gregorys lived in a large apartment on the first floor of a three-storey apartment house on Oglesby Avenue. Their home was gay and bright for the holiday season, with holly in the windows and Christmas decorations still hanging. The parlor was large, padded with expensive furniture, and the walls, even of the long hallway leading to the bedrooms in the rear, were crowded with photographs, paintings, and religious pictures. In the parlor, there was a thick and luxurious Oriental rug of dark hues, a shiny baby-grand piano, *Louis Quatorze* chairs, elaborately upholstered couches, a shiny new radio, pictures, and insipid statues of Dante and Beatrice which June had bought in Italy the previous summer.

All day, from dinner time on, members of the family and close friends had come and gone. The house had rung with laughter and buzzed with conversation. Cousins, sisters, brothers, in-laws, nieces, nephews, old friends, ex-employees had trooped in, wishing Tom and June a happy, healthy, and prosperous New Year and going down on the record as having paid their respects to the family patriarch. Nearly everyone who had come had remarked to some other guest that Uncle Tom just looked the picture of health, and that you wouldn't for a minute think he was as old a man as he was. Uncle Tom had devoted a great deal of time during the day explaining to one guest after another the precise time at which he got up in the morning, adding that no person was worth his salt unless he or she were an early riser. He experienced several lapses of memory when he could not recollect whether he had gotten out of bed at six or at six fifteen on the previous Tuesday morning. Once his memory had failed on another detail, and he strove to recollect whether he had drunk two or three cups of coffee for breakfast on Wednesday morning. About three o'clock, Aunt June had given her recital. She was paying ten dollars an hour in a downtown studio to take lessons in drama and elocution. She gave Channing Pollock's *The Fool,* and one of her sisters, two cousins, and one close family friend had either sobbed or sniffled. The guests had applauded her performance enthusiastically, and Charles Moses, the young bond salesman who now handled Tom's stock-market account, had lengthily expatiated on the artistic talents of Mrs. Gregory. Charles was a protégé of Mr. Gregory, having met him at a retreat given one summer at Notre Dame, where both of them had had the pleasure of shaking hands with Knute Rockne, the football coach. Tom had been almost immediately convinced that Charles was a lad with get-up and go to him, and he had taken the young man under his wing. Charles was now a frequent visitor at the Gregorys', and Mrs. Gregory thought he was the nicest young man. Besides his excellent talk and his politeness, there was his thoughtfulness. For instance, right after Mr. Gregory had bought a large farm, Charles had appeared with a present of three trees to be planted on the grounds. A day after he had given them this present, he sold Mr.

and Mrs. Gregory fifty thousand dollars' worth of stock in a new issue being floated by one of the public utilities corporations controlled by Solomon Imbray, the great midwestern utilities magnate. After Charles had finished discussing the artistic talents of Mrs. Gregory, O'Brien had spoken of them. O'Brien, an insurance man, was a protégé of Mrs. Gregory. He was a small and ingratiating man of about forty-five and, thanks to Mrs. Gregory, had sold policies totaling thousands of dollars to the Gregorys, to members of the family, and to close friends. He had also taken two trips to Florida with the Gregorys.

The day had passed rapidly, soberly, happily, a wonderful New Year's Day. At about six o'clock, when the day had already darkened and there was a sharp and whistling wind outside, the celebration continued. Many guests left, but others arrived, among them June's sister, Lizzie Brown, and her two beautiful daughters, Anna and Caroline. The women sat together in the parlor. The young folks were grouped by the piano, recollecting old-time songs. The men sat in the comfortable sun parlor, off the parlor, smoking expensive cigars and discussing affairs of moment.

II

"Tom, I look at it this way. A cycle is a natural thing, and every so often, because of the cycle, we have to have a depression. Then the cycle goes up, and we have good times," Frederick Van Duym said; he was June Gregory's only brother, a man of about forty-three.

"Now that's just what Mr. Gregory told me the other day when I was here," Charles Moses said, closing his right hand and swinging it downward in a gesture of agreement.

"It's too bad Al Smith lost to Hoover last time. I think that if we can elect him president in the next elections, we'll have better times. Better Times," O'Brien said, covertly watching Tom's face to catch the old man's response to his remark.

"O'Brien, get some of those cigars out here!" Tom said as if addressing a servant, and O'Brien scurried to obey orders.

"Now, I agree with what Mr. Gregory was saying only last week. America is too great a country to remain in the throes of a depression," Charles Moses said.

"Well, sirs!" Tom said, arising. He glanced querulously into the parlor. "O'Brien, hurry up with those cigars!"

360　CAN ALL THIS GRANDEUR PERISH?

"Yes, sir, Mr. Gregory, I got them as quick as I could," O'Brien said apologetically as he hustled back with a box of cigars.

"Pass them around!" Tom ordered.

O'Brien offered the box first to Tom. Tom took a cigar and bit off the end. Charles Moses was before him with a lighted match. O'Brien passed the cigars to the others.

"Well, sirs!" Tom said.

O'Brien dropped out to the womenfolk, and whispered to June Gregory for them to speak more softly and not have the young people sing, because they all wanted to hear every word while Mr. Gregory discussed business and conditions. He returned to the sun parlor.

"Well, sirs, one of the causes of hard times is over-capitalization, particularly of buildings. Here in Chicago, the bankers loaned out money right and left, on buildings, and mortgages were granted on them once they were put up. We have too many hotels, too many office buildings, too many apartment buildings, and they can never pay for themselves. The banks are getting in a bad way because they can't collect. We, in our business, get private reports on banks we deal with so we know when to withdraw our money in time, and I know that the banks are in a bad way. Soon they'll be owning all kinds of buildings, and they won't be able to liquidate. Well, sirs, when somebody asks you why are there hard times, you just tell them what I just told you."

"Isn't that so! Conditions are just as Mr. Gregory has described them," Charles Moses said ingratiatingly.

"Mr. Gregory's a great man. You don't want to miss a word he says," O'Brien said to Fred Van Duym, looking daggers at Charles Moses as he spoke.

"I think that Mr. Gregory has told us something very instructive," Charles Moses said.

"Well, sirs!" Tom said, ignoring Charles Moses, "I think that the solution for hard times is this. There are too many people in the cities, and not enough jobs for them. What has to happen is for some people in the cities who are not working to go back to the country. Here's what I think should be done. Let the government loan about five thousand people enough money to get started on a farm. Mind you, loan, not give. In a year, two, three years, they can pay it back with interest, and they can raise farm products. They'll have enough to eat that way, and they won't be tramping the streets looking for jobs where there are no jobs. And we got to do something like this, because, you know, we don't want this country to get like Russia. I had a priest here the other night who has seen Russia, and we can't let the same thing happen here. And it pays going back to the farm. Take my farm. I bought it, and invested in improvements. I spent over fifty thousand dollars on it. But, well, sirs, it will pay in a short time. In fact, it paid some last year. When the farmers had a milk strike, we were able to supply a dairy with plenty of milk. And if people do that, they'll lead a simple life that's wholesome," Tom said.

"That's what I call a bully idea, Mr. Gregory," Charles Moses said.

Tom beamed, a Santa-Claus smile on his face.

"O'Brien, get me that book I'm reading," he said.

O'Brien obeyed, returning with a copy of *Parnassus on Wheels* by Christopher Morley.

"Now, there is a description of the simple life here that I was reading the other night, and I marked it. I want you gentlemen to hear it."

III

"Lizzie, now that your girls are grown and in school, and your delicatessen store is sold, you ought to be able to get around more and enjoy yourself," Aggie Leary said to corpulent Mrs. Brown, whose reddish hair was beginning to show white streaks.

"Aggie, I'm never done with work, fixing and cleaning and tending to the girls' clothes. A mother is never done with work. But I'm proud of my girls," Mrs. Brown said.

"They're such lovely girls. Tom and I wish we saw more of them," June said.

"June, they're so busy with school and studies. Anna wants to be a lawyer, and she works so hard. And I think I'll let Caroline study dramatics. She wants to be an actress, but I don't know what to think. When I was a girl, it was considered a disgrace to be an actress. But then, maybe times have changed. You know all about acting, June, what do you think?"

"Lizzie, it would be wonderful for Caroline to study it, but you should never let her go on the stage. That ruins good sweet girls," said June.

"Lizzie, you should have heard June's recital. It would have made you cry," Ella Markham, another of the Van Duym sisters, said.

"Lizzie, June made me cry," Aggie said.

"I wasn't so good today," June said modestly.
"But, say, June, you've lost weight," Aggie said.
"I lost ten pounds on the Hollywood diet," June said, smiling.
"Is it a good one?" asked Mrs. Brown.
"It's wonderful, Lizzie," June said.
"Lizzie, what happened to the diet you were on?" Aggie asked.
"I lost two or three pounds, but I had so much housework to do for the holidays, I forgot. I got hungry and ate," Lizzie said, and they laughed.
"Lizzie is like me. She likes her steaks thick and juicy," Myrtle, Fred Van Duym's wife, said.
"Yes, but, Myrtle, you can afford it. You're not an old tub like me," Mrs. Brown said.
"Well, none of us are spring chickens any more," Ella Markham said.
"You said it, Ella," Myrtle Van Duym said.
"We're too old to be worrying about the vanities of the flesh. The soul is what should interest us," Ella Markham said.
"Ella, here, is as religious as Tom," Mrs. Brown said.
"Tom is very religious now. He wasn't, though, when he was younger. But now, my goodness, he wants everybody to live according to the letter of the Ten Commandments. Gracious, but he is getting more and more strict," June said.
"He's a wonderful man, Tom is," Ella Markham said.
"Yes, Tom is a good man," June said.
"Indeed, he is," Myrtle said enigmatically.
"A better and more religious man than Tom Gregory cannot be found," Ella Markham said.

IV

"He's an old tyrant, going around, spying on everybody to see what time they get up in the morning. Jesus, he certainly likes early rising. When he came around to see Mother last week at ten o'clock in the morning, and she wasn't up, she almost had fits. She's afraid of him, too! Everybody in the family is afraid of the old tyrant!" Caroline Brown said.
"But he's a nice old bear," Anna Brown said.
"I'll sell him to you cheap," Caroline said.
"You buy him, Doll," Anna said to her younger sister.

"And it won't do them all so much good for being afraid of him. He's got an iron constitution, and he'll bury most of the people who are here soft-soaping him to get into that will," Caroline said.

"Aunt June told Mother we're in it," said Anna.

"Don't count on it. He has more lives than a cat. He'll be the same as he is now at eighty, only more of a tyrant," Caroline said.

Peggy Markham joined them. She was a solidly built woman in her thirties, with large piano legs, the result of a childhood illness. She had a sweet but sad and faded face, and a kindly good nature.

"Well, kids, what secrets now?" asked Peggy.

"Does Uncle Tom come to your house, too, to find out what time you get up in the morning?" asked Caroline.

"You must be tolerant of Uncle Tom. He has such a good heart. He's older and more experienced than you kids, although maybe he does bend too much on the side of being a puritan," Peggy said.

"He's just an old puritan!" said Caroline.

"Why, Caroline!" said Anna.

The girls laughed. They saw that O'Brien and Charles Moses were struggling like Trojans, setting up camp chairs and card tables. O'Brien, perspiring and breathless, suddenly stopped before them.

"Mrs. Gregory says we got to play cootie," he said.

"God!" exclaimed Caroline.

"Kids, it's really little to do to humor Aunt June and Uncle Tom on New Year's Day. And they're really so good to everybody," Peggy said.

V

Uncle Tom sat alone in the sun parlor watching the proceedings. He smiled fatuously as if to reveal that he considered this game foolish, but that he humored such harmless folly. O'Brien and Charles Moses were distributing dice cups and pads of paper, while June was seating the guests, four to a table.

"Everybody's going to have a little sport now, Mr. Gregory," O'Brien said, sitting down beside Tom.

"Aren't you playing?" Tom asked.

"I thought I'd keep you company," O'Brien said.

"Go and play!" Tom said.

O'Brien jumped up and went to Aunt June in the parlor. She discovered that one more was needed to even the tables. She gave final instructions, and stated that when she gave the signal *go,* the game would start. She asked if they all understood her instructions. They chorused that they had. She gave the signal, and the guests played cootie.

Each player shook the dice in turn, and the object of the game was to get a cootie which totaled 21 points. Before a player could begin scoring, he had to get the body for his cootie. When he shook a one, he got this body, and marked a round ◯ on the pad to suggest the body. If he shook three, he got a head for his cootie, and he marked that ⊗ . To get each of the eyes, he had to shake a two, and he marked these ⊗ . A four gave him a nose, which was marked ⊗ . Three was a mouth, ⊗ . Sixes were arms and legs, and two of each were required for the complete cootie, which was then marked down ⊗ . The points totaling the twenty-one for the cootie were six for a body, four for a head, three for the mouth, two for the nose, one for each eye, and one for each of the arms and legs. As soon as a player at any of the tables got a complete cootie, he yelled, "Cootie!" All shaking immediately stopped. The players added their scores. Then Aunt June, the referee, gave the signal, and they began shaking again to get a cootie. The guests caught on to the game quickly, and each one shook the dice rapidly in order to hurry the progress at his or her table, for only one player could get a cootie for each game. Mrs. Brown, Myrtle, Fred Van Duym and Ella Markham were seated together at one table. Ella was slow in shaking, and inclined to talk. They ragged her and fretted because she was robbing them of their chances to get higher scores. Whenever they could, Charles Moses and O'Brien let out a remark that the game was fascinating, or very interesting, and that only a hostess like Mrs. Gregory could think of it for her guests to play like this at a large party. Tom sat alone, smoking, the Santa-Claus smile on his face. June moved officially from table to table, beaming with gratification. The dice-shaking was hurried, even frantic, and there was much good-natured laughter. Ella Markham couldn't be fast, and some of the older people, while shaking hastily, would constantly smile self-consciously at one another to hint that they did not and could not take the game with real seriousness. Fifteen games were played, and the complete scores were laboriously totaled. Caroline Brown was highest, Uncle Will Markham was second, to his own surprise, and Charles Moses was third. Prizes were given out to these winners, trinkets which June Gregory had purchased in Italy. There were buzzing conversation and good spirits. Tom Gregory circulated through the parlor remarking that he hoped they had all liked the sport. Charles Moses and O'Brien buttonholed June and told her what a wonderful idea it had been to have the guests play cootie, and that she was a wonderful hostess.

VI

The guests sat down at the long rectangular mahogany table in the dining room off the parlor, Tom at the head and June at the foot. There were cold turkey and pork, heated dressing, plates of vegetables, salad, olives, dates, nuts, and Chinese spices. Everyone ate heartily and talked. Tom repeatedly scrutinized Caroline Brown who sat a few places down on his left. Ella Markham, seated on Tom's right, asked him if he didn't think that Lizzie Brown's girls had grown up to be fine young ladies. Instead of answering Ella, Tom turned toward Caroline. She returned as simple a smile as she could muster, although he made her uncomfortable. She wished that Anna was in her place instead of at the other end of the table. Smiling, a slight blush on her cheeks, she was handsome, almost radiantly beautiful and virginal.

"Tom, don't you think that Lizzie Brown's girls are fine young ladies?" Ella Markham repeated.

"A young lady like you," he said to Caroline sternly, fixing her eyes, "just has to keep her feet on the ground. Don't forget, Caroline! Always keep your feet on the ground!"

"That's wonderful advice your uncle gives you, Caroline," O'Brien said.

"Yes, young lady, always keep your feet on the ground," he said, waving a finger at her.

"Mr. Gregory, Caroline is doing fine at Saint Paul's. And her sister, Anna, is making good progress at the University," O'Brien said.

"O'Brien, I always say that everybody must keep their feet on the ground, particularly the young," Tom said.

"What's that Mr. Gregory said?" Charles Moses asked Peggy Markham, who sat on his right.

"Uncle Tom was telling Caroline to keep her feet on the ground," Peggy answered, smiling artificially at Charles.

"My daughters always keep their feet on the ground," Lizzie Brown said.

"Of course, they do, with you for their mother," Charles Moses said

"Well, sirs, I always tell a young person to keep their feet on the ground," Tom repeated, again staring at Caroline.

"Mrs. Gregory, you certainly have wonderful nieces in Anna and Caroline Brown, and also in Peggy," O'Brien called down the table.

"The way I figure it is this," gray-haired, sad-faced gentle Will Markham said to Fred Van Duym, continuing a private discussion they were having. "Now, we have bad times. But we've had bad times before. Take my line, the building line. Things have been slack in building, and when they are bad in that line, they're slack in other lines, too. Take my own neighborhood in Hyde Park. In my own personal acquaintances, I know eight families that are doubling up because they can't afford to live singly. A man likes to have his own home, and things are pretty damn tough when families got to double up. But then, I think with things picking up as I expect them to do in the coming year, and like they've done in the past after hard times, these people will want to live singly again, and the building business will perk up. If it does, things in other lines will follow, and we'll have better times."

"I had to lay off some of my men. I hated to, but orders from the top, that's orders. I'm not a Gregory. I'm just manager of the warehouse, and orders means orders. I hated to lay off my men, though," Fred said.

VII

Two maids brought in coffee and three large homemade cakes.

"Did all of you people see my son's picture in the paper this morning?" asked Mrs. Gregory.

"Wasn't it wonderful!" exclaimed Ella Markham.

"Mrs. Gregory, you should be proud to have such a son," O'Brien said.

"What picture? What's this?" asked Myrtle Van Duym.

"Didn't you see the full-page advertisement of the New Year's sale at Peoples' Stores, with Eugene Gregory's picture at the top of the page?" said O'Brien.

"Why, no," Myrtle said.

"I'll get it. Will you pardon me, Mr. and Mrs. Gregory, will everybody pardon me a minute while I run away from the table to get the paper with Gene's picture in it?" O'Brien said.

CAN ALL THIS GRANDEUR PERISH? 367

"Sit down, O'Brien! They can see it later," Tom said.

"You know, folks, it proves what Mr. Gregory was just saying to us. His son has kept his feet on the ground, and that is why he's advertising manager of the Peoples' Stores, a big man with a wonderful future while he is still young, and when he advertises, his picture in the ad means something. The advantages of home life with Mr. and Mrs. Gregory, that has done a lot to put Eugene Gregory where he is today," Charles Moses said, and, listening to him, Anna and Caroline looked knowingly at one another.

"Ella, have you seen Mr. Gregory's farm since he put in his latest improvement?" asked O'Brien.

"Why, no," Ella said.

"You should. It's a model farm, a wonderful estate, worth every cent Mr. Gregory has spent on it," O'Brien said.

"Just a minute, O'Brien," Tom said.

"I was just telling the folks what a wonderful farm you have, Mr. Gregory," Tom said.

"The trouble with people is that they don't lead simple lives. You take the money they spend. People could live on much less money than they do. It isn't the necessities of life which costs people money. It's the luxuries," Tom said.

"Isn't it so! Women smoking cigarettes, committing all kinds of sins. Why, if I did the things that girls do now when I was a young girl, I would have buried my head in shame. I say that they have to go back to the good life like what we all lived when we were girls, obey the Ten Commandments, fear God, and stay in the Church," Ella Markham said.

"I tell you, folks, if people only would live according to the maxims Mr. Gregory lays down, this would be a much happier world," Charles Moses said.

"Fred, Mr. Gregory says wonderful things. People don't spend money on the necessities of life, it's the luxuries. Wonderful," O'Brien called down to Fred.

"You take the American worker. Even with the depression, there is a happy man. He lives the simple life, and he is happy and satisfied. He gets two and three dollars a day and goes to work with a light heart, a full dinner pail, none of the unnecessary worries of life. He knows that it isn't the luxuries of life but the simple necessities that count. I tell you, folks, how often I envy him myself. And Mrs. Gregory, here, she is as simple as the wife of an American worker," Charles Moses said.

"But, Charles, a lot of American workers are not working, and not happy on their pay," Caroline said, smiling sweetly. Charles gaped at her in surprise, momentarily at a loss for words. Just as he opened his mouth to speak, Caroline continued, "Charles, lots of people are so poor that they hardly have enough to eat."

"Caroline, is that really true?" June asked.

Tom diverted Caroline from answering her aunt, and waved his finger at her.

"Young lady, keep your feet on the ground!"

"You know, times are pretty bad," Will Markham began, but Aunt June arose, and the guests followed her from the table.

VIII

"Let's have some old-fashioned homey songs," Charles Moses said to Peggy.

Peggy went to the piano to play. Charles corralled the young people, and they gathered around the piano. Charles stood beside Caroline. They sang. The elderly women sat talking, and Ella Markham spoke about a sweater she was knitting for Will. Aunt June told Lizzie about Lily Dale, the spiritualist colony she had visited two summers ago, suggesting that Lizzie go there with her next summer. Lizzie asked June if there really was anything to spiritualism, and Aunt June said that there was. Ella Markham asked if it was against the Church, and June said that it really wasn't. Will Markham asked Tom Gregory what he had thought of Paris when he was there last summer. Tom said that he had stayed at the Hotel Crillon, and that it had cost him, he couldn't remember exactly, but that it had cost him something like twenty-five dollars a day, and the service was no better than the service at many an American hotel where it only cost you eight to ten dollars a day.

"And what about Ireland?" Will asked.

"Will, that's a great country," Tom said.

"It is, huh, Tom?"

"But you know, the real Irish don't come here. Only the slum Irish come over, and the real ones, the best people, stay there. And conditions are very good there, too."

"The poor aren't as hard up?" asked Will.

"No, they live on farms, and the poor people are happy and contented. They are good Catholics, have their feet on the ground, and live simple lives. But they are a bit lazy," Tom said.

The young folks droned through the chorus of *My Old Kentucky Home.*

"I saw an Irish play here, *The Playboy of the Western World.* It should have been stopped. It says that all Irish are fools. The Irish are wonderful people, that is, the best elements," Tom said.

The talk began to grow very lackadaisical, and the guests were constantly yawning. Charles Moses kept trying to talk to Caroline, and she kept unobtrusively avoiding him. Tom walked about, closely surveying the clan, listening to odd bits of talk. O'Brien followed him. A few guests departed. Tom suddenly looked at his watch.

"O'Brien, put the radio on," he said.

O'Brien hustled to obey. Tom sat next to the radio, with Lizzie Brown on his right.

"Everybody please keep quiet now. Amos and Andy," O'Brien said, and the conversation petered out.

"Darkies have such wonderful spirit and humor. They're such simple people when they keep their place," Charles Moses said, glancing at Tom Gregory.

He noticed the vacant chair beside Caroline. She caught his glance, and as he nonchalantly arose, she went out to the bathroom. He occupied the vacant chair. Tom sat listening to Amos and Andy, his face benign, softened, almost boyish. He kept smiling, a simple Santa-Claus smile, chuckling constantly. The others listened, some laughing, some chuckling, some smiling artificially. If anyone whispered, O'Brien shushed them. Tom sat enjoying Amos and Andy, smiling, chuckling, nodding his head.

"Ah, that's good," he said, smiling when the program ended.

He arose. He suddenly looked down at Lizzie Brown, who was yawning.

"Well, Lizzie, it's now 1931, and I don't think us old folks will be around much longer," he said.

He yawned, walked away.

The guests got up and departed.

1931–1937.

Mendel and His Wife

I

"Mendel! Mendel, won't you pay attention to me when I call you!" Ruby petulantly exclaimed.

Mendel sat in the garden, pondering as he smoked cigarette after cigarette, tossing the ashes and butts into the flower garden. He was a small, husky lad of twenty-four who looked older than his age, largely because of his full dark mustache. He had a thin ridged face with a long and prominently sharp nose, and his mop of dark hair was slightly kinky. Ruby was cross-eyed, but with a clear and lovely brownish complexion. She had high cheekbones, a broad expanse of face, and exceedingly thick lips that were almost always smeared with cheap lip rouge. There was a slight protuberance around her belly which made her appear perennially pregnant, and she was large-boned and bow-legged.

Before marrying Ruby, Mendel had been a soap-boxer in Chicago, speaking at Bohemian forums, in Bughouse Square and at the Bug Club in Washington Park. He had eked out his living by what collections he could take up. He had gone to the University for three quarters, and the principal fruit of his study had been Ruby. She had been a girlish co-ed who dreamed of the time when she would be a writer. Her father was a dentist, and her mother was a parlor communist and a member of the Party who had influential relatives in the Communist Party of Russia. The mother also attended the University, seeking at a late age to secure a degree. Both parents had opposed the marriage of Ruby and Mendel. Directly after they announced it, the parents had whisked Ruby off to California, but when they returned, both young people had refused to get a divorce. So Mendel had been taken in to live at the parents' home, and he and Ruby had been given separate beds at opposite ends of the apartment. The father was a light sleeper and whenever he heard Mendel going to Ruby's bed in the night, he awakened, and thwarted their intentions. Finally, Mendel had secured a hack writing job with a small Jewish publisher in

Chicago. He had been employed for a year and a half at a salary of fifty dollars a week, preparing and writing a history of art. When it was completed, the firm had paid a member of the staff of a local art museum a high price to allow her name to be signed as the author, and the book had been released in a gaudily expensive edition.

In his soap-box days, Mendel had styled himself an anarchist, but he had never troubled to think out his views consistently. Ruby had styled herself a communist. They had long discussions on communism versus anarchism, but Ruby always won them because she would break into tears. Mendel's self-styled anarchism began to weaken. When his hack job was finished, Mendel found that he had not succeeded in his aim of saving money on the job so that he could do his own writing. Ruby began a campaign to convince her parents that since both she and Mendel were creative persons, they should be sent to Paris for the sake of their art. They were sent to Paris, and they were now living in Fontenay aux Roses, and receiving an allowance of fifty dollars a month from Ruby's parents.

"Mendel! Mendel, I'm calling you!" Ruby said in exasperation.

He got up and went to her.

"Shall we have one or two eggs for lunch?" she asked.

They debated the question, Mendel taking the view that they should have two eggs. That entailed more discussion, and it was decided that they should have one egg. There was no fresh bread, and Mendel suggested that they ought to buy bread with their last two francs twenty-five. Ruby decided that they should have cigarettes, and she pointed to some stale bread lying on the uncleaned kitchen stove. The bread was almost as hard as a rock, and the mice had nibbled at it.

Mendel started downhill to the café. He was loose and gangly, and bow-legged. His arms, disproportionately long, curved down past his hips. His posture was a slumped one, and he dragged his feet and often walked pigeon-toed. He began to think, and put his long arms behind his back, so that they gave the faint impression of a tail. All the way down and all the way back, he seemed to be lost in thought.

When he returned, Ruby told him that she had toasted the stale bread. He carried the beautiful old cherrywood table from the dining room out into the walled-in garden. Ruby placed the coffee pot, which was unwiped after having boiled over, on the table, and coffee dripped. They sat down to eat. As they munched away, Mendel orated on the shallowness of all modern literature, including the works of those many contemporary writers whom he had not read. Over the coffee cups he delivered a second oration, on modern art. Ruby listened with adoring eyes riveted upon him. They smoked cigarette after cigarette, dumping their ashes onto the table, their landlady's heirloom. Then Mendel stacked the dishes in the sink with those that had already lain there unwashed for several days. He asked Ruby if she would wash the dishes. She said that she couldn't lest she spoil her hands. He said that he'd do them if he hadn't planned to write that piece of art criticism.

"But, Mendel, you promised to type my story for me this afternoon," she pouted.

They quarreled. She ran from him, wriggling her large buttocks, and sat crying in the dining room. Mendel could not bear the sight of his wife in tears. He went upstairs to type her story. It was a tale of mystery on an ocean liner, centering about a beautiful heroine who was quite like Mrs. Mendel Markowitz, minus the cross eyes, the bowlegs, and the large hips. Mendel cursed as he worked pick and hunt with two fingers. Ruby came upstairs to tell him that he was a dear. She promised to go into Paris next week and look for work as a stenographer so that they would have enough money to leave him free from worry while he went on with his writing.

They were living in a pavilion attached to a large stone house, and it lacked a bathtub. They were having dinner that evening with a Chicago lawyer whom they had picked up hanging around the American Express office on the Rue Scribe. His name was Mr. Smart. She undressed, draped herself in a long red robe and went down to the kitchen, which had a stone floor. Standing upon a smooth board, she carefully washed her toes, her knees, and her neck. She called Mendel down to wash her back. Then she washed her hands and face. Mendel was dispatched upstairs to get her toothbrush and the toothpaste. He came down empty-handed, and they ransacked the whole kitchen for these objects. They broke three dishes, but finally found the tube of Rubis Rouge paste lying in the soup they had saved from the previous Tuesday. The toothbrush was discovered under the stove. She washed her teeth. She went upstairs and put on a pair of khaki breeches, which emphasized the width of her hips, and a shirt. She went into the garden and opened a copy of *Ulysses* at the last chapter.

Mendel sat down at his desk by the open dining-room window, and started to write a critique of an art exhibit, determining that it would not be a mere catalogue as were most such critiques. He worked for five minutes when he was interrupted by Ruby. She wanted a glass of water, and he hastened to her with it. He wrote for five more minutes, when she called for a cigarette. Five more minutes, and she asked for a chair upon which she could rest her feet. After having filled two and a half pages, he put his art criticism aside and began on a story which he was titling *The Birth of a Writer*. It described a young American writer in Paris of whom he was exceedingly jealous. The theme of his story was that this particular writer was bourgeois. He rushed out to Ruby to read her what he had written. She was avidly reading. She yawned, exclaimed that Joyce was vulgar, and then listened while Mendel read to her. She said it was wonderful writing. He returned to his desk, jammed the incompleted manuscript into a pigeonhole, and started a poem which urged the masses to revolt. Suddenly, while describing that the workers have bloody fingers, he remembered that he had to have a shirt ironed. He asked Ruby if she would do it. She pouted and said that she would after a while. He arose, paced to and fro with his nose jutting forward and his hands behind his back, loudly complaining that she never did anything for him. She ordered him to quit disturbing her. He ironed his own shirt. She impulsively flung her book on the grass and came into the house complaining she had a headache. He heated black coffee for her. She then gave him a pair of her bloomers which needed washing. She had worn them for two months since he had previously washed them for her. He took out the washboard and rubbed away, growling to himself. She complained of nervousness and said that she had to take a walk. He said that if she waited until he was finished with her bloomers, he would go with her. She was too nervous to wait. She went downhill to the café, and bought a Pernod with two francs which he didn't know she had. She drank it almost in one gulp.

He was still rubbing away at her bloomers when she returned.

"Mendel?" she said.

"Yes," he answered.

"You know, when one goes to the bathroom, one's mind is so vacant. I think we ought to put up a bookshelf there."

"That's a good idea. And what books would we put on the shelf?"

"I don't know. What do you think?"

"There's a copy of Darwin's *Origin of the Species* which was here when we came. How about it? I might get it read that way."

"But that's only a textbook, Mendel. Suppose somebody came out here. We wouldn't want them to think that we read textbooks, would we?"

Mendel scrubbed and rubbed away.

"Where will we eat tonight?" she asked.

"I like that restaurant on the Boulevard Montparnasse. What's it called? Oh, yes, the Restaurant Sainte Cecille."

"But, Mendel, it only costs fourteen francs for dinner there and Mr. Smart has lots of money. I think we ought to take him to Foyot's. It's a hundred francs there."

"Have it your way," he said, still busy on her bloomers.

II

An hour late for the engagement, they met Mr. Smart. They had dinner at Foyot's. Afterward, they sat in the Café Select, and wangled him into taking them to the Rue Blondel. They ended up at Les Halles and had onion soup. Going home in the morning, Ruby said that Mr. Smart was nice, and that he must have lots of money. Look at all he had spent!

"He's bourgeois," Mendel grunted.

III

"Gee, Moses will be here soon," Ruby said with expectation in her voice.

"Yes, and I'm sure he'll give me a suit and some shirts," Mendel said.

"You need them so. And he'll take us around Paris. He'll want to see things," Ruby said.

"You know, Ruby, I think we ought to start a little bureau of our own. People are always coming around to us to be shown around Paris."

"We could have wonderful times, see everything, and we could make enough to live on, and then you'd be free for your writing. You know, Mendel, you must keep on with it. That poem you wrote about the Rue Blondel was wonderful. And that was a beautiful metaphor you used, describing the girl's breasts as the red apples of Eve. And you made *Eve* rhyme with *sieve*. That's a fine rhyme. But say, I'll be so glad to see Moses," Ruby said.

"Mos is one of my best friends," he said.

"I'll have to show him my story, too. When I was on campus, Moses used to like my writing, and he always used to tell me that it was swell, and that if I kept on writing I would some day be printed. I'm going to ask him if he thinks that I can sell my story," Ruby said.

"Moses is a stimulating talker," Mendel said.

"And, Mendel, you need people like him to talk to."

"One fellow like Mos to talk to is better than a pile of books. These American adolescents who come over here, they don't think for themselves. Parrots! They read books but what good does it do them? Parroting what liberal-minded bourgeois intellectuals like Bertrand Russell say. When the Red Army marches on Europe with its fifteen million soldiers, where will all the liberal-minded American adolescent writers be? They'll be mowed down."

"Yes, Mendel, they are all bourgeois. But the revolution is coming in Germany any day now. Bruning can't last, just as Fritz told me, and Fritz ought to know because he's a Party member. And after the revolution the bourgeois will all be killed. And then, Mendel, people like you will get your rightful place," Ruby said.

He grunted agreement.

"But, Mendel, I saw Danny sitting in the Select with Norris Gillette. Norris knows people here, and you got to meet them for your career. So be nice to Danny tonight if you see him and maybe you can get introduced to Norris."

"He's only an adolescent, though. And like all adolescents in this modern age, he's egotistic and selfish and only wants success. They all want success."

"They're little bourgeois worms. Oh, Mendel, Mendel, I can't wait until the German revolution and the Red Army marches into Germany to help it so that these bourgeois worms will all be killed."

Mendel was feeling in a good mood now. He washed the dishes. Ruby said that she needed a little walk. She went downhill to the café and had a Pernod, paying for it with money they had borrowed from Mr. Smart. Mendel sat down at his desk. He wrote an experimental poem entitled *Sex,* in which he strove to suggest sexual relationships and sex emotions by using words denoting colors. When Ruby returned, he read it to her. They decided that it was a fine and an original poem. Returning to his desk, he wrote four pages of an article on the nonsensuousness of Chinese art, and two and a half pages of an article on functionalism in architecture. Ruby got a pair of stockings and one of his shirts which needed washing. She heated the water and had Mendel drag out the washboard and tub. Then she made herself some black coffee. She looked at the shirt and stockings. She made a decision. She threw them in the garbage pail. After all, Moses and his wife were coming. They could get her stockings and give Mendel shirts. That saved her hands. She went to Mendel who was again at his desk.

"Mendel, we'll have to buy some oils," she said.

"Yeh," he answered without looking up from the article he was writing to prove that there were no artists in America.

"Mendel, my father and mother would be terribly disappointed if I didn't follow up my painting and writing here in Paris. After all, they sent me to Paris so that I could be an artist," she said.

Mendel continued with his article.

"Mendel, I'm speaking to you!"

He put down his pencil and listened.

"And I ought to have more stories done to show to Mos," she said.

"Well, I hope he brings me a suit," Mendel said.

"He will. Mos is a swell fellow. And, Mendel, you'll have to see what he thinks of the poetry you've written here," she said.

Bruce, a young artist on a pilgrimage, arrived. He was an American who was one of the most sought-after young men at the Thursday-afternoon dances held at the club for American students and artists conducted on the Boulevard Raspail by the liberal-minded Episcopalian minister. He came hoping that Mendel, known at the Café du Dôme as a brilliant young art critic, would, well, that he would write of his art exhibit now at the club on the Boulevard Raspail.

Mendel outlined his theory about the purity of art to Bruce. Bruce, like most painters, did not understand big words. He sat listening, nodding his head, trying to edge in a few hints about his exhibit. Ruby sat adoring Mendel. Then she slipped down the hill for another Pernod. When she returned, she found Mendel declaiming that Titian had made no contribution to painting.

"Mendel writes brilliant art criticism," Ruby interrupted.

Bruce was impressed, and said that Mendel was expressing his own ideals in painting. Mendel went on to an oratorical demonstration of the inferiority of Renoir.

"Mendel also writes the most beautiful poetry," Ruby said.

Ruby dug up some of Mendel's latest writings, four pages on functionalism in architecture, two and a half pages on an art exhibit, and the poems. Bruce read the manuscripts in discomfort, but nodded his head and said that they were all very good.

"What magazines do you write for?"

"Oh, Mendel could write for any newspaper or magazine, but he doesn't publish much because he strives for perfection. He has written a brilliant history of art that was published in Chicago."

Bruce asked to borrow a copy. Unfortunately, they had none. They talked a while. Bruce again said that Mendel expressed his own ideals in painting.

"Maybe you'll write a little piece about my exhibit," Bruce said cautiously.

Mendel said he'd be glad to do that. As Bruce left, Mendel touched him for twenty-five francs. Ruby took a five-franc note, ignored Mendel's threats, and went down the hill where she had two Pernods.

IV

"Mos ought to be along now," Mendel said, sitting with Ruby at the crowded Café Select.

"It's eight-thirty," she said.

"He gives me a pain. He comes to Paris for a week, and then he does nothing but go to the Cluny Library to look up dead manuscripts," Mendel said.

"And he hasn't taken us around hardly at all," she said.

"A week in Paris, and all he does is bury himself in a library," Mendel said with contempt.

"Marion has changed him. She's very nice, but then he only brought you three shirts and one suit. If he didn't have her as a wife, he might have given you a half a dozen shirts and maybe two suits," Ruby said.

"His talk about scholarship. Scholarship! These guys give me a pain with their scholarship," Mendel said, grunting out more scorn.

"Mendel, you've done scholarship. When you worked on your book, you were always able to go places, and you never gave up delivering your orations in Bughouse Square either," she said.

"They don't pulse with life. They have words instead of blood," he said.

"Mendel?"

"Yes?"

"Mendel, I'm nervous."

"Ruby, you must learn to control your nerves."

"I know, but I got a headache."

"Now, Ruby, you can't have a Pernod," he said, striving to be firm.

"Mendel, I'm so nervous."

"I forbid you to have a Pernod!"

"I'm so nervous, and I just got to do something. You got to give me the money for just one."

"I forbid you to have one! Get a *bock* instead."

"Give me the money!"

He again forbade her, and then he gave her the money and watched her go inside to the bar and drink a Pernod. When she came back, he forbade her to have any more, and she promised.

"Oh, Mendel, there's that Lithuanian who used to be the agent for an American publishing house over here. You must meet him," she said.

"He knows Katz, and I'll meet him through Katz," Mendel said.

"Mendel, I'm so glad that you aren't like Mos, burying yourself in a library. You do as much work as anybody, but you don't make a mole out of yourself," she said.

"I have to laugh at these people who are always working like little petty bourgeois. There's no life in them," Mendel said.

"And, besides, a writer has to go around and get color," she said.

"Yeh."

Moses and Marion joined them. Moses was a young rabbi from Decatur, Illinois, tall and thin, but solidly built and healthy-looking. He was reddish-haired, and he sported a reddish mustache which made him look older than he had a few years previous when he had been a student at the University. He was well dressed, wearing a neatly pressed light gray suit. Marion was a fleshy Jewish girl with a pouting expression on her moony face. After apologizing for being late, Moses suggested drinks. All but Ruby ordered a *bock*. Ruby ignored Mendel's ultimatum and said she wanted a Pernod. She started talking with Moses when Mendel began an arm-waving oration on the necessity of self-discipline. She did not even hear him when he reached the point of warning her that she was ruining her health. Moses sat back in his chair, limply at ease. He appeared to have quickly picked up the manner of many Americans in Paris, that of being able to lounge at a café table with facility and nonchalance. They talked, and Moses said that it was necessary, in the study of art, to focus one's attention on the movements and trends of a time, rather than upon individual artists and their particular products. Mendel agreed without having listened. Moses repeated himself.

"Modern youth is going to the dogs," Mendel interrupted. "These young sophisticates! They're all shallow. And modern art is the same. All these movements, Cubism, Vorticism, Dadaism, Futurism, all of them, you'll find that together the whole bunch of them discovered one little idea, one small aesthetic truth, and that's all," Mendel added, swinging his arms appropriately.

Moses picked up the discussion while Marion and Ruby talked.

"Mendel writes such beautiful poetry," Ruby said.

"Has he ever published it?" Marion asked.

"Oh, Mendel doesn't believe in showing and publishing his poetry. He doesn't write for the mob or to make a big name for himself. But he writes really beautiful things."

"I want to read them."

"Yes, you must," Ruby said.

"And Moses will, too."

"And Mendel does such brilliant art criticism," Ruby said.

"Moses was telling me about his art criticism."

"And Moses likes my writings. I hoped to have a number of stories ready to show him, but I couldn't. I just didn't have the time," Ruby said.

Gesturing fiercely, Mendel spoke in dispraise of ambition, and of those shallow young men who write in order to become successes.

"They aren't sensitive," Mendel said, concluding his diatribe.

"Yes, Mendel is almost too sensitive," Ruby said, overhearing her husband.

V

Lorenson, a painter, and a few other friends joined them.

"Since seeing Matisse all in a lump at his exhibit like I just did, I've come to value my own paintings more," Lorenson said.

"Oh, are you a painter?" Marion asked.

"Do you paint?" Moses asked.

"Yes, he's an artist. Lorenson, I was just going to tell Moses and Marion that I'm going to get oils and pick up my own painting again," Ruby said.

Moses attempted to describe precisely how he felt when he walked down a street. This led to a discussion of rhythm between Moses and

Lorenson. Botts and his wife came around. Botts was a genial, warm-hearted, and shabbily dressed Englishman who had, he claimed, written three plays, one of which had been produced by an amateur theatrical society in London. He now described himself as an economist, and wrote a monthly article for an English hemp and wool journal, and occasional other articles for British trade journals. His wife was a sculptor from Indiana, an ill-fed, scraggly-looking blonde girl. She complained that she couldn't afford clay for the statue of Saint John the Baptist she was doing, with Botts serving as the model. Botts outlined a theory he was developing in his next article. He said that the economic depression could be eliminated if birth control were dealt a death blow. If people had more babies, they would have more character, and, also, there would be intensified population pressures to make emigration necessary. Waste sections of America, Australia, and similar countries would be inhabited. New lands, new cities, new industries would be developed, and, thereby, new wants and new wealth would be created. Also, man would regain his lost pioneering spirit, which he so woefully needed. There was a long and noisy argument, and Mendel had the last word.

"When the Red Army marches into Germany, bourgeois like you and Keynes, your little tin god, will be mown down."

VI

They went to a dimly lit *bal* on the Rue de Lappe, Moses acting as host. The establishment was tight and narrow, with a bar on the right of the entrance. There was a series of wooden benches arranged around the room, bordering the small dance floor. The Markowitz group occupied a long narrow bench at the edge of the dance floor. The three-piece orchestra was at the other end of the hall. The ceiling was dotted with clusters of small electric globes, and these were switched from a dim white to a dim red, and then to an amber glow. The habitués of the place were all young. The males, *les titis,* were thin, small, and many of them seemed poorly fed. And they were dressed similar to the characters in René Clair's *Sous les Toits de Paris.* They wore scarfs and their caps were arranged at slanting angles. They had strained faces, with a kind of haunting artificial expression pasted on. The girls were dressed in cheap little skirts and blouses. The dancing was mechanical. The dancers moved in a steady waltzing whirl, scarcely talking.

"This is very proletarian," Ruby said.

"You find the real proletarians around here, and they're the only people in France who are intelligent," Mendel said.

"They dance with more spirit and abandon than other people do. The future of the world is in the hands of proletarians like these," Ruby said.

"It's very interesting," Moses said.

Botts tried to talk about economics and Harold Laski, his former teacher, but he was shut up.

"It's so lively," Ruby said.

Dance followed dance, and the dancers twirled around steadily like automata, their faces almost blank. The Markowitz group danced. Ruby sought out one little fellow who wore gray trousers, a dirty white shirt, no tie, and a gray peaked cap which was slanted over his right eye. She couldn't follow his steps, and their performance was clumsy. She tried to tell him in ungrammatical French that she was an American, and that she was for the proletariat. Then she said that there was going to be a revolution in Germany. He caught the word German, and said,

"*L'Allemagne, c'est mauvais, très mauvais.*"

He did not answer her when she stumbled on in French and English, but he graciously spun her around until the dance ended. Then their party left, and wandered around the Bastille section, and at dawn they ended up having onion soup near Les Halles.

VII

"You know, my mother and I are both interested in psychology," Ruby said as both girls, in their pyjamas, sat talking in the sunny garden. Ruby seemed more cross-eyed than usual, and Marion's pyjamas were tight, revealing her slabbed brownish skin just above the buttocks.

"Psychology is very interesting. I think that coming to Europe and meeting people, as we are, it improves one's knowledge of psychology because, after all, what is psychology but a knowledge of people?" Marion said.

"My mother and I took the same course in abnormal psychology at the University, and we were very interested in it. She sent me abroad to work on my writing and painting, and she would be terrifically disappointed if I didn't do a little reading in psychology, also. I'm going to start reading soon. I think I'll start going down to the American Library one or two days a week."

"That's a good idea," Marion said.

"My father is a dentist, you know, but he isn't a bourgeois. And my mother is a Party member. She was in the revolution of 1905, and do you know who's her cousin? Bulgachevsky!"

"Who's Bulgachevsky?"

"You don't know who Bulgachevsky is?"

"No."

"Bulgachevsky is a big man in the Party. He was in the Chinese revolution," she said.

"When was that?"

"I don't know, but a little while ago. There was a revolution in China, but the bourgeois had something to do with it, and it wasn't successful. My mother is going to get jobs for Mendel and me in Moscow when we get all the atmosphere of Paris," Ruby said.

"That's wonderful," Marion said.

"But what I meant to say is that of course I haven't lost my interest in reading, even if I don't do a lot of it right now. I'm progressing a lot, because I meet people, and I make a study of them. I apply and test the principles I learned in psychology at the University, and that kind of work, it's called field work, is more necessary than just learning theories," Ruby said.

"I wish I'd paid more attention to psychology in college," Marion said.

"You'd never have regretted it. Now take me, I can observe the people I meet and decide if they have obsessions," Ruby said.

"It's interesting when you have a knowledge of psychology. Moses has it," Marion said.

"So has Mendel. He gets people quick, and it helps him amazingly in his art criticism," Ruby said.

"It helps Moses, too," Marion said.

"My knowledge of psychology has helped me here in Paris. Now, there's a girl we met named Gwennie. She was deported from America because she's an anarchist like Emma Goldman. Well, it was because of psychology that I learned how to detect that she's a Lesbian. And you know, she wants to get me, but I wouldn't let a Lesbian touch me," Ruby said.

"Did you read *The Well of Loneliness?*" asked Marion.

"Yes," lied Ruby.

"Wasn't it a sad and thrilling book?" said Marion.

"I only like books about the class struggle," said Ruby.

"Moses always says that he isn't interested in politics and economics, but only art," said Marion.

"Mendel and I, we believe in the revolution," said Ruby.

Marion innocently asked Ruby if she and Mendel did anything for the revolution.

"Mendel writes," Ruby said.

There was a moment of silence.

"But I do have to study more abnormal psychology. Marion, have you read Freud?" Ruby asked.

"No, but I read Edwin Arlington Robinson, and I think that he's a wonderful psychologist," said Marion.

"I like Robinson," said Ruby.

"He's simply grand," said Marion.

"He is," said Ruby.

They began talking about sex, and talked on for a long time.

VIII

When Moses and Marion went on to Berlin, Marion forgot a coat and a dress. As Mendel put them on the train, he remarked that they might see the revolution in Germany. He also said that a letter had come from Ruby's parents, and that it looked like they would soon get money to go on to Russia if they wanted it. However, the departure was not cordial. Moses and Marion had spent considerable money on the Markowitzs, but Mendel and Ruby were disappointed. They had the word *cheap-skates* formed in the backs of their minds, but they did not mention it to each other.

They found other patrons, and the days spun along as they waited for further word from Ruby's parents and for the money that would enable them to go to Moscow. Ruby was hoping that Marion wouldn't write for the clothes she had left behind, but Marion did. She wrote three letters. Two weeks after the third letter had arrived, Mendel shipped the package to them. It had cost fifteen francs, but Mendel wrote asking Moses for twenty francs expenses.

Ruby discovered that the Lesbian, Gwennie, knew a number of writers. So she and Moses courted Gwennie, and invited her to dinner.

She asked Gwennie all sorts of questions, but she was disappointed because Gwennie made no advances toward her.

Another discovery of theirs was Scoopy, a consulting psychologist who also made a good income writing hack short stories. He was a thin, ugly, tubercular fellow with ears that stuck out from his skinny face and made him look ridiculous. Scoopy was always drunk, and he spent money liberally. His talk was merely an endless jabber, but Mendel would listen to him and constantly nod his head in agreement.

"You know who's here now? John Watson. John's a born psychologist. I'm going to meet him again next week in Moscow. I saw John last night. John thinks a lot of me. And, of course, it's mutual. He's a born psychologist. But there's one point on which John and I don't agree. It's this. John insists that a person cannot hold visual imagery in his memory and I insist that he can."

"Of course, he can. I'm an art critic, and an artist does," Mendel interrupted, but Scoopy paid no heed to him.

"Say, I've seen all kinds of Americans here. Why, Paris is just loaded with American writers this Sunday. But you say you met me in Chicago at the Sour Apple forum?"

"Yes, I used to speak there," Mendel would say again and again in answer to this question.

"Say, yes, I did see you there. I was with Brown. I was Secretary to Brown's Society for the Dissemination of Atheism."

"I remember."

"Say, I'm drunk. When a person drinks like I do, there's a reason for it. Well, I got a reason. I'm not just drinking to drink. I'm celebrating. I'm celebrating. My wife left me and I'm celebrating."

The Markowitzs thought that Scoopy was a swell guy. He took them around and paid all the bills. And they hoped he could be used to help them move. They had become dissatisfied with living in Fontenay aux Roses and with the long daily tram rides to Paris. They owed twelve hundred francs back rent. They asked Scoopy to pay it for them so that they could move. He promised to, but he disappeared as suddenly as he had come upon their horizon. Then their landlady evicted them and they found a small apartment in Montparnasse.

Constantly they lost old friends and made new ones. One of their new friends was Lorenson's girl, Sarah. But they lost Sarah just as they had others. She was paying the bill for drinks during the Bastille day celebrations. Ruby was drunk, and a party of American tourists were so amused by her antics that they kept calling her over for more Pernods. She continued leaving her own party to join the tourists. Sarah's pride was hurt. Angry, she left the table and would not speak to them again. Lorenson also stopped speaking to them, remarking that they had sponged off him enough. Their fifty-dollar allowance came the first of each month, and it lasted a week or two. And then there was the same old round of borrowing and chiseling. They acquired such a reputation as spongers that finally they could borrow no more and they often went hungry. Ruby would have to go through periods without drinking Pernod, and she became irritable. They quarreled with greater frequency and with intensifying bitterness. Mendel blamed Paris and the French for his plight. Ruby echoed him. He kept saying that as soon as the German revolution came, he would go there. And he was sure that it would happen following the Hoover Moratorium. But it didn't. He waited and fumed. And finally, just when the Markowitzs seemed utterly friendless, the money for their transportation to Russia came from her parents. They got their visas as tourists, and said goodbye to whoever would speak to them. They left for Russia in a pilgrim mood, hoping to find a better life thanks to the influence of Ruby's cousin, Comrade Bulgachevsky.

1931–1936.

Precinct Captain

I

O'MALLEY was a stocky man in his forties, with a solid, brick-like face, thinning reddish hair and narrow blue eyes. He had an air about him. He walked, he talked, he sat, he stood, he gesticulated with an air of authority. He was always playing his role in public, the role of a man who had been in the political game for twenty years. The fruits of his public service were a job as deputy sheriff in the county building and the title of precinct captain in his neighborhood near South Shore Drive and Seventy-first Street.

The primary fight put O'Malley on the spot. In the previous election, he had gone around and told all his people to vote for Kline for Governor. He had said that Kline was as fine a man as they would ever find in public life in the whole state of Illinois. He told them that Kline had a fine record. He said that it showed you what a fine country America was when it would elect a Jew. Many of his voters were Irish, and he told them that the Irish and the Jews had to stick together. Look what happened to the Irish in the old country. And look what happened to the Jews in, where was it, Jerusalem? Anyway, look what happened to them. He had thus argued that the Irish had to vote for Kline for Governor because he was a fine man, because he had a fine record, because he was a good Democrat, because the Party and the organization were behind him, and because it was a fine thing for the Irish and the Jews to stick together. If the Irish voted for a Jew, the Jews would return the compliment by voting for a mick. And to Jewish voters in his precinct he had said that they had to come out and stand by a man of their own race and repay him for his public service rendered to them, and to all of the people.

Now, O'Malley was in the hole. All those whom he had lined up to vote for Kline had now to be lined up to cast their ballots for Anderson against Kline. It was a hot primary fight, and the organization needed every vote it could garner in the entire county because Kline was certain to roll up a large downstate plurality. O'Malley was working night and day, ringing doorbells, rapping on doors, trying to compose letters to his voters, handing out cards and cigars, hiring one gang of kids and young men to put Anderson literature into mailboxes and another group to take Kline literature out of the same mailboxes.

Easter Sunday came two days before the primary election. He was still busy, with more people to see, more cards to dispose of, more Kline literature to be destroyed, more Anderson literature to be distributed. The organization was fighting for big spoils, and the machine was built up of such rank-and-file corporals as himself. They had to do the producing. If they didn't, the machine was sunk and they were sunk with it. In every ward the Kline people were putting together an organization. If they won, they could have their own ward committeemen, their own precinct captains, and then, where would O'Malley be? He had to hop to it, and he was doing the hopping. He went to an early Mass on Easter Sunday, received Holy Communion, and then, after a quick breakfast, he was out working. He had to see a printer and arrange for the printing of more cards and for the mimeographing of a letter for distribution to the voters on Tuesday morning. He had sat up almost all of Saturday night composing this letter. It told the Democratic voters of the precinct that their friend and neighbor was Patrick J. Connolly. He had served them long and well. He had guarded the public interest as if it were his own property. He had never turned a deaf ear to their needs and their appeals. And now Patrick J. Connolly needed them as they had needed him. He needed their votes so that he could be returned as ward committeeman, in which capacity he would continue to serve them as he had done in the past. O'Malley was pleased with this letter of his. It convinced him that the big-shots down in the City Hall weren't the only fellows who knew a trick or two. None of them could have written a better letter, a letter that would win more votes than his would. But it had been hard work. He had gone to confession, and after midnight he could not eat, drink, even take a sip of water. He had done the job, though. After arranging with the printer, he had his rounds to make. The ballot was so long, and he had to give instructions to the people on how to vote, what names to skip on it, what men to vote for. It was a tough job, and no matter how long he spent explaining the ballot, he still could not be sure that the idea had been put across. And some of his voters were so damn dumb! They might vote for Anderson, but not for Connolly. They might give a vote to some of the traitors on the ticket who had waited until their names were printed on the organization's list on the ballot before they had changed and come out for Kline. Ah, yes, his job was all grief during an election fight.

About four o'clock, tired and weary, he got around to the Doyles. The Doyles were nice people, and he was glad he had met them. He knew that Mr. Doyle must have once been a well-to-do man. He acted and talked like a gentleman. Now he was having hard times and the breaks had gone against him. And the boy, he was all right, too, a fine chap. They were poor because of hard times, and too proud to go on relief. He was going to try and see what he could do for them by way of getting a job for Doyle if he could manage it. The Doyles were the kind of people you called the worthy poor.

He walked in on them in their one-room furnished apartment over a store. The apartment gave the sense of overcrowding, and the furniture was old and scratched. It seemed almost to breathe out a feeling of its own unliveableness. O'Malley smiled and handed a box of candy to Mrs. Doyle, a fat, beefy-armed, bovine woman. He pulled out cigars for Doyle, a tall, thin, graying man whose blue trousers were frayed at the pocket and their narrow, worn cuffs were out of style. He also handed two cigars to the son.

"Well, Mildred, here's the best precinct captain in Chicago," Doyle said as Mrs. Doyle was dusting off the best chair for O'Malley.

"No, just the most worn out," O'Malley said.

"You poor man, you must be so tired. Here, let me make you a cup of coffee," Mrs. Doyle said.

"Please don't, Mrs. Doyle. I only got a minute. There's still a long list of people I got to see," he said.

"You work so hard. It'll be a shame if everybody doesn't turn out and vote for you," she said.

"You don't think they will?" he asked, his brows beetling in worry.

"Certainly they will," Doyle quickly said.

"Don't be giving me heart failure, Mrs. Doyle. After all, a man of my advanced age can't take too much," O'Malley said, smiling grimly.

"It looks good, huh, O'Malley?" said the twenty-five-year-old son, a rather emaciated, characterless young chap with badly decayed teeth.

"I think I got it pretty much set. Now, how have you folks got the people managed in this building?"

"Skipper, you needn't worry about this building. Say, it's in your vest pocket," Doyle said.

"That's the way I like to hear you talk," O'Malley said, smiling and lighting a cigar while Doyle and his son puffed on theirs.

"Mr. O'Malley, are you sure you wouldn't take a cup of coffee? It'll only take a minute to make it for you," Mrs. Doyle said maternally.

"No, thanks. Now, about this fellow across the hall, the Polack?"

"I'm getting up at six in the morning to see him. He's hard to catch," Mrs. Doyle said.

"Be sure and do it. We got to get every vote we can. We got a fight on our hands this time."

"You'll win. Everybody else in the building is going to vote for Anderson. And you know, Mr. O'Malley, there was somebody around putting folders for Kline in the mailboxes."

"There was?" he exclaimed, glancing angrily at Mrs. Doyle. "Say, I'll bet he was one of these birds with a fishhook for a nose."

"But wait until you hear the rest of the story. I spoke to him. He asked me who I was for. I said, why I was for Kline. But now wait a minute until I tell you all of the story, Mr. O'Malley. I said that I was for Kline and so was everybody else in the building. I said that I had talked to them for Kline, so he put his folders in the mailboxes, and I asked him for more. He gave me some. I said, 'Oh, Mister, give me a lot more. I want to give these to all of my friends in the neighborhood.' So I got a great big pile of Kline literature. And right after I saw that he was gone, I took the stuff out of the boxes and threw the whole shebang into the garbage can," Mrs. Doyle said.

"Good for you! Good for you, Mrs. Doyle! If all people were like you folks here, I'll tell you, my job would be a good deal easier than it is and I wouldn't be getting early gray hairs from worry."

"Say, what the hell, Skipper! Don't have such a low opinion of yourself. You're the best precinct captain in Chicago," Doyle said ingratiatingly.

"I only wish I was," O'Malley said with almost histrionic dejection.

"Why, of course you are, Mr. O'Malley," Mrs. Doyle said.

"Sure, but let me tell you something. Roosevelt's the best precinct captain we got."

"My, but isn't he a wonderful man!" Mrs. Doyle exclaimed.

"He's a real bird, all right, fine man. He's done a lot for the people and the country," Doyle said.

"Best president we had since Woodrow Wilson," young Doyle said.

"You're damn tootin', he is! Damn tootin'! And he's the best precinct captain we got. But I ain't worried none about putting him over in my precinct in the fall. What I'm worried about is the primary election this Tuesday. Now, are you sure you got everybody in the building all set?"

"Oh, yes, of course. There isn't one Kline person in the whole building," Mrs. Doyle said.

"Here's the way I handle them. I say that, of course, now, Kline is a fine man. He's governor. A fine man. Sure. But so is Anderson. Anderson is a fine man, and he is the one we got to put over. Kline has that Oriental strain in him that's in his blood. He's not one of us, and he doesn't understand our problems."

"Say, Mr. Doyle, you ought to have my job. You're a smart man. That's the ticket, and I'm going to use that line myself. Say, I wish everybody in my precinct was like you. And you got mostly Irish in this building, haven't you?"

"Yes, Irish and Catholic."

"Of course, there is the Polish man across the way, and Mrs. Hirsch. I don't like her. She's too dirty, and, say, she would talk a leg off you. Now the other day—"

"Who's she for?" O'Malley interrupted.

"Why, Anderson, of course."

"Well, tell her to stay that way. And don't forget to nail the Polack," O'Malley said.

"Of course, I will," Mrs. Doyle said.

"You know, folks, I can't understand an Irishman who would vote for Kline after what he done to us. It was us who put him in, and then he is a turncoat. Why, four years ago I went around and told everybody to vote for him. Why, I got out a bigger vote for Kline in this precinct than I ever got out for anybody except Roosevelt. The Irish didn't go against him because he's a Jew. And what does he do? He turns on us," O'Malley said, his words and tone giving expression to a puzzled, wounded feeling.

"He gave us the can, didn't he? But he ain't got a chance, has he?" the son said.

"Not a chance of a snowball in hell if all the others around the city get out the vote the way I'll do it. Now, take that big apartment building down the street here in the next block. There must be a hundred voters in that buildin'. Well, I got every Democratic vote in the joint," O'Malley proudly said.

"Good for you," Mrs. Doyle said.

"The woman who works in the renting office there, I spoke to her and lined her up. So when some dame comes around for Kline, why, this woman, she says to the Kline dame, she says that the tenants in the buildin' have just gotten sick and tired of everybody and his brother comin' around about votin' and puttin' cards in the boxes. She says to the Kline dame that she can't let anybody else go around botherin' and annoyin' her tenants, because if she does, a lot of them will move out on her. So this Kline dame, she is dumb. You know, she ain't never been in politics and thinks she can come in and lick somebody like myself who has been in the political game all my life. She's dumb, see! She asks the woman, are her tenants for Kline. The woman says of course they are, sure, because everybody is. She takes the Kline literature from this dumb dame and throws it all in the ash-can, just the same as you did, Mrs. Doyle."

"That was clever," Doyle said.

"You ought to meet that woman. She's a fine woman," said O'Malley.

"Well, she helped. And on this game, every little bit helps," the son said profoundly.

"You're a smart young fellow. Every little bit, every vote does count. Every one. And to think of how many votes I swung to Kline four years ago. For him to go and turn his back on the organization and the people that made him, bitin' the hand that fed him. Well, don't worry! I'm cookin' the goose for him in my precinct. We don't waste our time with traitors to us when we're the fellows that made them somebody," O'Malley said vindictively.

"Mr. O'Malley, I'm just so certain that Anderson will get the nomination," Mrs. Doyle said.

"So am I. But we can't take any chances. Every vote counts. Now, are you sure you got every voter in this here buildin'?"

"It's in the bag," the son said.

"Yes, we guarantee it," Doyle said.

"All of the people have promised me already, except that man across the hall, the Polish one. I'm getting up in the morning to make sure of him," Mrs. Doyle said.

"That's the way I like to hear you talk. And if we win, I won't forget how helpful you've been to me," O'Malley said.

"We're doing everything we can," Mrs. Doyle said.

"That's the ticket," O'Malley said.

"And, Mr. O'Malley, what about election day?" Doyle nervously asked.

"Here, I brought these sample ballots," O'Malley said, arising and pulling out long pink-sheeted ballots, one of which he spread out upon the narrow dining-room table. "Now, I got this all marked up just right." The family gathered around him. He became official, and almost coldly professional. His tone of voice changed. "You can all study this after I go, and I'm gonna leave some of these here for you to show to the people in the buildin' and to get them to study it. Now watch me carefully. See, you start here with Anderson's name at the top of the ticket. Now you go straight down until you get to Hogan for sheriff. You skip him. Any man that would turn on his friends the way Hogan did, he doesn't deserve a vote. Coming out yesterday and sayin' he was for Kline like he did on us. Be sure to skip Hogan, and tell your friends in the buildin' here to. And then you go straight down the list, Kaczmarski, Moran, Cogan, Connell, and then, here, you skip Schulman for county clerk. See, I got it here, and there's no X after Schulman's name. He is another one who turned his coat and betrayed his friends and the organization. And now here, don't forget, Connolly. See, right here! Tell all your people, absolutely, to mark an X after Connolly's name. See it, for ward committeeman. When you mention Connolly, you say: 'Your ward committeeman.' You see, what good is it going to do us if we get in the top of the ticket but don't get our own man, our own friend and neighbor, in for ward committeeman? So, don't forget it. Above all else, we got to get Connolly in," O'Malley said.

"Of course," Mrs. Doyle said with assurance.

"Now it should all be clear. See how they are marked with an X, and then, I got rings around the names of those you skip, like Hogan. You won't forget this and go votin' for the men I got ringed, will you?"

"Holy Moses, no!" Doyle said.

"You can study this sample ballot carefully after I go. And you know, you can take these into the booths with you when you vote, in order to see how to vote. We just got the rulin' on that, and it's O.K. to take sample ballots into the booth."

"We'll study it, Skipper, and show the neighbors what to do," Doyle said.

"If you're sure you can do that, you'll save me a lot of valuable time," said O'Malley.

"Of course we can. And we're glad to do it. You poor man, you must be so tired," said Mrs. Doyle.

"Well, I've been doing this for twenty years. I'm used to it, but, golly, a man does get tired toward the end of a hot primary fight," O'Malley said.

"And what about election day, Mr. O'Malley?" Mrs. Doyle asked.

"I've just been demonstratin' it to you, and I thought you all said you got the dope straight?" O'Malley asked, his expression changing.

"Yes, we understand that. But what I meant is, what time should we come to vote and, you know, Mr. O'Malley, you said something about your wanting us working around the polls, because you said we were so helpful to you," Mrs. Doyle tactfully said.

"Sure, you come around at six, and I'll get you fixed up."

"We'll be there," said Doyle.

"Then, if we win, as I fully expect to, well, as I just said, I don't forget them that sticks with me. If I did, I wouldn't be worthy of the name of O'Malley."

"Oh, we know it. And Mr. O'Malley, you look so tired, haven't you the time for a cup of coffee?" said Mrs. Doyle.

"Gee, no, I spent more time talkin' than I meant to. I'm so busy. I got to get these cards distributed," he said, taking out a stack of Connolly cards and giving some to Mrs. Doyle.

"You better leave a little more than that. I can distribute them," Mrs. Doyle said.

"Ah, that's the way to hear you talk," O'Malley said, handing her additional cards.

Leaving more cigars, he went out, followed by profuse farewells from all of the Doyles.

II

"He's such a nice man," said Mrs. Doyle.

"He's a sketch," the son said.

"We don't care what he is, as long as he gets us a job," said Doyle.

"I wonder? Maybe it would have been better for us if we had gone for Anderson, but let Arty here be a Kline man. Then we might have gotten somewhere either way," Mrs. Doyle said.

"Catch me voting for a Jew," the son said.

"Listen, Arty, we don't care what in the name of Jesus Christ he is, if he gives us a job. God, we want to get a job for one of us, or we can't go on! We can't be such choosers," said Doyle.

"Here, he brought this candy, and it's filling. If you watch it, Papa, so the sweets don't get in your teeth, and you do the same, Arty, it's filling," said Mrs. Doyle.

"I can't eat chocolates, not with these molars I got," the son said, as his father took a chocolate and chewed it carefully.

"I'm glad that he didn't take the coffee. We hardly have any canned milk left," Mrs. Doyle said.

"Yes, we'll vote for Kline, Anderson, or the Devil himself for a job," Doyle said.

"That's why I talked like I did, about the people here. You know, some of them won't talk to me if I say Anderson. They're Republicans. But we might as well let him think that we're doing everything in our power," Mrs. Doyle said, eating a chocolate.

"Yes, and we'll give him our votes. Golly, I hope that we put Anderson over," Doyle said, grabbing a caramel.

"We got to! If we don't, we won't be anywheres," said Mrs. Doyle while the son enviously watched his parents eating the candy, his tongue playing around in his decayed teeth.

"Damn it, I meant to pray for Anderson's success this morning at Mass, and I forgot to," Doyle said.

"You would! You're just like an absent-minded professor," said Mrs. Doyle.

"Couldn't help it. I meant to. And I can still pray until Tuesday," said Doyle.

"Well, I think that the Lord will provide for us by electing Anderson so you can get a job," Mrs. Doyle said, dividing the last two pieces of candy with her husband.

"And after election, Tuesday, we can get a swell meal. We'll have five dollars each. And, Ma, I think that we can spare ourselves a movie. Shirley Temple will be at the show that night," Doyle said.

"But, Pa, we'll have to watch that money. You know, the agent told us last month that he was giving us our last chance. If we get evicted, we got to have a little something, or where will we sleep?" said Mrs. Doyle.

"Goddamn it, Anderson has got to get in," said Doyle, pacing the floor nervously.

1936.

The Professor

I

THE Professor slanted his reddish, bull-dog face and frowned. He rubbed back a few strands of graying hair from his thick forehead. He slammed his pudgy fist against the desk and glowered.

"This morning I am going to be a tough guy like O'Neill," he announced brusquely.

The class laughed, and heads turned to simper at unkempt O'Neill, who occupied a rear seat.

"Ordinarily, I am a peaceable citizen, but this morning I cannot hold myself responsible for any belligerent activities which I may commence with the male students of this class in Advanced Composition. It is to be understood, however, that regardless of my disposition, I am too gentlemanly and chivalrous to strike any of the ladies. . . . Um. . . . Now that I have given fair warning, and in case any of the young men present are trembling lest I descend upon them like the wrath of Carlyle, they may leave the room. . . . I see that no one is leaving. . . . Well, you remain at your own risk, because after everything is said and done, a man over fifty cannot be held morally accountable for his deeds on a morning when the prunes he has eaten have not agreed with his stomach."

The Professor fumbled through the manuscripts before him while the class appreciated his humor. When it quieted down, he read a thriller by Harry Cogan, the neat, goggled, never-smiling young man who sat in the first row. After the reading, he blessed the story with banalities and opened class discussion. Two commonplace girls paraphrased his banalities, and Mr. Cogan agitated upon the precipice of a modest smile. The Professor asked Mr. Scroggins for his opinion.

"Well, Mr. Saxon . . . ah. . . . Now, on the whole . . . I think that the story is pretty good, and that it had many passages that are truly professional. . . . But I think . . . I think that Mr. Cogan has been careless in spots, using some very bad clichés such as . . . 'The steel dagger gleamed above green eyes in the hushed and lightless room.' That's bad."

The Professor nodded agreement, but added that such slips could perhaps be partially forgiven in one who could write sentences like "The night crushed speechlessly about them."

Frail Miss Durham timidly objected to the story because of the author's lack of sympathy with his character, Bastian McGraw. After hemming and hawing, the Professor countered that the character of Bastian McGraw was so weak and so vicious that a writer could scarcely be decently sympathetic toward him. The class then went dead, and Mr. Cogan took occasion to ask would it be all right if, after he had rewritten the story, he tried it on *The Saturday Evening Post*. The Professor answered that it wouldn't do any harm.

"Mr. Saxon, do you really approve of that story?" lean, ascetic, Adam's-appled Abe Ginsberg asked.

"Well, Abe, that depends upon what you mean by approve."

"I want to know if you approve of it?" Abe repeated excitedly.

"Um. . . . Considering that the author is a beginner, yes, I do. I believe that it shows promise. To the contrary, I don't approve of it in the sense that I would approve of a story by Poe, Kipling, O. Henry, Bret Harte, or Chekhov. Mr. Cogan is only starting out."

"You approve, then?"

"As I explained."

Abe smirked in arrogant derision, and the Professor asked O'Neill's opinion.

"I agree with Abe that it's lousy," said O'Neill, some of the girls tittering at his bluntness.

"But Abe didn't say precisely that."

"I do now!" Abe said, provoking added tittering.

An argument concerning the plot short story quickly developed. Abe, morally indignant, and O'Neill, youthfully cynical, attacked the Professor.

"Of course, you two are free to stick to your own views," the Professor began when the discussion had stumbled into an impasse. "Although, I should like to assure you that they will never get you anywhere. If a story hasn't plot and pattern, what can it contain? What can be its meaning? What can it offer as a bid to reader-interest?"

"It can have life, the Misery, the Rawness, the Squalor, the Tragedy, the Beauty, the Glory of Life!" Abe said loudly and in the manner of a zealous prophet.

"But, Abe, plot does not exclude that. For instance, have you ever read the stories of Wilbur Daniel Steele?"

"He's one guy I can't stomach," O'Neill interrupted.

"Well, may God have mercy on Mr. O'Neill's soul," the Professor remarked.

"I loathe Wilbur Daniel Steele's work, and I scorn all trick writing," Abe declared.

Losing some of its log-like lethargy, the class laughed. Abe denounced his fellow students, along with O. Henry. Mr. Scroggins asked the Professor to summarize and repeat his views on the technique of the short story. The Professor replied, giving a good paraphrase of any number of textbooks and commonly accepted views on the subject. O'Neill waved a book in the air, opening it on a page where a diagram was printed.

"That sounds just like this book. I picked it up because I thought it was a textbook on bridge-building. But I discover that all these diagrams are to tell you how to write a short story," O'Neill said.

"That's not funny," Scroggins said.

"No, it's a scandal," O'Neill said.

"It's sad!" Abe said, jerking nervously to his feet.

The Professor was secretly thrilled by Abe, his brilliant baby of a student, and he thought, too, that when he could stimulate Abe to such enthusiasms he wasn't doing his job of teaching so badly. The spirit was there, and Abe was possibly a genius, even if his ideas were wrong. In his own undergraduate days, the Professor had been similarly wrong, but ah, the lost zest and spirit and enthusiasm of those days, their hopes. Ah, the pathos of distance!

Continuing to argue with his two prize students, he suddenly seemed to hear himself talking as if he were two persons, one repeating the formulas of twenty-seven years, the other an uncomplimentary and dissatisfied listener. He winced inwardly, and halted the discussion by asking Miss Slocomb to read her story, *The Justifying Moment*. The story described a witty and sophisticated young author and a beautiful and charming girl who drove through moonlit woods, wittily and incisively discussing Life, Beauty, and their own souls. Suddenly the author revealed that he was disgusted with his level and boresome existence, and determined that he would experience one moment of high, abandoned, and romantic living, even though it caused his death. With unrestrained jubilation he drove the automobile into a tree and, arising from the wreckage, he declaimed to the high heavens that now all his life was worth while, because he had had his one grand and justifying moment.

Only half-listening, the Professor dwelt upon his own past, recalling ghosted memories that were cloaked with a consoling melancholy. Ah, those undergraduate days when he had thrilled with the ambition to become a great writer! And those fevered nights when he had written, written, written! And Muriel Smith, the girl whom he had thought he loved. She walked slowly into his mind, her each light step pressing the heaviness of loss upon him. He held her before him, a pale memory-image dripping bitter nostalgia, and he thought of her chestnut hair, her blue eyes, the lips that he had kissed farewell on many a zero winter evening when the moon was a frozen chip of snow in the sky and he was setting out for that long return journey back south to the campus dormitory. Ah, Muriel, and the manner she had had of resting her dimpled chin in a white palm. And those six months of anxiety after he had determined to propose, and he had slaved to write out his proposal in Shakespearean blank verse. And that night when he had read it so well, and the cruelly gentle feminine kindness in her rejection. Ah!

God, that girl's story! Ye gods and little fishes! A pity for her to think that she could write, almost a maniacal delusion! But it would be too cruel to hurt the poor thing's feelings by telling her so. And still, what in the name of all the gods there be could he say to her about it? What? Great Caesar's Ghost!

Sometimes he played bridge with Muriel and her husband, an advertising man, and all that was now merely a prank out of the irrevocable past, just as it should be. Neither of them regretted that she had rejected him. No, his regrets were merely the pathos of distance, regrets for a lost state of his own feelings.

That girl's story! Atrocious!

Miss Slocomb's watery eyes begged for praise. In veiled words he cautioned her about the use of scenes that might impress the reader as being exaggerated, because if a young writer was not careful, he or she was liable to break a leg in the pitfall of melodrama. He opened class discussion and permitted his students to wander on. He thought of Muriel, her of the dreams of his young manhood, of some of the best thoughts and emotions of his whole life. Lost to him! Ah! The loss was that of the emotions, and similarly he had lost that first emotional state for his wife whom he had loved, too, as a young man loves. He had slept in the same bed with her for twenty-five years, and she had borne him three daughters, and he had looked across the breakfast table into her bony face for an eternity of mornings. They had an indifferent affection toward each other, a casualized sympathy. Out of each other's sight, they did not think much of one another. They accepted each other. That was perhaps as it should be, and yet, ah, the pathos of distance. She had been a good wife, and Muriel could have been no better. But his wife had been at best only half sympathetic to all the things he had cherished the most. Now, old age was creeping upon both of them. He thought of *Modern Love,* Meredith's incomparable poem. Ah, how well it described emotions which many a couple must have!

"Don't you think, Mr. Saxon, that there are too many figures of speech in that story? Ones like . . . 'The moon was a newly minted dime cemented in the cloud-tiled floor of the sky' . . . now that, of course, is good. But just the same, the total effect is bad because there is so much imagery, particularly in the climax where swift action is called for," Mr. Brennan said.

"Quite so, George, good criticism," the Professor said.

Through his mind ran the lines:

> *At dinner she is hostess, I am host.*
> *Went the feat ever cheerfuller? She keeps*
> *The Topic over intellectual deeps*
> *In buoyancy afloat. They see no ghost.*
> *With sparkling surface-eyes we ply the ball:*
> *It is in truth a most contagious game.*
> HIDING THE SKELETON, *shall be its name.*

"I tried to infuse feeling and poetry in my story, the tones of woods and sky, and that was why I used so many images," Miss Slocomb said.

"The intention, of course, is laudable, but the trick is to get them in without putting bumps and obstacles upon the hill of rising action," the Professor countered.

He seemed to be listening calmly to his students. But feelings cracked and burst inside of him, falling into a weltering chaos. He knit his smashed feelings together with more lines from Meredith:

> *Thus piteously Love closed what he begat:*
> *The union of this ever-diverse pair!*
> *These two were rapid falcons in a snare.*
> *Condemned to do the flitting of the bat.*

Yes, he and his wife, and many other men and their wives, too, were all not so rapid falcons in a snare, condemned to do the flitting of the bat. And soon, relatively soon, would come . . .

"That's a bully suggestion, Miss Durham, and I think that Miss Slocomb should adopt it."

"I will, Mr. Saxon. I like criticism like that, because it tells me where I fail, and it is constructive," Miss Slocomb said.

Soon . . . last night he had again foundered over those headings in the biography of British authors . . . Soon . . .

"And now, Miss Durham, will you please read that sketch of yours, *Pinkish Dust?*" he asked.

Miss Durham coughed with embarrassment, arose, read from the poetry of Rupert Brooke to explain her title, and slowly went through her sketch.

Soon! Last night, those prophetic headings! . . . Oliver Goldsmith (1728–1774), William Cowper (1731–1800), William Blake (1757–1827), Newman (1801–1890), Robert Browning (1812–1889), Ruskin (1819–1900), Robert Louis Stevenson (1850–1894), Thomas Carlyle

(1795–1881), Matthew Arnold (1822–1888) . . . all his dead giants and poets.

And once in the springtime of another century, the young undergraduate, Paul Saxon, a boy from a small town in Indiana, had stood under an oak tree in Washington Park brooding upon life, chanting hopeful lines from Robert Browning. And then, young Saxon had not been so afraid. He had shaken his fist in the face of life, daring death. Then he had anticipated the grave as the last dark and adventurous tower to which he could come, like Childe Roland. Young Saxon had been brave in the springtime of another century.

The bell sounded, ending the class hour.

II

The chimes stridently tolled *Nearer My God to Thee* as the Professor and Abe walked across the campus. Abe glanced at the sun-polished ivied towers, the well-groomed lawns and blooming lilac trees. He remarked that it made him think of the middle ages. The Professor, noticing the lilac trees, thought how they seemed like shy and blooming virgins, opening their arms to their lover, the sun. And he suddenly reflected on how he had grown old teaching at this institution. He loved it. And some day he would have to leave it.

"Abe, you didn't understand me today. I don't think that a fellow like Cogan can write, or that he ever will. But he's a nice boy, sincere, and well-meaning, and I just can't hurt his feelings by being the one to tell him that he might as well give up the idea of writing now when he's young. I just can't be that cruel and tell him."

Abe was absorbed in his own thoughts. They passed through the campus men's club, one of the buildings in the northeast quadrangle. A poster announcing the Professor's play, *Sorry Old Fellow*, which was to be produced by the campus student dramatic association, stood in the corridor. The Professor hoped that Abe would comment on it, but the student was silent. Perhaps he even guessed that fear of rejection had prevented the Professor from submitting it to commercial producers.

They walked along a sunny street, and the Professor spoke of his own undergraduate days when he had known the grand infliction of the divine afflatus. He had piled work upon his instructors in every composition course, and after graduation he had been determined to become a writer. But first he had married and gotten a job in order to establish himself in emotional and economic security. He had written several novels that had been fair successes commercially, and he had contributed to *Lippincott's* and the other magazines of the day. One of his stories had even been reprinted in several anthologies. But after having completed the manuscript of still another novel, he'd destroyed it. Stealing a glance at Abe, he sensed that his student might be pitying him, and changed the subject, speaking in that witty, slangy manner that had given him local fame.

Smoking a cigarette, he rode downtown on an Illinois Central Suburban train. His attention wandered from the morning newspaper to his great Victorians. Sighing, he reflected how the scientific work of Darwin had crashed into the Victorian world like a comet, smashing all values and certainties. All its poets and writers had awakened in a universe that was crumbling. Persistent and terrifying questions had stared them in the face. Is there a God? Is there an after-life? Or is the universe blind matter and a brute survival of the fittest? Do we ascend from lower species, or do we come trailing clouds of glory from God Who is our home? Like grave-worms these questions had, he thought, crawled through the pages of Victorian writings, making it, for him, the saddest period in all English literary history. And he had been nursed in that world. Its values were his values. He was too old now to be casually agnostic like so many of his students. Too old! He was sadder than his poets. His Carlyle, mighty mind, knifed by Doubt. Newman, always with a skeleton in his closet. Poor Walt Pater, wearily obsessed with anticipations of Death, stretching the tired arms of his emotions toward Rome when the brain could not follow. Great Browning whistling to keep up his courage. And grand and wistful Robert Louis, also whistling. Tennyson, pitting his genius against unanswerable eternal problems in *In Memoriam*. Matthew Arnold hearing in his inmost ear only the melancholy, long, withdrawing roar of the River of Faith. Ah . . . for the world which seems

> *To lie before us like a land of dreams,*
> *So various, so beautiful, so new,*
> *Hath really neither joy, nor love, nor light,*
> *Nor certitude, nor peace, nor help for pain;*
> *And we are here as on a darkling plain*
> *Where ignorant armies clash by night.*

Doubt, doubt had been the cancer of their spirits, as it was of his. Would it always be so? Would men never know? Always life going on, and man never knowing? Always! Never?

The train ran parallel to the lake that was plated with sunshine, its waters churning, the white caps and waves slashing against the beach. Ah, how fresh and young the lake! How lightly it bore the weight of the many centuries that had walked over its back! If man could only bear the weight of the eternal years thus! Alas! And Matthew Arnold's sleepless ministers of Nature were out there

Their glorious tasks in silence perfecting.

Ah, sad, how all men came questing to the shingles where the waters halt, questing, asking, begging an answer. They stood at the seashore before the mystery of life. And the waves roared and broke, speaking no word of certitude or consolation. And. . .

Paul Saxon (1876–19??) . . . Percy Bysshe Shelley (1792–1822) . . . . Paul Saxon (1876–????).

Yes, Paul Saxon, sorry old fellow. . . . One day he would be alone in a six-foot coffin, under the ground for the worms and the rats of Graceland Cemetery. His farewell from life and man and his poets would be shovelfuls of dirt rattled on his coffin, first one shovelful rattling, then others plumping in heavy succession. The seasons would roll on, and springs would come, and the suns of many, many Maytimes would shatter over his mounded grave. But it would be calm and peaceful down there, no, no, no, it would be lonely. Tonight he would have dinner with Louise, his oldest daughter, and he would see one of his little granddaughters. There would be an excellent meal, and afterward a lively round of bridge. Louise was no longer named Saxon. He was the last Saxon, the last of his line, and when the gravediggers would have heaped fresh dirt upon his coffin the sun of Saxon would have set. And it was going to be lonely there, under the ground, away from the sunlight, with only the worms and the rats.

Foolish to worry like that. . . . Foolish defeatism! Unnecessary morbidity! He was still hale and hearty, his teeth were healthy, his limbs flexible. Many of life's goods were still in store for him. And he had the right attitude toward life. The idea was to keep busy and active, not to contemplate black thoughts. He did that. He had his teaching, his newspaper work, his social life, golf, bridge, his interest in college athletics, brilliant students like Abe to nurture, first nights at the theater with people pointing him out and saying there goes Paul Saxon, literary banquets where he met interesting people, plenty of excellent meals, books to read, conversations. Conversation itself was an art, and he had mastered it. Many considered him one of the best conversationalists about town. Ah, no need for pessimism. All these things got him through his days tolerably well. . . . But at night, those few minutes when he lay awake, unable to take his eyes off those headings. Ten or fifteen minutes before sleep . . .

George Meredith (1828–1909) . . . Paul Saxon (1876–19??).

III

In his private office at *The Chicago Questioner* the Professor wrote the daily piece for his column, *Contrasts*. It was a review of a book by Gladys Fairchild Kennilworth, a member of the Gold-Coast society set which the Professor had never quite completely attained. He contrasted her volume with *An American Tragedy*. Unlike Dreiser, this local author was sincere. She did not write a somber portrait, false to life because it represented people as will-less automata, like rats in a maze. Rather than being so unbalanced, Gladys Fairchild Kennilworth presented human beings as free, exercising that independence of will which was the bounty of their Creator. And her writing was sheer beauty. In each of her gemlike tales the meaning had transcended the local and the immediate, swooping up, like a glorious bird on the wing, into the empyrean realm of the universal, and thereby becoming fine art.

Reading his piece over, he decided that it was good, and that the author would appreciate it, too. And he breathed easily because Andrew Aiken Fletcher, owner of *The Questioner,* was a very erratic man. Employees on any of his papers throughout the country never knew when he would take a dislike to something one of them wrote. The Professor felt that at all events his job was safe for one more day, because there was nothing in this column that was likely to displease the erratic Mr. Fletcher.

Lighting a cigarette, he looked at his fan mail, letters containing challenges to fights and games of golf, notes assuring him that he did not know the simple ABC of bridge, corrections of his grammar, appreciations of his common sense, decency, and capacity for leadership, suggestions for future columns, praise from former University students for a recently written eulogy of Coach Harry Haggin Jackson, the grand old man of the gridiron, requests for autographs written in feminine handwriting. Out of the batch he suddenly found a letter from one of his former prize students, a boy whom he liked, and in whom he had placed great faith. It concluded:

Both you and Harry Haggin Jackson are getting more pathological every day. Look out or the freshmen and the sophomores will get wise to you.

He maintained his equilibrium with an effort. He sat motionless. He grew angry. But then he decided that the letter was mean, petty, unfair, warped. He lamented that youth was so hard, and cold, and unsympathetic, and brutal. Youth, ah, youth! Because these cruel strains were in the very grain of youth, it lacked understanding and rarely accomplished anything genuinely human. He decided that this was a good idea for a column one of these days.

He went to the window and nervously glanced down at the diminished specks of human beings on the sidewalk. He termed it the urban ant heap, and decided that it, too, would serve as a column he might write.

He returned to his desk and stared at the wall calendar. Another day for him who was the last of his line, whose name was writ on less than waters, writ on the pages of a yellow journal that was drowned each noon hour, whose name was writ not on waters, but on oblivion, and whose sun was setting in the west of life. Ah, me!

Ah, many a time and oft in these last years he had fumed, to revolt and abandon everything. He thought of Browning's poem on the lost leader. Had he, too, sacrificed everything for a few handfuls of silver to make life comfortable? Suppose he should write a novel laying naked his soul, a human document to drip tears through the ages as the record of one defeated man? But he lacked the ability and the courage to destroy and burn all his bridges, and to speak out in hard truths. A man of fifty doesn't usually revolt. That was just the theme of *Sorry Old Fellow*, and it was a good play, too. He had to play the game. Hadn't he written recently that playing the game was the ethical basis of sports and also of life? His words turned and came back on him like retched-up food.

To be, or not to be; that is the question.
Whether 'tis nobler . . .

Hamlet Saxon smoked another cigarette. His face seemed to have become suddenly old and worried and mean. It carried an expression of smallness, cheapness and spite that was rarely noticeable. Aging Hamlet Saxon sat in the newspaper office, smoking a cigarette.

Too late now! No one would see Paul Saxon, last of his line, taking the dusty road at daybreak, walking to the far horizon with only the city of God at the other end of the road. That was merely poetry. He sat at his desk, thinking that he had often been called *The Happy Warrior*. He sat. The Happy Warrior sat, his cigarette ashes dropping over his littered desk.

Kelly Malloy, city editor, waddled in, interrupting the Professor's thoughts. Younger than the Professor, Kelly looked more shopworn. He had several unnecessary chins and his stomach bubbled out ridiculously. His eyes were the blue eyes of a mischievous boy corpsed in lazy fat. His manner was familiar, much to the Professor's discomfort.

"Professor, I'd like to talk to you. Say, do you know you're the only professor I ever met who talked and acted like a human being?" Kelly said, a remark he had been making ever since Mr. Saxon had been on the paper.

Kelly spoke of a perplexing problem in bridge which bothered him. The Professor provided an analysis that was acceptable, because Kelly always accepted the Professor's analyses on such matters. Then Kelly spoke of the latest gang murder, but the Professor could not suffer him. He grabbed his hat, pleaded a luncheon engagement, and was gone.

For teaching two classes and doing his newspaper work the Professor received seventeen thousand dollars a year. His day's work was done, and he stepped out of *The Questioner* Building just as the one o'clock whistles blew. Joining the flow of pedestrians, he felt less spry than usual. He was troubled, and tried to forget himself by observing the passing people. He noticed bleary-eyed men and women moving furtively, many of them looking pinched, underfed, crass. An aging woman with powder in the sad creases of her face. Ah! Sometimes the city streets seemed to him like walking morgues. He informed himself that the people on the downtown streets were dabs of mud spun against his perceptions by the perpetually revolving and sometimes cruel wheel of life. He told himself that the passing people were an inundation of human beings whose faces were breaking waves of joy and sorrow. But in the souls of all these men and women there was the compensation of Faith. In the souls of all these people, Faith endowed them with dreams and hopes which they hugged tightly within the manger of their hearts. Ah, there was another crackerjack column he would soon write!

He tried to douse his mood by laughing at himself. He had always prided himself on having a real sense of humor. Now it would not work. He realized, as if finally, that he had come to a point in life where he could no longer be light and gay. He had to be serious, to squeeze sustenance and hope from every one of his little doings. He was a failure, and, yes, something of a clown. But he must be serious and feel that he was importantly contributing to the things that were human and valuable. Life was no longer a game, a race to be run, an experience to be exploited, a gilded rack upon which to hang figures of speech and poetry. It was something very, very precious, and he wanted to clutch that preciousness tightly within himself . . . forever. . . . And some day his grip would relax, weaken, stiffen, and the preciousness would drop like some beautiful choked thing. Dead!

Weep for Adonais!

1932–1937.

Children of the Times

I

"Just think, I had a hunch to pick that horse. Say, I could slap my can all the way around the block," Morton said.

"I wanted to tell you to play Broken Back," Anne said.

"Why didn't you? I might have done it then," he said.

"Honey, you were so set on Horse Feathers," she whined.

"You're just another second-guesser," he said, grimacing as he turned away from her.

"Honey!" she said, bewildered as she looked at his broad back.

He sat on the couch, a ruminative expression on his pocked face. She dropped down at his feet, gazed up at him, waiting for a change in his mood.

"All I needed to do to get two and a half smackers was to follow my hunch. I didn't, so I haven't got a sou in my jeans. Goddamn that horse I bet on!" he said.

"Don't take it so hard, Sugar," she said.

"A hell of a lot of good sympathy does. It doesn't put one red cent in my jeans," he said.

"Honey, that's how it is. Sometimes you have luck, and sometimes you don't," she said dully.

She picked a pile of newspapers from the floor of their small and disorderly parlor and placed them on the foot of the couch. There were three hand-me-down chairs in the seedy room, a scratched and battered radio, and the overstuffed couch on which he sat. In one corner there was a bookshelf piled with books she had forgotten to return to drugstore rental libraries. She sat down beside him, neither of them speaking for several minutes.

"Gee, I wish I had a million dollars," she said.

"You want nothing less than a nice little handout to tide you over, huh, kid?" he said, laughing ironically.

"So long as I'm wishing, I might as well wish for something," she said, smiling grimly.

"Now, take me! I'm not a chump or a sucker. I'm just the world's goddamnedest fool for not playing a hunch. If I only slipped my four bits on Broken Back. Two and a half bucks! Kid, sometimes that's a lot of dough. And it would have given us something for the races tomorrow. You know, I got a hunch that Eagle Eye is going to walk off with the purse in the fourth, and it'll pay big odds. I just shouldn't kick my toilet around the block. I should do it a second time as an encore performance," he said.

She kissed him on the forehead and tousled his curly hair. He brooded, unresponsive.

"Christ, you don't know how it hurts my pride to lose my last sou on a no-good horse," he complained.

"Me and you both, Sugar," she said.

He began pacing back and forth across the room.

"Sugar, don't be so nervous," she said.

"I got more on the ball than some people think," he said, ignoring what she had said. "And some day I'm gonna get mine. I don't say as I know just how I'm gonna do it, but I know that I'll be getting mine. I got something on the ball besides a measly old roundhouse outcurve," he said.

"I know you have!" she said with intense faith.

II

She tidied up the apartment while he took a nap. She looked at him lying on the bed, his shoes off, his mouth open, a sleepy expression making his pocked face obtuse. He snored. She kissed him, and covered him with a blanket. She kissed him again, lightly caressed his hair. She stood over him for a moment.

"My Sugar!"

She went into the small kitchen. There was not much food left because they had already eaten most of what they had gotten through their relief order. She dug up some cold ham and potatoes. She washed the potatoes and put them in a pot to boil. She washed a shrunken lettuce.

When he awoke a half hour later, supper was ready and the table was set. He came into the kitchen, sleepy-faced, his open shirt revealing a hairy chest. He yawned as he sat down, and remarked how he wished there were more to eat.

"Well, Sugar, it ain't my fault," she said apologetically.

"I know it. I was just wishing," he said.

"I'm glad we have this much left," she said.

"I'm always glad to get something, and I'm always twice as glad to get twice as much as I get," he said.

"Well, Sugar, the investigator should be around with our new relief ticket tomorrow, and we'll have a better supper tomorrow night. Only I hope she doesn't look at our radio again and wonder how much money you can get from a second-hand radio," she said, serving him, placing a larger portion on his plate than she was reserving for herself.

"If she does, tell her to go to hell. I'm tired of them. And I wish to Christ that those Goddamn Salvation Army workers, or university Phi Kappa Craps or whoever they are running this relief racket would let us get cigarettes on our tickets," he said.

"They rub your face in dirt every time you turn around. If they'd get me a job, I'd be much better pleased than I am taking their tickets," she said.

"Don't worry, kid, our luck will change. I'm going out to see a fellow about a job tonight," he said.

"But, honey, you didn't tell me," she said, suddenly disappointed.

"I'm telling you now, ain't I?" he said with a mouthful.

"Gosh, it's a fine time to be telling me," she said.

"You ain't got dough for a movie or to do anything, so what the hell difference does it make?" he said.

"But, gee, honey, it came as a surprise. It ain't that I don't want you to go out if you can get a job, but just that it came as a surprise. I get lonesome alone at night when we ain't got a cent or anything to do," she said.

"I got to go out. I might be able to land a job as a basketball coach for one of these suburban high schools. I forget which one it is, though," he said.

"Gee, Sugar, really?"

"I can't say for certain, but it looks pretty sure. I meant to tell you, but I got so damn sore about that horse that it slipped clean out of my noodle," he said.

"If you do, Hon, maybe we can buy a car," she said.

"And a lot of other things. That's what I'm thinking," he said.

She served coffee and two pieces of stale cake that she had gotten the day before from a girl friend she had visited.

"I think I'm going to get this job, and then we'll just be sitting pretty," he said.

"My Sugar!" she proudly exclaimed, going to him, kissing him, rubbing his head.

"Save it, kid!" he said, bored. "Let's get through with supper. I want to get my coffee drunk and listen on the radio to see if there are any new reports on that Bixby kidnaping before I go out."

She went back to her chair. They drank their coffee.

"It's a smart mob that arranged that snatch, smart, I say," he said.

"But it's so awful, kidnaping a baby like that. The poor father and mother! Why, if anybody kidnaped you, I don't know what I'd do," she said.

"If they kidnaped me?" he said, laughing. "What would they snatch me for? Relief tickets? Or maybe they'd want a couple of my torn shirts for ransom, and an old pair of my britches."

"I hate that word, *britches*. It's an awful word," she said.

"Ain't a spade a spade, and don't I wear britches, and ain't they old? Kid, get me straight! I don't believe in being highfalutin," he said.

"That's why I love you," she said.

He went to the parlor and turned on the radio while she washed the supper dishes. He heard jazz music, and then a news broadcast which stated that there were no new developments in the Bixby kidnaping. She came in, and asked if there was anything new on the kidnaping. He said no.

"Gee, I hope they get the baby back," she said.

"So do I. But all I'm saying is that the mob that pulled this snatch is smart. They'll get plenty for it, because Bixby can afford to loosen up his kick," Morton said.

He went to the bedroom, and soon reappeared wearing a clean shirt with a thready collar, and a gray sweat-shirt.

"Honey, you're not looking for a job like that?" she said.

"What's wrong?"

"Wear your coat."

"This is all right."

"No, it isn't. You wear your coat."

"If I wear this, I'll look athletic like a basketball or baseball coach ought to look," he said.

"Please wear your coat, Sugar."

"Say, who's gettin' this job? You or me?"

"You are, but you're not going out to coach tonight," she said.

"Do you know more about basketball, or don't you?" he asked.

"That hasn't anything to do with it," she said.

"If you don't know as much about basketball as I do, don't tell me how to get the job," he said curtly.

He left without kissing her goodbye. She cried. She turned on the radio until the music made her too blue. She turned it off and played solitaire. She kept hoping that her Sugar would come home soon, so that they could play a little rummy before they went to bed.

III

When he left the apartment, Morton walked down toward Sixty-seventh and Stony Island Avenue. He stopped at the first drugstore and bought a package of cigarettes with fifteen cents which Anne did not know he had. His tongue and mouth had been dry, and he had been jittery for a smoke. He felt better as soon as he had a cigarette in his mouth. He felt free, too, glad to be out of the house. Anne, now, sure he cared about her, and he wasn't taking any run-out powder on her. But he liked to get off by himself now and then. And he wanted to look up Bleary, the guy who had told him something about knowing a lad who had the dope on how he might try and get that job as a basketball coach. That job would be just up his alley. He inhaled, strolled on, imagined himself as a coach, and then maybe getting on as the baseball coach, too. He could see himself batting out grounders to the kids, bawling them out, giving them the real lowdown on the game. He wished that he was a guy with enough stuff for the big leagues. If he was a little younger, and able to get at it every day, he might make the grade. If he had followed it closely when he was a kid! But now, at twenty-nine, hell, that was another of his lost opportunities.

He paused to look at a Ford Model V in a show window, and he became all eyes of yearning and admiration. It was a honey with its new streamlines, the curves, the curving doors, the shiny blue plating over the engine, the low radiator cap. He would want nothing better than just such a buggy. He lit another cigarette and walked on, thinking of the automobile. He joined a group of fellows in front of a drugstore on the corner of Sixty-seventh and Stony Island and asked if anyone had seen Bleary.

"Not for three days," a tall, skinny lad said.

"I wanted to see him," Morton said.

They did not seem particularly friendly. Some of them were strangers. Others he knew by name, and had spoken to them several times. He knew Bleary best, but he didn't know him too well. They talked about horse races and automobiles, and Mort described the Ford he had just seen. A fellow named Sweeney joined them.

"Say, Sweeney, seen Bleary?" Morton asked.

"I seen him this afternoon," Sweeney said.

"Did he say anything about drifting around here tonight?" asked Morton.

"Didn't mention it, one way or another," Sweeney said.

"I wanted to see him. He gave me a tip on a lad who could tell me about landing a job as a basketball coach. He said he'd see me around the corner here and wise me up some more on the proposition," said Morton.

"I don't know nothing about that. I seen him downtown today," Sweeney said.

"Any luck?" a fellow named Hoyle asked Sweeney.

"Nope, no soap," Sweeney said, making a deprecatory gesture with his palms spread outward.

"Things are tough in this man's town," the tall, skinny lad said.

"If any of you lads hear of a place where they ain't tough, don't keep it a secret," Morton said.

"I been looking for a job for two years," Sweeney said.

"I tried to nose in on this C.W.A. racket, but I didn't get to first base," Hoyle said.

"My brother-in-law got one of them jobs. He's an engineer, and they told him to go downtown on Michigan Boulevard and then count the automobiles passing by. He did it like a dumb cluck for a couple of days. And then he asks himself why anybody, even the government, would want him to count automobiles. So he takes in a show every afternoon and guesses the number," a fat lad named O'Malley said.

"He's in clover. How did he get it?" asked Morton.

"He knows Barney McCormack, the politician," O'Malley said.

"Anything new in the papers about the Bixby snatch?" asked Hoyle.

"No, not according to the radio. But say, don't you lads think that the mob pulling off the snatch was damn smart?" Morton asked.

"Every one of 'em ought to be strung up by the balls," Hoyle said.

"I don't question that. All I say is that they're smart," Morton said.

"I don't like that kind of smartness," Hoyle said.

"Neither do I. But you got to admit they're smart," Morton said.

"I don't like it," Hoyle said.

"But still, you got to admit what the lad said. It must be a smart mob. They ain't left a clue, and all they do is stand in the way of collecting fifty grand. Anybody who gets fifty grand is damn smart," Sweeney said.

"That's just my argument," Morton said.

"Some guys get nothin', and others collect fifty grand," O'Malley said.

"My brother, now, he's married, and he hasn't been workin' for a year, and he has two kids. When he talks about the relief people who come around to see him, why, he speaks like he's damn near becomin' a communist," the tall, skinny fellow said.

"That won't get him any gravy. Tell him to pull along with Roosevelt and give the President a chance. He's only been in the White House a year. When a rookie comes up to the big leagues, nobody expects him to burn up the league in his first year. Hell, Roosevelt's like a rookie in the White House. Give him a chance," said Sweeney.

"And he has the interest of the little guy at heart, too," Morton said.

"Sure he does. He knows the box score," said Hoyle.

"I think he's pretty good," Morton said.

"And there's something pretty good, too," the tall, skinny fellow said, pointing at a passing girl.

Morton hung around talking until about eleven-thirty. When he left, he told them to tell Bleary he'd been looking for him.

IV

"Where did you get it?" Anne asked in surprise when Morton let himself in with the key and pulled in a large, friendly police dog after him.

"He followed me home," Morton said.

"I wonder if he's got an owner?" asked Anne.

"There's a tag on the collar with his name, and the owner's name and address. His name is Boozer, and the guy that owns him is named Smith and lives on South Shore Drive," Morton said.

"He's a swell-looking dog. Maybe we'll get a reward. Here, Boozer!" Anne said.

The dog came to her, wagged its tail, looked up with begging, liquid eyes.

"He's panting. He needs some water," Anne said.

Morton took off his hat and coat while Anne led Boozer into the kitchen and gave the animal some water.

"He was awful thirsty," she said, returning, the dog at her side.

"I suppose the mutt's hungry, too," Morton said.

"And we haven't anything to give him, poor dog!" Anne said, caressing Boozer's narrow head and pointed nose.

"He ought to be worth some dough," Morton said while the dog gazed beggingly at Anne.

She bent down and read the tag on the collar. She patted the dog again, cooed to it.

"We'll watch the newspapers and see if a reward is offered," she said.

"Yeah," Morton said meditatively.

Boozer went to Morton, put his snout in Morton's lap.

"Good dog! Too bad we ain't got any pork chops for you," Morton said, patting the animal.

"We might get five dollars reward for him. Gee, Sugar, wouldn't that be swell," she said.

"That ain't any too much," he grumbled.

"Well, what do you want for nothing?" Anne said.

"Anything I can get. All I was sayin' is that five dollars ain't any too much dough," he said.

"I'll throw an old coat on the kitchen floor and he can sleep on that tonight," Anne said.

"Yeah," Morton exclaimed, still in meditation.

The dog, unrewarded for its begging, finally went to a corner and sprawled out.

"Did you see the man about the job?" she asked.

"No, but I left word for him. He'll be around tomorrow night and I'll get it all settled then," Morton said.

"Gee, I hope so, Sugar," Anne said.

"Well, my ship is overdue in the harbor by now," Morton said.

"Maybe Boozer is going to bring us good luck," she said.

"Maybe," he said.

"Was there anything new in the papers about the kidnaping?" she asked.

"No, except the Bixbys got another ransom note," Morton said.

"Maybe it was the same ones who took the Lindbergh baby," she said.

"Who knows?" Morton said.

"I hope they didn't kill the poor little thing," said Anne.

"Just think, kid, that mob might collect fifty grand out of this snatch," Morton said reflectively.

V

"I walked past the apartment hotel where that guy Smith that owns Boozer lives. It's built like an armory. Any guy living in a cage like that must have plenty of dough," Morton said, taking his coat off.

"We ought to get five dollars then," Anne said.

"The hell with the reward," Morton said.

"But, Sugar, you're not going to give Boozer back to him for nothing, are you?" she said in surprise and disappointment.

"See any holes in my head?" he asked.

"But what?"

"The guy has dough, hasn't he?"

"I suppose so," she said, still surprised.

"Well, he's got to pay more than five bucks to get his dog back," Morton said.

"But you can't tell him how much to give us. He did say in the ad in the papers that there would be a liberal reward and no questions asked. I don't think he'll be a cheap skate," she said.

"Listen! Is that guy Bixby gonna dictate to that mob what he'll pay for his kid alive, or isn't he?"

"What's that got to do with it?"

"Plenty!" Morton said knowingly.

VI

"Now, I call that a good note," Morton said, looking at the sheet of paper on which he had been writing.

"Sugar, I'm afraid! We might get five dollars and be legal. This way we might get into awful trouble, and we got trouble enough with neither of us working. The investigator was hinting again today that we ought to sell our radio," Anne said.

"What do you mean, not working? This is work. I been working on this ransom note all afternoon," he said.

"I'm afraid!"

"Can the worry. I'm running this show," he said.

"But if anything happens to you, Sugar, it's like as if it happened to me, too. I'm part of you," she said.

"Can the stuff. Here, read me this note," he said, handing her the paper.

She looked at the note he had written.

DERE MR SMITH—BOOZER IS SAFE YOU WILL HERE MORE IF YOU TELL ANYONE WE WILL KILL BOOZER DEAD WE MEAN BUSINESS

She read it aloud.

"It sounds pretty good, doesn't it?" he said.

"I don't know," she said abstractedly.

"Why don't you? Sure, it does," he said.

"You didn't spell 'dear' and 'hear' right," she said.

"That's what makes it a better letter," he said.

"Why?"

"He'll think we're real tough if we can't spell, just like the mob that grabbed the Bixby kid didn't spell all the words right in their ransom notes," he said.

"Please don't send it, Honey."

"Are you yellow?"

"I'm afraid, and it isn't worth it," she said.

"Twenty-five bucks! Say, are you bugs? What are you talking about?"

"I wish you wouldn't. Honest, please don't send it."

"Listen, who wears the pants in this menagerie?" he said.

"Maybe the man doesn't care about Boozer," she said.

"He cared enough to advertise, didn't he?"

"Well, he might give us five dollars, and we won't have no trouble. This way, we might even get arrested."

"For Christ sake, do you think I'm dumb? I'm smart, and you just let me handle it," he said.

"But how do you know he won't get the police after us?"

"If he does, he can start mourning for his Goddamn dog!"

"But you wouldn't kill Boozer, would you? He's such a lovely dog," she said.

"Give me the letter!" he said.

He folded the paper and put it in his pocket. He went to the bedroom for his coat and hat. When he came out, she was crying.

"Listen, you ain't Greta Garbo. Quit the sobbing!" he said, leaving. She continued to cry.

VII

"You shouldn't have spoken to him on the phone," she said.

"Why not?"

"He could have traced the call."

"Only the cops can trace a call. And this guy is afraid. I know. I've been watching his house, and he's got a kid. Well, that's probably why he wants the hound back. And then, too, I got him thinking we're a mob, and that we'll bump him off if he does any squealing on us," Morton said.

"If you got that job as a basketball coach, you wouldn't be doing this," she said.

"I told you I'm going to see Bleary tonight for sure. And after I do, we're set, and everything is going to be home-cooking for us. He must be sick, because he hasn't been around to see me," Morton said.

"Honey, please don't do this," she said.

"Listen, I'm all set to collect. The guy has the notes, and I got him on the phone. He ain't squealing to the police. See! He ain't!"

"How do you know?"

"I know. He wants his dog," he said.

"Sugar, please!"

"Don't start going yellow on me! What the hell kind of a babe are you? I thought you said you'd stick with me through thick and thin after that time I laid you and we got married. What about it?"

"But, Sugar, I'm so afraid," she said.

"All right, stay home then! I'm all set. I'm going to be standing on the corner with a tin can in my hand, and he'll have somebody pass me by and drop the dough in the can. You are a block away with Boozer around the corner, and if you get the signal from me, you come out with the dog. If not, you run, and for Christ sake, don't lose the God-damn hound."

"But why that way?" she asked.

"Listen, for Christ sake, who's running this show? You or me?"

"But, Sugar."

"How can we kidnap a dog and collect ransom if we don't do it mysterious? What the hell do you think kidnaping is, huh?"

"But, Sugar, if you say so, all right. Only I'm afraid. Suppose you get caught?"

"I won't! And listen, I knew I was always gonna get some racket, and this looks just like my racket. It's going to be a sucker proposition, like taking candy from babies," he said.

They went out the back way. Under the porches, he rubbed his face in dirt. He sent her into the basement with an empty milk bottle, and she carried it back filled with water. He poured the water on black earth, and then plastered the mud on Boozer. Leading Boozer by a rope, they left.

Morton took his position at a corner and waited with a tin can in his hand. She waited a block down, at Seventy-third Street. She trembled as she watched. Every man approaching Morton caused her to shudder. He stood, casually holding the can, proud of himself. He knew it was going to work smooth as a whistle. And with twenty-five bucks, he could do plenty. They could eat swell. He might probably even get a suit on a five-dollar deposit from a tailor he knew. A stranger approached. Morton watched him closely out of the corner of his eye. The man was small, well dressed, mild-looking. He seemed to recognize Morton. Morton said nothing. He eyed the fellow closely. The man came nearer, dropped money in the can.

"Keep moving, and you'll get your dog! And if you let a bat out of you, you'll go home in a long box, with your eyes on the sky!" said Morton surlily.

Morton watched the man walk on. He took his hat off, and drew the money out of the can. He flung the can in the street, the signal for Anne. Seeing the fellow walking on according to schedule, he walked away. Two Federal agents popped out of a doorway and followed him.

The man approached Anne. She called to him that Boozer was around the corner, tied to a rail. She ran. The dog barked. The man chased her, and two Federal agents came out of a building and joined the pursuit. She was captured as she tried to turn in an alley.

Mort strolled on home, confident, whistling. Anne would get there by the time he arrived. He was going to clean himself up, go down to Rolfe's bookie place, and lay five whole smackers on New Hope. He had a hunch on New Hope. Just as he stepped in his hallway, he was grabbed from behind by two Federal agents and, after a short struggle, subdued. They put a gun into his back and followed him upstairs in order to search his apartment. Then he was taken off.

VIII

In court, Mort and Anne were found guilty of using the mails for purposes of extortion. They were given the maximum penalty of ten years as an example to others who would stray into the paths of crime.

1934–1937.

Wanted: A Chauffeur

I

"Why, Charles, you've been a stranger. You haven't been around to see us for months, and you know you're always welcome," Mrs. Brown said, looking up from her work by a window in a corner of the dining room; she was sewing on new curtains, and she sat surrounded by goods and scraps.

"I was thinking, and I said to myself, 'Now today is such a lovely Sunday, I'll just spin over to the Browns and see if Mrs. Brown and Caroline would like to go for a little drive with me.'"

"Oh, Charles, that was so thoughtful of you, and I'd just love to, but I have to finish sewing these new curtains. But maybe Caroline would like to go. Sit down and make yourself at home. Don't act like a poor relation," Mrs. Brown said.

"Of course. I'm an old friend of the family. At least, I hope that I'm considered so."

"And you are dressed up so nice."

She looked at him, a dark, thin young man in his early twenties. He was wearing a freshly pressed pair of white duck trousers with a blue serge coat. He sat down, pulling his trousers at the knees.

"Yes, Charles, you look wonderful, just like a young gentleman," she said.

"Well, Mrs. Brown, I believe in dressing in good taste. It's good for business."

"You're so sensible. I'm sure that you'll go far in the world. I said that to myself the minute I met you at my brother-in-law's," she said.

"Mrs. Brown, you're certainly a good housekeeper, just like my mother," Charles said.

"I try to give Caroline a good home since my other daughter married, a nice respectable home where she can bring decent young men like yourself to see her," Mrs. Brown said.

"Thank you, Mrs. Brown, and let me say that you certainly have the right idea."

"I try to be a good mother. But, Charles, Caroline will be ready in a minute. She's dressing," Mrs. Brown said. She raised her voice. "Oh, Caroline, Charles Moses is here waiting to see you."

"All right," Caroline called back petulantly.

"But how have you been, Mrs. Brown?"

"Very well, thank you, Charles. I go swimming down at the lake nearly every night, and it's good for me," she said.

"Say, that's great," Charles said with manufactured enthusiasm.

"You must come down some evening and go swimming with us off the rocks," she said.

"It would be fun. You know, we could bring sandwiches and we could swim, and then all sit around and sing in the moonlight. I'd like that."

"How is your business, Charles?"

"Very good, Mrs. Brown. In fact, I just bought a new car," he said with modest pride.

"Then it must be very good. I'm glad to hear that, because I like you, Charles. I think you're a young man with gumption and ambition. You know, you're going to be a real success. I'll bet that your mother is proud of you. I would be if I was your mother."

"I try to be. I work my hardest to be a success, because I believe in hard work. And I owe it all to my mother, and to the virtues she instilled in me at her knee when I was a youngster," said Charles.

"That's why I like you, Charles. And you say business is good again?"

"The market has picked up, and this time I think it's for good. You know, there's been more money made these last few weeks on La Salle Street than there has been since 1929. Why, dead accounts that I've had, they've suddenly come to life again. Money seems to be coming back into the market."

"Do you think it's because of Roosevelt?"

"I think he's done a fine job to bring back prosperity."

"You do? I'm a Republican, and voted for Hoover last fall. I never trusted the Democrats."

"Of course, Mrs. Brown, I don't mean to infer that Hoover didn't do as well as he could. The market crash was just necessary. We needed something like it to bring us back to our senses, to put us with our feet on the ground, as your brother-in-law, Mr. Gregory, always says. It was just that it was necessary, and when it happened they blamed Hoover and he had everybody against him."

"The Democrats wouldn't help poor Hoover. They would have stood by and seen us all starve to death before they would have helped Hoover to bring back prosperity. I guess poor Hoover just had too many against him," Mrs. Brown said.

"That's just the way I analyze it, Mrs. Brown. I say that conditions just became so bad that the upturn had to come. All that I meant about Roosevelt is that he has taken the right steps in this New Deal, and this N.R.A. that he's starting is going to help insure a business upturn. It ought to restore the confidence of the people in business. And that's what happened. As I was saying, there's been more money made on La Salle Street in these last few weeks than in years. And I guess I better knock on wood, because I'm making about seven hundred and fifty dollars a month."

"You deserve it, Charles. You're such a hard worker and such a smart young man."

"I try hard."

"Oh, Caroline! Caroline! Charles Moses is waiting," Mrs. Brown called.

"I'm coming."

"Yes, Charles, I suppose now that you're doing so well, you'll be settling down and marrying."

"Well, now, if I did find a girl, a sensible Irish or Anglo-Saxon girl, now, well, there's no reason why I shouldn't. Of course, she would have to be sensible. Me, now, I'm a Syrian, but I don't come from the lower classes in my country."

"Charles, anybody with two eyes in their head could see that you didn't. And over here, we're all Americans, except the Jews. Say, don't you like what this Hitler is doing? We ought to have somebody like that over here to make the Jews know their place."

"Of course, I don't follow that much. I guess that if Hitler is all right for the Germans, that's their business. The Jews bring things on themselves. They're so money mad, you know."

"That's what I always said, and that's why I like Hitler. But, Charles, you've certainly done well. There are few young men from Syria who made good and have became as Americanized as you have. Your mother certainly must be proud of you."

"I've been in this country since I was a little tot, and, of course, I say that anybody who doesn't try to make his mother proud of him isn't worth his salt. Syria, Mrs. Brown, is like all other countries in this one respect. The best people, with few exceptions, don't leave the country. My parents were great exceptions. So people in America see the worst of our people, the riffraff who come here and become waiters and bus-boys."

"It's the same with the Irish. The scum Irish came here, not the best Irish. But I was just thinking, your mother must be proud of you. You must come and see us often."

"Well, thank you, I will."

"Caroline!"

"Coming, Mother, dear," Caroline called superciliously.

II

Charles got in at the wheel of the new automobile, with Caroline beside him. He started off easily and turned the car in the direction of Jackson Park.

"I was thinking to myself that I would come down and see you today. And do you know why? Well, because you and I, we always get along so well together," Charles said.

"Why, Charles, you're so observant," she said, smiling enigmatically. She added, "Your new car is keen."

"I've only had it four days. Of course, there are lots more expensive cars on the market. But then it runs, and it doesn't look bad."

"Don't be so modest, Charles. It's simply gorgeous."

"I'm glad you like it," he said, looking at her. He became suspicious, noticing her enigmatic smile. "I really am glad you like it. Honest."

"Charles, isn't the lake lovely?" she said. Her tone of voice seemed to confuse him, and he screwed his face up in an expression of discomfort and uncertainty.

The Buick curved onto the park drive which ran parallel to the lake.

"The lake is," he said, no longer uncertain. "You know, I like to drive here at night, when the moon is out. It's romantic then. Even if some people might not think so, I have a poetic and romantic streak in my nature," he added, gazing at her intently.

He stepped on the accelerator, and the speedometer registered thirty miles an hour.

"Been to the World's Fair yet?" he asked.

"A few times."

"I was there the other night with a party of friends. Only we didn't stay long. The lights at night are very nice, and I'm going to go back and see all of the worthwhile exhibits. But, say, I forgot to give you a little music. Like music, Caroline?"

"I adore it. It's such a relief to hear music rather than some people talk," she said impishly.

"I feel the same way about it. You know, whenever I'm in the car with people who . . . well, people who bore me . . . but, of course, I don't mean you, Caroline . . . but with people who bore me, why, I can turn on the little radio," he said.

"I'm insulted," she said in feigned hurt.

WANTED: A CHAUFFEUR

"Now, Caroline! Gee, you know, it wasn't personal. Why, why would I come down to ask you to go out for a d..., if I meant "Maybe you wanted to show off the car." e with me?"

"Well, I did, but I wanted you to like it. Didn't I say that you always get along so well together?"

"Yes, but you said you got bored with people."

"But I meant some people. But you, gee, you got to believe me, Caroline."

"All right. Maybe I was over-sensitive," she said, almost laughing at him.

"I just meant other people, not a pretty and sensible girl like you. I just thought that you might like to hear the radio while we were driving here by the lake," he said, switching on the dial on the dashboard. Getting a symphony orchestra, he quickly turned to another station. "I like music to be a little peppier. That was kind of slow. This jazz band we got is faster, more pep. Of course, I don't want you to think that I don't like good classic and religious music, because I do. I'm a music lover, you know. But I'd rather have music that's peppier, good fast dance tunes."

She smiled out the window on her right.

"Say, that reminds me, Caroline. Since you and I get along so well together, it would be swell if we could go to the Fair some night and have supper there, and then maybe dance a little in the Belgian Village. I hear that it's a beautiful and a romantic spot at the Fair."

"It would be grand. I'd love it," she said.

They drove on, past the bathing beach, not conversing for a space.

"You know, I've been thinking," he said.

"How strange!"

"What?" he asked, puzzled.

She smiled at him, disarmingly.

"You know, for a second there, I thought you meant you couldn't imagine me thinking," he said.

"Charles, how could you? Now I'm hurt."

"Please don't be. We don't want to have misunderstandings," he said.

"Charles, you said you were really thinking. About what?"

"Well, I'm twenty-seven now. Of course, people often tell me that I don't look my age. But I am twenty-seven. And you know, I get sort of . . . well, lonesome, and like I wish I had a companion. You know, I'm what you might call a domestic person, the kind who would appreciate a home and a wife, an Irish or Anglo-Saxon girl from a good family, who could be a real partner to me in life," he said, glancing at her, his eyes begging.

She met his stare impersonally. He drove out of Jackson Park and onto the South Shore Drive.

"Ever play golf?" he asked, rather embarrassed, and nodding toward the fenced-in golf course of the South Shore Country Club.

"No, but I'd love to."

"It's an interesting game. I'm learning it. Good exercise when you're in business like I am. In fact, golf is the business man's game, and I find that I can do a lot of business, too, while I play. I want to perfect my game. I've even played here on the club grounds a couple of times," he said with beaming pride.

"I see that you associate with the best people, Charles," she said.

"I make it a principle to. It's good business, and when you try and see the best people, you have stimulating contacts that improve your mind and character," he said.

"Well, that's something you need," she said.

"Everybody does. Nobody is perfect. But as I was saying, Caroline, now, here I am—"

"Yes, I know that," she interrupted.

"I'm making seven hundred and fifty dollars a month, and I have a car and an apartment. I can afford things, and a wife, if I met the right kind of a girl. What do you think of my getting married, Caroline?"

"It would be just grand."

He looked glumly out of the window, and drove on for a block in silence.

"Don't you think that my salary and commissions would be enough for a couple to live on comfortably, and still let them save and invest for that rainy day?"

"Surely, if the girl wasn't a spendthrift like me," she said.

"Caroline, you're not that. You're a sensible girl with her feet on the ground, just like your uncle always says. And for me, I'd want a girl who would be sensible about money and know the value of it, and wasn't the kind who would try and make a fool out of a fellow."

"That would be impossible, *Charles;* no girl could make a fool out of you," she said with deadly sweetness.

"Well, Caroline, even if I do say so myself, it wouldn't be so easy.

"Gosh, but you're a pretty girl," he exclaimed in genuine wonder.

"Charles, if you continue flattering me that way, you're liable to make me flattering you. Honest, cross my heart, I mean every word of it."

"I'm examining the small dining room and the rose-patterned dishes in the cupboard, they went into the small and spotlessly clean kitchen. He poured out beer and produced pretzels from the pantry.

"Say, Caroline, can you cook?"

"A little," she said, smiling girlishly.

"Could you come here some night and cook a meal for me? Of course, if you want me to, I'll have a chaperone along, only that might spoil it. But, gee . . . it would be such fun, and it would be just wonderful, if you would."

"I can't promise whether or not you'll live through the experience."

"Say, I'll bet that you could cook a swell dinner. I'll bet you're a wonderful cook, just like your mother, and your aunt, Mrs. Gregory. Say, would you do that for me?"

"I'd be charmed to."

"Honest?" he asked with dog-like gratitude.

She nodded.

"How about making it Wednesday?"

"I'd love to, but I couldn't make it Wednesday."

"Thursday?"

"We'll have to wait. There are several things I have to do next week, and I'm not sure on just what days I've got to do them. You call me up around the end of the week."

"But will you be able to make it real soon, anyway?"

"Yes."

"I'll give you the money, and you can buy the groceries."

"Yes, Charles," she said mockingly, her smile confusingly friendly.

"It'll be fun, too. Say, Caroline, you know, every time you and I see each other, I'm able to see more clearly how you understand me."

"Yes, Charles. And we have such interesting subjects for conversation," she said, swallowing the remains of the beer in her glass.

"Say, I never realized that. But isn't it so? One of the reasons we get along so well together is because when we see each other, time runs so fast."

"But that reminds me, Charles, I must be getting back home."

"Gee, I was thinking that we might have dinner at a nice place near here, and then do something, maybe go to the Century of Progress."

"It'd be such fun. And, Charles, it's so thoughtful of you to ask me. I'd love to do it, if I only could. But I have an engagement tonight that I simply cannot break, much as I would like to."

"Now, isn't that just my luck," he exclaimed with a forced laugh.

They left the apartment.

"Say, are you doing anything tomorrow night?" he asked as he stepped on the starter.

"I'm sorry, Charles, but I'm going to be busy."

"Gosh, a fellow has to put in reservations to go out with you, doesn't he?"

"Now, Charles, don't tease me that way."

They drove several blocks in silence, and he began to show his discomfort. He turned onto the drive, and went toward Jackson Park. They drove on in stiff silence.

"Say if I had a girl like you for my wife, I'd be just as proud as a peacock, and I'd sure treat her as swell as I could. A girl like you is just what I need. And now that I'm making seven hundred and fifty dollars a month, and my prospects are good, with prosperity back again, I feel that it's about time I was getting married. And all my wife would have to do is manage our home, and take me to the office in the morning and call for me at the end of the day's work. I don't think that I have any bad faults, either."

"Don't be absurd. Charles, finding a girl should be the easiest thing in the world for a successful young man like yourself."

"You think so?"

"Of course, I do."

"I don't know. There aren't many I've seen. And, gee, Caroline, I get so lonesome, and think of how I'd do everything in my power to make the right girl happy if she was the right girl, one who is sensible, and keeps her feet on the ground, a girl like yourself," he said when they were again in Jackson Park.

IV

"Charles, thank you so much for the drive and the lovely time I had," Caroline said, emerging from his automobile.

"Oh, don't mention it. Thank you for coming with me. And, say, when are we going to go out again? It's been so nice today, we ought to go out together often."

"Yes, we will. You'll have to call me up, Charles."

"Can't you make a date now?"

"I'd love to if I could, but I have my dates all mixed up."

"I guess you must be popular. Can't I put in a reservation for some night next week instead of having to wait in line?"

"Call me up, Charles."

"You can't let me know now?"

"It'll be easier if you call me up."

"But will you try and keep a night open for me if I do? You will, won't you, Caroline?"

"How could you ask such a question? You know I will."

"Because there's so much we can do together, and so much we have to talk about."

"Yes, there is."

"Well. . . ."

"Goodbye, Charles, and again, thank you for such a lovely time."

"Now don't forget?"

"How could I forget you, Charles?"

He watched her walk to the doorway, disappear. He was wistful. He sat in the car, apparently thinking. Then he drove off.

1933–1936.

The Scoop

A LARGE *Chicago Questioner* delivery truck parted the traffic as it roared northward toward the Clark Street bridge. It shook the street, emitted carbon monoxide gas from its exhaust pipe, punctuated the atmosphere with the shrillness of an open cutout. And thundered onward.

It was the first truck to be used for deliveries. Dennis McDermott, a circulation slugger, stood on the tail gate and hung onto a stout rope. Husky and handsome, he expressed his pride in a characteristic leering frown. He enjoyed the honor of having been assigned to this new truck while the other sluggers remained at work on horse-drawn vehicles.

Bumping, the truck rattled over the Clark Street bridge. Dennis was tearing through the scenes of his boyhood. He had grown up on the Near North Side, been educated on its streets, and he had served as an altar boy at the Holy Name Cathedral. Nuns had even looked at him with masked wonderment, incapable of understanding why such an intelligent-looking boy, who seemed so holy and so devout in his acolyte's cassock, should always be fighting the way he was. That had been before he had been ejected from school for the third and final time in his seventh grade. His father had been an Irish immigrant and an unskilled worker. A precinct captain in Bart Gallivan's organization had gotten him a job as a street cleaner, and that had elevated Dennis' father to one of the most minor positions in the neighborhood political aristocracy. Dennis had always had before him the example of the local hoodlums, and in his small-boy manner he had emulated them, leading his gang in expeditions to roll drunks, and in fights against neighborhood gangs of Jews and wops. Reckless and possessed of volatile courage, he had grown up to be a tough guy, hired as a slugger and strikebreaker, employed in the taxicab wars, and then by *The Questioner* in the newspaper circulation war. Twice, he had been arrested in hold-ups. Duke O'Connell, from Dennis' own neighborhood, had become State's Attorney, and he had sprung Dennis both times. He stood on the tail gate of the truck, delivering papers to the old corners, even to corners where he had sold newspapers himself. And just as earlier sluggers had gypped him by subtracting papers from his order and charging him for them, so he was now gypping newsboys who were acquiring an education similar to his own in the same kind of system.

He clutched his supporting ropes more tightly as the truck curved about a corner. It drew up to a newsstand and Dennis flung down a bundle containing forty-five copies of the paper.

"How many?" asked the newsboy, a tired-looking kid of twelve or thirteen with a hole in the knee of his left stocking.

"What you ordered. Fifty!" Dennis said in his habitually bullying voice.

"Last night there was only forty-five. I counted 'em," the kid said with a nervous and uncertain air of defiance.

"I said there was fifty!"

"Well, I counted 'em!" the kid said, a whine creeping into his voice.

Dennis squeezed the boy's left ear between two strong fingers, and asked him how many there had been.

"I counted 'em!" the kid said, his voice cracking.

Dennis gave him a back-handed slap in the mouth and said that there had been fifty copies. He collected for the papers and jumped on the truck as the sniffling newsboy opened the bundle.

"How's it going, Wop?" Dennis asked Rocko Martini at the next stop.

"All right, Irish," Rocko replied, winking.

While Rocko opened his bundle of papers, Dennis quickly said that he and a pal were pulling an easy house job on Saturday night and they needed somebody for a lookout. He'd been watching Rocko, and he knew he was all right. If Rocko wanted, they'd let him in with a fourth of the take. Rocko agreed, and Dennis made a date to meet him after work to give him the lowdown.

After two uneventful stops, the truck drew up to a stand where two newsboys were jawing each other. Dennis leaped down and stood over them, sneering, his hands on his hips. He noticed that a freckle-faced kid had a bundle of *The Chicago Clarion*.

"What's the idea, huh?"

"This guy's trying to bust into my business," *The Questioner* kid said.

Dennis looked at the freckle-faced boy, and the latter drew back a few paces.

"This is my corner, ain't it, Denny?"

"Well, I can sell my papers where I wanna. It's a free country, ain't it?"

"So that's the story!" Dennis said, grabbing the freckled kid's papers, and shoving him. The kid reached for his papers. Dennis twisted his arm, booted his tail, and warned him not to be seen selling papers on this corner again. He tore the papers up and told *The Questioner* kid to let him know if the punk came back.

Dennis delivered papers to Shorty Ellis, the punk he didn't like. Ellis was always giving *The Questioner* inside place on his stand. He told his driver to go around the block, and jumped off the tail gate. He sauntered back to Ellis. He pointed to the copies of *The Questioner* which were placed on the inside.

"Didn't I tell you where to place our papers?"

"Well, Muggs was around and told me to place his in the same spot."

"He did?"

"Yes."

"What did I tell you?"

"I don't see why you guys can't leave a kid alone to sell his papers."

"You don't, huh!" Dennis said, catching a look in Ellis' eyes that he didn't like.

"Change 'em!"

"And then Muggs'll come around and crack my puss."

"Change 'em!"

Ellis did not obey the command. Dennis slapped his face. Touching the red flush on his cheek, Ellis drew back, pulled out a pocket knife and, waving it before him defensively, told Dennis to let him alone. Dennis advanced on the boy. Ellis, still brandishing his knife, scratched Dennis' wrists. Dennis lost his temper and flashed a razor. When the boy again struck out defensively, Dennis slashed his throat, almost from ear to ear. The boy fell, his head nearly dismembered, his blood gushing over the sidewalk. Dennis looked around. No one had seen the fracas. He knew the kid would die quickly. He hastened away and leaped onto his truck. It raced back to *The Questioner* office. He saw the night editor, Kelly Malloy, who had worked himself up from a copy boy and was now only in his thirties. Malloy always talked hard, but he had a soft, womanish face. He had been given the job in a change that was calculated to jack up circulation, and Dennis was the best circulation man on the force. When Dennis assured him for the fourth time that no one had seen him slash the boy, he breathed a sigh of relief. Then he slapped his hands together and said that the story was worth an extra. He became a dynamo of energy.

Very soon Dennis was back on the truck with an extra which bore the headline:

NEWSBOY MURDERED; SLAYER UNAPPREHENDED
North-Side Boy Slashed With Razor In Suspected Neighborhood Gang Fight

At that time *The Questioner* was conducting, as a circulation stunt, one of its wars on crime. On the editorial page of the extra there was

guy a better appetite, and he would get healthier. If only he would get a break, have some rich babe go gaga over him, clean up heavy on the ponies, or maybe enter and win a dance marathon and get himself signed up for Hollywood.

"Gee, it would be the nuts to be a big-shot and just loll around on the beach on these nice warm days. You could have a swell broad by your side, and have your Marmon roadster parked waiting for you with James to spin you wherever you wanted to go, and after a swim you could take your mama along and dash out to a roadhouse and get a real feed," George said.

"Yes, wouldn't it be the nuts," Jack said.

"It wouldn't be no ordinary beach where, what the hell do you call 'em, the hoi polloi go. No, sir! It would be a private beach of some ritzy joint like the South Shore Country Club, an exclusive dive whose members would be all filthy with dough."

"I'd get 'em off on these hot days, sitting in my white flannels with some rich jane on the veranda of a club like that, sipping my liquor," said Jack.

"And I'd be sipping a Tom Collins," said George.

"Then wouldn't life be the nuts, and I don't mean maybe. You could play a round of golf early in the morning before it got too hot, and then rest a while, and then take a dip in the lake, and then dine like the King of Italy, and then just loll away the afternoon, or maybe go to the races and play for some small change, you know, a thousand bucks or so, and maybe have your own stable, and keep a harem in swell apartments, and take turns sleeping with them. I tell you, life would be the nuts then," said Jack.

"And you could winter in Florida, and now and then take a quick little hop over to London and dash across to Paris for some French cutie, and you could take in the season at Deauville, and then top it off by jazzing some Spanish senoritas who would be hotter than pepper," said George.

"It would be the nuts," Jack said.

"Yeah," said George.

They strolled along for a period in silence, puffing away at their cigarettes. George had, or believed that he had, a pain in the heart. Heartburn! He would have to cut down on his smoking. But he might just as well finish off the one he was smoking. No use wasting it. He wasn't getting enough exercise, though. He would have to watch that, and get in a lot of tennis and golf and swimming this summer, and next winter he would go ice-skating and take in some gym regularly. He would get up early in the morning and take a little hike before breakfast. Goddamn it, it was lousy, getting up, dashing for a train, and half of the time not getting a seat. And at noon a guy had to dash out and eat at the counter of some joint jammed with jabbering broads. And then having to work all day, too. He wished he had a job working outside. But then most outside jobs were common, laboring ones, and they had no future. It would be the nuts, though, if he could land a good selling job, maybe traveling, seeing America, riding swell on Pullmans, stopping at high-class hotels and getting himself a new broad every night in the week. That would be the meow, all right. Tomorrow morning he would be getting up early and dashing for the train, and then he'd be sweating all day in the office. Jesus Christ! Some guys just didn't know how lucky they were.

"I'm gonna play Blood'll Tell tomorrow," said George.

"That goddamn nag," said Jack.

"You watch. I'm playing it to place. You watch and see, because I got my system, and it don't go wrong," said George.

"Well, if you want a real tip, take this. Play Mickey Gallagher in the fourth," said Jack.

"That dopey nag!" said George.

"All right, you wait and see," said Jack.

"I got my system," said George.

Coming to Jackson Park, they entered by a path through the bushes and came out upon a golf course. It was already dark, and the park was deserted, except for a few passing golfers. A foursome, two couples, passed. Jack and George both agreed that the two girls looked like swell lays with perfectly grand toilets on them. They slowly passed along the grass stretch. Looking back, they could see the rising hulk of the Westgate Hotel on Stony Island Avenue, and, further along, the ugly red pyramid of a chain motion-picture palace on Sixty-third. They discussed going to a movie, but decided not to, because it was too swell a night to be wasted on the movies. It was nice out, all right, they agreed, and they walked on. Jack said that he would just like to have about five percent of what guys got in Jackson Park in the summer time. George said that if he did, he would be dried up in no time. Jack said that he had a lot of stuff. It made George secretly worried because it made him ask himself, as he always did, was he sterile? He had never knocked up a jane. Maybe he was. But he couldn't tell anyone of this fear, not even Jack. Jack would laugh at him, and all of the lads would get wind of it. He would be razzed until Doomsday. But there was no real reason to be worried. And still this fear kept coming back to drum away at him.

Jack spoke of a pig he had recently picked up. Afterward, when he got home, he had washed his mouth for fear that he might have been contaminated by her kisses. George told the story of the lousy bitch he had gotten one night at the Gardens a couple of years ago, when that was the place to go for free and easy tail and they had that hot band there, the Tennessee Melody Gang, with a swell guy like Voltaire Raymond beating the drums. Yes, sir, that had been a red-hot band, all right, you bet. Anyway, George said that he had taken the broad over to the island in Washington Park, and they had gotten along real nice, and she had seemed to be one blazing party and he was beginning to think that he was going to get something pretty nice and maybe pretty regular when, damn it if she didn't turn out to be a dirty degenerate.

"That's a nice sky," George said as they sat under a tree at the edge of the golf course.

"Yeah," said Jack.

"Gee, I wish I had a lot of bucks," said George.

"Who don't?" said Jack.

"Now if I was in some racket like Al Capone," said George.

"You'd get your ears shot off," said Jack.

"It would be worth taking the chance," said George.

"Baloney," said Jack.

They lit cigarettes, and George tried to convince Jack that he wouldn't mind taking the chances that go with being a big-shot in the gang wars. Then they began talking of the good old days when they were at Saint Stanislaus High School.

"Remember the time that Father Hans kicked us out of the class in geometry, and we organized a singing society of our own in the basement and damn near raised the roof?" said George.

"And Dan was in school," said Jack.

"Too bad about him. He was a swell guy, and, you know, he would have been a dandy athlete. He got too smart. He wasn't smart, like Shanley and those guys in school. Why, Christ, he was the biggest drunkard in the class, next to Marty Mulligan. And then he went goofy. I hear he's a communist, and married a rich broad or something."

"Well, that's not so bad, if he did marry a rich broad."

"He always used to come to dances with a new broad every time, and he usually had a keen one."

"Yeah, he was a good guy," said Jack.

"And now he's writin' a lot of junk, and he went and lost his religion," said George.

"It all goes to show how you never know what a guy's gonna become. Now, there he was, a swell football player, and nobody would have thought he was smart. And then he went and became too smart and turned into an atheist," Jack said.

"You never can tell about life," said George.

"And, say, remember that game in Joliet when we broke the window in a suburban car?" said Jack.

"Yeah," said George.

"And we put on some good benders in those days, too," said Jack.

"Yeah," said George.

"Those was the days," said Jack.

"I wish we had 'em back," said George.

"Don't I!" said Jack.

Nostalgia ached inside of George, and he started singing the popular songs of other days. He remembered the song *I Hear You Calling Yoo Hoo* that they were playing at Louisa Nolan's dance the first time he had danced with that broad Sally Schmalski who had taken him over to Jackson Park, and *I'm Runnin' Wild* that he had heard when he took Clara Eldridge to Fraternity Row, the swell cabaret downtown. Thinking of Clara, he started singing:

> *You're the kind of a girl that men forget;*
> *Just a toy to enjoy for a while:*
> *For when men settle down, they'll always find,*
> *An old-fashioned girl with an old-fashioned smile;*
> *And you'll soon realize that you're not so wise,*
> *When the years bring you tears of regret.*
> *When they play "Here Comes the Bride,"*
> *You'll stand outside,*
> *Just a girl that men forget.*

and if the book is good, why, then, when that friend says that another book is good, he waits until next June, and he buys it, and when he goes to Montana, why, then he reads that book if the radio does not interfere with his reading when he lies down in the afternoon.

Mr. Lunkhead is what is called a he-man. He likes he-man hobbies, and he-man sports, and he looks like a he-man. So he likes to ask a question. What are your hobbies? He is actually not interested in your hobbies. The question merely permits him to tell you of his hobbies. And he has one favorite hobby. He says, well, and then he pauses, and there is a very slight noise in his throat, well, his favorite hobby is old clothes. He likes to wear old clothes. You tell him that old clothes are your favorite necessity, and he says, yes, it is great fun to get out into the open and to put on old clothes and be natural.

He has a philosophical bent, and so he likes to ask questions like what makes a person tick. He will, for instance, see an attractive young woman, and he will say to her that he wonders what makes her tick. He smiles condescendingly at her, and tells her that he is fifty-six years of age, and that the secret of his success is that he does everything in moderation, and that a person is as young as he looks and as youthful as he thinks he is, and if he never does anything to excess, why, there is no reason why he should not reach the age of fifty-six without looking it. And so he wonders what makes a young girl tick.

And then one might ask him what he does all day when he is not in Montana wearing old clothes. And he will say, well, he got up in the morning and he ate breakfast and he looked at the newspaper. And then he came in from Long Island in a motor boat. And he went to his office. And he had a pile of mail on his desk. But he did not read it. Why didn't he read his mail? Well, he has a theory about not reading your mail in the morning. There might be some bad news in it, and bad news can always wait a day or two. So he only reads his mail after it is two or three days old, because then, one may assume, the bad news will not be quite so bad. And then he had conferences. There were perhaps some people who wanted his bank to sink some money in the purchase of a golf course. Well, that did not seem a good investment, so he was thumbs down on that. And there were some more conferences. And there was lunch. He had lunch in his office, just a sandwich, because he believes in moderation, he says. And then there was another conference. And a friend called him up. He knew what the friend wanted. He wanted to borrow some money. So he invited the friend and the friend's wife to supper. And then he had an engagement for tea with a charming young lady, and they talked about the philosophy of life, which undoubtedly meant old clothes, moderation, and how to become fifty-six years old without looking your age. And then he had supper with the friend, and since the friend's wife was along, the friend was too sensitive to try to borrow some money. And so another day passed into eternity, and Mr. Lunkhead, the banker, traveled on from the age of fifty-six to the age of fifty-seven without looking his years.

1936.

The Oratory Contest

I

FACING the bathroom mirror, Gerry O'Dell practiced for the contest, and he imagined the thunder of applause that would greet him at the conclusion of his oration. His mother called him, and he said that he was coming. He met his dad in the hallway, and Mr. O'Dell looked at his narrow-faced, small, sixteen-year-old son with a mingling of pride and humility.

"Well, Gerry, how do you feel? The old soupbone in your throat loosened up?" the father asked.

"Yes, Dad," Gerry nervously answered.

"Gerry, your mother and I are mighty proud of you, and we'll be giving you all the . . . the moral support we can tonight. Don't get worried because you're speaking in public, or because of the size of the crowd. Ah, anyway, Gerry, oratory is certainly a great gift for a boy to have," the father said, putting his hairy hands into his blue trouser pockets and rocking backward on his heels. "Gerry, if a man has the makings of a great orator in him, he need have no fears of getting ahead in life."

"George, don't be making the boy nervous. Gerald, supper is ready," the mother called.

"Martha, I was only explaining to him," the father apologetically explained.

him to be interested in her writings? She was deeply depressed. But she counteracted her gloomy mood by insisting to herself that she was worthy in her desires, and that he might perceive and nurture the spark of sincerity within her.

On the first class day, Mr. Saxon gave an assignment for each of the students to write two poems, one rhymed, and one in free verse. Angela went to the telephone exchange that day with despair in her heart. But suddenly, while working at the board, she was inspired with two ideas describing the pangs of those who reach toward the Unattainable Beyond in order to touch the gossamer drapings of Truth and Beauty. She left work in almost an agony of impetuosity, rushed home, sat at her desk with her rhyming dictionary before her, and slaved over the poems until two-thirty in the morning. She tumbled into a ready sleep, confident and excited. She awoke, ashamed of what she had written. She thought of cutting class, but that would have been cowardly. She steeled herself. She timidly laid her assignment on the desk with a shaking hand, and spent the entire class hour in a state of excited apprehension. She felt that her work would seem so poor that she would be dropped from class. For two days she remained in this mood. She was so distressed that she could scarcely even smile at the many witticisms Mr. Saxon expressed in class. On the third morning, he entered the classroom with the manuscripts under his arm. He spent the last fifteen minutes of the class hour reading some of the poems, his selections from among the most absurd and sentimental handed in. Angela brooded, silently prayed that he would not read hers and publicly disgrace her. When the class bell sounded, it rang joyously within her. She was saved, at least for one more day. But then Mr. Saxon announced that he wanted to speak with Miss Angela Malloy after class. She trembled, her plain round face red with blushing. She approached his desk in the emptied room, halted about five feet in front of it. He looked at her, his pudgy face set in a frown. She stood in speechless embarrassment. He smiled, completely disarming her.

"Angela, I am going to call you by your first name; I want to tell you that your poems were the best ones handed in to me. Your work is very promising, and very beautiful. I hope you will show me everything you write. And you must write, write, write, write. You have the spark. You mustn't let it be extinguished. Do not limit yourself to class assignments. Write as much as you can, and please let me see it all," he said.

It was disturbing to Angela when she had to go to work that afternoon and sit at a telephone board with common, ordinary girls. The next day Mr. Saxon read her poems in class and eulogized her. The class was new, unadjusted to college, and no one disagreed with Mr. Saxon's judgment, not even the gruff-voiced, curly-haired boy whom Angela hoped to know.

From that morning on, Angela's college career became one of steady triumphs. Mr. Saxon repeatedly lauded her work in class, and at the end of the quarter he said that it had been more artistic and promising than that of any other member of the class. In fact, it had been two years since he had had the pleasure of reading freshman work as promising as hers. He hoped she would continue and that he would see her again in his advanced classes. He was convinced that neither Willa Cather nor Zona Gale had written so well as Angela did when they were her age. She wrote so beautifully that she even made him fall in love with her.

Angela acquired a literary reputation on campus. Strangers sometimes pointed her out as the girl who wrote beautifully. It was often predicted that she would some day do big and fine things. And as each school quarter passed, her reputation grew. Slowly, her head began to turn, but for two years she crowded in enough work to maintain a straight A average and to win scholarships. Most of the courses she took were snap ones in Lit. At the end of her sophomore year she was promoted at the telephone exchange to the position of supervisor, with a salary of thirty-five dollars a week. She had more spending money, and her work was less tiring. She drifted into the society of the campus literati.

She met many promising writers and actors who were going to do big things. They were hard-boiled young people, free in their talk, self-assertive in their knowledge, superior in their feeling for their own advanced aesthetic sensibilities and tastes. They loved talking, and drank much, and their way of life was a new world to Angela. In no time she became emancipated. Her figure had improved, though she remained homely. She tried to dress stylishly, but her taste in clothes was so erratic that she often looked like a travesty. And her favorite remark became, "But a woman must have a career." By autumn of her third year she was emancipated to the point where she discussed homosexuality. She constantly sought to extend her masculine acquaintances, with particular preferences for those who were literary. She

of a girl whose only attraction was the vulgar physical thing. Life again was joyousness. She bought a new dress which nicely emphasized her figure and made her look less homely. And the next morning in the Coffee Shop she met another interesting male, a frail blond student who agreed with her on Yeats and Masefield. He was writing a term paper on the poetry of Mark Turbyfill, and they discussed it, almost point by point. A bond of common appreciation was established between them, sealed when he recited what they both considered to be a brief little gem of Turbyfill's:

> *In the doorway,*
> *The little birdies sit,*
> *Keeping time*
> *To their thoughts.*

Angela then matched his quotation, describing it as one revealing a blood-red passionate feeling, and though she was not certain of the exactness of her quotation, it ran something like this.

> *And I guard you deftly,*
> *Gathering you*
> *With love-bright fingers,*
> *Into the reinforced blood-red walls of my heart.*

Life went on blithely for Angela. With Mr. Saxon's help she was granted an honor scholarship which would permit her to do literary research in her senior year and, also with his help, she was given a job as coach for the dramatic club of the telephone operators. Working with her girls, she decided to write a play of her own. She announced her intention to everyone she saw in the Coffee Shop. In fact, she said that the play had just about written itself in her head, and that all she had to do was to transcribe it. She jotted down a few scenes and read them many times in the Coffee Shop. After reading these fragments, she would outline the remaining scenes, detail by detail. Over and over again she described how her principal character was a mad old virgin who lived alone. From her window she could see into the living room where her sister and brother-in-law lived. Hating both of them, she was able, by watching from her window, to participate vicariously in their lives. When the window was open she could hear almost everything they said. Of course, it was obvious, Angela always said, that the parallel development in her plot was unique. The scenes switched back and forth between the two apartments, and the tragedy at the end resulted from the fact that a gable was constructed, obliterating the sight of what went on in the home of the sister and brother-in-law. The final scene describing the old virgin would then be a crescendo of poetic madness. Also, the play was to be more than merely a tragic drama. It was to be constructed like a poetic symphony. Each character would speak in a personal and individual rhythm which would, in turn, blend into one splendid and magnificent whole. And Angela would permit the Theatre Guild to do the play with Lynn Fontanne and Alfred Lunt playing leading roles.

Angela was graduated. She had planned to go to New York immediately, but changed her mind, deciding to remain in Chicago until she completed her play. She opened up a salon on the Bohemian Near North Side, and shortly afterward she lost her job. She had to get work immediately, and landed a job selling classified advertising over the telephone for *The Chicago Questioner*. She continued living what she considered a full life, surrounding herself with interesting people, talking and planning, reading fragments of her play over and over again. Billie disappeared from her life without regret on the part of either of them, and others came and went in his place. Every Sunday for over two years she had tea and open house. A group of emancipated young ladies like herself were always present, welcoming the males who came around. She entertained aesthetic cabinet-makers, house-painters with ideas on modern art, dancers, gypsies, embryo young writers, college literati turned into copy writers, advertising salesmen and cub reporters. And she always lounged on a couch in either a gypsy or oriental costume, dominating the talk. She would talk of the quest for the Unattainable Beyond which was the true ideal of the artist, and suddenly she would switch into a description of Bunny and Mel. They were both good eggs, lusty guys. Almost every Sunday morning at about one or two A.M. they would appear under her window, dressed in tuxedos, leaning drunkenly on one another, singing *How Dry I Am*. They were really very interesting and so funny that it was killing. But they drank like gentlemen. Bunny came around to see her often, but she was, of course, interested in him only because of his higher nature. She gave him all she had, but in a spiritual way. And when she heard that he chased other girls, she would deny it. Talk never ran out at Angela's salon. Under the stimulus of tea and gin, the conversation persisted. When nothing else was left to talk of, Angela would hold up her stubby toes, describe in beautiful language how they wriggled, and why her feet were callused.

Suddenly Bunny abandoned Angela without warning. She was heartbroken. She felt that life was futile. She lacerated herself for not having accomplished anything. Sunday came, and she did not know how she could survive seeing anyone. But she dressed in her gypsy costume and waited for her guests. They came, and soon they were discussing rumors they had heard concerning an affair Bunny was supposed to be having with a mulatto. Angela arose dramatically and stood in the center of the group.

"Bunny, I'm through with you! I'm through! I'm through! Some day I'll do big things. It may be today! It may be tomorrow. It will be some day. I'm through with you, and I'll do big things. I'll never compromise my desire for space and the twelve winds of heaven. Bunny, goodbye!"

The talk went on. A dancer who lived downstairs got drunk and ran to the bathroom. She filled the tub and sat in it, crying, and had to be lifted out and dragged to her own apartment, where she was put to bed. The talk went on.

Angela's life went on, until one day she received a note from Mr. Saxon. He had heard of an editorial job which was open on a fraternal organ in a small town in Indiana. She landed the job through him. She held a final Sunday with her friends and left, promising to do big things, to be heard from, to complete her play and see it on Broadway with Lynn Fontanne and Alfred Lunt. She left for Indiana. Soon she married the editor. She had babies and postponed writing the play until some time in the future.

1930–37.

A Noble Guy

I

MR. MORRIS LEVIN crossed his squat legs, puffed nervously at his cigar, and glanced at the silken leg of Miss Stolberg. He dictated.

"My dear Mr. Weber . . . It grieves me to write you this letter

". . . no, change it . . . Much as I regret writing you this letter . . . uh . . . I find . . . no, make it . . . I feel that it is . . . ah . . . absolutely necessary . . . Let's see, now . . . Owing to business conditions . . . No, make it this way . . . Much as I regret writing you this letter, business conditions force . . . no, make it . . . require me to do so. Continue . . . your rent is now overdue, and since I have waited a considerable time, I have now no other choice than . . . ah . . . to ask that you remit your check by return mail or . . . otherwise, make it . . . no . . . or else I . . . no, it will be necessary for us to commence proceedings for dispossession. Sincerely yours."

He gulped in the sight of her legs. She sat trim and chic in a black silk dress, her legs crossed, the right one exposed to the knee. Continuing to find fascination in this sight, he dictated other letters. Four of them were substantially the same as the one he dictated to Mr. Weber. One other was to a Mr. O'Mara, who had remitted only half of his rent, and Mr. Levin begged to inform him that there was still twenty-five dollars due. He trusted that Mr. O'Mara would remit by return mail. Three other letters were short notes to be sent out with new leases. Finally, he dictated a long pep letter to his salesmen.

The office boy came in and said that Mr. Weber was outside waiting to see him. He told the boy that Mr. Weber should wait. He asked Miss Stolberg to type the letter to Mr. Weber immediately and to bring it in while he was speaking with that gentleman.

He sat alone for about twenty minutes, casually glancing over old papers and nervously puffing away at his cigar. When he calculated that Weber had waited a sufficient time to be impressed, he pressed the button for his office boy. He told him to bring in Mr. Weber.

A little man in his early thirties appeared, and Mr. Levin quickly observed that he was wearing an old suit. Mr. Levin told him to sit down. Weber obeyed. He pulled out a soiled handkerchief and wiped his face.

"Yes, sir?" Mr. Levin said, turning a fishy smile on Weber.

"I meant to see you sooner, Mr. Levin, but . . . well, I wasn't able to."

Miss Stolberg quietly entered the office and laid a typewritten letter before Mr. Levin. He pretended to read it carefully. Weber sat anxiously on the edge of the chair.

"Oh, yes, a coincidence. I was just sending you a letter, Mr. Weber, but since you are here, it will be unnecessary," Mr. Levin said, handing the letter to Weber and continuing to talk while the tenant read. "If you have the remittance for your rent, you can give it to my cashier and she will give you a receipt. That will settle our business quite happily."

"That's what I came to see you about, Mr. Levin," Weber said meekly.

"Of course, you will understand, Mr. Weber, that there are some things we do not like to do, but we have no choice in the matter. You will understand that it is a business we are conducting here. And there is some little cost to us in running expenses, upkeep for our offices and buildings, and, well, if we do not collect our rents, it's going to be impossible for us to keep our heads above water. Rents are the life blood of the real-estate business. And any business, like any human being, must have . . . life blood."

Mr. Weber laid the letter on a corner of the glass-topped desk and glanced pleadingly at Mr. Levin.

"You see, Mr. Levin, my wife has just had a baby and . . ." Weber began haltingly and apologetically. "And there's some question of the little fellow. The doctor only gives it an even chance to live, and . . . Mr. Levin, I just couldn't . . . ah . . . get out. If I do, it will kill the baby . . . And I haven't the rent. I'll try and have it as soon as possible for you. What I came here for was to ask you to have just a little more patience."

As a gesture of thinking, Mr. Levin protruded his lower lip over the upper one. He rubbed his hairy hand over his sleek, well-barbered face. Mr. Levin thought.

"Well!" he exclaimed.

He continued to think.

Weber gulped, swallowed saliva. Mr. Levin touched his bright blue cravat and slowly asked Weber when he thought he might have the rent.

"I think . . . I think that I might have some of it . . . next week."

"Working?"

"Yes. That is, I have a commission job selling a new and original line of novelties that look like they might go well. I'm plugging at it hard, but it takes time to get a proposition like this one going right."

"Hmmm!" exclaimed Mr. Levin.

Weber watched Mr. Levin closely.

"It doesn't sound so good," Mr. Levin said reflectively.

Weber fidgeted.

"When could you try to make some remittance?"

"I could try and make it next Friday."

"You couldn't make it Monday?"

"I'm afraid not."

"Wednesday?"

"No, sir. You see, Mr. Levin, I got to pay for my stock on Monday and I don't get anything over expenses made before Friday. But I—"

"All right," Mr. Levin interrupted. "I shall expect some remittance next Friday. Then we can see further."

Mr. Levin made notes on a pad.

"And thank you very much, Mr. Levin. I appreciate this favor more than you think, and—"

"Don't mention it, old man. I'm always glad to help out a fellow human being," Mr. Levin said, interrupting.

II

Friday came and Weber was unable to make any remittance. The baby's condition remained serious. Mrs. Weber complained of pains and a feeling of general weakness. Her recovery would be slow, and some time in the future it would be necessary for her to have an operation because her womb had dropped. They could not afford sufficiently nourishing food, and this added to her worries, helping to sap her very meager strength.

On Friday, the Webers were fortunate to have any supper. The work he had described to Mr. Levin amounted to selling novelties from door to door, thereby earning a mere pittance for food and medicine. They had no relatives to whom they might appeal. They did not know where they could turn.

After supper, Weber looked at the sleeping baby. All it had known, and all that it might ever know in this life, was a brief and blind period of primeval pain. And it looked, he felt, just like its daddy. If God would only save it, get him a decent job, that was all he asked.

He turned away from the second-hand crib and looked out the window at the lazy life of Euclid Avenue. He heard an Illinois Central suburban train pulling into the Bryn Mawr station. People passed along the street. He watched them, almost crying. Only one thought seemed to be fastened upon his mind. Did these people passing below him, did they have worries about their next meal, and about their families?

He told himself that things would have to get better. Hard times must have reached rock bottom by now, and business had to pick up. Maybe soon he might even be back at his old job, selling paints. A man must have faith. He must have faith in the future. But people couldn't, he couldn't, go on suffering. Something had to be done! Yes, *something had to be done!*

That he should have a baby in these times! But even so, he was proud and glad that he had. He prayed and he begged God, please, please to let it live. He returned to the crib and again looked at his sleeping son. Jimmy Weber! His son! Sleeping so peacefully now. Perhaps it was getting better. God, if it only was!

Nellie Weber washed the dishes. He sat down to read his indispensable newspaper. These days when he lived in such insecurity, when he had so much to worry him, his newspaper was his only escape. The radio was gone. They could not afford to go to the movies. They couldn't even go out and take a walk together on account of the baby. And anyway, he was never in the mood to walk, because it only made him worry the more. These days he couldn't drive his own problems out of his mind. When he picked up his newspaper, he could escape from all that, and he completely forgot himself.

He read his newspaper. The Lindbergh kidnaping story was still on the front pages. He thought of how horrible it was, and he hoped that the villainous gangsters who'd done such a terrible thing would be captured. And if they were, hanging would be too good for them. Poor Mr. and Mrs. Lindbergh! The heart of every father and mother in America went out to them. And there were still divorces, murders, politics. On the second page, he read of a mother who had murdered her baby and committed suicide because there was no food in the kitchen. Well, he did not condemn that poor mother. It was a way out. There was a way out for a man, after all. He turned and noticed an item on the third page which told how a rat had gnawed a baby to death in the home of an unemployed Negro in the Black Belt. Awful! Ah, yes, just as he had told himself. And there was news of the Bonus Army in Washington, but he wasn't sure now whether or not it would be good to give them the bonus. And there was mention of a bread riot. He quickly flipped the pages to the less disturbing news, and read about shows, ball games, society people who were still giving parties, getting married, going away. Everybody hadn't been affected by hard times. He read that money was needed immediately if relief was to continue in the city. He felt that he should be given relief. But he had a job, and when he had applied for relief, they had not given him anything. A job! Going out, frantic, bitten with shame, not knowing if he would come home to find his baby living or dead, knocking on doors, having them slammed in his face, realizing that if he failed to sell something it might mean starvation for his family. A job! He read on, slowly and carefully. He didn't want to finish with the paper, because then he would have nothing to do but worry.

Mrs. Weber noticed his cloud-faced absorption. She got angry and cursed him for wasting three cents on a newspaper. He tried to pacify her, but she only became the more angry and excited, flinging cruel and cutting words at him. He lost his temper and slapped her. She screamed. They dragged up nasty memories from the past, faults, neglects, misunderstandings, and hurled them at one another like so many knives. The baby began to cry. Suddenly Mrs. Weber lapsed weakly into a chair and sobbed. He rushed to her side and tried to kiss her tears away. She drew his head to her breasts. He cried like a small boy, his body quivering. He helped her to her feet, put his arm around her, and they went to the crib. She picked up the sick, crying baby, and changed its diaper. He sat on the couch. She joined him.

"Talk to me the way you used to before we were married, dear," she said.

III

Mr. Levin waited until Monday for Weber's remittance. Then he dictated another letter. Weber appeared humbly at his office the next morning. His shabby suit was neatly pressed, only adding to his silent shame. He dropped his shifty, beaten eyes, unable to look at Mr. Levin squarely. Levin gave him a fishy stare, and kept shaking his head adamantly. Weber begged. The baby had had another spell, and they had almost lost it Saturday, when it had coughed and vomited nearly all night. It couldn't take any food, and he was very worried. He was worn out. He and Mrs. Weber had not slept for three nights, and lack of sleep was telling on the missus. She was not strong enough for the ordeal she had to face. He was nearly out of his head because of the whole business, and he didn't know what to do. The doctor could give him no hope or consolation, because the baby's case was extremely critical. He would pay his rent at the first possible opportunity, only he begged Mr. Levin please to have a little more patience and give him more time.

Mr. Levin lapped his under lip over his upper lip. He rubbed his hand across his forehead. Weber suffered through five minutes while Mr. Levin thought. Then Mr. Levin remarked that he was not conducting a relief bureau . . . but that under the present circumstances he would wait another week before taking any action. Weber's expression of gratitude was cloying.

After Weber's departure, Mr. Levin called in Miss Stolberg. Dictating, he eyed her closely.

"Dear sir . . . it grieves me to. . . ." He interrupted his dictation and said, "I don't like to be dispossessing people, but I got to. Rent is the life blood of this business."

"Yes, sir, it sure is hard all around," Miss Stolberg said.

"I try to be as decent as I can with my tenants, considering all the circumstances. Take this fellow, Weber. I'm keeping him when he can't pay rent. That's more than many an agent would do for him. Would that crook Bailey do it? Not in a hundred years. But I do. And I do it, knowing in advance that Weber won't be grateful to me or appreciate what I have done for him. I tell you, there's no gratitude in human beings. They don't appreciate nothing you do for them. But even so, I'm not evicting Weber. I believe in being human and kind whenever I can. So I keep on sheltering him and his family, even though he doesn't appreciate my generosity. But then, it isn't in people to be different."

He shrugged his shoulders and continued his dictation.

"Don't go yet," he said to Miss Stolberg when she arose to leave.

She sat down.

"Maybe you have a nice boy friend? Don't marry him if he can't pay your rent," he said.

"I don't take any of them too seriously," she said, smiling curtly.

"Mm, smart girl! You're a smart girl," he said, leering.

IV

Another month, and another letter to Weber. Weber returned to the office. His baby still hovered between life and death. He pleaded with Mr. Levin in God's name.

"Ummm. . . . Well . . . I should go on keeping you forever? I should be a philanthropist? Yes?"

"My God, if I move my baby now, it'll die."

"Well, old man, hold your horses. I don't want to see any unnecessary suffering in this world. My faith is always to help my fellow man. I believe in universal help. But then, I should go bankrupt? I have obligations to meet, and I must answer to my associates and my clients. When I say now this fellow, and this one, and that one, and the other family, they owe rent, they ask me why. I say they have no money. They say, all right, institute proceedings for dispossession."

"But, Mr. Levin, my wife and baby . . ."

Levin went into thought. He said that he would make an exception in this case, only it would involve fighting with his associates over it. Weber thanked him.

"Don't mention it, old man. I believe in helping my fellow man when it's possible. . . . But maybe you could make some little remittance to me?"

"I'll try at the very first opportunity."

"Maybe this week you can give me something, even if it's only five dollars, just to show your appreciation?"

"I'll try."

"When can I expect it?"

"I'll try and do it on Friday."

"All right, and good luck to you."

V

Mr. Levin shook his head on hearing the news, and reflected that it was sad. He signaled for Miss Stolberg. He told her that the Weber baby had died that morning.

"How awful!"

"Well, I did my bit. I kept him for three months, and didn't dun him, like many a realtor would. Now, if he had been renting from that crook Bailey, he would have been thrown out the first week."

"It's a pity!"

"Well!" he said. He paused. "All right, I'll give you some dictation." She posed for dictation.

"My dear Mr. Weber . . . It grieves me . . . ah . . . greatly . . . no, change it to . . . It grieves me beyond the power of words to express to write you this letter. However, it is . . . no, that'll never do . . . however, it is my duty to my associates to do so, and I have no other choice in the matter. Unless your check for rent is remitted by return mail, I shall have to institute proceedings for dispossession. This is final, because I cannot let this unprofitable situation continue. I have permitted it for three months, and I cannot do so any more . . . no, make it any additional leniency. . . . No, cut that and change it to I have no other alternative to choose. Sincerely yours."

She got up to leave, but as she went, he called after her:

"Miss Stolberg, try and put a little sympathy in that Weber letter. You know, a personal human touch."

1932.

A Hell of a Good Time

I

JACK REILLY'S wife had to leave town to attend the funeral of a relative. She would like to have taken Jack along, because that would have made a better impression on the clan, and, also, she did not trust her man out of her sight. She feared he would get drunk with that good-for-nothing friend of his, Joe O'Brien. But if Jack were away from the office, he would be docked, and in addition there was the extra train fare. Before leaving, she made him promise not to see O'Brien. Suspicious, she said she hoped he would act like a decent and honorable man and keep his promise, and that, after all these years, he would begin to show some of the sense the Lord had given him.

Jack was a dried-up-looking man around fifty, who worked as a clerk for a wholesale grocery concern. He was getting bald, his cheeks were hollowed, and he was almost toothless. But he dreamed of somehow, some day, getting some money, escaping from his nagging wife and making some kind of a great big splash in the world before he went to his grave.

His wife's departure was his first opportunity to have a big time in nearly a year. On his first free night he telephoned his friend. And Joe, red-faced, fleshy, a widower, came out to Reilly's apartment on the South Side. He greeted Jack like a long-lost brother, and planked a bottle of bootleg gin on the table.

"Say, Joe, we're gonna have a hell of a good time," Jack said as they tipped glasses for their first drink.

"That's O.K. with your Uncle Dudley," Joe said.

"Joe, the lid's off tonight, and the top of the sky's the limit. The old woman is away. Ha! Ha! Jesus, Joe, wouldn't the old rip be sore if she saw us this minute? But, Joe, how's tricks?" Jack said.

"Can't complain. Business is fair, and, say, I got myself a young jane who's got everything. She's married to a plasterer, and sometimes in the daytime I go see her, get a feed, and Jack, that little gal is a piece that's got everything a man wants."

"Congratulations! And, you know, I got a little chicken, too. Mary, she's a waitress, and she was pure as a lily till I met her," Jack said, leering insinuatingly as he spoke.

Each silently thought that the other was a damn liar, and they clinked glasses.

"You're a sly devil," Joe said, and Jack beamed. "Reilly, I always thought you should get wise to yourself. If you'll excuse me for saying it, I always felt that that old lady of yours was a goddamn battering ram and that you've always been too good for her."

"I know it, friend. It was the greatest mistake of my life. I hate her, the goddamn bitch!" Jack said, decisively emptying his glass. "But what the hell is a man going to do? I can't get a divorce, and if I could, I'd only get socked for alimony. I got to put up with a lot."

"I know how your old lady hates my guts. And, well, I don't fancy anything in her, either," Joe said.

They drank to the eternal damnation of Mrs. Reilly.

"To hell with her, Jack. Tonight we're going to have a hell of a good time, just like the old days," Joe said.

They tipped glasses.

"Say, I saw Kitty Shannon the other day. She's married a German and had a regiment of kids. You wouldn't know her. Did she turn out to be a tub! I say, did she!" Joe said.

"Kitty was a sweet girl," Jack said dolorously.

"But come on, bottoms up!" Joe said.

"Here's looking at you!" Jack said. He drank, and continued, "Joe, Kitty Shannon was as fine a girl as ever walked the street. She was just like that song, *My Wild Irish Rose*."

Jack commenced to sing the chorus of that song.

"For God's sake, have a heart," Joe interrupted.

"Joe, I liked Kitty Shannon. I liked her," Jack said.

"We all liked Kitty. She was hot stuff. Wasn't I ready to give her the works on the front porch one night, when I'll be damned if her old man didn't damn near catch me with my britches down," Joe said.

"Joe, she was a grand girl."

"Come on, let's go!" Joe said, sticking the bottle in his hip pocket and putting on his hat.

"We're going to have a hell of a good time tonight," Jack said, slamming the front door.

II

"Joe, times'll never be the same," Jack said as they staggered along Fifty-seventh Street. "Now, take those punks runnin' around nowadays, gettin' drunk by smelling a cork. They ain't like the lads we was in our day. Joe, nowadays they're only punks."

"You said it, my friend."

"Christ, Joe, if I was only young again!"

"Me, too, pal," Joe said.

"These modern girls, they're the real stuff, and they need the likes of what we used to be. Take my Mary, she always says she wouldn't trade me for these cookie-dusters that try to sneak feels off her while she's serving them lunch."

"And, Jack, these modern girls don't even wear pants," Joe said.

"Don't I see 'em getting off of street cars! If I was only the man I was in my best days!"

They stopped in a hallway and drank from the bottle.

"Why, hello, Kitty!" Jack exclaimed at two young girls who were dressed in organdy, and who passed them, walking westward, just as the two pals emerged from the hallway.

"Pal, you're too old for that game," Joe said, taking Jack's arm after Reilly had turned to gape after the girls.

"Say, I still don't need no monkey glands," Jack said, turning for a final glance after the girls.

They went into the lavatory at the Fifty-seventh Street entrance of the Illinois Central suburban station, and finished their bottle. Outside again, they walked by the studios of the Fifty-seventh Street art colony. They paused before a lighted window and studied a painting of a bronze dancing girl who was covered only by a golden veil.

"Now, just give me a hootchie-kootchie like that," Jack boasted.

"It's only a picture," Joe said.

"I don't care. Just give me a fling at a hootchie-kootchie like that one," Jack said.

"That's no way to talk about pictures. Pictures are art, and the artist doesn't have dirty thoughts like yours when he paints it. All he sees in it is art."

"Listen, Jack Reilly knows a lot of art for a hootchie-kootchie like that."

"Come on, Reilly, you're drunk."

"And I'm gonna get drunker," Jack said.

"Put it here, old pal, and shake on that," Joe said, and they shook hands enthusiastically.

They crossed Stony Island Avenue and trailed along a gravel path in Jackson Park.

III

"Say, Joe, look at that moon!" Jack said, the two of them sitting on a bench.

"Beautiful!"

"Joe, the moon, poetry and love makes a guy wish he was young again," Jack said.

"Moonlight and roses bring memories," Joe said.

"Joe, you didn't know it, but I'm a poet at heart, an Irish bard. And some day I'm gonna write a beautiful poem about moonlight, and roses, and Kitty Shannon, and love, and memories," Jack said.

"Pal, all of us Irish are poets at heart. That's why we never get rich like the Jews. We're a race of bards and scholars," Joe said.

"Joe, remember when we used to take Kitty and Nellie out?"

"Could I forget?"

"Ah!" sighed Jack.

"When Father Time sets the clock, there's no turning it back," Joe philosophized.

They boasted about women, and then they were silent. They surveyed the moon.

"Kitty was a dandy girl, and I used to like her. Oh, Christ, why did I ever marry the rip I married!" Jack suddenly said.

"The day you did, I asked God to have mercy on my poor friend Jack Reilly."

"I wish she'd died! But she's got an iron constitution. But, Joe, mark my words! Some day I'm just going to ups and leave her, and I won't even say, 'Bye, bye, bitch!' But as I was sayin', Kitty, she was different."

"And remember Nellie's golden hair?" Joe said.

"But, say, look at that chicken," Jack said, pointing at a girl passing beneath the rays of an arc light, her arm crooked in the elbow of a young lad.

"That's what I call a lulu," Joe said.

They watched the couple disappear, and they were again silent, until Jack tried to sing old-time songs. A passing group of sixteen- and seventeen-year-old kids yelled for him to shut up.

"Say, go home and get washed behind the ears," Jack yelled at them.

"Please, Jack!" Joe said persuasively.

"I ain't afraid of them!" Jack said as the kids made lip noises. "Say, beat it home to mama before your diaper pins break!"

"Please, Jack!"

"Say, grandpa!" one of the lads snarled as he approached them.

"Jack . . ."

"I ain't afraid! I ain't afraid!" Jack said.

"No?" snapped the lad, while his companions grouped themselves behind him.

"No," Jack said weakly.

"Boys, he's just a little bit under the weather. Don't pay any attention to him. He don't mean what he says," Joe said.

"Listen, you dried-up old . . ."

"Well, I ain't afraid," Jack reiterated in a tremulous voice.

The kid turned Reilly's hat around backward, gave him a lip-fart, and walked away with his companions, all of them laughing sarcastically.

IV

"Pretty good stuff," Joe said, seated with Jack at a corner table in a dingy speakeasy on Lake Park Avenue below Fifty-fifth Street.

"It's good, all right. I know the guy who runs this joint. Sure, it's good stuff," Jack bragged.

A HELL OF A GOOD TIME

"Let's have another," Joe said.

Reilly called the waiter and ordered in a tone of over-familiarity.

"Good stuff," Joe said to the waiter ingratiatingly.

"It's the real article," Jack said, grinning at the waiter.

The waiter served them and said that the liquor had come straight from Canada. Joe paid without giving any tip.

"Looks like a pretty tough place," Joe said, sipping.

"It is," Jack said, and Joe's face showed worry. "But it's all right. The guy runnin' it is an old friend of mine."

"You know, Jack, I don't fancy getting mixed up in any dago gang wars or anything like that."

"It's all right."

"You know how I feel, pal. Of course, I wouldn't mind a good old-fashioned fight like we used to have in the old days. But I don't want to be gettin' tangled up in the wrong places. Joe O'Brien never avoided a fight or failed to stand by a friend. But he never courted trouble. You know me, Jack?"

"And, Joe, you know Jack Reilly?"

"We're buddies."

"Through thick and thin," Jack said, stretching his hand across the table and shaking with Joe.

"Take those kids we saw in the park. Jack, now if they had really been hostile—" Joe said.

"I wasn't afraid of them. You know, Joe, that Jack Reilly isn't yellow," Jack said.

"If those kids had really been hostile, we'd have taken their britches down and spanked their tomatoes red for them. But they were only kids. What do a couple of old-timers like us want to do pickin' on kids in the cradle?" Joe said.

"Yeah, Joe, just so you know I wasn't afraid," Jack said.

They had another drink.

"And now for some girls," Joe said, arising.

"That's our ticket," Jack grinned.

They staggered to the bar, bought a half-pint of gin, and left.

V

They barged up and down streets. Now and then they paused in an alley or a doorway to drink. Shortly after eleven o'clock, while they

"Sure, I know Tom," the guy said, sliding the words from the side of his baboon lips.

"Well, he hangs around Sixty-first now, and the lads down there are no tennis players, but Barlowe can take most of them with one hand," Red Kelly said.

"Well, as I was sayin', he was champ down at Forty-seventh. Me and him onct fought a draw. As I was sayin', he is good, and I mean . . . good."

Benny Taite joined them, and they told Benny about the guy.

"Me and Tom used to have swell times down there," the guy said.

"Any time we get in dutch with bigger guys from another neighborhood, Tom will stick up for us," Red Kelly said.

"He likes us kids," Benny Taite said.

"He's a prince dat way. But don't never cross him none, becuz den he's jus' hell on wheels," the guy said.

"Him and my brother pal together a lot, and whenever they get shoved in the can, my old man, he's Sergeant Kelly, he gets them out," Red Kelly boasted.

"I know 'im. He's down at Twenty-second Street, ain't he? I onct got brought into him when I was caught in a raid on a can house, and he let us out. He's a good bull," the guy said.

"That must have been another one. My old man is at Grand Crossing."

"Oh, I know 'im, too. I was onct playin' indoor ball out at the playground there against all the ginnies and Polacks. A wop flashed a knife on me, so I let 'im have it, and dere was a riot, and dey called de paddy, and it was lucky for dem wops dat dey did. But your old man, he turns us loose. He's a good bull, too."

"My old man's pretty good," Red affirmed.

"Yeah," grunted the guy.

He shoved more tobacco into his mouth, and passed the plug around. Some of them bit off large hunks, and they stood around with their jaws puffed out so that they looked like bad cases of the mumps.

"Well, Tom would have to be a real guy becuz he's from Forty-seventh and de Grove," the guy said, professionally emitting a flood of tobacco juice.

"He always hangs out at the poolroom at Sixty-first and the L now," Red said knowingly.

"Didn't you say something about your brother? He never hung out at Forty-seventh and de Grove, did he?" asked the guy.

"My brother, no. He's always hung out at Sixty-first, but they're plenty tough up there, too," Red Kelly said.

"They don't eat nobody's crap," Weary said challengingly.

"Well, we always had a swell bunch," the guy bragged.

"That's what I always heard," Paulie said ingratiatingly.

"Dey was real lads," the guy said.

"Barlowe should go in the ring," Weary Reilley said, and they nodded agreement.

"We pulled some damn funny tricks, me an' Tom. Now onct, we was in Greasy Mike's hashery. Mike, he was a white Greek, doh! Well, we was onct in Mike's about one in de mornin', me an' Tom, and we didn't have nottin' to do, so we calls up goofy Bill Bellows. Bill, yuh know, was just one of dem goofy guys. De kind dat's a little off in de belfry and has de bells always ringing when dey shouldn't be. Dere's a guy like him in every gang. He always took tings serious, and you could be kiddin' de life out of him, and he wouldn't know de difference, see! Whenever we tol' him a joke, we hada tie an alarm clock on it so's he'd wake up in time to laugh. Well, on dis particular night, Bill had been around braggin' about how he always knocked de molls for a couple a rows, and he'd gone home to turn in early. Well, we jus' decides to pull a fast one on 'im. We calls him up, and Tom does de talkin', but it was all my original idea. Bill, he answers de phone like he was walkin' in his sleep, and Tom, he sez . . . he sez . . . 'Lissen you sonofabitch! Lissen, what de hell do you mean, sleepin' wid my wife. Huh?'"

They laughed.

"That's funny, all right," Paulie said, wiping a slobber of tobacco juice off his chubby chin.

Davey Cohen came around with a butt in his mouth and he listened.

"Well, Bill was kinda surprised, and finally it dawns on de dope dat he wasn't jus' dreamin' of de birdies, see! Say, I'll bet he ruined his pyjamas right den and dere. He sez, goofy-like . . . 'What wife? Who is dis? I ain't been sleepin' wid nobody but myself, you must have de wrong number.' So Tom, he sez, tough, too, he sez . . . 'Don't pull dat on me, Bellows! You're de bastard I mean, and you jus' cut it out or I'm comin' over and drill yuh. Get dat! I'm gonna drill yuh!'"

They laughed.

"Well, Bellows was jus' about scared shitless, and he doesn't know but what some guy is gonna come over an' croak 'im."

They laughed.

"Say, we'll have to try that on someone," Studs Lonigan said.

"We'll pull something like that on Diamond Tooth," Weary suggested.

"No, a dick can always trace a call," Paulie said.

"We'll figure out some guy to pull it on," Red said.

"Well, anyway, de joke works jus' to perfection. We wisens up all de lads to it, and nex' time Bill comes around, Tom, he walks up to Bill and sez . . . 'Say, Bill, dey was some guy aroun' here lookin' for you. He was a plenty tough-lookin' slugger. Know 'im?' And Bellows, he gets white as a ghost, and asks us all kinds of questions, and gets nervous and looks up and down de street quick. Say, it was a riot. And den de lyin' bastard tells us, braggin' dat de guy was an i-rate husban' whose wife was batty over him, and he sez, he does . . . 'Yeah, I know 'im and I ain't afraid of de fathead, but I don't wanna be mixin' in no brawls over a low, cheatin' frail.' But he was white as a sheet, an' it was funny. He kept tellin' us about dis ting, and he didn't never catch on dat we pulled his leg. But, as I was sayin', Tom he was funny dat way, and he had a real sense of humor."

They laughed.

"We had a good bunch, but now dere all scattered. Dere was Patsy Scanlan, and he was a game kid, game as you make 'em. He had guts, and when I say guts, I mean guts. Onct, de gang of us cornered a jigg, black as coal, and greasy as oil. He was head'n shoulders over Patsy, but Patsy lights into him like a bat out of hell, an' dey go to it, an' Patsy makes a real go of it, too, until he gets tired becuz de shine is so big. Den we piles in and we knocks de eight-ball for a goal and gives him de royal clouts. Say, we sent dat nigger back to State Street wid a mouthful of blood where his teet shoulda been. Patsy was game, dat was his trouble. Poor Patsy. De bulls, dey caught up wid 'im in a little stickup, and he got ten years up de road. And den dere was Bill Durange, as fine a fellow as ever walked de earth. But he got plugged in a fracas in a gamblin' joint. And Sticky-Fingered Toby Malone. It's funny, becuz he was de biggest crook in de bunch, and him walkin' a beat now. He had ed-u-cated fingers, he did, and de way he worked 'em in a store was jus' nobody's business. But he's makin' his on de force and he's turned out to be a real flat-foot. But, say, him a cop, dat's a real joke. Oh, we had a bunch, all right, down at Forty-seventh and de Grove."

"We got a pretty good bunch here," Red Kelly said.

They told him about guys in their bunch who weren't around, like Kenny Kilarney. Kenny was funnier than a vaudeville show, like the stunt he pulled last week on Big Fat Jeff, the baby elephant, who was only thirteen and weighed more than Jess Willard, the world's champ. Kenny had taken Jeff in back of the Fifty-eighth Street elevated station and crapped right in his ear. And then another time, Kenny had got a rope, and they'd captured old Nate, the crazy guy who was Father Time's oldest brother and who drove a grocery wagon for Herschfield's. They'd taken him right off the wagon and hung him by the shoulders to a telephone post, and let him hang until old man Herschfield had to come and cut him down. And it was Kenny who had thought up the bright idea of taking along pepper when they went over to Washington Park, cleaning up on Jews and niggers, and throwing the pepper in their eyes.

Lucy Scanlan passed. The guy noticed her, and said there was a girl they ought to get. Studs Lonigan scowled. They talked about girls and gangs.

"And yuh know, we had a guy down at Forty-seventh and de Grove dat was like dat, George Dillon. He had a sense of humor, too, but he got killed on a freight, ridin' de rods out to de West Coast. Onct, we was all over in Jackson Park, when we was kids, like youse is, and we meets one of 'em wid a hook nose that almost looked like a question mark. Well, we held him, and George hits dat nose wid a stream at five feet. Now dat, I calls marksmanship."

"We'll have to have crazy Kilarney try that," Davey said.

They talked on, and stained and splattered the sidewalk with tobacco juice.

"Say, dat remin's me. We used to have a lad named Spike Keefe aroun' de corner."

Weary's fourteen-year-old sister, Fran, passed.

"Say now dat's de kind of stuff you birds should gang up on. We always used to," the guy said.

Weary Reilley glowered.

"Anyway, one day, Spike and me, we tackles five niggers an' . . ."

"Say, it even pours out of your ears," Weary Reilley sneered in interruption.

"It makes me think of poor Mr. Rogers. You know, he lost his home and automobile, and he's a broken man, poor devil," Jack said.

"I have no pity for him. Not with that one he has for a wife. The Lord took away from her because of her false pride. When the Rogers had it, they acted like they were just too good for words. The Lord gives, and He takes from those who have false pride," Aunt Martha said with stern self-righteousness.

"I feel sorry for any man who has lost his home, especially on Thanksgiving Day," Mrs. Hicks said.

"So do I, but not for them," Aunt Martha said snippily.

"So be it, but, folks, I sure do want to say that I ate enough," Jack said, looking at the well-hacked turkey. "But what I want to ask is, has anybody not got his or her fill?"

They all chorused that they had had enough.

"We always want you to eat your fill at our house on Thanksgiving Day," Jack said.

Sonny, Jack's boy, asked for a second piece of cake, and Jack wondered whether or not it was good for him, not that he objected to the boy eating, but he just wondered if it was good for the boy. Mrs. Hicks interceded, and Sonny got his cake. Then Sissy Hicks asked for more cake, and got it. The adults smiled tolerantly at the children.

"Well, boy, you sure got a tapeworm," Jack said, watching the boy gobble his cake.

"Now, John, you know it's Thanksgiving Day," said Mrs. Hicks.

"Oh, Mother, I was only kidding him," Jack said apologetically.

"But the little man sure has got a tapeworm," Uncle Joe said; he belched.

"All growing and healthy children eat a lot," Aunt Martha said.

"Seeing how the Lord has provided for all of us so that we can eat our fill, it makes me think that with these bad times there's many the poor family in Chicago today without a turkey. That's why we should all thank the Lord especially on this day," Mrs. Hicks said.

"But, Lizzie, you know there were baskets given out to the poor. Didn't you read about the baskets which *The Questioner* and *The Clarion* gave? People are too good to allow the poor to go hungry today," Aunt Martha said.

"Nobody starves in this day and age, even in hard times," Uncle Joe said.

"I certainly hope to God that no one does. And it's such a cold day,

You can hear that wind rattling the windows," Mrs. Hicks said.

"But, Jack, the little man here has got a tapeworm, at that," Uncle Joe said, laughing until his face reddened and his belly heaved.

"I don't think I ate any more than anyone else did," Sonny said in a high-pitched voice.

They laughed.

"The boy is right. I'm so full that I don't want to do a thing but sleep," Mrs. Hicks said.

"I think we all got tapeworms today," Uncle Joe said.

"Well, I know that my innards aren't empty. I et my fill," taciturn Cousin Ben said.

"When Ben troubles himself to speak and says that, he is full to the gills. I'm glad and I know that we gave him enough to eat," Mrs. Hicks said.

"Well, I say that my innards aren't empty," Cousin Ben said.

The radio filled the room with saccharine music.

"Yes, Mother, when Ben says that, it proves beyond all shadow of a doubt that you gave the folks a real old-fashioned Thanksgiving feed," Jack said.

"You know, I always like things to be nice and special on Thanksgiving, because I like to see everybody get his fill," Mrs. Hicks said.

"You know. I've just been thinking. After a dinner like this one given us by Jack and Lizzie, a fellow really feels pretty good. He feels so good that he feels like there wasn't a trouble in the world, like business depressions, or communism and Russia, or unemployment, or Prohibition," Uncle Joe said.

"I most surely do wish something would be done about this depression, because these days there are so many beggars coming to the back door. I'm afraid, because you never can tell what they will do to you. Why, only yesterday a man came, and he talked as if I owed him a living, and he had the dirtiest old clothes on. I was frightened almost out of my wits. I thought that I would scream for the police. But I just fixed him. I slammed the door right in his face and switched on the burglar's lock," Aunt Martha said with indignation.

"If you ask me, now this here depression is a bum's dream. All these bums who never would work and never wanted a job, why, now they got an excuse and they say, it's hard times and they can't get work. I wouldn't give them a red cent. Whenever they hit me on the street, I tell 'em to go to the charity organizations," Uncle Joe said.

"Do you really think that there are people who don't want to work?" asked Mrs. Hicks.

"Country's full of 'em," said Cousin Ben.

"Well, I say that something ought to be done," Jack said.

"I guess that if anybody really wants work, he can find it. There's always something to do, if a man will look for it and not stand on his high horses," Mrs. Hicks said.

"Well, things don't stack up the way they used to, and I tell you it's the fault of the people of this country. They never should have elected Hoover," Jack said.

"You're right," Uncle Joe said with an air of profundity.

"And I say this. There ain't going to be a depression much longer. We're going to give Old Man Gloom a kick right in the seat of his pants. Mark my words if we don't! I mean the people of the good old U. S. A.," said Jack.

"Think so, Jack?" asked Cousin Ben.

"Think so? I know so! It's all a matter of psychology. If everybody gets the right psychology, and thinks prosperity, why it follows, just as sure as black is black, that we're going to get prosperity back again," said Jack.

"I hear psychology is such a wonderful thing," Mrs. Hicks said.

"Psychology is nothing but mental health. That's what it is, mental health. A sanitary, healthful, optimistic outlook," Jack said.

Ben said he guessed that Jack was right. Uncle Joe said that he knew things would pick up by spring at the latest.

"But, folks, you know, for good, solid, one-hundred-percent comfort, there's nothing like this, a good family dinner with everybody having his fill, and then a good cigar and some sound, right-thinking conversation to stimulate the mind," Jack said.

"Me, I'm so full, I fear I'm going to burst," Aunt Martha said, giggling.

"I ate enough," Mrs. Hicks said.

"I et my share," Cousin Ben said.

The radio brought in another sermon. Jack decided that they had heard enough sermons for the day, and ordered Sonny to get them some snappy music. Sonny obeyed, and the room was loud with jazz. Sonny had to turn it down.

"You know, I've just been thinking of something," Cousin Ben said.

"What, Ben?" asked Mrs. Hicks.

"I've been thinking of how I couldn't eat another bite, even if I wanted to," Cousin Ben said.

"I wanted you to have your fill, all of you," Mrs. Hicks said.

Sissy asked if she and Sonny could go to a movie, and there was a debate. Jack didn't think that it was quite right for them to leave the family on Thanksgiving Day with their aunt and uncle and their Cousin Ben around. Uncle Joe laughed, and gave them the money, and Jack relented. They left. The adults got back to talking about which side of the family each of the children resembled.

"But, folks, look at him. Now, could you fancy that?" Jack said, pointing at Uncle Joe.

"Tickle him, Jack," said Cousin Ben.

"Let the poor man sleep. He ate too much," Mrs. Hicks said.

"I'm so full, I could sleep myself," said Aunt Martha.

"Well, don't for one minute think that I didn't eat enough," said Jack.

"And yours truly here is just stuffed like an owl," said Cousin Ben.

"But, Lizzie, where are you going?" Jack said, seeing his wife collecting bones.

"I'm just getting these bones for Rover," she said.

"Lizzie, you know that you should only feed the dog twice a day. You'll spoil him. If you do, he'll always be begging, sticking his snout into our plates when we're eating," Jack said, seemingly injured.

"But just this once. It's Thanksgiving Day," said Mrs. Hicks.

"Have it your way. But when the brute is spoiled, don't say I didn't warn you," Jack pouted.

"If Rover feels the way we do when he gets those bones, he'll just roll over and hit the hay," said Cousin Ben.

"I gave Rover the bones, and it would warm your heart to see the poor beast eat. You know, he's such a smart dog, he's almost human," said Mrs. Hicks, returning from the kitchen.

"A good dog. He has a sort of human nature to him," Cousin Ben said.

"It's the truth," Mrs. Hicks said.

"Anyway, folks, know what?" said Jack.

"What, John?" asked Aunt Martha.

"I'm glad you all ate enough," he said, laughing.

"Look at him sleep. He ate enough," said Aunt Martha.

"Joe always stows away enough grub," said Jack.

"I'll feel sorry for you waiting all that time," Marion said.
"Well, who was it?"
A gleam came into Marion's eyes. She twisted her lips ironically.
"It might have been George Peters," she said.
Eloise struggled to control herself. Wench! They walked along in silence, but suddenly Eloise became overly cordial. She would kill this wench with sweetness and bide her time instead of showing her hand. They went to Eloise's. Marion stole the attention of Jackie O'Keefe from both Eloise and Mrs. Russell. That night, Eloise went over to Marion's for supper, pretending that they were going to study together. Afterward, Peter, a high-school boy from Tower Tech., came to see Marion, bringing Michael along. Michael made a play for Marion but she didn't respond. He had to remain satisfied with Eloise. The two of them sat side by side on the couch in the McGowan parlor. Marion's mother was out, and Marion took Peter with her into her bedroom and closed the door. Eloise went to the bathroom, and she listened against the door which led into Marion's bedroom. She heard merely a low echo of conversation, but she could not catch what was being said. She heard Marion suddenly giggle, and Eloise made a face, expressive of her jealousy. She left the bathroom and tried to peek through the keyhole of the door which opened into the hallway. She could see nothing, and decided that it would be just like Marion to hang something over the doorknob, covering the keyhole. She returned to the parlor, boiling inside.

"So you're a Saint Paul girl," Michael said, trying to make conversation.

"Yes," Eloise sighed in a voice wearied beyond her years.

"Well, it isn't a bad school," he said.

"No, not for you when you don't have to go to it," she said.

"Plenty of nice girls go there," he said.

"Who, for instance?" she said, her interest having suddenly perked up.

"Rose Macauley, lots of 'em," he said casually.

Eloise frowned, emitted a wordless exclamation of scorn.

"Well, what's the matter with Rose?" he asked.

"Everyone to his own taste. But do tell, now what is your name?"

"Mike," he said, flustered by her tactics.

"Well, everyone to his own taste, my dear George," she said.

They sat without speaking. Mike awkwardly moved his hands and wriggled about, restive.

"And, pray, what school do you attend?" she asked.

"Tower Tech."

"Oh, Tower! Yes, Tower! Tower!" she exclaimed, fidgeting for a word, hoping to find some withering comment with which to slay him. "Tower!" she repeated, forced to make the intonation of her voice substitute for the unfound withering sarcasm she had intended.

"Yes, I go there," he said defensively, and to make more conversation.

"Do you like it?"

"Well, now, I do and I don't," he said weightily.

"What does that mean?"

"There's some good fellows there, but, well, I guess I don't just like any school too much. What guy does?"

"I'm sure I can't answer that. Fellows are not one of my strong interests, so I can't speak for them. I know girls like school. I do," Eloise said archly.

"You must be different, then," he said.

"Not particularly," she said, striving for the sophisticated weariness of a motion-picture actress.

A pause. Mike smoked.

"Give me a drag!"

"Oh, you smoke?" he said.

"Who do you think I am, my grandmother?" she asked, taking his cigarette, puffing it, returning it to him stained with rouge.

"I didn't know," he said.

A pause.

"I see you're a modern girl," he said, trying to appear witty.

"Why?" she asked, posing.

"Aren't you?"

"What do you mean?" she asked belligerently.

"Oh, nothing. You're a modern girl. You smoke, and you—"

"And I don't," she interrupted.

"Well, I only said you were a modern girl. Now, if I'd said something else—" he began.

"You'd apologize," she interrupted.

"I never apologize," he said, trying to appear forceful.

"Snag that! You have a Tower Tech. sense of humor," she said, jumping up from the couch, walking around and wriggling her buttocks. She sang, swaying her shoulders and wriggling as she did so.

> *Every star in the sky*
> *Seems to wink as we go by, Mary Ann.*
> *Every rosebud blooming in the heather*
> *Seems to whisper "Go on together."*
> *I can't wait until the time*
> *When we'll hear the church bells chime,*
> *I'll be yours, and you'll be mine, Mary Ann.*

"That's a good song," Eloise said, flinging herself back on the couch. She held out her hand for a cigarette, and he gave her a Lucky Strike. He lit it for her.

"How did you meet Marion?" she asked.

"I didn't. That is, I just met her tonight. Pete's been talking a lot about her, and said he'd bring me to see her, and, well, he did tonight."

"And you saw me?"

"Yes, why?"

"Now, go ahead, say you're disappointed."

"Why should I?" he asked gallantly.

"Because maybe you came here tonight expecting to get something I won't give," said Eloise.

"What do you mean?"

"Don't be so innocent, Tower Tech."

Another pause. He puffed, uncomfortable.

"I know how fellows are. You came here expecting something that I won't give," she said, snapping her fingers; she hummed a jazz tune, ogled at him. Clumsily, he tried to put his arm around her.

"Stop that! I'm not that kind of a girl."

He didn't know whether she was kidding and teasing, or whether she meant what she said. He glanced away, nonplussed, and his eyes lighted upon a jumbled watercolor drawing of a peacock which hung on the wall above the baby-grand piano and must have been drawn by an insane person.

"See anything green?" Eloise asked snippily.

"Yes, the grass," he said, his composure restored as he pointed at the drawing.

"Mr. Tower Tech. Smart Aleck," she said.

"Not particularly smart."

"What do you think of Conrad Nagel?" she asked.
"Not particularly," Mike said.
"I think he's darling," Eloise said.
"What do you think of Mike Schlivsky?" Mike asked.
"Very conceited," Eloise said.
"Should I say what I think of Eloise Russell?"
"Pray, don't bother!" she said haughtily.
"Well, I was going to."
"I really don't care what any fellow thinks of me," she said.
"A proud and mighty wench she is," said Mike.
"Take love! Phui. Speak of love and you speak nonsense to me," she said.
"Yes, I guess love is nonsense to most girls nowadays," he said philosophically.
"They just decide that the man ain't living that is worth throwing their heart away on. I wouldn't throw my heart away on any man," Eloise said.
"Neither would I on a girl, I guess," Mike said.
"I'm not so sure," said Eloise.
"Why? You hardly know me."
"I can see what type you are."
"What type?"
"Very romantic. *Très romantique*," she said.
"You know French, too?"
"I study it," she said.
"Like French?" he asked.
"It's very nice. *C'est très intéressante*," she said.
"It's supposed to be a beautiful language, all right," he said.
"*C'est très belle*," Eloise said.
"Maybe sometime you'll write me a letter in French?" he asked.
"The man I do that for has never been born. I should say not! *I should say not!*" she said, springing to her feet, walking about the room, tossing her head from side to side to emphasize her determination. She returned to the couch. He put his arm around her.
"I'm not that kind of a girl," she said, putting his arm back in place.
"So you're one of these icebergs," said Mike.
"No, just selective," she said.
"That's a compliment," Mike said ironically, lighting another cigarette. "Anyway, if you're selective, look me over! Here I am!"

"Where?"

"Gee, I wouldn't call myself conceited," he said pointedly.

"No, just *selective*."

"Nobody can be as conceited as a Saint Paul girl."

"Don't you mention Saint Paul girls!"

"Not much. They're nearly all conceited."

"They're not!" she said with feigned anger.

"Well, then, they're not. It's only that they think the world was made for them."

"It was. It was made for all pretty girls," said Eloise.

"Yes? They're only pebbles on the beach," said Mike.

"Tower Tech. fellows aren't even that. They're only grains of sand."

"You mean they're the beach," Mike said.

"Your physiology is wrong," said Eloise, reaching over languidly and taking one of his cigarettes. "But say, where is Tower Tech.?"

"Ninety-eighth and Eggleston," he said.

"Did you learn that comeback in class or read it in a funny book?" she asked.

"I read it," he said.

"I thought so," she said wearily.

"Well, that's where Tower Tech. is," he said, grinning.

"And Saint Paul's is in Mexico," she said.

"It might as well be for all the good you can get out of its girls," he said.

"What do you mean? We have girls like Marion McGowan at school," she said icily.

"Say, they're in that room a long time. I wonder what they're doing," Mike said.

"Let's find out," Eloise said.

"No, we better let them alone," said Mike.

"Well, you must want girls like her, not like me," Eloise said.

"I meant what I said. Most Saint Paul girls are wet blankets, icebergs, too hoity-toity," he said.

"How many of them do you know?"

"Enough."

"You sound like sour grapes. You must be like the fox who couldn't get the grapes because he didn't know how to climb the tree to get them," she said.

"Well, if you ask me, Saint Paul girls usually *are* the sour grapes."

"I didn't hear anybody ask for your opinion. But if you want to know something, they might be sour grapes. But there's lots of fellows from Tower Tech. and other schools that would like to taste such sour grapes."

"Which they'll never get," Mike said dryly.

"Why should they?"

Mike had no comeback. They sat silent until Eloise spoke again.

"Do you really think there's nothing to a boy and girl being together except necking and that sort of thing?"

"What do you mean?" he asked.

"Just what I said."

"Explain yourself, woman," he said.

"Don't call me woman!"

"All right, Sheba."

"If you get smart, I'm just going right on home."

"And get your shoes and ankles all muddy."

"Oh, that never happens to me," she said coyly and suggestively.

"Meaning which?"

"If the weather looks bad, I bring galoshes and an umbrella along."

Again he was stumped for a comeback. He tried nonchalantly to show an interest in his cigarette.

"We got sidetracked. What did you mean about a fellow and a girl when you spoke of it a little while ago?" he asked.

"Can't a boy and girl be just friends, without all this necking, and can't they just dance, and go out together without having themselves all messed up in a necking party?"

"Can't it snow on the first of August?" he asked.

"I'm serious."

"And I'm not fooling."

"You wouldn't even fool your grandmother, would you?" Eloise asked.

"No, because I haven't got one," Mike said.

"That's cute," Eloise said.

"Sure it is."

"Don't act so conceited. There are plenty more cute fish in the pond," Eloise said.

"Do you go fishing much?" he asked.

"I don't have to. They come after me in schools," she said.

And his old man made him work around his buildings, tending furnaces, sweeping sidewalks, mopping hallways, polishing mailboxes, cleaning out cellars. Goddamn it, some day he was going to be a bigshot.

And Eloise. Tomorrow he would take her to a movie. They would sit in the darkness, and he would hold her hand. Eloise! She was such a wonderful girl, once you knew her. He would hold her in his arms and kiss her.

"Boy, you got it hard!" Pete said.

"I was just looking out the window," Mike said.

"You got it hard. When you going to buy the ring?" Pete said, and Mike thought to himself that Pete did not know how much he would like to be buying the ring. "I thought you once told me she was just a teaser?" Pete added, smiling ironically.

"I made a mistake. She's a swell girl."

"She liberal-minded?" snickered Pete.

"You always did have a dirty mind," Mike said.

"You sure got it bad," Pete said.

X

"Gee, kid, I'm sorry you can't come with us tonight," Eloise said to Marion.

"I won't be missed," Marion replied as they walked along Cottage Grove Avenue, homeward-bound from school.

"We'll like to have you and Joe come along and make it a double date," Eloise said.

"That's nice of you to say so. But you two just moon all over the place. And, Russell, I thought you used to say that Mike was a dope?" Marion said.

"He's nicer than most of the fellows I know," Eloise said.

"Why don't you quit playing around then, and go ahead and make him?" Marion asked.

"McGowan, you're just an evil influence," Eloise laughed.

"The kid's weakening," laughed Marion.

"You lose them when you let them go too far, and then, too, they don't respect you then," Eloise said.

"Who told you that, your grandmother?" asked Marion.

"Well, isn't that true?" Eloise asked in an insistent voice.

"You'll learn," Marion said.

They strolled on. Eloise thought of Mike. He was so nice. She loved those lips of his, and he had such nice dark hair. She liked straight hair better than marceled hair. These fellows with their curly hair, they were show-offs. There was nothing show-off about Mike.

"What does Mike's father do?" asked Marion, pointedly gazing into Eloise's blue eyes.

"He's an engineer," Eloise said.

"Russell, you're so funny, I could kiss you," Marion said.

A fellow stopped with an automobile and signaled to them.

"Should we let the chump ride us home?" asked Marion.

"I don't ride with strangers," Eloise said.

"No girl gets anything she doesn't want," Marion said.

"Let's walk, McGowan," Eloise said.

They went on, ignoring the fellow. Eloise again thought of Mike. These days she wanted to do almost nothing other than that. She sat in school and thought of him. All the kids teased her about being in love. They were jealous, that was all. They wanted to be in love themselves, and when they were, they acted just the same as she did.

"Come on upstairs awhile, McGowan," Eloise said, in front of the building where she lived.

"I got to go home and go shopping with the mater," Marion said.

Eloise watched Marion walk on. She was glad that Marion wasn't coming. She wanted to go upstairs, play the radio, and think of Mike, and then take a long time bathing, sitting in the tub full of lukewarm water, looking at herself in the water, feeling the water all over her, thinking of Mike.

XI

"Good night," Eloise said lingeringly and softly as she stood with Mike in the lower portion of the hallway.

"Good night," Mike said yearningly.

They stood facing one another. She took a step toward the door which opened into the inner hallway and the stairs. He watched her with begging moon-calf eyes.

"It was a wonderful time I had," he said.

He watched her. She blew him a kiss.

"Just one more kiss," he asked huskily.

She went to him with opened arms, embraced him. They kissed in a long embrace. They relaxed, faced one another, breathless, embarrassed. Her light dress was crushed and rumpled.

"Don't go up yet," he pleaded.

"I got to," she answered.

"Why?"

"Mother told me to be home at twelve-thirty, and it must be after that already," she said.

"If you're a little late, it won't be so much worse to be still a little more late, will it?" he asked.

"Daddy gets angry if I stay out too late," she said.

He looked at her. His excitement, his desire for her, his love were almost painful. His face was distraught. And he had never seen her like this. Her eyes seemed so large, so very soft. She seemed feverish. He took her hand and it was warm. He kissed her cheek, and it was feverish. They looked at one another. They did not know what to do.

"Kiss me once more, Michael, before I go," she said.

They embraced. They relaxed again, limp.

"Take a walk with me in the park?" he asked.

"I got to go up! I must! Call me up tomorrow morning," she said.

She blew him a kiss, turned, ran up the steps, turned the key, went through the door and upstairs. He watched her disappear.

XII

"Mother went out and won't be back," Eloise said, letting Mike in.

They kissed, and went into the parlor, a well-furnished and large room with conventional furniture, and two new and gaudily modernistic chairs. No one thing in the room seemed to match anything else.

"What did you do today?" Mike asked, awkwardly sitting down.

"Oh, nothing much. What did you do?" she asked.

"I worked and waited till it was time to see you," he said.

He seemed shy. He did not know what to do. He sat on the edge of a chair.

"Where did your mother go?" he asked after a lapse in their conversation.

"She went downtown shopping with Jackie O'Keefe, the boy who lives upstairs. I told you about him. She wanted me to go, too, but I said I simply had to stay home and study."

"I'm glad you didn't go," he said.

"You are?"

"Aren't you glad you didn't?"

"Yes."

"You know, Eloise darling, you're so different from what you seemed to be the first time I met you," he said stutteringly.

"How? Am I showing the wear and tear of going out with you last night?"

"I just meant that you're much nicer," he said.

"Wasn't I nice then?"

"Yes, of course, but it was different. You're different."

"So are you. When I first met you, you were always pulling a line on me," she said.

"I didn't know you," he said.

"Now do you know me?"

"I want to know you always," he said.

"That's a nice thing to say to me," she said.

"Eloise, let's get engaged?"

"We're so young, Mike," she said.

"We can be engaged anyway. Others are. Pete was once engaged to Jenny Birkofer," he said hastily.

"And what happened?"

"She gave him the gate," he said.

"Have you got an engagement ring to give me?" she asked.

"No, but I brought along my class ring from grammar school. I was hoping that maybe you'd want to wear it," he said, trying to be casual.

He fumbled through his pockets and brought out the ugly, squat, gold class ring that he had bought and worn when he was graduated from grammar school almost three years ago.

"How many other girls have worn it?"

"None," he said gravely.

"Is that so or is it just a story you're telling me?"

"Honest, Eloise! You know I love you, and you know I couldn't lie to you. Here, please wear it," he said, looking at her askingly.

"Well, it is nice. Let's see how it fits," she said.

He watched her putting the ring on, and smiled. He took her hands and pulled her to his lap. She draped her left arm around his shoulder. He kissed her. They tumbled sidewise and lay together kissing.

"Are we, or aren't we?" he asked breathlessly.

"What?"
"Engaged."
She kissed him.

XIII

Her eyes were red from crying. She felt sore. She stepped into the tub of lukewarm water, and she kind of wished that the bath could wash away what she had just done. She had become engaged this afternoon, and she was no longer a virgin. Mother was always complaining that a woman's lot was such a hard one. Was this what she always meant? Why did girls want to do this sort of thing when it hurt them so much? It had hurt her terribly. She sniffled. She began to cry again. She wiped her tears away with the wetted back of her right hand. She looked at herself. She must not act at supper so that Mother and Daddy would know. But how could they know? They couldn't. Unless she had a baby? How soon would she be able to tell if she would have a baby? How soon would it show? But maybe it wouldn't. Other girls did it and didn't have babies. She didn't know. She knew hardly anything about all these things.

She drowsed, sunk lower into the tub, splashed and ruffled the water lightly until only her head, covered with the blue bathing cap, was above the water. She liked the smell of the bath salts and the perfume which she had dumped into the water. A tear fell down her cheek. She hadn't expected things to happen this way, either. She had just thought it was going to be nice to have Mike come to see her, and they could kiss and pet. But she had not wanted to let it happen. She had just been swept off her feet. Eloise Russell being swept off her feet! She had never thought that any fellow would be able to do that to her. Not to Eloise Russell. She looked at her slender wetted body glistening under the water. And so that was what everybody giggled about, and got married to do, and that was what led to girls being disgraced? Such a thing! So awful! UUGH! She wanted to scream. And that Eloise Russell should let herself do that! She was disgusted with herself. She felt that she ought to go right out into the kitchen and turn on the gas. She would be found dead and naked and it would be in the papers, and everybody would be wondering about the Eloise Russell mystery.

She lay back in the tub. And she had been afraid and wondered what to do about the sheet. But she had to laugh. Poor Michael! He had been so scared that his face had been almost white. She had had to think of what to do. She had made the bed, and taken the sheet downstairs and had Mike put it in the furnace and burn it.

She had a date with Mike tonight, and what could she say to him, and how could they look each other in the face. When she was being hurt so much, she had hated him. Oh, so that was what it was all about, was it? She could kill herself for being such a fool.

Eloise Russell, you are a fool!

Eloise Russell, you are a Goddamn fool!

She heard her mother entering the apartment. It was getting late. She soaped herself, lolled back again, and then got daintily out of the tub. She looked at herself. She felt her legs, her breasts. She looked in the mirror. Her face was always God-awful with no powder on after a bath. She slowly dried herself. She began to sing. She liked herself now. She didn't hurt now, either. Well, suppose it did happen. She was a woman of experience, even though it had been something awful. Any girl to be a woman of experience had to go through something awful, didn't she? Putting on her bathrobe, Eloise sang, and then she went to her room to dress.

XIV

After lunch, Mike went for a walk. Eloise was going downtown this afternoon with her mother to get some new clothes, and he wouldn't be able to see her until after supper. Waiting until after supper seemed as if it would be so long. After-supper seemed so far away. Time was so funny. When you wanted it to hurry, it seemed to pass so slowly, and when you didn't want it to seem to go so fast, it seemed to zip right by you. Yes, after-supper seemed a long way off.

He was glad that his Saturday chores were done. But he had had a scrap with his father doing them. The old man had noticed him not paying attention to what he was doing when he had cleaned out the basement. So the old man had lost his temper. He couldn't like his old man. The old man was just too dictatorial. The old man felt that a kid of seventeen should be treated as if he was just a runt in short pants. As far as the old man was concerned, Mike knew that he might just as well be ten instead of seventeen. He was ashamed of his old man, too. The old man spoke broken English. In the bank this morning, the old man had made a scene. He had bellyached that he would keep two thousand more dollars in this bank than he did if the bank didn't make so much trouble and ask questions. It had all happened because the teller had looked closely at the old man's signature on a check. Mike had felt as if he could have fallen through the floor right there in the bank. The old man barking like a foreigner so that everyone present knew he was a foreigner, making a scene that a civilized American wouldn't make, boasting that he could keep more money in the bank than he did if the bank didn't make so much trouble about formalities. Suppose one of Eloise's friends had been in the bank, the mother of one of the girls she went to school with, and he was recognized as the son of such an ignorant foreigner of a father. Gee!

And after-supper was such a long ways off. Two o'clock to three, three to four, four to five, five to six, six to seven, seven to eight, and then he could put in his appearance. Gee, when he first met Eloise's parents he had felt that he would give them both away. But Eloise said that her father and mother liked him. He seemed like such a nice shy boy to them. And Mrs. McGowan liked him too. No one suspected what was going on between him and Eloise. They all, all the fellows and girls he and Eloise knew, all knew that they were going together and had a crush on one another, but none of them knew what they were doing. He walked along at a drooping gait, unaware of the streets he passed, singing softly to himself.

Yes, after-supper was a long time away.

Gosh, to think that some fellows thought that Marion McGowan and some of the other girls were better than Eloise. He could just fix Eloise's lovely face in his mind, and it was so wonderful just to think of her. Ah, love was such a wonderful thing. All his life he and Eloise would be in love like this, even when they were old. And it would always be so wonderful. Think of it, all of their lives they could love each other, and think of it, when they got married, they would be together and love each other all they wanted to in their home instead of in the park, and in her hallway, and in taxicabs as they now had to, afraid that they would be seen and caught almost every minute of the time. Eloise had said that they had to stop making love in the hallway because if they got caught, it would be awful.

A girl across the street, she was pretty, but not so pretty as Eloise. Everything he looked at, thought of, everything he did, it was as if Eloise was with him, watching, looking on, knowing and feeling just what he felt. Eloise seemed to be a part of all the world now. She was part of the moon at night, and part of the sun in the daytime, and part of the air, and the grass, and the wind, and part of all the songs he heard over the radio.

Oh, yes, when he was out of school and making big money as an engineer, and he and Eloise were married, and they had a house of their own, to make love in. Ah!

He wandered on, singing to himself.

Yes, after-supper was a long ways off.

XV

"We can't tonight, Michael," Eloise said, sitting beside him on the inner hall steps.

Mike looked at her, let down and disappointed. He took her in his arms, kissed her.

"Please, Mike, we can't," she said.

"Why?" he asked in a rush of breath.

"We just can't."

"I don't think anybody will catch us."

"It ain't that," she said.

"If we sneak down in the basement, like we did last night, nobody'll catch us," he said, trying to be persuasive.

"It isn't that," she said.

"What is it, sweet Eloise?"

"I don't like to say it because I'm afraid to say it even to myself," she said.

Mike knew. His face became glum.

"Are you sure?"

"I'm afraid. I'm afraid to talk about it. Kiss me, Mike, kiss me and tell me you'll always love me," she said, throwing herself into his arms.

He kissed her. Again she sank back on the stairs, almost lifelessly, her dress crushed and rumpled. He looked at her helplessly, his face marked with rouge.

"Maybe it isn't," he said with weak hope.

"I'm afraid. I should have had something happen to me. It hasn't," she said gloomily.

"Can't we do something? Maybe get some medicine. I heard a fellow say there was medicine that made everything all right."

"No, we can't," she said.

just tell the clerk what you want, and you'll get it," Pete said, snapping his fingers as he still tried to remember.

"You never got it yourself?"

"Never needed it. But Johnny has. You ask him, if I can't remember it. He'll tell you. He was sweating his pants off because he had a baby knocked up, and he told his older brother. His brother got it for him, and Johnny said the stuff worked like a clock."

"You really mean that, and that then we'll be all right with nobody knowing?" Mike asked enthusiastically, his face relaxing.

"Sure. You'll be all right. Say, that isn't any trouble. You'll come out of it without any trouble. If that's all that's worrying you, why drop it. You ain't in any trouble. It's merely the little formality of paying about six bits or so, and letting Eloise take the stuff, and then everything is hunky-dory. Get a load of yourself. You've got no worries. That's nothing," Pete said.

"You're sure?" Mike asked with hopeful anxiety.

"Yeah. Can the worry, Mike. That ain't nothing. That happens every day in the week, and a guy goes to a drugstore, and there you are, settled," Pete said.

Mike had to leave. He walked home with a light heart. All these visions and fears which he had had, seeing himself arrested, put in jail, seeing Eloise in disgrace, fearing that it might kill her and that he might be held for her murder, fearing their being found out, all these were gone. He would get the name of that medicine, and then—well, Eloise would take it and that would end all their trouble. If she got in trouble again, the medicine would settle it, and well, this was never going to be any worry to them in the future. Ah, it was swell, too, to be relieved of such worry, to have no more fears. He walked on home, singing gayly, smiling as he hadn't smiled in over a week.

XVII

"Mike, are you sure I'm not getting fat and showing it?" Eloise asked, standing before him, her figure trim and slender as a young tree in her organdy dress.

"I can't see any signs," Mike said, scrutinizing her closely.

"You're not saying that just to make me feel good?" she asked suspiciously.

"No, honest, Sweets, I can't see any signs of it," said Mike.

"Well, I can when I get up in the morning. I look at myself and my tummy seems to stick out, and I get so worried and afraid for fear my mother will notice it and find out what's the matter with me," she said.

"But, Eloise, I tell you you don't look any different than you did before you found out that this was wrong with you," he said.

She ran to him.

"You're tired of me, aren't you, because I'm like this?" she said nervously as she clung to him.

"No, Sweets, honest, I'm not," he said, gripping her firmly.

"Swear you're not!"

"Swear!" he said, trying to smile.

They kissed in a long embrace.

"Sweets, I tell you that this medicine is all right, and that it won't be any trouble," Mike said, sinking back in one of the modernistic chairs in the Russell parlor.

"How do you know?" she asked nervously.

"Well, Johnny and some girl were in the same kind of a boat, and his brother got this medicine, and that was the end of it," he said.

"You told Johnny?" she said, jumping to her feet.

"Honest, I didn't," he said.

"Well, how did he find out?" she said, her eyes flashing anger.

"I remembered when it happened to him, and he talked about it."

"Is that what fellows do, talk about us girls, tell what happens to us, and what you do to us? You're awful," she said, beginning to cry.

"Why, no, honest," he said, confused, unable to bear the sight of her tears and showing his discomfort.

"Yes, it is! I know it is! I know it!" she snapped.

"Honest, Sweets," he began.

She left the room, and went to the rear of her apartment. He arose, gazed out the window down at the quiet spring street. He watched some kids playing tag. He saw an automobile pass. He mopped the perspiration from his brow. He wished that he had never gotten into this. He tried to think of something he could say to make her believe him. He had only told Pete, his best friend, but he couldn't let her know that. He hated to lie like this to her, and he was sorry he'd told Pete. But if he hadn't, how would he have found out about this medicine which was going to get them out of this fix? Gee, if she would only let him give her the medicine.

He was suddenly aware of her presence behind him. He turned. She was smiling as she used to smile just a little while ago, before they had learned of her pregnancy.

"Mike, I was just nervous and afraid," she said humbly.

They embraced, and then she sat on his lap on the couch.

"Mike, you haven't told any of the fellows you go with about us, and about this . . . condition of mine?" she asked.

"Honest, Sweets, I haven't."

"Let me look you in the eye."

She gazed at him, and he tried to be honest in his expression. He told himself, look honest, look honest, and he looked straight into her vapid blue eyes.

"I believe you," she said.

"Eloise, if you take this, I'm sure that everything will be all right," he said, trying to force conviction into his voice.

"How do you know?"

"I know. Didn't it work for Johnny?"

"I don't believe it. It must have been a false alarm. I tell you I heard my mother talking with my aunt, and they were saying that awful things happened to women because they took medicine when they didn't want babies, and the medicines didn't do any good. I won't take it. Honey Mike, I'm afraid to take it," she said spiritedly.

"Then what'll we do?" he asked helplessly.

They looked at each other, two frightened children. She squeezed his hands. He was afraid that she was going to cry again. They nervously lit cigarettes.

XVIII

"Pete, are you certain that the stuff will work on Eloise?" Mike wanting reassurance asked, after they got off the car.

"You know it did when Johnny was in dutch. I tell you, you haven't got any need to worry," Pete said, striding along beside his friend.

"Suppose she won't take it?"

"What does she want to do, be the band leader at her own funeral? Tell her not to be a damn fool. Say I said that."

"I can't do that," Mike said gravely.

"Why?"

"She doesn't want anybody to know. Pete, you got to promise me, as my best friend, that you won't mention it to anyone," Mike said, his tone of gravity persisting.

"Sure. But what the hell should she care? I wouldn't if I was Eloise. Hell, she and you only did something that is natural, and then something else natural happened to her. That's only the way the world goes round and round," Pete said lightly.

"Pete, promise me you won't mention this about me and Eloise to anybody?"

"You know me, Mike."

"But, gee, what should I tell Eloise to make her do this? I tried and tried until I haven't got any new arguments to convince her with," Mike said hopelessly.

"Tell her it won't hurt her, and that it will turn the trick. She doesn't yearn for materhood and a scandal, does she? She doesn't want to get both of you in dutch up to your ears, does she?"

"No. Jesus, Pete, I'm damn near going nuts about it all," Mike said, slouching.

"Well, then, tell her that. She'll see the point, and do it. It's the easy way out of it, and there won't be any trouble, and nobody is going to be the wiser over it, nobody but you and Eloise," Pete said.

"There's something in what you say," Mike said, again grave.

"Sure, there is. And come on, Mike, quit acting like you were the County Morgue," Pete said.

Mike smiled, but it was a grim smile. They walked along in silence.

XIX

"McGowan, what am I going to do?" Eloise asked, sitting in Marion's parlor.

"Populate the world, I guess," Marion said.

"McGowan, you're awful! I'll never speak to you again. If you were in trouble like I am, and you came to me, I wouldn't say such awful things to you. It's not witty, either," Eloise said in an injured voice.

"Come on, Russell, don't be so ridiculous. You act like you were petrified," Marion said.

"Well, I'm in trouble," Eloise pouted.

"What every girl knows," Marion said, and Eloise cried. Marion's manner changed immediately. "Don't, Eloise. I didn't mean it. I was only trying to make you feel good and snap you out of your blues."

"I don't know what to do. Tell me," Eloise sobbed while Marion gently kissed and petted her.

Eloise looked up, grinned, wiped her eyes. Marion smiled.

"Kid, I don't know what to tell you. We don't get that in zoology and physiology."

"McGowan, should I go to the library and see if there are any books with something about my condition in them?" Eloise asked, a new hope lighting her face.

"I don't think you'll find help there," said Marion.

"How do you know? Have you read the books?" asked Eloise.

"No, but I'll bet there isn't much in them," said Marion.

"I'm afraid to take that medicine," said Eloise.

"I asked a lot of people, and they all say that the medicine isn't worth a damn," said Marion.

"Look at me! I stick out like a cow," Eloise said, jumping up and thrusting out her abdomen, her voice and manner one of self-laceration.

"No, you don't. You don't show. You're sticking your stomach out. Here," said Marion, going to Eloise and pushing her abdomen in. "Here, stand straight as you always do, like that. You don't show." Marion retreated several paces, and closely looked at Eloise from both the front and the side. "It doesn't show."

"Honest?"

"It won't for a couple of months yet. You have time."

"When I get up every morning, I look at myself. My breasts seem swollen."

"They don't to anybody else. You have brassieres, what the hell. They don't show."

"McGowan, I'm going crazy. Oh, if something doesn't happen to me, I'll jump into the lake," Eloise said.

"Don't go getting tragic now, Russell," said Marion.

"You're just mean and have no sympathy. I'll bet you're even glad this has happened to me. If you came to me in trouble, I wouldn't be so cold to you," Eloise said melodramatically.

"I'm not cold. I just don't see where you are doing any good by getting yourself overworked," said Marion mildly.

"I have reason to," Eloise said tragically.

"Maybe something will happen, kid. Have you taken a lot of exercise?" asked Marion.

"Oh, God, I'll go crazy if I run up and down any more stairs. You should see me in the morning! You'd scream, McGowan. Bending and twisting, God, you'd think I was an acrobat," Eloise said, smiling girlishly.

"Well, you got to try more," said Marion.

"I'll exercise, but there's two things I don't want to do. I don't want to take that medicine, and I don't want a doctor to go poking into me, killing me. I won't! I won't! And if I do, I might be ruined for life," Eloise said shrilly.

"You might be ruined anyway," said Marion.

"Mike is saving money. The poor boy hardly even eats lunch, to get money to send me to a doctor," Eloise said, wiping away the tears which were smearing her face.

She went to the bathroom, and returned, her face powdered.

"McGowan, do I look like I've been crying?"

"No, not much, dear."

Eloise went to the tall mantelpiece mirror and studied herself. She drew away and looked at her image sidewise.

"Eloise, maybe it will happen. Maybe it's only a false alarm," said Marion.

"Oh, kid, if it only is. I'll do anything. I'll never let myself get caught again like this," said Eloise.

"You'll even resume your vows of chastity, won't you?" laughed Marion.

"I'm going to," Eloise said with determination.

"Poor Michael," said Marion.

"He can wait and suffer. Marion, the woman always pays, doesn't she?" Eloise said seriously.

Just then the telephone rang. Marion ran to it. Eloise was nervous. She went to the hallway to hear what Marion was saying.

"Russell, it's Mike," Marion called and Eloise ran down the hallway to the telephone.

XX

There was a spider in her head. The spider was ugly, and it made her sick to her stomach. She could not clearly make out where she was. Around her there seemed to be walls like varnished floors. She was so sick and so sad that she wanted to cry, and there was that spider in her head, and she could feel it pressing, getting bigger. Her head was swelling, and as it grew bigger, she felt herself puffing out, and her arms and her legs, and all of her puffed up and out. She was like a balloon, and she would never be pretty and slim again, and the spider in her head was ruining her, and it would mark her for life. She wanted to run. She told herself that she would run. She tried to run. She said to herself: Run! And she couldn't run. She couldn't move. She could only swell, with a spider in her head slowly getting bigger, until her head would be bigger than a balloon with a spider in it. Maybe the spider would kill her. She looked around, and she no longer saw herself surrounded by walls like varnished floors. She did not know where she was except that wherever it was, it was dark, and it seemed to be getting blacker just as the spider got bigger, and she felt herself swelling and puffing up. She began to walk. She was suddenly running, and she could not get out of this place, wherever it was, whatever it was, that was getting darker, darker than dark skies. It was dark like death, and maybe the spider was killing her, and as she died, the world got blacker. Maybe she was dead already. Maybe being in Hell meant that you never stopped swelling, but only got bigger and bigger, and the spider in your head got bigger and bigger. She halted. She gazed around her. There was no one near her. There was nothing. The earth seemed all around her, and there was nothing on the earth. The sky was black. The clouds were black. She wanted to find somebody and have them help her get the spider out of her head. She wanted Mike, Marion, Daddy, Mother, anybody. She wanted to cry. She could not even cry. She could only feel that awful spider pressing in her head. She tried to run. It was getting bigger. It was getting darker. She ran through the darkness. The spider was coming out of her head.

  and

      Eloise awakened in her own bed, sweating and trembling, the sheet tossed off her onto the floor, her silky nightgown wrinkled up around her neck. She sensed the darkness of the room as if it were a dread presence. The sadness and fright from her dream lingered like sad music. She heard a train. She feared to move. For a moment she was unable to realize where she was, and she felt that she was having a baby in disgrace, and dying. She rubbed her eyes. She sighed with relief, realizing that she was in her own bed, and that it was night, and that she had only been dreaming. She was still safe, but the sadness and horror of her dream lingered. She turned onto her left side and cried herself to sleep.

XXI

"I've done everything, and here I am in this fix," Eloise said, sitting beside Mike on a bench in Jackson Park.

It was a sunny afternoon, and he had cut school and picked up Eloise when she got out of classes. They had walked slowly, gloomily, hardly speaking, to Jackson Park, and had found this bench. A breeze blew in back of them, and now and then the mild wind ruffled her blonde hair.

"You didn't try the medicine?" he asked anxiously.

"I won't! It will hurt me, and it's no good. It's dangerous to take medicine for that. You don't know what it will do," she said.

"What are we going to do?" he asked disconsolately, almost in despair.

"That's a fine question to ask me. You got me into this, and then you say what are we going to do?" she said bitingly.

He was too despairing to answer her angrily.

"I'm certain my mother is suspicious. I felt that her eyes were looking right through me this morning," Eloise said in a bitter voice which seemed to lacerate both of them.

Mike was petrified with fright. Visions tormented him. He would be arrested. He would go to jail, and both their lives would be ruined. His father would find out, and beat him. He would have to run away and be a bum, and anything might happen to him. Eloise would die. He would go through life a marked and unhappy man whose career would be ruined, and he would die in the gutter. Pete, all the fellows he knew, none of them would have anything like this happen to them, and they would all be successes in life. Marion wouldn't get into trouble and be disgraced, and maybe die like his Eloise might.

But the silence between them was too oppressive. He had to speak.

"Did your mother say anything?" he asked, almost gulping out his words.

"No! But she was looking at me, and I felt that her eyes were like hat pins stuck into me. I could have screamed! And I got sick to my stomach in the morning, too. I vomited yesterday morning."

"Maybe we better tell your mother, and say that we're going to get married. I'll quit school. Maybe I can get some kind of a job. I might maybe be able to drive a taxi or do something," he said like a man in torture.

"Don't you dare tell my mother! If you do, I'll kill you!" she said almost like a wild cat.

"Eloise, Sweets, I'll do anything. I want to stick by you," he said.

Her head fell onto his shoulder. He put his arm around her. She held his hand.

"Let's pretend there's nothing the matter with me," she said girlishly.

"Let's, Sweets," he answered like a condemned man.

"And we're going to a dance tonight and have a keen time," she said.

"Yes," he said.

They sat, gazing across a stretch of grass, watching waddling pigeons land, hunt for food, fly away, listening to chattering sparrows, hearing from a short distance the noise of passing automobiles.

XXII

"What's an abortion like, Pete?" Mike asked as they sat in an ice-cream parlor on Seventy-first Street, with their emptied soda glasses before them.

"You get rid of a baby that way," Pete said.

"I know that," Mike said.

"What do you ask me for then?" asked Pete.

"I meant, what does it do to a girl?"

"Gets her out of trouble," said Pete.

"No, I mean, is it dangerous?"

"How should I know?"

"Pete, I'm serious. This isn't a matter for kidding. It's almost three months now, and I can see that Eloise is getting fat, and maybe soon everybody will be able to tell what her condition is. And Eloise said that she found out from some girl that if she is to have an abortion, she has got to get it done before three months. It's nearly that already," Mike said.

"Well, I don't know much about it. Johnny says that it ain't no worse for a girl than a dose is for a guy," Pete said.

"How bad is a dose?"

"Say, I ain't a clinic."

"We got to do something," Mike said with determination.

"You know the old saying," said Pete.

"What?" Mike asked, grasping for some straw of hope.

"Join the navy," said Pete.

"Hell of a lot of comfort you are," said Mike.

"I told you what to do. Give her the medicine," said Pete.

"She won't take it."

"Did you impress on her that if she doesn't, it's her funeral?"

"I told her everything."

"Nothing won't change her mind?" asked Pete.

"Nothing," said Mike.

"Well, old chap, I hope it's a boy, and listen, don't call it Peter. Me, I want my own bastards named after me, and not anybody else's," said Pete.

"Jesus, I don't know what to do. Please don't kid me, this is terribly serious," Mike said.

"Sure it is. Don't I know? Ain't I watched you moping around like the last rose of summer for almost three months? Don't I know that you just got through school and the exams by the skin of your teeth? Sure, it's serious, and, Mike, I wish to hell I could help you or do something, but what can I do, except try to make you cheer up a bit and hope for the best?" Pete said with real comradeship.

"Boy, and have I done some tall hoping!" said Mike with a grim smile.

"Maybe it'll work out. Sometimes girls just lose their babies. I think it's called a miscarriage," said Pete.

"That's why Eloise tried to do so much exercising, and she's taken physics, Jesus, she's taken them, but it's done no good."

"Well, all I can say is that I don't see any use in hoping for the worst. Maybe if you hope for the best, the best will come. That's what my old man is always saying, although I don't see where he gets any of the best. I don't know," Pete said.

"Well, let's scram out of here anyway," said Mike.

XXIII

"Mike, why didn't you make me go and have something done sooner? I can't wait any longer. Look! And don't tell me that you can't notice any difference in me," Eloise said, her arm in his as they walked through Jackson Park.

He noticed the protrusion of her abdomen. He had nothing to say.

"My mother is suspicious, too. She tries to hint around and ask me questions. I keep telling her about how I have been eating candy, and I made Marion talk to her, and just drop it in how I do nothing but eat candy and sodas, and that I better stop it before I get fat."

"Is your father suspicious, too?"

"Daddy is so worried about business that he doesn't notice anything. A man is not like a woman. You men never see anything, even when it is as big as life before your eyes," she said.

"What'll we do?"

"I don't know. Last night I felt like jumping in the lake," she said.

"Eloise, please!" he said, turning pale.

"What's the use of living and being disgraced?" she asked.

"I can take care of you," he said.

"How?" she snapped sarcastically.

"I can get a job doing something," he said.

"Give me a cigarette!" she said.

He handed her one, and under a tree held the match to it. He grabbed her and kissed her. She cried, and then she powdered her face around the eyes to hide the marks of her tears.

"We should have done something about it before," he said as they strolled on.

"I was afraid. Why didn't you make me do something?"

"But, Eloise, I tried to get you to take medicine," he pleaded.

"It's no good, and it hurts a girl."

"What can be done?"

"I got to go to a doctor. Give me the money you saved up," she said.

"But will anything happen to you?"

She did not answer. He looked at her. She seemed sad. He turned away, because he was almost crying. He sneezed and blew his nose in order to hide how upset he was.

"Eloise, you can't do it!"

"I got to!"

"I won't let you!"

"I got to do something! I'm showing. Any day now my mother will discover what's really the matter. She would have already except that she is so interested in herself that she doesn't pay a lot of attention to me," Eloise said.

"We'll tell her and get married. We'll get along somehow. I have three years' high-school education, and that ought to help me to get some kind of a job," he said resolutely.

"I told you never again to mention that! I won't let you!"

"But, Eloise, I don't want anything to happen to you," he said.

"You're just afraid. And I let myself get into all this trouble because of somebody who is afraid," she said bitterly.

"I'm not afraid!" he said.

"You are!"

"I'm not! I wouldn't care if it was me. But it's you, and I'm not going to let anything happen to you," he said.

"Give me the money you saved!" she said.

"I won't!"

"Give me the money!"

"I won't! I'm going to go and tell your mother and father, and do the right thing," he said.

"You . . . you fool!" she said in tears.

She left him, walking fast. She broke into a run. He chased her, unaware of strangers who paused to watch the scene.

"Don't come near me," she screamed, turning as he almost reached her.

"Eloise. Eloise. Please," he begged.

Running on, she tripped. He helped her up. She was in tears. She took his arm, and they walked off.

XXIV

Eloise got off the Sixty-third Street car several blocks past Western Avenue. It was about three o'clock, and the day was very sunny. She walked slowly along a street with narrow sidewalks. To her left there was a large vacant lot, and kids were shouting as they played in it. Ahead of her and on the other side of the street, she could see some girls jumping rope, and she wished that she was still a little girl doing that. Then she wouldn't be in this trouble. Yes, she was afraid of what she had to go through. She didn't see why such a thing had to happen to her, and why she had to go through this awful business. She wondered what kind of a woman it was that she was going to see. She held a slip of paper and an address in her hand, and she walked along slowly, trying to read the addresses on the houses, many of them frame structures in bad repair. She heard a train. The house must be down a way from Sixty-third Street, she guessed. That made her glad. She slackened her pace. It was all right if she walked slowly and got all her thoughts collected. She had time. It didn't matter if the woman did this thing to her at fifteen minutes after three, or at twenty minutes after three, or even at half past three. She felt her swollen abdomen. Her mother said this morning that she was getting fat, but Daddy hadn't noticed anything. But her mother was really getting suspicious, asking questions, hinting, trying to trick and trap her. It had to be done right away or she would be found out. And she was glad that it was going to be over and done with. Just think, in a week, she would be breathing a sigh of relief, going about as if nothing had ever happened, and she would have this terrible thing over and done with. God, wouldn't that be wonderful! And never again was she going to let herself get into this condition. Never!

She found the house, a wooden two-story frame one, its paint peeled to the extent that it was a dirty and rather dusty silver in color. The small yard in front of it was rank with weeds, and there were small vacant lots on both sides, also rank with weeds, and strewn with tin cans and broken glass. She slowly walked up the steps, wishing that she didn't have to go through this, telling herself that she would go away and come back tomorrow. She knocked on the door hurriedly before she lost her courage and ran away. She heard a husky-voiced female inside asking who it was. She said that she wanted to see the woman here. The door opened.

God, what an old witch! Eloise told herself impulsively at the first sight of the woman.

The woman was corpulent and apparently in her fifties, with uncombed gray hair, a coarse face lined with wrinkles, and large dirty hands. Her apron was also dirty. Eloise looked at her, shuddered.

"Come in!" the woman said in a cold and unsympathetic voice.

Eloise timidly stepped inside. She was led into a cluttered dining room. The floor was carpetless and unswept. The table was covered with an unwashed blue cloth, and the luncheon dishes lay soiled upon it. On the sideboard there lay exposed bandages.

"Who sent you to me?" the woman asked, sitting down and frowning at Eloise.

Eloise was unable to speak.

"Who sent you here? What did you come to me for?" the woman asked, still maintaining her coldness.

"I came . . . I want an . . . I want an abortion," Eloise said meekly.

"You got in trouble, I suppose. Are you married?"

"Yes," Eloise said, holding out her left hand with the five-and-dime-store wedding ring she had bought.

"Where's your husband?"

"He's at work. He works in the daytime."

"How old are you?"

"Nineteen," said Eloise.

"Come closer to me! Let me look at you!" the woman said, and Eloise obeyed, trembling under the woman's gaze. "What did you lie for? You're not nineteen, and I don't believe you're married."

"I am," Eloise said so inconclusively and in such a childlike voice that the woman smiled ironically.

"How far gone are you?"

"It's not three months," Eloise quickly answered.

"It isn't?"

"No, I'm certain it isn't."

"We'll find that out."

"But it isn't."

"You girls should learn how to take care of yourselves, and then you wouldn't be coming to me with your troubles," the woman said.

"Will you do it?" Eloise asked, anxious to get it over with, hoping that the woman would say no, wishing that she had the courage to run away.

"I don't know. You know it costs money. I can't be taking chances of getting myself in trouble with the police by doing such things. Don't you know it's against the law?"

"Yes," Eloise said.

"Why do you come to me and ask me to violate the law?"

"I . . . can't . . . I can't have a baby."

"Well, if I do it, it'll cost you fifty dollars."

"But I haven't . . . I haven't got that much."

"Then I can't do anything for you," the woman said coldly.

"What'll I do?" Eloise said, turning pale.

"That's not my trouble, it's yours. I didn't get myself knocked up," the woman said brutally.

Eloise began to sob.

"I don't see why you girls come crying to me with your troubles. What's your name?"

"Eloise."

sight. Again she glanced out the window. Why didn't he come? She told him that he should come right over. She sat down and waited, her youthful face pale, grim, the lips tight, clenched. The bell rang. She hastily looked at herself in the mirror, powdered, went to the hall. She pressed the buzzer for the downstairs door. She opened the door and waited, not knowing how she would act toward him.

"Hello," Mike called as he came up.

She did not answer. She heard him, and then he was on the landing, smiling. He came toward her, put his arms around her.

"Hello, Sweets!"

He tried to kiss her. She abruptly jerked out of his arms and walked into the parlor. Mike closed the door and followed her, entering the room with a quizzical expression on his face.

"What's the matter, Eloise? Aren't you all right?"

She swung around to face him with hard, glittering eyes. He looked at her, hurt and puzzled.

"But, Eloise, what did I do? I've never seen you act like this."

Her glare became fiendish.

"But, Eloise, are you sick?"

"Yes, I'm *sick!*"

"But it wasn't my fault," he said meekly.

"It doesn't matter! I know only one thing now! I never want to see you again!"

"But, Eloise . . ."

"I despise you! I never want to see you again!"

He stood before her, humble, wounded, indecisive.

"Eloise, you got me wrong, let me explain . . ." he said, and then paused to flounder for words.

She shuddered. She faced him, her body rigid.

"Get out!" she screamed.

Mike looked at her with pleading eyes. He made a helpless gesture with his hands. He turned. He walked very slowly to the door. He looked back and saw her eyes on him unrelaxed and unrelenting. He left.

She ran to her bedroom, flung herself on the bed, cried. She sat up, wiped her tears away. That he should have done that to her! No man would ever again! From this day forth, she would use men like pawns. She vowed that she would! She went to the mirror and powdered her face to erase the marks of her tears.

1931–1937.